Households of Faith
Family, Gender, and Comi

MW00715042

Households of Faith examines a variety of religious traditions with a particular focus on the way in which religious communities define gender identities. The authors explore the boundaries drawn in religious discourse between the private and the public, offering a revisionist perspective on the theoretical framework of separate spheres. By analyzing gender relations within the matrix of the family, they explore both the conflicts and the interdependency of gender roles.

Households of Faith has a broad scope, extending from a consideration of church ritual in New France, to demographic analyses of New Brunswick and the Eastern Townships of Quebec, to the intersection of gender and ethnicity, the construction of family in Aboriginal communities, and the changing definitions of sex roles and the family itself among both clergy and laypeople.

NANCY CHRISTIE, a former Webster Fellow in the humanities at Queen's University, is an independent scholar and the co-author of the award-winning *A Full-Orbed Christianity: The Protestant Churches and Social Welfare in Canada, 1900–1940* and *Engendering the State: Family, Work, and Welfare in Canada*, which was awarded the Sir John A. Macdonald Prize.

MCGILL-QUEEN'S STUDIES IN THE HISTORY OF RELIGION

Volumes in this series have been supported by the Jackman Foundation of Toronto.

SERIES TWO   In memory of George Rawlyk
Donald Harman Akenson, Editor

Households of Faith

Family, Gender, and Community in Canada, 1760–1969

Edited by
NANCY CHRISTIE

McGill-Queen's University Press
Montreal & Kingston · London · Ithaca

© McGill-Queen's University Press 2002
ISBN 0-7735-2271-9 (cloth)
ISBN 0-7735-2330-8 (paper)

Legal deposit quarter 2002
Bibliothèque nationale du Québec

Printed in Canada on acid-free paper

This book has been published with the help of a
grant from the Humanities and Social Sciences
Federation of Canada, using funds provided by the
Social Sciences and Humanities Research Council
of Canada.

McGill-Queen's University Press acknowledges the
financial support of the Government of Canada
through the Book Publishing Industry Development
Program (BPIDP) for its activities. It also
acknowledges the support of the Canada Council for
the Arts for its publishing program.

**National Library of Canada Cataloguing
in Publication Data**

Main entry under title:
　　Households of faith: family, gender, and community
　　in Canada, 1760–1969
　　(McGill-Queen's studies in the history of religion)
　　Includes bibliographical references and index.
　　ISBN 0-7735-2271-9 (bound)
　　– ISBN 0-7735-2330-8 (pbk.)
　　1. Family – Canada – Religious aspects –
　　Christianity. 2. Sex role – Canada – Religious aspects
　　– Christianity. 3. Gender identity – Canada.
　　I. Christie, Nancy, 1958– II. Series.
　　HN39.C2H68 2001　261.8'3585'0971　c2001-900990-9

This book was typeset by Dynagram Inc. in 10/12 Palatino.

Contents

Acknowledgments

The conceptualization and development of any collaborative work of this type naturally involves the incurring of many debts. My principal debt is to Donna Andrew, who not only provided encouragement and sensible advice regarding the "long eighteenth century" but, most importantly, was crucial in helping me to clarify my ideas on the interrelationship of gender and family. Natalie Davis assisted in the early stages of this project; Carl Berger, Mark Noll, and Arthur Silver generously offered detailed historiographical suggestions. More particularly, I would like to thank not only the anonymous readers but also Ollivier Hubert and Arthur Silver for taking the time to read and comment upon the introduction to the volume. At the Aid to Scholarly Publications Programme both Louise Robert, the executive director, and Simon Lapointe, the grants officer, were extremely helpful at a critical stage of the assessment process. For the intellectual evolution of this volume, I owe a tremendous debt to Michael Gauvreau for cheerfully undertaking the onerous task of translation, which has contributed in no small way to bringing the new Quebec historiography of religion to an anglophone audience.

No acknowledgments would be complete without my expressing my deep appreciation to the staff of McGill-Queen's University Press. Most importantly, I thank Don Akenson and Roger Martin for taking a great leap of faith in enthusiastically supporting the publication of this volume. Professor Akenson's personal commitment to religious history and his intellectual acumen greatly improved the overall shape of the manuscript. In particular, I wish to thank him for enabling me to streamline the introduction thematically. At the copy-editing stage, the work of Elizabeth Hulse markedly improved the manuscript. As always, Joan McGilvray is a treasure and makes the final production of the book an actual joy.

Lastly, I would like to thank the contributors to this volume, for without their excellent scholarship and continued enthusiasm for expanding the scope of religious history in Canada, it would not have reached fruition. Not only did all the contributors participate in two intensive workshops, but they patiently endured a lengthy assessment process. For their constant support I thank them.

Contributors

NANCY CHRISTIE is a former Webster Fellow in the Humanities at Queen's University and has taught at the University of Manitoba and the University of Winnipeg. She is co-author of *A Full-Orbed Christianity: The Protestant Churches and Social Welfare in Canada, 1900–1940* (1996), which won the Harold Adams Innis Prize, and the author of *Engendering the State: Family, Work, and Welfare in Canada* (2000), which was awarded the Sir John A. Macdonald Prize by the Canadian Historical Association in 2001. She is currently completing a manuscript on the social history of the family.

ENRICO CARLSON CUMBO obtained his PhD in history and ethnic studies from the University of Toronto in 1996. He has lectured and written on various aspects of Canadian immigration history and ethnicity and on the Italian immigrant experience in particular. Current and forthcoming publications include studies of Italian Catholic popular piety, the Sicilian immigrant conception of fate, the origins and diversity of Italian-Canadian Protestantism, Italian religious foodways, and the construction of ethnic identity in boxing.

PATRICIA DIRKS is associate professor of history at Brock University. Her research focuses on religiously based voluntary organizations and programming for late-nineteenth and early twentieth-century English-Canadian Protestant youth. She is currently completing a manuscript that analyzes developments in Protestant religious education in this period.

KENNETH L. DRAPER is academic dean at the Canadian Bible College, Regina, Saskatchewan. He has recently completed a thesis at McMaster University entitled "Religion Worthy of a Free People: Religious Practices and Discourses in London, Ontario, 1870–1900." In concert with his partner, Carla, he attempts to care for four young children and, where possible, explores the relationships between religion and liberal society in the nineteenth century.

MICHAEL GAUVREAU is professor of history at McMaster University. he is author of *The Evangelical Century: College and Creed in English Canada from the Great Revival to the Great Depression* (1991) and co-author of *A Full-Orbed Christianity: The Protestant Churches and Social Welfare in Canada, 1900–1940* (1996), which won the Harold Adams Innis Prize. He is currently completing a cultural history that explores the relationship between Catholicism, modernism, and Quebec's Quiet Revolution.

OLLIVIER HUBERT is assistant professor in the department of history at the Université de Montréal. His research centres on the concept of sociability in rural communities in pre-industrial Quebec. He is author of *Sur la terre comme au ciel: La gestion des rites par l'Église catholique du Québec (fin XVIIe – mi-XIXe siècle* (2000).

CHRISTINE HUDON is professor of history at the Université de Sherbrooke. She is the author of *Prêtres et fidèles dans le diocèse de Saint-Hyacinthe, 1820–1875* (1996) and has published various articles on the social history of religion.

HANNAH M. LANE is a PhD candidate and part-time lecturer at the University of New Brunswick. She has published or presented papers in church history, women's history, and business history. Her dissertation on "Methodism and Economic Life in Mid-Nineteenth Century St. Stephen, New Brunswick" is part of a larger project on religion, gender, and class in nineteenth-century St Stephen, New Brunswick, and Calais, Maine.

J.I. LITTLE teaches history at Simon Fraser University. His most recent book is *Love Strong as Death: Lucy Peel's Canadian Journal, 1833–1836* (2001), and forthcoming in *Labour/Le Travail* is another edited collection, "A Canadian in Lowell: Labour, Manhood, and Independence in the Early Industrial Era, 1840–1849."

SUSAN NEYLAN is assistant professor at Wilfrid Laurier University. Her book *"The Heavens Are Changing": Nineteenth-Century Protestant Missions and Tsimshian Christianity* is forthcoming from McGill-Queen's University Press.

MARGUERITE VAN DIE holds a joint appointment in history and theology at Queen's University. The author of *An Evangelical Mind: Nathanael Burwash and the Methodist Tradition in Canada, 1839–1918*, she continues to research and write on religion and community life in nineteenth-century Canada.

Households of Faith

Introduction: Family, Community, and the Rise of Liberal Society

Over a decade ago, in discussing how to establish new critical analyses of gender roles and boundaries, Linda Kerber wrote that "no area is more inviting or more ignored than that of religion."[1] This collection of essays has taken her exhortation as its starting point, and through an investigation of both religious discourse and experience, it traces the way in which the Protestant and Roman Catholic religions have conceptualized the family and gender relations within it, as well as the evolving relationship between the institution of the church, the family, and the community between 1760 and 1969. In Canada the history of the family has developed into a lively field of scholarly inquiry, and the discourse on family (and gender relations) has been studied from the perspective of political debate, the development of the state, the legal system, and the workplace, but apart from Lynne Marks's path-breaking treatment of small-town Ontario,[2] there has been no ongoing exploration of the way that religious discourse has idealized the family or how spiritual practices within families have shaped the institutional church.[3] Recently, particularly among American historians, there has been an insistence on contextualizing gender relations within the family, while at the same time the family has been reproblematized as a decidedly political terrain, an arena from which broader social and cultural forces were never entirely absent, but which was both complementary of and fundamental to the interests of church and state.[4] It is this new conceptual framework of the interconnectedness of the triad of state, church, and family which forms the baseline from which *Households of Faith* proceeds. Influenced by the theoretical perspectives developed by the cultural history of early modern Europe, this book works from the presupposition that any social order is not rendered meaningful by a monolithic cultural system but, rather, that every individual understands his or her own identity in terms of categories established by a multitude of value systems and solidarities which overlap and intersect. And following the lead established by Michel Foucault, who postulated that each institution formulates a unique discourse as the result of its own particular interests and needs,[5] I argue that it is important to add the ideological constructs of Christianity to our evolving understanding of how such orthodox binary opposites as public and private, individual and community, high and popular culture, patriarchy and separate-spheres ideology, and male and female sexual roles may have operated within religious discourse and practice in a way that differed considerably from legal, medical, state, or workplace imperatives.

The now standard interpretation of the nineteenth century, given its most complete formulation by Leonore Davidoff and Catherine Hall in *Family Fortunes: Men and Women of the English Middle Class, 1780–1850*,[6] is that it was an era characterized by the rise of the affectional, individualistic family, the ideal of companionate marriage, which emphasized equality between the sexes but in which there were increasingly rigid boundaries between male and female spheres. This social transformation in gender roles, according to economic and labour historians, occurred as a result of the expansion of capitalism and the market economy, which eroded the function of the home as a centre of economic production and narrowed its role to one of reproduction and moral education, activities dominated "naturally" by women. This revolution in gender relations, according to this historical interpretation, was forged as a result of the industrial revolution by an emerging evangelical middle class, which then imposed its gendered ideology of work and home either by education or by emulation upon working-class culture. However, not only has the model of a middle-class imposition of separate spheres been revised by Anna Clark in her recent account of British radicalism,[7] but the work of Amanda Vickery and Margaret Hunt on the language and practice of domesticity in the eighteenth century has exposed serious deficiencies in the alleged corollary between capitalism, evangelicalism, and separate spheres. Through their analysis of both the gentry and the "middling sort," these scholars have called into question the class basis of the language of domesticity, and by so doing, they have also challenged the periodization of separate spheres. If, as they argue, the domestic ideal predated the industrial revolution, can social developments have derived largely from economic change? More-over, by positing gentry culture as the crucible of the cult of domestic-ity, they implicitly challenge the centrepiece of Davidoff and Hall's interpretation: that evangelicalism was the ideology that primarily undergirded the concept of separate spheres. Indeed, as part of her reassessment of this paradigm, which sees in the progressive rigidifi-cation of gender boundaries a restriction of women to a private do-mestic domain, Vickery has argued, in her recent monograph on British women, that the nineteenth century witnessed a blossoming of women's roles in the public realm, largely as a result of evangelical thought.[8]

American historians have also placed the concept of the progres-sive bifurcation of gender spheres between workplace and home un-der critical scrutiny. Nancy Grey Osterud, for example, has shown that the model does not apply to rural economies, where gender in-terdependence was a necessity in the workplace, thus calling into question the very notion that public and private were gendered cate-gories during the nineteenth century.[9] The emphasis that Osterud places upon cross-gender cooperation, in which women sought gen-der integration rather than a single-sex cultural environment sepa-rate from men, has been enhanced by the work of a range of family historians who have taken the inner dynamics of households as their terrain of study. In reconsidering the function of the family, these his-torians have placed household and community in a continuum, thus adding to the complexity of our understanding of the gendered cate-gories of private and public. As a result of her analysis of antebellum New England, Karen V. Hansen has created a new category that she terms the social, an equivalent to Mary Beth Norton's more precise definition of the public, as one divided between the formal public, which comprised church and state, and the informal public of family and neighbourhood. In Norton's model the private constituted an al-most negligible social category,[10] a view that persisted well into the nineteenth century if one accepts the observation of Elizabeth Fox-Genovese that women had little individual self-identity, for one's identity was defined by the collective, first by the family and then by one's spiritual community.[11] What the work of Norton and Genovese makes clear is that without a well-developed notion of privacy, in terms both of self-hood and of the family, there can be no real articu-lation of separate spheres as feminist historians have so defined them. In this new formulation, family was a distinctly public institu-tion, one intimately connected with notions of community and the wider civic culture. And as the work of George Belmer and Katherine Lynch on state policy in Britain and France has shown, by the end of the nineteenth century the family had been defined even more decisively by both working-class welfare clients and middle-class reformers as the central mediating force between the individual and the wider community, leading to what Belmer has called an increasingly "mutual infiltration of spheres."[12] In this new interpretive framework which has emerged from the recent work of historians of early colonial America and the American South, the institution of the family has re-emerged as a crucial nexus of social and political relationships that are translated into the dynamics of gender interaction within the household. In this new historical framework the family is identified as the primary mediator between individual and community.[13]

The new family history, then, not only has resurrected the concept of the household as a conceptual tool but, by so doing, has overturned the opprobrium of the first wave of gender theorists, most notably Joan W. Scott, who rejected gender analysis in terms of kinship and family because family history has traditionally ignored power relationships within the home.[14] Where Scott saw the marketplace and polity as the fulcrums of gender inequality, revisionist historians of the family have now reaffirmed it as the primary site where gender hierarchies were negotiated and defined. Thus Julie Hardwick, in her study of notarial households in France, has concluded that political hierarchies are created and reaffirmed by relations within the household, which she sees as "hierarchies of power," thus reversing Joan Scott's belief that gender hierarchies in the home are imposed as a result of external relationships of power. As Hardwick notes, "The person and familial have a symbiotic relationship with the public and political."[15] Similarly, Margaret Hunt has argued that changing political idealizations, social relationships, and cultural identities flowed imperceptibly from micro-transformations taking place within the family.[16] Thus, if the household or the familial is seen to be the nexus of broader cultural and social relationships and thus the bedrock upon which gender hierarchies are constructed, this interpretation inevitably raises the question of the role of men within the family. Indeed, the question of how men related to women was first raised by historians of courtship, most notably Karen Lykstra, Ellen Rothman, and Peter Ward. These historians have emphasized gender interdependence and, by reading men's as well as women's correspondence, have criticized the idea of a culture of female sisterhood.[17] While to some extent their conclusions were ignored because courtship was seen to be such an anomalous stage, in which one might naturally uncover gender cooperation, new gender historians who have emphasized the roles of both women and men, such as Barbara Melosh,

Donald Yacovone, Ginger Frost, Mark E. Kann, Angus McLaren, and Lisa Wilson, have shown that masculinity, like feminine identity, was believed to be best developed within the domestic sphere. Donald Yacovone, for example, in his examination of men's correspondence with other men, has shown that they frequently expressed virtues commonly attributed to women. Analyzing court records for broken engagements, Ginger Frost has concluded that domestic life was the foundation of male self-identity well into the twentieth century, while the work of Mark Kann and Angus McLaren has demonstrated that men were regulated by public discourse and institutions just as were women, although the criteria of disorderly conduct differed. This cumulative work on masculinity has rendered a much more complex picture of the interplay between individual and familial roles for both men and women. The conclusions offered by these historians of masculinity on the cultural and emotional life of the family have been further clarified by the legal historian James A. Hammerton, who shows that the ideal of companionate marriage was attenuated by the fact that men seeking divorces adhered firmly to an older patriarchal notion of familial hierarchies, while the female defendants believed in equality between the sexes within marriage. Finally, the recent work of Lisa Wilson on fatherhood in colonial America has defined the family as a sphere of gender mutuality and inequality where individuals, including men, saw themselves closely bound by ties of obligation and duty. What these new studies of masculinity make abundantly clear is that there can be no simple equation between domesticity and separate spheres or a gendered division between private and public.[18]

These new critical perspectives on family, community, and gender have thus dismantled the older feminist conceptual tool of separate spheres. Indeed, by rigorously reintroducing the masculine into a territory traditionally seen as exclusively female – namely, the family (or household) – the new gender historians have reconceived the family in terms of what Carole Shammas calls a "patriarchal domesticity," a formulation that has distinctly reinserted power into the family arena by placing the male head at the apex of the hierarchy of "family governance."[19] By framing the question in terms of family governance, both Shammas and Norton explicitly situate the family unit as a part of the "public," as an institution which, as Norton reminds us in her study of Puritan New England, was intimately connected to – and indeed, often interchangeable with – church and state. The starting point for her analysis is a comparison of two disparate world views. The first is that of Sir Robert Filmer, who outlined a conception of political power in which the family, religion, and the state were viewed as analogous institutions, thus emulating patriarchal governance as the primary principle of obedience upon which all social order was founded. The other telos of Norton's scheme is the thought of John Locke, who severed the connection between family and state by arguing that the state was founded upon contractual relationships, a view that many political commentators have taken as the point of origin for a concept of individualism.[20] Shammas likewise begins her overview of colonial American social development with the notion of patriarchal governance. Starting with the question of how British ideologies were superimposed and then renegotiated within a New World environment, she has convincingly argued that patriarchy was reinvigorated in New World societies because of two crucial elements: the need for a small state placed greater emphasis upon male governance within the family, while the weaker presence of state churches and the consequent religious diversity in turn removed the church as the central mediator between the family and government. Both Norton's and Shammas's historical models break with orthodox periodization, which focuses on the American Revolution as the critical juncture for the introduction and rapid diffusion of both Lockean ideas and the notion of "republican motherhood"; for in their interpretive scheme, patriarchy grew unabated throughout the post-revolutionary period largely as the result of legal constraints and the continued need of a laissez-faire state for familial governance by men.[21] As these historians of patriarchy have concluded, patriarchal social relations were not conducive to the creation of rigid gender separations; rather, this hierarchical framework implied the interdependence of bonds both within the family and between household, community (church), and state structures.

The theoretical framework thus constructed by Norton and Shammas has direct implications for Canada, another settlement society, one framed by both French and British social systems. As in colonial America, Canada, during its phases of both French and English settlement, had a relatively weak state, compared to the European parent societies, a situation that persisted well into the early to mid-twentieth century. Moreover, the concept of church establishment remained embryonic, despite the designs of imperial officials, and as settlement expanded, both French and English Canada took on greater affinities with the American example of religious conflict and diversity.[22] Here, then, was an environment ripe for the assertion of "patriarchal domesticity," an ideal promoted and fostered by both Protestant and Catholic churches in a polity in which the family was viewed as the foundational edifice of the social order. It is the purpose of this volume, therefore, to elucidate the way in which the idea of patriarchal governance evolved within the Canadian cultural environment. How long did Filmerian patriarchy survive? When and how long did a concept of a social maternalism take root, and at what time did the notion of individualism overwhelm the communitarian ideal? And how long did the notion of familial unity or tribalism pertain within religious communities?

FROM THE PATRIARCHAL FAMILY TO SEXUAL INDIVIDUALISM

The theme of patriarchal domesticity is taken up in this volume by Ollivier Hubert, who provides a needed corrective to the literature on the evolution of the modern, nuclear family. He revises the trajectory of the evolution of the family offered by its most prominent interpreter, Lawrence Stone. While Hubert agrees that the nuclear family was emerging by the end of the eighteenth century, he argues that its roots lay not only in Protestantism but were emerging at the same time in Roman Catholic societies,[23] though, unlike Stone, he does not believe that the "affective individualism"[24] of Stone's English Protestant families was a feature of family and parish life in New France/ Lower Canada. In this regard, Hubert's essay parallels that of Jack Little, in so far as he demonstrates that a familial model of society was formulated by a clerical elite, who saw the family, as the Puritans would have it, as a "little church, a little commonwealth."[25] Using a consensual rather than a conflictual model which views the social practice of religion as neither simply clerical or merely popular culture, Hubert demonstrates how in this period there was no conception of individual behaviour, but that all pious performances occurred in a communal space. One attended and performed the ritual of mass within one's family group in a pew, while even an ostensibly private act such as the sacrament of confession was closely scrutinized and monitored by the parish community, as was the individual behaviour of priests. Thus, he states, the Catholic Counter-Reformation of the sixteenth and seventeenth centuries did not bring about a radical individuality as some historians have maintained, for the individual was doubly encompassed in communal ties, through both the family and the parish.[26]

Moreover, Hubert describes two vectors of social cohesion. The early family functioned primarily as a mediator between the individual and the bond of community, in which the church functioned as the main space in which these ties were enacted, while a vertical hierarchy of social ranks looked upwards towards the godly Father, a system which, in turn, drew a direct symbolic connection between the authority of the earthly father and the sovereignty of God. In this way, the dominant patriarch functioned as the principal conduit between family, church, and community. It was because of this crucially important role that the clerical elites so forcefully attempted to replace older forms of masculine sociability – which often included fighting, drinking, and leaving the church during mass – with a newer ideal of Christian masculinity, which became increasingly defined in terms of paternity.[27] The nuclear family, consisting of a patriarchal father and dependent wife and children, became the symbolic structure in which the husband's power was derived through the fulfillment of his domestic duties.[28] The family thus became the essential medium of the sacred.

This theme is pursued in turn by Jack Little in his exploration of intertextuality, in which the prescriptive literature of the Reverend James Reid from the Eastern Townships of Quebec is juxtaposed against his own lived religion and family experiences. Little takes issue with the dominant historiographical paradigm, as articulated by Mary Ryan and most recently in Canada by Jane Errington, which reads the nineteenth century in terms of an evolving discourse of separate spheres in which there was a clear gender dichotomy between workplace and home. By studying a moderate Anglican, Little has offered a novel corrective to the burden of literature which often erroneously links the language of domesticity with evangelicalism. Moreover, by studying an era prior to the period of state formation and industrial growth, he also dissents from those who have interpreted domestic ideologies as flowing directly and deterministically from materialistic categories, most notably the growth of industrial capitalism.[29] Most importantly, Little demonstrates that the notion of separate spheres is a theoretical construct which has little application to Christian conceptualizations of the family. During the period he studies, the family was not seen as a private sphere; rather, both the church and, by extension, the community at large were regarded as direct extensions of family relationships. More signficantly, Little drastically revises the separate-spheres paradigm by showing that the ideal of companionate marriage propounded by the churches from at least the Reformation was one in which the husband and father took a leading, if not prominent, role in the moral education of his children, and in this way the ideology of James Reid echoed the formulations of Anglican leaders such as the Reverend John Strachan, who stated that a man was "a social being only within the family."[30]

Far from diminishing during the onset of industrialization, Christine Hudon demonstrates, in her demographic analysis of French-Canadian Protestant families in the Eastern Townships of Quebec, the degree to which the familial model of social relationships was actually reaffirmed by geographical mobility and social dislocation. Within the broader intellectual continuum between church, family, and community, she suggests, familial interests often conflicted with those of the church, and indeed, group identities were forged primarily within the framework of kin relations. Not only does Hudon emphasize the independence of lay popular religious culture, thus revealing a more dynamic interplay between popular practices and elite clerical ideologies, but she shows that the fact that Catholic women converted upon marrying Protestant men tended to reinforce patriarchal dominance over religious sensibilities within the family. In this way, one can conclude, as does Enrico Cumbo, that the family often functioned as a bulwark of resistance to modern values attendant upon industrialization. The implications of these familial religious strategies for the elaboration of ultramontanism in Quebec is that church leaders in the long term relaxed prohibitions relating to the degrees of consanguinity in marriage in order to shore up strict religious divisions at the elite level, while at the same time popular practice was countenancing greater interaction between Protestant and Catholic communities.[31]

The essays by Cumbo, Hannah Lane, and Susan Neylan, read together, powerfully illustrate the degree to which the familial model of society testified to by clergymen was to a remarkable degree shared by the Christian populace, but in addition, they reveal that the way in which religion was experienced was much more variable than historians have previously understood. In a intensive demographic analysis of small-town New Brunswick, Lane argues that there was a high degree of religious fluidity, for people moved frequently among the major and minor Protestant denominations. What is distinctive about this movement, however, is that it was not a matter of purely individual choice. Rather, Lane makes abundantly clear that conversion or a change in church membership was a family strategy, and she thus dissents from the perspective of historians of the Great Awakening, who interpret that movement as the critical watershed between an older religious tribalism and a more "modern" individualist temper because of the supposed priority placed upon conversion as a solitary act.[32] While, like Hudon, Lane is aware of the frequent reality of conflict between husbands and wives, the overwhelming pattern of religious adherence suggests that such conflict was resolved and mediated through the family, a conclusion that goes far to underscoring that the primary identity in the nineteenth century was a familial one which transgressed religious demarcations. Further, Lane's study of church adherence in New Brunswick argues that the uniquely irenic character of Canadian Protestantism was very much the creation of popular religious practices, and in so doing, she provides a deeper analytic explanation for the Protestant consensus of which William Westfall has written.[33] Her treatment of this subject, however, questions the long-standing interpretation of the nineteenth century as a period of massive denominational conflict and boundary-making, suggesting that this was but a clerical invention. Methodologically, Lane's findings underscore the unreliability of studying the past along rigidly denominational lines.[34]

In keeping with the central question as to whether particular religious ideologies are imposed from above, the essays by Susan Neylan and Enrico Cumbo show that, while specific ethnic and racial groups may have on the surface shared in the rituals of a particular religious faith, they nevertheless refashioned these religious dispensations in their own cultural terms. Studying the missionary campaign to convert the Tsimshian in British Columbia, Neylan shows how the missionaries' insistence upon imposing their own vision of the nuclear family was to some degree effective, in so far as Native kin networks tended to convert, not as individuals, but in family groups, but that the Native understanding of what the family constituted was vastly different from that which the missionaries believed they were impressing upon them. Indeed, as Neylan concludes, the missionary impact upon Native culture paradoxically resulted in thus strengthening traditional kinship networks. Concomitantly, the overriding need to convert the "other" in turn reinforced the familial emphasis within white missionary society. With her interpretation of overlapping cultural interests, Neylan thus provides a much more nuanced and dynamic model of cultural relations, which allows for the concept of both superimposition and change from below.

In a similar vein, Cumbo explores the issue of cultural contact, in which adaptation to the New World in fact helped to reaffirm traditional ethnic culture mediated through family identity. He offers an in-depth analysis of the importance of family worship to the process of immigration of Italians to southern Ontario at the beginning of the twentieth century. If tribalism and family coherence formed a powerful counterweight to individualism within established communities, family strategies were the very fulcrum of the process of immigrant community-building. Like Neylan, Lane, and Hudon, Cumbo argues that religiosity must not be studied merely in terms of church attendance or from the view point of clerical leaders, for as he so well demonstrates, if one were to take this perspective, one would be forced to conclude, as did the largely Irish-dominated priesthood, that the Italians were simply irreligious. Just as Hudon has argued for Quebec, so Cumbo shows that what we have come to know as the devotional revolution was a much more protracted process and one that must be qualified with reference to the question of ethnicity beyond the Irish mainstream.[35] What Cumbo so cogently argues is that Italian men and women were very religious; however, the core of their piety occurred for men in festivals and parades and for women in the context of family devotions. He thus not only draws our attention, as do many of the other essays in this volume, to the gendered complexion of religious experience but, more profoundly, insists on the methodological importance of private religion to a broader understanding of the Canadian religious experience. Historians such as Patricia Bonomi have pointed out that churchgoing was only one measure of religious belief and one that was profoundly affected by such variables as community cohesion, family tradition, and geography.[36] More significantly, by studying ethnic identity in the New World environment from the perspective of religion rather than the workplace, Cumbo clearly demonstrates that ethnic imperatives reinforced gender interdependence and that because traditional religious practices were in fact enhanced as they were transported from Italy to Hamilton, they staved off the forces of modernization.[37]

Female piety and the way it came to be progressively identified as the predominant link between the family and the larger sacred household of the church is the theme of Marguerite Van Die's essay. In an investigation of various facets of female participation within the church – through charity, temperance, Sunday school, participation in revivals, and direct provisioning of church and minister – she concludes that it was "precisely because church involvement allowed women to place their domestic life within a communal framework that they could assert that such apparently private concerns as intemperance, poverty, and family relations were in fact public." Van Die's essay thus calls into question the very applicability of the concept of separate spheres to any assessment of women's religious life. Personal salvation and individual piety, from this perspective, served to uphold the traditional continuum between family and communal bonds that had animated religious ideology since the end of the eighteenth century. Her analysis leads to the conclusion that, far from being constricted by the imposition of an ideology of domesticity, women's activity in the public sphere was actually expanding during this period.[38] Because the work of women in charities and church continued to be subordinate to the financial and official leadership of men, Van Die's is a study in what Carole Shammas calls "patriarchal domesticity," and it goes a long way towards explaining why in Canada the idea of domestic moralism focused on women did not spawn distinctly female-led reform networks, as occurred in the

United States. In Canada the notion of a "republican motherhood," in which women's role as moral educators legitimated their public presence, was strangely truncated, largely because, as the essays of Kenneth Draper and Patricia Dirks illustrate, by the late nineteenth century, public concerns over how to educate males to assume both their more individualistic civic duties and their communal family responsibilities hastened the reassertion of "patriarchal governance." This development occurred for two reasons. As the spiritual interests of mainstream Protestantism became increasingly intermingled with the imperatives of social reform and the creation of government policy, family and church were once again tightly fused, but, as Draper suggests, this older emphasis upon the family as the basis of society increasingly served the needs of a modern liberal society. Moreover, as young men moved increasingly to cities after the 1880s, fears arose regarding parental authority and spurred a renewed assertion of patriarchal governance.

If, as Van Die so rightly contends, women's behaviour – seen beside the contributions of Draper and Dirks, who focus upon the growing discourse that sought to keep men tied to church and church-led organizations – did not form the cusp of modernity, we are confronted with the need to explore the process of "modernization" from a specifically gendered perspective, one that must focus upon the problem of men rather than upon women. If the practice of women's participation within religious organizations persisted well into the twentieth century – the only real break appears to have occured in the 1950s, when United Church ministers began for the first time to expatiate upon the problem of getting a sufficient supply of volunteer female workers, upon which the edifice of Christianity so depended – then it is incumbent for historians to examine more closely the behaviour of men as the harbingers of those individualistic values that historians have associated with the modern liberal temper.

This, in fact, is the starting point for Kenneth Draper, who situates the preponderance of interdenominational activity and the expansion of church-based institutions – namely, the YMCA, the WCTU, church-run orphans' homes, and the newly professionalized mass revival services, the whole apparatus of a burgeoning theology of social Christianity – in the gender disorder of the post-1880 era. Indeed, as Draper so effectively demonstrates, because the churches saw as their principal social task the proper formation of male citizens within a liberal social order, they embarked on a new trajectory which, in the twentieth century, witnessed the elaboration of social Christianity and the erection of a panoply of religious organizations functioning beyond the purview of the church congregation, all directed to propping up the stability of the family. Likewise, Patricia Dirks examines in detail the discourse on masculinity that emerged in a revitalized Sunday school movement and within the YMCA, and she demonstrates how the Protestant denominations were at the forefront in newly conceptualizing adolescence as a particular life stage. But more significantly, she traces the persistence of a preoccupation with the problem of encouraging men to attend church; however, in the context of Draper's article, the absence of men from church had now become a euphemism for a perception that older community ties were breaking down. His analysis delineates the way in which liberal society both encouraged individual male ambition and at the same time created new "familial" institutions by which to constrain and discipline male behaviour. Thus together Van Die, Dirks, and Draper argue that female behaviour and character remained largely static, and that because male activities changed with ever-greater alacrity, they fell under increasing scrutiny and regulation. Although, as Van Die contends, much of the impetus for this organizational activity appears to have flowed from social maternalism, Draper argues that maternalist priorities were in fact a species of patriarchy. Indeed, his conclusions reinforce those of Wally Seccombe regarding working-class family life in Britain, in which the notion of individual self-advancement was harnessed to men's responsibility to their families.[39]

To understand this cultural reorientation, it is important to briefly investigate the flurry of prescriptive literature on the family that emerged between roughly 1880 and 1900. Two things are significant about the literature produced in this period. The moral economy of the family was for the first time directly linked to the fortunes of the nation or state, for as the Reverend Nathanael Burwash so eloquently stated in his introduction to *The Gospel of the Home*, published in 1903, the home is the "corner-stone of national prosperity," while the author of this same volume, the farmer D.C. Hossack, noted that "good homes will protect the state."[40] As never before, then, the family became an appendage of the liberal state, and its men were to be its dependable foot soldiers. With the emerging discovery of an endemic unemployment problem, greater attention was paid to the ideal of family self-sufficiency, which in turn hinged upon family formation and male responsibility[41] – hence the second novel departure within the ideology of domesticity, an overweening preoccupation with the changing behaviour of young men. As never before, clergymen and public commentators hastened to use their pens to reinforce the ideal of family interdependence. While small sections of their publications were devoted to instructions for women, it is of particular note that the female virtues described there were no different from those that had been prescribed since at least the seventeenth century.[42] Certainly, there were passing references to the "new woman", and writers hastened to tame the new aspirations of women for education by arguing that female intelligence must be made indispensable to a happy and pious home. Nevertheless, before we simply assume that this social change meant the introduction of full-fledged separate spheres – namely, a distinct gendered dichotomy between home and work – it should be recognized that clergymen admonished women to work, for, should they become widowed in the future, they might at least be qualified to support themselves and their children.[43] Nevertheless, this period did witness a growing emphasis upon the ideal that the "woman has the greatest power in the home"[44]; however, the notion of the primacy of moral motherhood remained contested. There is no better illustration that older traditions which saw women as mere economic appendages of patriarchal men persisted and that the concept of the moral mother as an active agent within the family was still in an embryonic state in the 1870s than the revealing statement by Burwash that a woman was but "a dowry to her husband."[45] And, if a nascent notion of separate spheres was emerging, gender mutuality, in which a moral woman and an affectionate husband were united by the duty of Christian nurture of their offspring, continued to predominate.

The theme of women's behaviour was, as I have argued, a minor one. A great deal more space was allotted in the literature of the day to the potential deliquency of young men. It is crucially important to recognize that, while women were explicitly directed that they could choose to be either married or single, men were admonished time and again that their only choice was marriage.[46] If this period marked a constriction of gender roles, this fell most heavily upon men. Not only were fathers encouraged to avoid both the temptations of all-male associational life and church office-holding because these would remove them too often from the domestic sphere, but young men were cautioned against fraternal orders for fear that such activities would lead to later marriage or unruly courtship practices beyond the reach of family and church.[47] The role of the Christian household was directed to creating a viable "civil society" by rescuing single men from their selfish preoccupations and turning them into "steady, energetic, and useful citizen[s]." This ideal of "highest manhood" depended most affirmedly upon the man's "conjugal role" as paterfamilias, and, as the Reverend John Laing made clear, family responsibilities thus tutored men in the necessity of labour and the avoidance of the sins of idleness.[48] Late-nineteenth-century pamphlets on Christian domesticity were thus perorations on a single theme: the regulation of male behaviour, which hinged upon the dual recognition of individual ambition and family duties. Fathers were instructed to develop their "feminine" qualities and to express their emotions in an affectionate manner to their spouses and children, while sons were enjoined to recognize early that "life is a struggle of individuals," so that they could competently earn a good wage and secure an independent existence for themselves and their families. In addition, young, upwardly mobile male clerks were told to carry the template of the pious home into the world by erecting a family altar in their boarding-house room. And most importantly, men were directed to make sacrifices for the larger felicity of the home.[49] The principal purpose of this church-produced advice literature was to teach men about the public value of family formation; but as was underscored so often, the construction of this "patriarchal piety," the "godly household"[50] of the church, and liberal society itself was to depend increasingly upon the foundation of maternal nurture within the home.

As the articles by Draper and Dirks make abundantly clear, however, the public perception that older forms of family and community were breaking down was not a feature of the 1840s, as some scholars have previously believed;[51] rather, the 1880–1914 era was a decisive period of social change, for not only were gender relations reconstituted, but the very purpose of the family was recast and inexorably linked to the fate of the state. To account for why this era was one of such crucial social and ideological transformation in Canada, one must understand also the decisive way in which public commentators were beginning to reconceive what constituted the central integrative forces within society. In short, we need to examine the changes occurring within the tenets of liberalism itself. By the late nineteenth century, as liberal thinkers jettisoned older political and constitutional formulations of the commonweal,[52] they redefined civil society as an interdependent web of social relations. This new view of the social structure insisted that society cohered largely through the integrative forces of morality and character. In short, from the point of view of Edwardian liberalism, social order flowed directly from the shared principle that all individuals must behave with an imperative sense of responsibility to the whole.[53]

This movement towards a collectivist-liberal vision, which naturally placed a much greater emphasis upon the training of individuals within the citizenry, was given further impetus, as well as its peculiarly gendered cast, during the first decades of the twentieth century, when the increasing public apprehension concerning the rise of illegitimacy, unemployment, family desertion, and mass family dependency underscored the universal need for a vast web of social institutions by which the next generation of citizens – most notably men – could be educated in those public virtues of work, thrift, self-discipline, and family self-reliance. This increased public awareness of the pressing need to discipline men, to force them to realize their profound duty to their families of dependent women and children, necessarily placed an ever-greater emphasis upon the role that patriarchal governance must play in preserving civil society.

While it is true that the conservative pronouncements of both Protestant and Catholic church leaders that the state was usurping the traditional functions of the family were not a true assessment of reality, the fact that church authorities perceived events in this way was decisive for the way in which they reinterpreted the public functions of both religion and the family. After World War II, in response to what appeared as a precipitate expansion in the welfare state, lay and clerical leaders within the United Church eschewed the tenets of social Christianity and at the same time redefined the family as a singularly private domain.[54] The Catholic Church also moved towards defining piety as a much more individualist and private experience, even though as an institution it preserved a greater concern for the church's role within the sphere of social reform than did the United Church in this period.[55] However, in the wake of the creation of the modern welfare state, both Catholic and Protestant church leaders believed that civil society and the state had become bifurcated; henceforth the family was no longer seen to be symbiotic with the state, as it had been since 1880. Now the primary function of the family was to forestall the inroads of state expansion and its corrolaries: bureaucracy, depersonalization, and alienation. Henceforth the primary purpose of the family was to foster individualism.

The new welfare state had also created, from the perspective of church leaders, a disordered tangle of gender relations. On the one hand, in the face of growing aspirations for work among married women, clerics wished to shore up the breadwinner ideal; however, at the same time, they did not wish to wholly capitulate to the notion propagated by the state that the primary bonds of the family were provided by economic security. In the main, male clergymen hoped to reinforce the notion of the moral, Christian home; however, they also feared that within the domestic sphere the traditional notion of gender mutuality was under assault by a reinvigorated matriarchy. The primary conundrum faced by the post-war churches therefore revolved around the question of how to keep the home a haven in a heartless world of industrial anomie for men and, at the same time, prevent women from finding their creative selves in the workforce. The ideal solution lay in a positive, healthy, sexuality, for this naturally created a mutuality between the spouses, while at the same time, it highlighted psychological dichotomies between the genders.

Despite certain differences in emphasis, therefore, both the Catholic and the Protestant churches once again were at the forefront in redefining the ideal Christian family, especially in the face of growing fears regarding divorce. By the early 1960s the modern nuclear family had again been reconceptualized, and it was now expressed almost wholly in terms of the conjugal couple. The key to preserving marriage as an enduring institution was believed to flow from the individual's satisfaction from sexual pleasure, especially as it pertained to women. As Michael Gauvreau argues in his essay in this volume, however, these new principles of marital felicity were not imposed from above, despite the anxieties of priests regarding the issue of divorce; rather, the campaign for marriage-preparation courses and premarital instruction which he explores emerged as a result of a campaign from urban, working-class women in Montreal, and as he demonstrates, it formed the fulcrum of a new feminist movement defined around the notion of the primacy of the sexual person. The rise of what Gauvreau terms "personalist feminism" marked the symbolic end of the influence of maternal feminism within Quebec.[56] Not only did church leaders place a new priority on psychological differences between the sexes, but the reification of "sacred sex," as I argue in my essay, now linked the perpetuation of the spiritual with the more individualistic experience of coitus. The long-standing vision of a continuum between family, church, and society was expunged in these post-war decades, largely by the negative reaction of Protestant church leaders to the stark reality that married women would henceforth be actively engaged in paid labour. Because married women were entering the workforce in critically large numbers, church leaders believed that gender dichotomies between work and family were being eroded, and in response, they constructed a new, psychosexual definition of gender difference.

Here was a profound break with the past, for the individual now fulfilled the role once occupied by the family.[57] The primary identity and the basis of the social order was no longer the interdependent family; rather, society was seen to be simply an aggregate of individuals whose sensibility of self derived first and foremost from a sense of sexual identity. Indeed, the new priority placed upon an individual's sexuality as the key to social identity explains why homosexuality became problematized in the church-based publications of the early 1960s. This period was thus a fundamental watershed in the evolution of Canadian society, for not only did it lead the Protestant churches towards a position of moral relativism (marital sex and homosexuality were no longer deemed sinful), but it in no small way forged as well our contemporary "discovery" of "gender roles," a perspective whose provenance lay within the orbit of a purely individualistic ethos of the sexual self. The church-led discourse on the new concept of what it termed "gender identity" drew upon both conservative and progressive perspectives, for while sex was meant to solve the modern angst of depersonalization brought about by technology and urbanization, the reification of the elemental character of the sexual relationship served also to evoke the new "democratic, fraternal, individualistic model" of society, whereby it was accepted that, because "man is made in the image of God," individual freedom could be pursued without leading to social and political "anarchy." Here in a modern guise was a reassertion of John Strachan's cautionary tale of social unrest, except that where Strachan and his contemporaries had evoked the metaphor of family, the church leaders of 1969 proclaimed the temperate beneficence of the "life-style" of individual sexual liberation.[58]

NOTES

1 Linda Kerber et al., "Beyond Roles, beyond Spheres: Thinking about Gender in the Early Republic," *William and Mary Quarterly,* 3rd ser., 46 (July 1989): 582.

2 Lynne Marks, *Revivals and Roller Rinks: Religion, Leisure, and Identity in Late-Nineteenth-Century Small-Town Ontario* (Toronto: University of Toronto Press, 1996).

3 See, for example, Bettina Bradbury, *Working Families: Age, Gender and Daily Survival in Industrializing Montreal* (Toronto: McClelland and Stewart: 1993); Suzanne Morton, *Ideal Surroundings: Domestic Life in a Working-Class Suburb in the 1920s* (Toronto: University of Toronto Press, 1995); Cecilia Morgan, *Public Men and Virtuous Women: The Gendered Languages of Religion and Politics in Upper Canada, 1791–1850* (Toronto: University of Toronto Press, 1996); Nancy Christie, *Engendering the State: Family, Work, and Welfare in Canada* (Toronto: University of Toronto Press, 2000); Cynthia R. Commachio, *Nations Are Built of Babies: Saving Ontario's Mothers and Children, 1900–1940* (Montreal and Kingston: McGill-Queen's University Press, 1993); Franca Iacovetta, *Such Hardworking People: Italian Immigrants in Post-war Toronto* (Montreal and Kingston: McGill-Queen's University Press, 1992); Kathryn McPherson et al., eds., *Gendered Pasts: Historical Essays in*

Femininity and Masculinity in Canada (Toronto: Oxford University Press, 1999); Mona Gleason, *Normalizing the Ideal: Psychology, Schooling, and the Family in Postwar Canada* (Toronto: University of Toronto Press, 1999); Mary Louise Adams, *The Trouble with Normal: Postwar Youth and the Making of Heterosexuality* (Toronto: University of Toronto Press, 1997); Joy Parr, ed., *Childhood and Family in Canadian History* (Toronto: McClelland and Stewart, 1982); Franca Iacovetta and Mariana Valverde, eds., *Gender Conflicts: New Essays in Women's History* (Toronto: University of Toronto Press, 1992); Bettina Bradbury, ed., *Canadian Family History: Selected Readings* (Toronto: Copp Clark, 1993); Janet Guildford and Suzanne Morton, eds., *Separate Spheres: Women's Worlds in the 19th-Century Maritimes* (Fredericton: Acadiensis Press, 1994); Margaret Conrad, ed., *Intimate Relations: Family and Community in Planter Nova Scotia, 1759–1800* (Fredericton: Acadiensis Press, 1995); Lori Chambers and Edgar-André Montigny, eds., *Family Matters: Papers in Post-Confederation Family History* (Toronto: Canadian Scholars' Press, 1998); Elizabeth Jane Errington, *Wives and Mothers, Schoolmistresses and Scullery Maids: Working Women in Upper Canada, 1790–1840* (Montreal and Kingston: McGill-Queen's University Press, 1995); Peter Gossage, *Families in Transition: Industry and Population in Ninteenth-Century Saint-Hyacinthe* (Montreal and Kingston: McGill-Queen's University Press, 1999); Marks, *Revivals and Roller Rinks*; Royden Loewen, *Family, Church, and Market: A Mennonite Community in the Old and New World, 1850–1930* (Toronto: University of Toronto Press, 1993).

For analysis of religion and women, see, for example, Sharon Cook, *"Through Sunshine and Shadow": The Woman's Christian Temperance Union, Evangelicalism, and Reform in Ontario, 1874–1930* (Montreal and Kingston: McGill-Queen's University Press, 1995); Mariana Valverde, *The Age of Light, Soap and Water: Moral Reform in English Canada, 1885–1914* (Toronto: McCLelland and Stewart, 1991); Brian Clarke, *Piety and Nationalism: Lay Voluntary Associations and the Creation of an Irish-Catholic Community in Toronto, 1850–1895* (Montreal and Kingston: McGill-Queen's University Press, 1993), 62–96; and Denyse Baillargeon, *Making Do: Women, Family and Home in Montreal during the Great Depression*, trans. Yvonne Klein (Waterloo: Wilfrid Laurier University Press, 1999).

4 See, for example, Nancy Isenberg, *Sex and Citizenship in Antebellum America* (Chapel Hill: University of North Caroline Press, 1998), xiv; Mary Beth Norton, *Founding Mothers and Fathers: Gendered Power and the Forming of American Society* (New York: Alfred A. Knopf, 1996); Jean Friedman, *The Enclosed Garden: Women and Community in the Evangelical South, 1830–1900* (Chapel Hill: University of North Carolina Press, 1985); Helena M. Wall, *Fierce Communion: Family and Community in Early America* (Cambridge, Mass.: Harvard University Press, 1990); and Stephanie McCurry, *Masters*

of Small Worlds: Yeoman Households, Gender Relations and the Political Culture of the Antebellum South Carolina Low Country (New York and Oxford: Oxford University Press, 1995).

The concept of community is a particularly useful one in an era when class relations are ambiguous and the language of class has not been fully developed. Moreover, the notion of community incorporates the informal public or civic culture as well as state structures, such as courts, the legislative process, and administrative bureaucracies. For an excellent example of how to use community as a primary conceptual tool, see David Garrioch, *Neighbourhood and Community in Paris, 1740–1790* (Cambridge: Cambridge University Press, 1986); see also the essay Ollivier Hubert in this volume. On revisionist interpretations of class relations, see David Cannadine, *The Rise and Fall and Class in Britain* (New York: Columbia University Press, 1999); Penelope J. Corfield, ed., *Language, History and Class* (Oxford: Basil Blackwell, 1991); Patrick Joyce, *Visions of the People: Industrial England and the Question of Class, 1848–1914* (Cambridge: Cambridge University Presss, 1991); and Dror Wahrman, *Imagining the Middle Class: The Political Representation of Class in Britain, c. 1780–1840* (Cambridge: Cambridge University Press, 1995).

5 For excellent revisionist discussion of the work of Michel Foucault, see Roger Chartier, *On the Edge of the Cliff* (Baltimore: Johns Hopkins University Press, 1997), 51; Barbara B. Diefendorf and Carla Hesse, eds., *Culture and Identity in Early Modern Europe, 1500–1800: Essays in Honour of Natalie Zemon Davis* (Ann Arbor: University of Michigan Press, 1993), 1–4; and Roger Chartier, *Cultural History: Practices and Representations* (Cambridge: Polity Press, 1988), 61. To appreciate the way in which the type of discourse or institutional context significantly changes gender outcomes, see Barbara Z. Thaden, *The Maternal Voice in Victorian Fiction: Rewriting the Patriarchal Family* (New York and London, Garland Publishers, 1997), 12, which shows that, while fiction emphasized maternal authority in the home, courts upheld patriarchy. On the theme of legal codes upholding patriarchy, see Bettina Bradbury, "Debating Dower: Patriarchy, Capitalism, and Widows' Rights in Lower Canada," in Tamara Myers et al., eds., *Power, Place and Identity: Historical Studies of Social and Legal Regulation in Quebec* (Montreal: Montreal History Group, 1998). For a more dynamic conceptualization of the interplay between elite and popular culture, one that circumvents the issue of social control, see Tim Harris, "Problematizing Popular Culture," in Harris, ed., *Popular Culture in England c. 1500–1850* (New York: St. Martin's Press, 1995). For an older view that explores imposition from above, see Peter Burke, *Popular Culture in Early Modern Europe* (London: Temple Smith, 1978); and Keith Wrightson and David Levine, *Poverty and Piety in an English Village: Terling, 1525–1700* (London: Academic Press, 1979).

6 Leonore Davidoff and Catherine Hall, *Family Fortunes: Men and Women of the English Middle Class, 1780–1850* (Chicago: University of Chicago Press, 1987). For a similar argument in Canada, see Errington, *Wives and Mothers*. For the United States, see Mary P. Ryan, *The Cradle of the Middle Class: The Family in Oneida County, New York, 1790–1865* (Cambridge: Cambridge University Press, 1981); Kathryn Kish Sklar, *Catherine Beecher: A Study in American Domesticity* (New Haven and London: Yale University Press, 1973); and Barbara Welter, "The Cult of True Womanhood, 1820–1860," *American Quarterly* 18 (1966): 131–74. On the rise of the affectional family, see Lawrence Stone, *The Family, Sex, and Marriage in England, 1500–1800* (New York: Harper and Row, 1977); Alan McFarlane, *Marriage and Love in England: Modes of Reproduction, 1300–1840* (Oxford: Basil Blackwell, 1986). For critiques of Stone and McFarlane, see John R. Gillis, *For Better, for Worse: British Marriages 1600 to the Present* (Oxford: Oxford University Press, 1985); and Jean-Louis Flandrin, *Families in Former Times: Kinship, Household and Sexuality in Early Modern France* (Cambridge: Cambridge University Press, 1979).

7 Anna Clark, *The Struggle for the Breeches: Gender and the Making of the British Working Class* (Berkeley and Los Angeles: University of California Press, 1995); Wally Seccombe, *Weathering the Storm: Working-Class Families from the Industrial Revolution to the Fertility Decline* (London and New York: Verso, 1993). For the creation of gender boundaries in the Canadian workplace, see a synthesis of the latest literature by Ruth Frager in "Labour History and Interlocking Hierarchies of Class, Ethnicity and Gender: A Canadian Perspective," *International Review of Social History* 44 (August 1999): 217–48.

8 Margaret Hunt, *The Middling Sort: Commerce, Gender and the Family in England, 1680–1780* (Berkeley: University of California Press, 1996); Amanda Vickery, *The Gentleman's Daughter* (New Haven and London: Yale University Press, 1998); Vickery, "Historiographical Review: Golden Age to Separate Spheres? A Review of the Categories and Chronology of English Women's History," *Historical Journal* 36 (1993): 383–414. For two excellent studies that explore, through a cultural approach, the emergence of more fixed gender categories, see Anthony Fletcher, *Gender, Sex and Subordination in England, 1500–1800* (New Haven and London: Yale University Press, 1995); and Randolph Trumbach, *Sex and the Gender Revolution*, vol. 1, *Heterosexuality and the Third Gender in Enlightenment London* (Chicago: University of Chicago Press, 1998). For a critique of gender spheres, see also Peter Williams, "Constituting Class and Gender: A Social History of the Home, 1700–1900," in Nigel Thrift and Peter Williams, eds., *Class and Space: The Making of Urban Society* (London: Routledge, 1987). For critiques of the role of evangelicalism in delineating gender boundaries, see the essays by Ollivier Hubert and J.I. Little in this volume. For the argument

that evangelicalism contributed to the expansion of women's public role, see Linda Colley, *Britons: Forging the Nation, 1707–1837* (London: Pimlico Press, 1992), especially the chapter "Womanpower." For a similar argument in the Canadian context, see the essay by Marguerite Van Die in this volume.

9 Nancy Grey Osterud, *Bonds of Community: The Lives of Farm Women in Nineteeth-Century New York* (Ithaca and London: Cornell University Press, 1991). See also Karen V. Hansen, *A Very Social Time: Crafting Community in Antebellum New England* (Berkeley: University of California Press, 1994), 23. For the Canadian context, see Marjorie Cohen, *Women's Work, Markets, and Economic Development in Nineteeth-Century Ontario* (Toronto: University of Toronto Press, 1988).

10 Hansen, *A Very Social Time*, 1–8; Norton, *Founding Mothers and Fathers*, 23.

11 Elizabeth Fox-Genovese, "Family and Female Identity in the Antebellum South: Sarah Gayle and Her Family," in Carol Bleser, ed., *In Joy and in Sorrow: Women, Family and Marriage in the Victorian South, 1830–1900* (New York and Oxford: Oxford University Press, 1991).

12 George K. Belmer, *Friends of the Family: The English Home and Its Guardians 1850–1940* (Palo Alto: Stanford University Press, 1998), 5; Katherine A. Lynch, "The Family and Public Life," *Journal of Interdisciplinary History* 24 (spring 1994): 665–84.

13 Elizabeth Fox-Genovese, *Within the Plantation Household: Black and White Women of the Old South* (Chapel Hill: University of North Carolina Press,1988), 83; Lisa Wilson, *Life after Death: Widows in Pennsylvania, 1750–1850* (Philadelphia: Temple University Press, 1992), 5–6; Hansen, *A Very Social Time*; Stephanie McCurry, "The Politics of Yeoman Households in South Carolina," and Victoria Bynum, "Reshaping the Bonds of Womanhood: Divorce in Reconstruction North Carolina," both in Catherine Clinton and Nina Silber, eds., *Divided Houses: Gender and the Civil War* (New York and Oxford: Oxford University Press, 1992); Norton, *Founding Mothers and Fathers*; Christine Adams, *A Taste for Comfort and Status: A Bourgeois Family in Eighteenth-Century France* (University Park, Pa: University of Pennsylvania Press, 2000). For the employment of the household as a unit of gender analysis in Canada, see, most notably, Bradbury, *Working Families*.

14 Joan W. Scott, "Gender: A Useful Category of Historical Analysis," in Elizabeth Weed, ed., *Coming to Terms: Feminism, Theory, Politics* (New York and London: Routledge, 1989), 94.

15 Julie Hardwick, *The Practice of Patriarchy: Gender and the Politics of Household Authority in Early Modern France* (University Park, Penn.: Pennsylvania University Press, 1998), 221.

16 Hunt, *The Middling Sort*, 8.

17 Karen Lykstra, *Searching the Heart: Women, Men and Romantic Love in Nineteenth-Century America* (New York and Oxford: Oxford University Press, 1989); Ellen K. Rothman, *Hands and Hearts: A History of Courtship in America* (New York: Basic Books, 1984); Peter Ward, *Courtship, Love, and Marriage in Nineteeth-Century English Canada* (Montreal and Kingston: McGill-Queen's University Press, 1990). Lykstra has criticized Carroll Smith-Rosenberg because her conclusions are based on reading only women's letters. See C. Smith-Rosenberg, "The Female World of Love and Rituals: Relations between Women in Nineteeth-Century America," *Signs* 1 (1975): 1–30.

18 On the history of masculinity, see Barbara Melosh, ed., *Gender and American History since 1890* (London and New York: Routledge 1993); Donald Yacovone, " 'Surpassing the Love of Women': Victorian Manhood and the Language of Fraternal Love," in Laura McCall and Donald Yacovone, eds., *A Shared Experience: Men, Women and the History of Gender* (New York and London: New York University Press, 1998); Ginger S. Frost, *Promises Broken: Courtship, Class and Gender in Victorian England* (Charlottesville and London: University of Virginia Press, 1995); Patricia R. Hill, "Writing out of the War: Harriet Beecher Stowe's Averted Gaze," in Clinton and Silber, eds., *Divided Houses*; Mark E. Kann, *The Gendering of American Politics: Founding Mothers, Founding Fathers, and Political Patriarchy* (Westport, Conn., and London: Praeger, 1999), especially the chapter "Disorderly Men"; Angus McLaren, *The Trials of Masculinity: Policing Sexual Boundaries, 1870–1930* (Chicago: University of Chicago Press, 1997); James A. Hamerton, *Cruelty and Companionship: Conflict in Nineteeth-Century Married Life* (London: Routledge, 1992); Ralph LaRossa, *The Modernization of Fatherhood: A Social and Political History* (Chicago: Chicago University Press, 1997); Lisa Wilson, *Ye Heart of a Man: The Domestic Life of Men in Colonial New England* (New Haven and London: Yale University Press, 1999), 1–10.

19 Carole Shammas, "The Domestic Environment in Early Modern England and America," in Michael Gordon, ed., *The American Family in Social Historical Perspective*, 3rd ed., (New York: St. Martin's Press, 1983), 129; Shammas, "Anglo-American Household Government in Comparative Perspective", *William and Mary Quarterly*, 3rd ser., 52 (January 1995): 105.

20 Norton, *Founding Mothers and Fathers*, 4–11. See also the interpretive overview by J.C.D. Clark in *English Society, 1688–1832* (Cambridge: Cambridge University Press, 1985); also Susan D. Amussen, *An Ordered Society: Gender and Class in Early Modern Europe* (Oxford: Basil Blackwell, 1988); and Rachel Weil, *Political Passions: Gender, the Family and Political Argument in England, 1680–1714* (Manchester and New York: Manchester University Press, 1999). Weil has critiqued the direct application of contemporary

gender categories to historical periods where family and community were the vehicles for exploring such questions.

21 Shammas, "Anglo-American Household Government," 117–20; Mary Beth Norton, "The Evolution of White Women's Experience in Early America," *American Historical Review* 89 (June 1984): 593–619. Not only has Norton critiqued the influence of "republican motherhood," but the expansion of patriarchy is a theme of many legal historians. See, for example, Susan Staves, *Married Women's Separate Property in England, 1660–1833* (Cambridge, Mass.: Harvard University Press, 1990), 214, where Staves argues that the removal of the strict settlement did not liberate women but actually reinforced patriarchal attitudes. For a similar argument, see Bradbury, "Debating Dower"; Lori Chambers, *Married Women and Property Law in Victorian Ontario* (Toronto: University of Toronto Press, 1997); and Peter Bardaglio, " 'An Outrage upon Nature': Incest and the Law in the Nineteenth-Century South," in Bleser, ed., *In Joy and in Sorrow*. For critiques of "republican motherhood," see "Introduction" in McCall and Yacovone, eds., *A Shared Experience*; Norton, "The Evolution of White Women's Experience." For the concept of "republican motherhood," see Linda K. Kerber, *Women of the Republic: Intellect and Ideology in Revolutionary America* (New York: W.W. Norton, 1986); Jay Fliegelman, *Prodigals and Pilgrims: The American Revolution against Patriarchal Authority, 1750–1800* (Cambridge, Mass.: Harvard University Press, 1982); Errington, *Wives and Mothers*; and Morgan, *Public Men and Virtuous Women*.

22 On the question of a weak state in Canada, see Allan Greer and Ian Radforth, eds., *Colonial Leviathan: State Formation in Nineteenth-Century Canada* (Toronto: University of Toronto Press, 1992), especially articles by Douglas McCalla, "Railways and the Development of Canada West, 1850–1870," and Peter Baskerville, "Transportation, Social Change, and State Formation, Upper Canada, 1841–1864," which explore the intermittent nature of state expansion. For the weakness of the state in the early twentieth century and the continued state promotion of patriarchal families, see Christie, *Engendering the State*. On the weakness of church establishment, see Judith Fingard, *The Anglican Design in Loyalist Nova Scotia, 1783–1816* (London: SPCK Press, 1972); Curtis Fahey, *In His Name: The Anglican Experience in Upper Canada, 1791–1854* (Ottawa: Carleton University Press, 1991); and Nancy Christie, " 'In These Times of Democratic Rage and Delusion': Popular Religion and the Challenge to the Established Order, 1760–1815," in G.A. Rawlyk, ed., *The Canadian Protestant Experience, 1760–1990* (Burlington: Welch Publishing, 1990). On the legal promotion of patriarchy in New France, see André Lachance and Sylvie Savoie, "Violence, Marriage, and Family Honour: Aspects of the Legal Regulation of Marriage in New France," in Jim Phillips, Tina Loo, and Susan Lewthwaite,

eds., *Essays in the History of Canadian* Law, vol. 5; *Crime and Criminal Justice* (Toronto: University of Toronto Press, 1994).

23 On this point, see also Kathleen Davies, "Continuity and Change in Literary Advice on Marriage," in R.B. Outhwaite, ed., *Marriage and Society: Studies in the Social History of Marriage* (London: Europa Publications, 1981); and Margo Todd, *Christian Humanism and the Puritan Social Order* (Cambridge: Cambridge University Press, 1987).

24 Stone, *The Family, Sex, and Marriage in England*, 22.

25 John Demos, *A Little Commonwealth: Family Life in a Plymouth Colony* (New York: New York: Oxford University Press, 1970). See also Gerald F. Moran and Maris A. Vinovskis, *Religion, Family, and the Life Course: Explorations in the Social History of Early America* (Ann Arbor: University of Michigan Press, 1992); and Hansen, *A Very Social Time*.

26 For a similar argument in another context, see Sandra Cavallo, "Charity as Boundary Making: Social Stratification, Gender and Family in the Italian States," in Hugh Cunningham and Joanna Innes, eds., *Charity, Philanthropy and Reform from the 1690s to 1850* (Basingstoke: Macmillan Press, 1998), 111, 120.

27 Here Hubert revises the notion that Christian manhood was the creation of a mid-nineteenth-century middle-class ethos. For this interpretation, see E. Anthony Rotundo, "Learning about Manhood: Gender Ideals and the Middle-Class Family in Nineteenth-Century America," in J.A. Mangan and James Wolvin, eds., *Manliness and Morality: Middle-Class Masculinity in Britain and America, 1800–1940* (Manchester: Manchester University Press, 1987), 43–5.

28 Although this early modern conceptualization of family was patriarchal, its interdependent nature rendered women's subordination less problematic. It was only with the rise of individualism that women's encapsulation within the household became of the private household becames overtly disadvantageous to women. For this sensible argument, see Louise Tilly and Joan Scott, *Women, Work and the Family* (New York: Holt, Rinehart and Winston, 1978), 43. See also Norton, *Founding Mothers and Fathers*; and Margaret J.M. Ezell, *The Patriarch's Wife: Literary Evidence and the History of the Family* (Chapel Hill: University of North Carolina Press, 1987). The best work discussing the rise of Lockean individualism and the suppression of women is Carole Pateman, *The Sexual Contract: Aspects of Patriarchal Liberalism* (Stanford: Stanford University Press, 1988).

29 For a recent restatement of this overly deterministic and overly reductionist view of the impact of industrial capitalism upon the growth of religious and moral thought, see Franca Iacovetta and Wendy Mitchinson, eds., *On the Case: Explorations in Social History* (Toronto: University of Toronto Press, 1998), 9, which links "capitalist state formation" and "the

concomitant creation of a moral culture infused by bourgeois values." The notion that industrial capitalism was as pivotal an agent of social change as this related to the family has now been largely dispelled by historians who have stressed the resilience of family structure and values. See, for example, Tamara K. Hareven, *Family Time and Industrial Time: The Relationship between the Family and Work in a New England Industrial Community* (Cambridge: Cambridge University Press, 1982); Hareven, "The History of the Family and the Complexity of Social Change," *American Historical Review* 96 (1991): 95–124; Michael Anderson, *Family Structure in Nineteenth Century Lancashire* (Cambridge: Cambridge University Press, 1971); Katherine A. Lynch, *Family, Class and Ideology in Early Industrial France, 1825–1848* (Madison: University of Wisconsin Press, 1988); and Sonya O. Rose, *Limited Livelihoods: Gender and Class in Ninteenth-Century England* (Berkeley: University of California Press, 1992).

30 Quoted in Errington, *Wives and Mothers*, 25.

31 In seventeenth-century France the Catholic Church permitted marriage between Protestants and Catholics because it feared that prohibitions would excite religious rivalry, thus preserving the authority of the church. See Keith P. Luria, "Rituals of Conversion: Catholics and Protestants in Seventeeth-Century Poitou," in Diefendorf and Hesse, *Culture and Identity in Early Modern Europe*. On ultramontanism in Quebec, see René Hardy, *Contrôle social et mutation de la culture religieuse au Québec, 1830–1930* (Montréal: Boréal, 1999). On the flexible nature of the Catholic Church's position in Quebec during the nineteenth century, see Serge Gagnon, *Mariage et famille au temps de Papineau* (Ste Foy: Les Presses de l'Université Laval, 1993).

32 On this point, see Norton, "The Evolution of White Women's Experience," 609. For the "individualist" interpretation, see Paul Johnson, *A Shopkeeper's Millennium: Society and Revivals in Rochester, New York, 1815–1837* (New York: Hill and Wang, 1978); William McLoughlin, *Revivals, Awakenings and Reform: An Essay on Religion and Social Change in America, 1607–1977* (Chicago: University of Chicago Press, 1978); Ryan, *The Cradle of the Middle Class*; George A. Rawlyk, *Wrapped Up in God: A Study of Several Canadian Revivals and Revivalists* (Burlington: Welch Publishers, 1988).

33 For the argument that a Protestant consensus emerged in the years after 1850, see William Westfall, *Two Worlds: The Protestant Culture of Nineteenth-Century Ontario* (Montreal and Kingston: McGill-Queen's University Press, 1989).

34 For the persistence of the denominational approach to the study of religion in Canada, which sees religious progress in terms of the tighter definition of the boundaries between the various institutional churches, see the synthesis by John Webster Grant, *A Profusion of Spires: Religion in Nineteenth-Century Ontario* (Toronto: University of Toronto Press,

1988). This approach still has currency among a large constituency of historians, as evidenced by the subject matter of many of the recent essays in G.A. Rawlyk, ed., *Aspects of the Canadian Evangelical Experience* (Montreal: McGill-Queen's University Press, 1997). For a critique, see Donald Akenson, *Small Differences: Irish Catholics and Irish Protestants 1815–1922* (Montreal and Kingston: McGill-Queen's University Press, 1987).

35 For the classic statement on the "devotional revolution" as applied to the Irish experience, see Emmet Larkin, "The Devotional Revolution in Ireland, 1850–75," *American Historical Review* 77 (1972): 625–52. Recently, Brian Clarke has applied the concept to the experience of Irish Catholics in Toronto in *Piety and Nationalism*. Recent studies of Quebec ultramontanism have, however, suggested the need for qualification and nuance, particularly concerning the sudden or "revolutionary" nature of the process. See Christine Hudon, *Prêtres et fidèles dans le diocèse de Saint-Hyacinthe, 1820–1875* (Sillery: Septentrion, 1996).

36 Patricia U. Bonomi, *Under the Cope of Heaven: Religion, Society and Politics in Colonial America* (New York: Oxford University Press, 1986), 87–8; Sara Mendelson and Patricia Crawford, *Women in Early Modern England* (Oxford and New York: Clarendon Press, 1998), 230.

37 For an opposing interpretation, see Franca Iacovetta, "From Contadina to Worker: Southern Italian Immigrant Working Women in Toronto, 1947–1962," in Jean Burnet, ed., *Looking into My Sister's Eyes: An Exploration in Women's History* (Toronto: Multicultural Historical Society, 1986).

38 This line of argument is confirmed by Jan Noel, "Women and Social Welfare in the Montreal Region, 1800–1833: Preliminary Findings," in Elizabeth Muir and Marilyn Whiteley, eds., *Changing Roles of Women within the Christian Church in Canada* (Toronto: University of Toronto Press, 1995), 261–83; and Diana Pedersen, "'The Power of True Christian Women': The YWCA and Evangelical Womanhood in the Late Nineteenth Century," ibid., 321–37. For the application of this insight to Britain, see Colley, *Britons: Forging the Nation*, 263, and Vickery, *The Gentleman's Daughter*. As Vickery states, "The rising tide of religious Evangelicalism did not efface woman in public, rather it reoriented the public life of the more serious-minded away from worldly entertainment towards good works. By the end of the eighteenth century, the institutionalization of fashionable benevolence had created altogether new platforms for female association and public action" (288). For a similar argument, see Ruth Bloch, "American Ideals in Transition: The Rise of the Moral Mother, 1785–1815," *Feminist Studies* 4 (1978): 100–26; Paula Baker, "The Domestication of Politics: Women and American Political Society, 1780–1920," *American Historical Review* 89 (June 1984): 620–47; Mary P. Ryan, "The Rise of Women's Networks," in Judith L. Newton, Mary P. Ryan, and Judith R. Walkowitz, eds., *Sex and Class in*

Women's History (London and Boston: Routledge, 1983); and Bonnie Smith, *Ladies of the Leisure Class: The Bourgeoises of Northern France in the Nineteenth Century* (Princeton: Princeton University Press, 1981).

For critiques of "republican motherhood" and separate spheres, see Catherine A. Brekus, *Strangers and Pilgrims: 1740–1845* (Chapel Hill: University of North Carolina Press, 1998). For a critique of Joan Landes, *Women and the Public Sphere in the Age of the French Revolution* (Ithaca: Cornell University Press, 1988), see Keith Michael Baker, "Defining the Public Sphere in Eighteenth-Century France: Variations on a Theme by Habermas," in Craig Calhoun, ed., *Habermas and the Public Sphere* (Cambridge, Mass. and London: MIT Press, 1992). On the conceptual need to combine patriarchy and domesticity, see Carole Shammas, "The Domestic Environment in Early Modern England and America," 129, with her concept of "patriarchal domesticity"; and Barbara Katz Rothman, "Motherhood under Patriarchy," in Karen V. Hansen and Anita Ilta Carey, eds., *Families in the U.S.: Kinship and Domestic Politics* (Philadelphia: Temple University Press, 1998).

39 Seccombe, *Weathering the Storm*, 203. For this argument in the Canadian context, see Christie, *Engendering the State*.

40 D.C. Hossack, *The Gospel of the Home* (Toronto: William Briggs, 1903), preface by Rev. Nathanael Burwash, unpayed.

41 For a recent treatment of the public "discovery" of the phenomenon of unemployment in the late nineteenth century, see Peter Baskerville and Eric Sager, *Unwilling Idlers: The Urban Unemployed and Their Families in Late Victorian Canada* (Toronto: University of Toronto Press, 1998); and Christie, *Engendering the State*.

42 On the persistence of female virtues, see, Vickery, *The Gentleman's Daughter*.

43 Women were freed from legal disabilities against working during the nineteenth century because it was feared that they would become a burden on the state. On this point, see Norma Basch, *In the Eyes of the Law: Women, Marriage and Property in Nineteenth-Century New York* (Ithaca and London: Cornell University Press, 1982), 25. The alternative to having women work in order to avoid the expansion of welfare provisions was to induce men to fulfill their family obligations by marrying.

44 Hossack, *The Gospel of the Home*, 18, 92. See also Rev. John Laing, *The Family: God's Appointed Institution for the Establishment and Maintenance of True Religion. Being an Address Delivered to the Synod of Hamilton and London, April 1878* (n.p.), 7.

45 "Introduction" to Hossack, *The Gospel of the Home*.

46 Hossack, *The Gospel of Home*, 84; Annie S. Swann, *Courtship and Marriage and the Gentle Art of Home-Making* (Toronto: William Briggs, 1893), 126–7.

47 On fraternal orders, see Mark C. Carnes, *Secret Ritual and Manhood in Victorian America* (New Haven and London: Yale University Press, 1989).

Carnes sees the rise in male ritualism as a distinctly gendered rejection of the feminization of evangelicalism (14). On male associational culture in Canada, see Kealey, "The Orange Order in Toronto," in Gregory Skealey and Peter Warrian, eds., *Essays in Canadian Working Class History* (Toronto: McLellan and Stewart, 1976), 13–34; and David Sutherland, "Voluntary Societies and the Process of Middle-Class Formation in Early Victorian Halifax, Nova Scotia," *Journal of the Canadian Historical Association*, new ser., 5 (1994). Sutherland argues that these largely male organizations attracted both artisans and the lower-middle-class men who were predominently in their early thirties. He concludes that these societies replaced kinship networks and were used for upward mobility. While it is not a central theme of his article, his research reveals that men and women also met at fetes held by these organizations, thus circumventing family control of courtship (241–8). On the trend towards later marriages in this period, see Marvin McInnis, "Women, Work and Childbearing: Ontario in the Second Half of the Nineteenth Century," *Histoire sociale/Social History* 24 (1991): 237–62 and Chad Gaffield, "Children, Schooling and Family Reproduction in Nineteenth-Century Ontario," *Canadian Historical Review* 72 (1991): 81.

The argument presented in this volume stresses apprehension concerning the breakdown of family control of courtship and marriage, rather than a view which states that women's sexual liberation and the attendant problem of illegitimate children resulted from their ability to secure paid labour. For the latter line of argument, see Edward Shorter, "Illegitimacy, Sexual Revolution, and Social Change in Modern Europe," in Robert I. Rotberg and Theodore K. Rabb, eds., *Marriage and the Family* (Princeton: Princeton University Press, 1980); and Carolyn Strange, *Toronto's Girl Problem* (Toronto: University of Toronto Press, 1994).

48 Laing, *The Family*, 8. See also, Presbyterian Church of Canada, General Assembly's Committee on Uniformity of Worship *Aids for Family Worship* (Montreal, 1900); Anglican publication written by John Ker, *Family Prayer for Busy People* (Montreal: E.M. Renouf, 1908); and Presbyterian Church of Canada, *The Book of Family Devotion* (London: Oxford University Press, 1913). This advice literature was not restricted to Protestant churches. For its presence within Catholicism, see Neil McNeil, *What Every Christian Father Can and Should Do* (Toronto: W.E. Blake & Son, 1910).

49 Hossack, *The Gospel of the Home*, 8. The frequent allusions to young men leaving family farms points to the period between 1870 and 1900 as a crucial watershed in Ontario. On this point, see Gordon Darroch, "Home and Away: Patterns of Residence, Schooling and Work among Children and Never Married Young Adults, Canada, 1871 and 1901," *Journal of Family History* 26 (2001): 220–50. For two decades between 1871 and 1891, Douglas McCalla has demonstrated a doubling of the urban population,

which, in the absence of massive external immigration, came from the province's rural areas. See McCalla, "The Ontario Economy in the Long Run," *Ontario History* 90 (1988): 99. For this transition, see also David Gagan, *Hopeful Travellers: Families, Land, and Social Change in Mid-Victorian Peel County, Canada West* (Toronto: University of Toronto Press, 1981). For two arguments on the problem of the emergence of separate-spheres ideology in the rural context, see Margaret Derry, "Gender Conflicts in Dairying: Ontario's Butter Industry, 1880–1920," *Ontario History* 90 (spring 1998), 43, in which gender mutuality is stressed. The study of middle-class culture in rural Ontario is still embryonic, but see the important article by Gordon Darroch, "Scanty Fortunes & Rural Middle-Class Formation in 19th Century Rural Ontario," *Canadian Historical Review* 79 (December 1998).

50 John E. Lanceley, *The Domestic Sanctuary, or, The Importance of Family Religion* (Hamilton, Ont.: Spectator, 1878), 120.

51 For Canada, the classic statements of this interpretation remain Susan Houston, "Politics, Schools, and Social Change in Upper Canada," *Canadian Historical Review* 53 (1972): 249–71; and Alison Prentice, *The School Promoters* (Toronto: McClelland and Stewart, 1976). This older argument is based upon the premise that a rising middle class created new state institutions in response to the breakdown of community attendant on urbanization in 1840s Upper Canada.

52 See, especially, Egerton Ryerson, *Civil Government – the Late Conspiracy: A Discourse Delivered in Kingston, U.C., 31 Dec. 1837* (pamphlet, 1838). Contrast the view in this publication with the statement by John Strachan, who saw social peace as flowing upward from the family.

53 For the rise of the new liberalism in England, the key volume remains Stefan Collini, *Liberalism and Sociology: L.T. Hobhouse and Political Argument in England, 1880–1914* (Cambridge, Cambridge University Press, 1979). For a discussion of this process in Canada, see Nancy Christie and Michael Gauvreau, *"A Full-Orbed Christianity": The Protestant Churches and the State in Canada, 1900–1940* (Montreal and Kingston: McGill-Queen's University Press, 1996).

54 For the church's conception of family relationships in this era, see, for example, Rev. George Pidgeon, *The Christian Family* (sermon at Bloor Street United Church, 30 January 1944); United Church, *Family Religion* (n.d). This pamphlet argues vociferously against the secular definition of the family, for it states: "A home is more than a place where children grow up to provide manpower for a country, and thus perpetuate the greatness of the nation." See also D.A. MacLennan, *The Christian Family at Home* (United Church pamphlet, 1947); and United Church, Board of Christian Education, Family Life Committee, *Family Nights at Home* (pamphlet, 1952). It is significant that the United Church periodical *The Christian*

Home began in 1960. Interestingly, the first issue featured a picture of a father reading to his sons. For a more sustained treatment of this process, see Nancy Christie, "The Spectre of the New Leviathan", in Christie and Michael Gauvreau, eds., *The Post-War Interregnum: Ideologies of Citizenship 1943–1955* (McGill-Queen's University Press, forthcoming). For an excellent contemporary overview of the Canadian family, see Frederick Elkin, *The Family in Canada* (Ottawa: The Vanier Institute, 1964). This was the first extensive treatment of such themes as immigration, leisure, the household economy, familial relationships, and deviant behaviour.

55 Michael Gauvreau, "From Re-Christianization to Contestation: The Catholic Church and Quebec Society, 1931–71," in *Church History: Studies in Christianity and Culture* 69 (2000): 803–33.

56 From this perspective, Gauvreau postulates that modern feminism in Quebec did not emerge out of the political ferment of the 1960s, as has previously been argued, or from the "sexual revolution" following access to the birth control pill, or from the fact that married women began to enter the workforce in ever greater numbers from the late 1950s onwards. For this line of argument, see, most notably, The Clio Collective, *Quebec Women: A History* (Toronto: The Women's Press, 1987), 336–7. For the importance of maternalist arguments in Canadian feminism, see Linda Kealey, *"A Not Unreasonable Claim": Women and Reform in Canada, 1880s–1920s* (Toronto: Canadian Women's Educational Press, 1979); Denyse Baillargeon, " 'Frequenter les goutes de lait': L'experience des mères montréalaises, 1910–1965," *Revue d'histoire de l'Amérique française* 50 (été 1996): 29–68; Andree Levesque, *Making and Breaking the Rules: Quebec Women, 1919–1939* (Toronto: McClelland and Stewart, 1994); and Christie, *Engendering the State*.

57 On the rise of a distinctly individualistic temper as a feature of post-war culture, see *The Church and the Secular World* (United Church of Canada, 1950), 63; and Elizabeth Roberts, *Women and Families: An Oral History, 1940–1970* (Oxford: Basil Blackwell, 1995), 14. For the insistence on private religion as an aspect of post-war culture in Canada, see National Archives of Canada, MG 28 I 11, Canadian Youth Commission, vol. 44, "Analysis of Youth Commission: Intensive Interviews," "Religion and Morals" (1947), 13. For a recent overview of the 1960s, see Arthur Marwick, *The Sixties: Cultural Revolution in Britain, France, Italy and the United States, c. 1958–1974* (Oxford: Oxford University Press, 1998), passim., especially 33–4.

58 See Canadian Council of Churches, *The Biblical and Theological Understanding of Sexuality and Family Life: Report of a Study of the Faith and Order Commission* (November 1969), 21, 43. It is not coincidental that this statement by the Canadian Council of Churches appeared the same year as the report of the Royal Commission on the Status of Women in Canada.

The Age of Patriarchy

Ritual Performance and Parish Sociability: French-Canadian Catholic Families at Mass from the Seventeenth to the Nineteenth Century

OLLIVIER HUBERT

In 1970 John Bossy, relying upon a number of anthropological insights, published a seminal study that employed a close scrutiny of liturgical texts to offer a new interpretation of the social and cultural transformations which accompanied, and in certain respects characterized, the Catholic Counter-Reformation.[1] In his estimation, one of the essential functions of the rituals managed by the medieval church was to periodically re-establish internal peace within communities by allowing social tensions to find an outlet through the public expression of conflict, followed by their suppression through reinternalization. According to this interpretation, post-Tridentine rituals were less effective in maintaining social peace because they overemphasized sacramental liturgies. Counter-Reformation Catholicism thus replaced a model of a harmonious society that all segments of the community had a hand in building and maintaining with one that rested on an order which was more apparent than real because it was imposed by clerical elites, and which ultimately rested, not on grand occasions of public penance and pardon, but on the individual avowal of sins within the privacy of the confessional.

Bossy's notion of an imperceptible individualization and privatization of social tension and its resolution following the Counter-Reformation certainly accords well with what a number of scholars have concluded concerning the evolution of sociability and structures of social control.[2] But was Bossy not premature in asserting that post-Tridentine ritual was fundamentally "individualist and asocial"?[3] In this case, his conclusion flows from a partial

reconstruction of what might have been the reality of a ritual performance, because it relies mainly upon liturgical texts read according to an overriding assumption that the social meaning of the rites
slowly dwindled. Bossy postulates the overly schematic assertion
that these rituals, whose purpose was clearly defined in the clerical
discourse as serving community cohesion, effectively fulfilled this
function during the Middle Ages. From this, he argues that the relative disappearance of this priority in Counter-Reformation liturgies, in which the notion of physical sacrifice was masked by a
more intellectualized sacramental culture, had the quasi-automatic
effect of weakening the bonds that united those that assembled to
hear mass. By adopting this line of interpretation, Bossy leaves little
room to understand ritual as a complex social phenomenon.

It must be stipulated at the outset that a purely religious analysis of
the liturgical evolution which followed on the Counter-Reformation
would lead to the conclusion that an individualization of ritual practices and an interiorization of belief did indeed occur, both through
the collapse of an older apparatus of ritual and the elaboration of a
new one. However, does this analysis inevitably lead the historian to
believe that the impact of these changes was sufficient to overthrow
the entire ritual culture of a population and that, in the aftermath of
the Council of Trent, a liturgy which had been viewed as a public institution of reconciliation was now simply a means of individual salvation? This article proceeds from a more nuanced assumption that
ritual always possesses a plurality of meanings. In the micro-societies
examined here – namely, the rural French-speaking Catholic parishes
of Quebec that were established between the seventeenth and the
nineteenth century, in a temporal context sufficiently long after the
enactment of the Council of Trent's reforms to lend credence to
Bossy's contentions – I see little evidence to support the hypothesis of
an "individualist" ritual culture. These parishes remained characterized by a pattern of social relations largely founded upon the community, a sociability that was demonstrated in the way that people lived
the ritual. This phenomenon was all the more significant because in
Quebec the ideal type of Catholicism set forth by clerical elites was
profoundly shaped by the Tridentine model. While changes in rural
culture in Quebec did occur over the course of two centuries, these
transformations came about relatively late in the period and were
progressive and complex. They were diffused by a number of means:
among others, by the church's institutional ritual, which purveyed a
series of new representations of social roles and models of behaviour.
This constituted a development whose implications went far beyond
mere adjustments in the liturgy, one that cannot simply be encapsu-

lated through reference to a process of individualization. Rather, it formed a part of a much larger process of cultural mutation, in which interpersonal relations were at once privatized and institutionalized. Further, in Quebec one of the most arresting features of this process was the superimposition of new models upon older practices, in which older modes of social regulation founded upon custom and local power actually survived but increasingly felt the impress of newer types of clerical control, methods that were more hegemonic and centralizing and aimed at short-circuiting the more traditional types of social interaction.

The parish community assembled in the interior space of the church, a weekly ritual theatre that doubled as a social theatre, was the specific environment in which different social groups defined themselves, measured their strength, and ultimately faced one another in a setting rife with the potential for mutual conflict. There was in these relationships a variable geometry that linked each individual to many groups at the same time and compelled a perpetual negotiation over status. In these pre-industrial rural societies, the common space was, first and foremost, the physical fabric of the church, for the countryside did not offer the extended panoply of venues for organized sociability which was available in urban areas. Yet even in the latter the church remained one of the important settings where one expressed one's rank and status. However, in rural areas the church, as the place where religious rites were performed, acquired an unparalleled significance, a fact that explains the local community's concern with the costs entailed in building and maintaining the church. It and its ancillary buildings were therefore above all other locations, the stage for meetings and display. Through membership in a group – the family – rather than as an individual, one gained a place in the jockeying for position that characterized life in these small communities, because the pew was rented to a particular family. It is significant that some bishops, in the accounts of their periodic pastoral visits, noted the number of *feux*, which was the basic unit of state tax, a procedure that identified the nuclear family as the lowest social common denominator. These senior clerics always made a careful accounting of the number of pews in each church and the total income that the vestry derived from their rent. Pew rents formed the essential basis of the parish revenues and, significantly, of how pew entitlements came into the possession of each family. Beneath this episcopal concern lay a lengthy history of managing the pews, occasional polemics, judgments that sought to resolve disputes, and adjustment to regulations.

What all this history consistently affirmed was the will of local families to annex the pews to family property. In New France up until the early years of the eighteenth century, the pew frequently appeared to be an integral part of the family estate, as the legal ability to auction it was transmitted directly to those who inherited the property.[4] However, during the 1720s, as the church made its first systematic attempts to create a parish structure, it sought to gain a certain control over pew entitlements, thus asserting its privileges in the matter of setting the level of dues. On this subject, the church became embroiled in conflict with the Conseil Supérieur. Bishop Jean-Baptiste de Saint-Vallier demanded that the parish vestries "secure the pew rents and the right to auction the pews after the death of those who own them, giving preference to widows and children."[5] In articulating this policy, his overriding concern was to enable the church to avoid dependence on the state. It ultimately became the general rule because it established a balance between the financial needs of the parish vestries, which were empowered to repossess the pews whose rents had not been paid, while safeguarding the interests of families.[6] Indeed, possession of the pew was tied to the father. A widow would keep the pew of her dead husband, but would lose it if she remarried. Because the paltry size of church buildings was a serious problem in parishes experiencing demographic growth, local vestries sometimes passed bylaws prohibiting the rental of pews by unmarried parishioners, even though they might be long-standing residents of the community.[7]

The issue of pews was thus absolutely central to the negotiating of relationships within the community. It underscored the immediate link between the ritual life of the parish, in which pew rents were invested in the financing of worship itself, church decoration, sacred objects, vestments, candles, and the established, legally recognized family – that is, the nuclear family defined around the person of the male habitant as head of the household. As well, the occupation of a pew was, for families, a source of legitimacy and standing in the community.[8] Every Sunday all the legitimate families would display themselves to one another and be recognized as such. A minimum level of prosperity was required, since the family whose pew rents fell into arrears would lose its pew. However, the social fact of possession was the key, because in order to eject the owners, the vestry would, at least by the nineteenth century, have to secure a court judgment against the debtors.[9] But was there a social hierarchy expressed during mass, articulated around the place occupied by families in the nave of the church? It is undeniable that in rural parishes the collective ritual of the mass was an important setting for bringing to the fore and validating social gradations. It must be remembered in this context that the place in which the ritual was performed was itself highly polarized. The Blessed Sacrament stood at the centre of a sacred space. However, not all parts of the church were equally sacred, as there existed a series of ascending levels of sacredness, organized into concentric circles, as one proceeded through the church door towards the altar.[10]

The necessity of carefully determining one's place in the church was most evident in the matter of precedence and in receiving honorific recognition, questions that much occupied people in the early modern era. The general limits to this fundamentally religious ceremonial dance were set by the state authorities, which determined the place that individuals and their families would occupy on these occasions. The general criterion was the function that they fulfilled both in the wider colonial society and in the parish micro-society. Here was a symbolic reward that acted as one of the primary axes of local administration. The protocol that was apparent during these ceremonies at once imposed its own order and also conferred legitimacy upon this hierarchy by closely associating it with a ritual process that possessed the ultimate validation of divine institution. Thus we have the spectacle of military officers, members of the Conseil Supérieur, the higher clergy, and officers of justice engaged in a struggle for a more prominent place in processions, seeking special attention during the rite of aspersion, clamouring to be the first to receive communion, and most significantly, attempting to secure a more prestigious pew within the church, one closest to the Blessed Sacrament just below the altar rail. This jockeying for position was characteristic of all rural parishes, where churchwardens, seigneurs, captains and militia officers, and even members of the church choir engaged in a constant assertion of precedence.[11] In 1768 Governor Guy Carleton required that the same honours – namely, the first pew in the middle row on the epistle side of the church – as was accorded the captain of militia under the French regime be henceforth conferred upon the head bailiff.[12] The inhabitants who were "expropriated" by this decision sometimes resisted, but the petty local officials usually got their way. For example, the bishop recorded in his visitation book that at Nicolet, Étienne Dumas, the under-bailiff, "took hold of the son of Louis Beaubien and rousted him out of the pew because the young man was loath to give it up."[13] At the beginning of the nineteenth century, Charles de Saint-Ours, a seigneur and aristocrat and a parishioner of L'Assomption, complained that "the [visibly vacant] seigneurial pew presently occupied by the servants of M. Roy [the *curé*], about whom I will not trouble you with my comments would be better occupied by the militia staff officers of L'Assomption and Lavaltrie."[14]

Beyond these privileges, which derived from one's function in the state structure, there were more subtle rankings linked to wealth, status, length of residency in the parish, and level of religious involvement. In principle, the law elevated financial status as the criteria for pew assignment. A *mandement* issued at the end of the seventeenth century clearly instructed the churchwardens to "auction [the pews] at the front door of the church, so that those who will contribute most to the church will secure them."[15] The "King's Regulation for the conceding of pews in the churches of Canada," proclaimed on 9 June 1723, was even more explicit: the annual rent that the buyer had to pay was the price set at auction, and the pew would only be conceded to the highest and final bidder.[16] Certain customs also reinforced the importance of wealth; thus those who donated land to the church would receive in exchange a free, well-situated pew, the first below the altar on the right if they were seigneurs. In 1790 a landowner obtained a pew for a pledge to furnish twenty-five cords of wood annually to the *curé*, which the latter promised would be "the first pew below that of the *curé* himself."[17] However, Allan Greer has observed that, at the beginning of the nineteenth century in the Richelieu valley, the habitants were frequently able to circumvent the system by not engaging in bidding, thus compelling a sale at the lowest price. This practice served to buttress their demand for a hereditary system of transmitting pew entitlements.[18] In this way, they engaged in a defence of their privileges as small proprietors in the face of a rising rural bourgeoisie that increasingly had the means to monopolize the best places in church. In the absence of a more detailed study of this issue over time, it is difficult to understand the exact relationship between position occupied in the church, wealth, and length of residence. However, given the present state of knowledge, it is reasonable to posit the following hypothesis: in the eighteenth century, length of residency was a more decisive factor than wealth. But during the ensuing century this relationship was reversed as the sale of pews to the highest bidder was progressively detached from any lingering hereditary constraints.[19]

Be that as it may, the interplay of economic imperatives evident in the process of pew auctions and ideals of family continuity that emphasized hereditary transmission of pew entitlements ensured that one's position in the church – "higher" close to the sanctuary and "lower" towards the main door – was assigned to families as a function of their economic status and their length of residence in the parish. Indeed, among peasants the two attributes were often linked. As for the poorer and less-established families, they were almost invariably relegated to the back of the church. In this respect, it is significant that the clerical discourse assigned a lesser value to peripheral areas in the church building, a view which associated social disqualification and moral deprivation. Thus the rood-loft, the most outlying part of the church, had a bad reputation because it escaped the surveillance of those charged with maintaining good order during the ritual, the *curé*, his assistant, the beadle, the churchwardens, and the parish constables. For Bishop Jean-Olivier Briand the loft was "gathering-place of all libertines and undevout elements, or, should I say, the blasphemers."[20] Some parishioners were relegated to even worse situations, compelled to sit on the stairs that led to the loft.[21] In this respect, the church door was regarded as practically a profane zone which could be likened to an airlock between two worlds. Here the newborn infants waiting to be baptized, and the "marginal" individuals – women who required churching after giving birth and penitents required to perform public penance – were forced to wait before reintegration into the parish community. As well, the poorest parishioners and men who wanted to leave quietly as the sermon began tended to frequent the area around the church door.

In these rural Quebec parishes it would be impossible to reduce social legitimation to the sole determinant of economic status. There were so many other overlapping elements at work that, in the final analysis, the study of local hierarchies must proceed from the premise that they were complex entities firmly archored in a specific historical context. From the foregoing discussion, however, one can conclude that a person's place in the church during mass was fixed by the highly formalized ordering of who occupied what particular pew. Further, in this scheme of social ranking, individuals were classed as members of family groups, and the status of the latter was a function of the father's position in society. Not only was this representation of the family highly patriarchal, but it articulated the image of local society as a hierarchical group of families. Consequently, individuals participated in the ritual of Sunday mass first and foremost as members of families. These local hierarchies of families constituted the basic social framework in a society undergoing rapid development and where social mobility was high and church buildings were few and far between. What conferred a sense of order and continuity was the indefeasible reality of owning and occupying a pew. Even when parishes could afford to build a more commodious church, the pews were simply transferred to the new building and all assumed their former places in the social hierarchy.

In these social settings the family was not, first and foremost, a set of intimate relationships divorced from the public sphere. Rather, attendance at Sunday mass exposed the family to the persistent scrutiny of other families, which acted as a powerfully constraining form of social control, one that the *curé* at times sanctioned and on other occasions attempted to moderate. In Quebec the social power of the clergy was certainly a reality, but it was a power that was exercised within certain bounds which parishioners considered legitimate. In this respect, ordinary believers were hardly silent and submissive in the face of clerical dictates. From parish correspondence – letters of clergy commenting on conflicts that shook particular communities, but also letters from habitants, in the form either of petitions drafted by the village notary or of individual missives directed to the bishop – we can see that these small societies were constantly fraught with tension caused by malicious gossip. The church posed as the arbiter of these social divisions, which it sought to appease under the rubric of maintaining peace and order. Its tactic in healing these local tensions was to present the image of an ideal society and to periodically employ exceptional rituals to inspire the hope that such an ideal could be realized. Thus the visit of the bishop was held up as the perfect occasion on which to regenerate society, through the image of the Good Shepherd coming down into the middle of his flock; the arrival of the bishop in the village was likened to the coming of Jesus Christ into the world.[22] Clerical accounts of these visits invariably present them as a time of outpouring of grace, when old enmities were reconciled and gossip ceased. On these occasions the ritual apparatus was greatly enhanced through processions, the presence of a large number of priests from outside the parish, precious and colourful vestments, and specific and rarely seen ceremonies.

Above all, however, mass confessions were the order of the day; serious cases of sin reserved for episcopal decision were granted absolution either by the bishop or by one of the confessors attached to the clerical delegation.[23] Ordinary parishioners, however, saw in the presence of outside confessors, made most evident through the addition of portable screens to the altar rail, the perfect occasion to escape the prying scrutiny of their own parish *curé*; the next day, communions were very numerous. In this way, periodic mass confessions acted as a safety valve for those who sought to escape the daily uncertainty of living with unacknowledged and unpardoned sins and the opprobrium of suspicion emanating from their neighbours. Jubilees functioned as another such periodic occasion when the high drama of reconciliation and restoration of order was re-enacted. In 1767 *curé* Degeay described the crowd, the spectacular conversions, and the palpable transformation of attitudes that had occurred in his parish of L'Assomption. "Eleven hundred persons," he stated, "took communion with much edification to themselves; often I had to stay in the confessional from 5 in the morning to 10 or 11 in the evening … By what I have seen during the fifteen days after Easter, the fruits of the jubilee have endured. Many people have been restored to good standing in the community, and many of the reconciliations with God appear to me to be sincere."[24]

In an era before the large-scale diocesan missions characteristic of later-nineteenth- and twentieth-century Quebec Catholicism, the ritual events surrounding the jubilee and the episcopal visit enabled the church to articulate a vision of society and an ideal of social relationships that should prevail. According to this scheme, the ritual of confession and pardon was not merely a formal or private procedure involving individual sinners, but must lead to concrete and visible acts of reconciliation. It was administered within the context of a theology of fear, by which the destiny of the entire group was linked to the conduct of each of its members. Indeed, divine wrath would punish the whole for any breaches of God's law committed by any of its parts. Thus nothing happened which was exclusively a transaction between God and the individual. To be sure, on occasions of mass confession, parishioners waited single file in front of the portable screens that temporarily replaced public sessions of penance and absolution. But personal interaction with the priest and individual repentance were always integrated into a dynamic process that was fundamentally collective in nature. Furthermore, the ritual, even when scripted as a private conversation between priest and penitent, remained in actual fact subject to public scrutiny and comment.

In examining this clerical literature which prescribed an idyllic portrait of social reconciliation, we must be keep resolutely in the foreground the fact that the ritual was something that cannot be abstracted from a framework in which it operated in a permanent and reciprocal dynamic, at once controlling and subject to the control of the constant attempt by local families to affirm and enhance their status. Ritual was in fact the keystone of an apparatus of custom which served to normalize individual behaviour. And as we have seen, individual behaviour was itself determined by membership in the family and in the microcosm of the parish group, which exercised a double vigilance over any transgressions. The concepts that governed behaviour both in the family and in the parish society were honour and scandal. The church did not work at cross-purposes with the rules of the game; rather, it claimed to be the chief umpire. And herein lay the key to its power at the local level, because it had sole possession of the administration of the rites during which social boundaries were publicly asserted and exclusions from and reintegrations into local society managed. The entire community was involved in the definition of scandal, and no one, not even the parish *curé*, was immune from the potential for dishonour. Here is a subtle relationship between the institutional ritual and the wider society that must be explored in more depth.

Honour was the prized possession of families, especially those with little in the way of worldly goods. It was, however, a fragile treasure, always subject to the hasty and often inaccurate verdict of wagging tongues. For parishioners, the preservation of honour was a constant and essential concern. What would it serve to possess a well-situated pew if family honour was lost? The position in the parish church that might have testified to the status of a household could overnight, through the public revelation of transgression, become the scene of its humiliation. Was it not out of concern to spare his family's reputation that, during rituals of public penance, the sinner voluntarily chose to leave the community? In the seventeenth and eighteenth centuries the public sinner, whether excommunicated or not, was generally excluded from church for periods of time which varied according to the gravity of the transgression. This exile was followed by a fairly lengthy process of reintegration, with an obligatory period spent standing at the rear of the church.[25] In these instances the concern was not to lessen the dishonour that attached to the individual but, rather, to preserve the community from the taint of scandal by temporarily excluding the delinquent from society. The empty place in the pew was an eloquent reminder that dishonour besmirched the entire household. Religious representations added elements drawn from Christian myth to reinforce social exclusion. As in the clerical discourse on disasters, individual sin was the root cause of misfortune that hit everyone without distinction; the particular offence of one family member drew calamity upon the entire household. This concept ineluctably drew people into a mental framework shaped by the biblical story of original sin, a mindset in which the sins of wives and daughters had particularly disastrous consequences for family honour.

In a general way, the church recognized that honour was fundamental to the standing of families. As the dispenser of social rituals of penance, it had the primary duty to ensure that accusations made in the form of rumour were well founded. Thus *curés*, in their reports of "parish abuses" directed to their episcopal superiors, always highlighted "scandalmongering" and "libel."[26] Paradoxically, however, local gossip networks played an important part in the very diocesan administration that sought to curb their abuses. Gossip reached the bishop through two main channels. When rumours involved the *curé*, the outraged parishioners wrote directly to the bishop in the hope of securing a replacement. As a model for all his people, the ideal priest had to be above all suspicion, a Procrustean bed which ensured that his behaviour would inevitably arouse it. He was certainly the most scrutinized and monitored member of the parish. Indeed, the parish priest was often cast in the role of defending his family honour, since a widowed mother or sister would often live with him. In a wider sense, however, the priest's honour was attached to the broader spiritual fraternity of clergy, over which the bishop acted as a father and, in this capacity, was forced to receive all the ugly rumours concerning the conduct of his scattered progeny. Quebec's diocesan archives contain a sizable concentration of these, at times anonymous but frequently signed, letters of complaint and denunciation. For example, in 1792 the *curé* of Lachine was accused of paying court to women. He defended himself maladroitly to the bishop, declaring that if he were engaged in such activities, he would not be doing so in the light of public scrutiny. "If I had the indecency to take young women for drives in my carriage," he stated, "I would not be doing so at Lachine, and even less so in Montreal."[27] Around the same time the *curé* of Sainte-Rose attempted to hide his amorous activities by going out at night. However, he did not succeed in shaking off the village spies:

Joseph Filliatreau, François Quenneville, André Nadon, former churchwardens, Michel Desjardins, syndic, Michel Marié, Amable Desjardins, Jean-Marie Morriseau, all inhabitants of the parish of Ste Rose of Ile Jesus, have the honour to inform you that for over five years Mr. Galet our *curé* has, according to the common knowledge of the whole parish, constantly frequented the house of Joseph Giroux, one of the choristers of this place, and that the said Giroux had living with him his sister Marie Giroux, and that some time ago the aforementioned *curé*, to the great surprise of the said parish, carried off Marie Giroux at night and took her to one named Joseph Bargue, surgeon at Terrebonne, where a few days ago she was delivered of a child.[28]

What was in store for this illegitimate family? Perhaps the enforced separation of the priest and the woman, with the unwed mother confined to a convent, a resolution that occurred a few years later at Saint-Paul (Joliette).[29] The eternal problem of Catholic discipline was resolved in this case, as it often was, by having the parties to the transgression removed from the scene. In instances of suspected sexual impropriety by members of the clergy, merely circumstantial evidence was sufficient to start the gossip mill running. Because their honour and good standing was at the mercy of the opinions of others – and this fact explains why the church reprobated slander as a serious abuse – *curés* were always prompt to defend themselves, and bishops were especially punctilious about monitoring the ages of priests' female servants and housekeepers. Transgressions against chastity bore the brunt of the parishioners' outrage, but letters accusing priests of drunkenness came a close second.[30] Drunkenness and illicit sex were the main areas where clerical behaviour incurred public censure, to such an extent that these sins were constantly chastized during the ritual performances themselves.

The second channel of local gossip was none other than *curés* themselves. Some seem to have had their ears in constant readiness to receive rumours, while most at least made a show of collecting parish goings-on. And what parish would have lacked a few good souls ready and willing to retail neighbourhood gossip? In one way or another, all manner of anecdote and hearsay would have passed through the *curé*. What would he had done with all this information? What he chose to do in these circumstances could make all the difference between a good priest and a poor one;[31] the good priest acted prudently, with an eye to best preserving the honour of the families involved, while the "bad" priest allowed himself to be swayed by rumour and engaged in hasty public denunciations of the supposed delinquent activity. One parishioner of Lachine complained that his parish priest "even in his Sunday sermons indulges in sallies and remarks which, although delivered obliquely, leave no doubt in the minds of all present that they are directed at me personally or reflect upon my character and private conduct." This individual stated that he preferred to absent himself from church rather than attend Sunday mass "for fear of experiencing more of these mortifications."[32] This priest made himself the most powerful transmitter of scandal, but, as *curé* Giroux informed Monseigneur Ignace Bourget, in these instances the parish priest often walked a tightrope.[33] Giroux stated that it was necessary to preach "in such a way that those guilty of this or that vice or the fomentors of such and such a disorder understand that it is not their neighbour who has committed or will commit the sin that I denounce; to make matters more clear, I provided a few details." The priest's action touched off a flood of gossip, and soon the parish was threatened with social discord.

This type of clerical behaviour was fraught with so many implications for community harmony that parishioners rightly denounced it to the bishop. In 1825 fifteen inhabitants of Sainte-Rose complained that *curé* Belair had surrounded himself with a circle of informers and spies over which he exercised "absolute power." On the strength of their unsubstantiated reports, he allowed himself to "oppress, insult, and use the most insulting and disagreeable language" to parishioners and was unwilling to hear anything that they had to say in their own defence. In the estimation of these people, Belair, "by acting solely on the basis of *hearsay*,[34] created a situation in which the guilty will escape censure while the innocent are punished."[35] Nonetheless, the clergy's verbal exhortations did not carry the social weight of ritual sanctions against sinners. These penalties, particularly in rural areas, would not have been regarded lightly. As Serge Gagnon has abundantly and perceptively shown, the clergy were very scrupulous, in the case of serious transgressions, about determining a scale of punishment commensurate with the nature of the sin.[36] Parish priests would invoke a penalty only after carefully weighing all elements of the case and always attempting to take the particular circumstances into account. Bishops, on the other hand, were more concerned to ensure that a common standard was firmly applied. Yet even they were aware of the need for flexibility if there were extenuating circumstances, and they rarely favoured extreme solutions. Finally, the clergy was always concerned to abstract the process of judgment from the parish rumour mill by carefully collecting testimony and frequently relying upon the advice of expert witnesses, usually doctors. In many of these situations, which usually involved illicit sex, illegitimate birth, or suicide, the historian can discern the anxious intervention of families who stood on the brink of dishonour.

The second great responsibility undertaken by the church in protecting the reputation of families was to ensure that the ritual events themselves did not act as mechanisms to reveal scandal or as occasions of scandal. The official ideology was that the purpose of ritual was to resolve scandal, not to cause it, a goal that was very difficult to realize in practice because the rituals themselves were public, and thus settings for the exercise of collective scrutiny by the congregation. Here was a fundamental ambiguity, a telling illustration of the divergence between the institutional church's desire to individualize religious practices and the mechanisms of the performance itself, which revealed the maintenance of a parish ritual that was embodied and understood in collective terms. This tension was most tellingly illustrated by the way in which the complex ritual of confession and communion was interpreted and administered by the clergy and lived by ordinary parishioners.

One of the great achievements of the Tridentine church was the isolation of the sinner in a process of avowal and individual pardon of sins, with forgiveness taking concrete form in the ritual consumption of communion. The secrecy of the confessional was the fundamental criterion in this process, and it explains the proliferation of wooden confessionals in church naves after the sixteenth century. However, the building of these structures makes sense only within the context of a ritual practice that remained public in character. Clerical prescriptions, as codified in the diocesan *Rituel*, were explicit. The duty of secrecy was binding not only on the priest but also on anyone who had "heard anything of the Confession while the Penitent was confessing: this obligates Confessors ... to ensure that people remain at a reasonable distance from the Confessional, and to warn the Penitents if they are speaking too loudly."[37] Furthermore, the *Rituel* instructed the priest, "If the Confessor is obliged to refuse or defer absolution, he must comport himself in such a way that such a refusal or delay brings no scandal upon the Penitent, and so that it not come to the attention of those present, he will say over the person who has confessed his sins the following prayer." This prayer took the form of a benediction spoken aloud "so that those present do not know that [the priest] has refused or deferred absolution."[38] But running counter to this practice, there existed an abundant prescriptive literature that sought to limit – or at least, precisely structure – the intimacy of dialogue in the confessional, especially that involving female penitents. The *Rituel* established a policy that was regularly republished:

[The place where confessions are held] must always be the Church and not the Sacristy, the latter reserved for the hearing of the clergy's confessions. However, if confessions are sometimes held there because of extreme cold or other necessary circumstances, the confessions of women must not be heard there, but those of men alone, and certainly never those of women who are alone. [The priest] will sit in a Confessional which must be located in the Nave, in the place most able to be seen, and it will be decorated with trellised windows for the hearing of Confessions, which must be made, as much as possible, during daylight hours.[39]

In practice, however, these ideal arrangements did not take form in the rural areas of Quebec before the second half of the nineteenth century. The rigours of the climate dictated that the presbytery occasionally and the sacristy invariably were used to hear confessions between November and May. This was such a well-established breach of practice that the first confessional in every parish was always located in the sacristy. In the poorest parishes, because of the cost of a second piece of furniture, confessions were heard in the sacristy even during the summer months. The bishops of the nineteenth century were outraged at this practice and insisted that the confessional be placed in the nave or that, at the very least, portable screens be installed at the two ends of the altar rail.[40] Even if in practice the sacristy was a very open setting, linked to the nave by a covered walkway, the episcopal intervention reiterated that the true purpose of the ritual arrangements was to carve out a private space, but in the setting of a public environment – that is, under the surveillance of a parish community that refused to be deprived of the right of scrutinizing the behaviour of its members. What drove the bishops in this matter was not simply a diffuse fear of women but also the concern to prevent rumours, which originated in situations charged with ambiguity and were always regarded as possessing the power to ruin the honour of the families of those confessing. However, the confessional, a closed structure that sheltered the individual at the same time from prying eyes and from rumour, because it was ideally located in the nave and a screen separated the body of the priest from that of women, seems to have been introduced only haltingly into rural Quebec.[41] Moreover, the constant whispering of the parish community even intruded upon the supposedly private, intimate dialogue of the confession itself. The "ecclesiastical power to judge"ensured that, for the essential Easter confession, parishioners could not easily escape their local *curé*. Bishop Jean-François Hubert tightened the screws in 1793 by proclaiming that, unless given extraordinary powers, *curés* could only confess their own parishioners and those from adjoining parishes located less than three leagues away.[42] A whole system of "tickets" or affidavits, given to the priest when "foreign" penitents sought absolution or communion outside their home parishes, expressed in concrete form the desire to prevent anonymity, to block the abstraction of the penitent from the daily round of comment and gossip that characterized the parish microcosm.

Communion was an even more public act. Because it was conditional upon securing absolution, this ritual had even more potential to inflict damage on reputations. The power that priests had to "not dispense" (*passer*) communion to parishioners could, on occasion, become an ignominious trial, as illustrated by the experience of Mme Quévillon, a parishioner of Saint-Vincent-de-Paul, who had the misfortune to fall out with her local priest and thus had to seek absolution in a neighbouring parish.[43] The *curé* of Saint-Vincent demanded an affidavit of absolution, which she stated she did not need because her "way of living,"as she said, was "known" to all. Thus began a personality conflict in which the bishop was forced to arbitrate. Mme Quévillon wrote:

Monseigneur have pity on me, I am crushed with sorrow. I throw myself into your paternal arms, help me, because nothing affects me more than being deprived of Holy Communion ... I cannot present myself to take it without your assurance that I am free to do so, without exposing myself to having it refused. If this happens to me a third time, I believe that I will die of sorrow from the scandal that has already resulted ... I have taken communion many times without the priest refusing me because I always took Communion with someone else and on the 21st the Octave of the Blessed Sacrament, I was in church but he confessed no one even though many wanted to be confessed and asked him to go to the confessional and I saw him frequently appear from behind the altar where he appeared to be watching to see if I was still there or not ... As he thought that I would present myself for Communion at the mass he said to an altar boy that he had confessed no one and that he would not be present to say the Confiteor ... Not knowing this I presented myself and was refused Communion and he said to one of his altar boys that if I asked why he had not said the Confiteor to tell me that I was a madwoman ... the 10th of this month having presented myself for communion with another person who had presented themselves with me and he passed over me in front of a number of people because on that day there was an anniversary service which caused a great scandal ... Now I fear that he is as capable of slander as of refusing me Communion in public.[44]

This squabble dragged on, and even episcopal efforts to resolve it were fruitless. It serves to illustrate how religious rituals, through their public character, played a primary role in the articulation of rural sociability.

However, we must elucidate the dynamic that linked this sociability, founded upon mechanisms of customary control, to the institution that maintained a tight rein over ritual procedures. Let us pause for a moment to consider the meanings attached to the concepts of honour and scandal and their interrelationship. The French lexicographer Antoine Furetière, in his *Dictionnaire universel*, defined honour as an act that "testified to the homage or submission which one renders to another" in either words or actions. He then stipulated that "we owe honour and respect first and foremost to God and holy things, to Kings and Magistrates, to one's parents and to virtue."[45] These categories were founded upon the obligation of law: the son honoured his father, not because of the particular virtues of the latter, since the category of virtue was subordinate to that of fatherhood, but simply because of the kinship tie. That God was the first recipient of homage was the perfect indication that honour was a sacred act transcending individual choice, and it defined a social order that was given from on high and not built by human will.

Thus we come back to the initial portrait of families sitting in their church pews. Here was an image of order that was itself a process of legitimation: the honour rendered to God by the worship also consecrated parental authority and that of the king and his family, which was always mentioned during the course of the mass. The family thus took precedence over the individual during the ritual, as a sacred and unquestioned social structure. From this perspective, the Christian image of the Holy Family acquired an enhanced value. In effect, the purpose was not simply to define a clerical representation of the ideal family but also to worship it: that is, to legitimate the family as itself a sacred institution. The importance of the devotion accorded in Canada to the Holy Family is well known to historians.[46] It took firm root as early as the seventeenth century, and its popularity was undeniable and strongly sustained by the church. This devotion was conveyed in a number of ways that suggest a profound and extensive diffusion: women's confraternities established in many localities, congregations of girls, use of members of the Holy Family as tutelary figures, liturgical feasts and devotions,[47] printed books, and above all, a veritable plethora of iconography. Reverence for the sacralized family filtered down to the parish churches in the form of statues and tableaux and penetrated ordinary homes through the medium of engravings. This voluntary exaltation of the Holy Family by elites who participated in the organization and the peopling of Quebec undoubtedly constitutes a compelling element in the interpretation of the founding of new societies by historians, precisely because of the emphasis that they place upon the role of the family in the process of settlement.[48]

Thus it is necessary to link the overrepresentation of this familial archetype, Jesus-Mary-Joseph,[49] with the construction of a twofold cultural paradigm. This worship effected a junction between the horizontal family, of which the terrestrial trinity was the model and constituted the foundation of society, with the vertical family of the celestial Trinity. The process was abundantly illustrated by the iconography of the Holy Family, where there was reciprocity between the symbolic gradations in the system of identification: patriarchy built upon the image of God the Father, which in return sustained the father's role in the family.[50] The preaching of fear made abundant reference to the depiction of an authoritarian God, who was loving but of an implacable severity towards humans, considered incorrigible children. In these portrayals, Jesus was at the same time a child protected by his parents and, as the son of his heavenly Father, subordinate in the vertical scheme. It was apparent that the church, inspired by the Holy Spirit, who occupied an intermediate position within the celestial Trinity under the authority of the Father, nonetheless held a position of authority with reference to the child. Thus we can see how the clergy moved to identify spirit, church, and mother. As in the case of the analogy between God and father, there was a shared representation of maternal functions, such as physical and moral guardianship and the transmission of values. Again, this pattern shows the desire to bring the two representations into close proximity and at the same time to impose a single model. The portrayal of the two trinities in conjunction thus instituted a double paradigm: the family was the basis of society (horizontal trinity), and the church was in a special position of social authority (vertical Trinity). And such was the concept of social order established by the ritual arrangements in the church: ranks of ordered families sat across the middle axis of the church, which from the nave moved upward to the choir, where the *curé* officiated before the Blessed Sacrament under the reredos, which in some churches was dominated by the figure of the eternal Father. Here was the ideal of order defined by the rendering of honour to one's superiors.

However, a slippage in the meaning of honour allowed Quebec Catholics to move back and forth between these rigid categories of order to one being constantly redefined and renegotiated through the process of mutual scrutiny that occurred within the space of the church nave. Furetière's commentary captured something of this more general and less formalized process when he wrote of "the homage due to virtue and merit." We have thus entered into a more dynamic and less static meaning of the term, in which the rendering of honour was not a function of duty but the mark of recognized value. Such an honouring, which signified at once virtue and merit, is suggestive of a constant evaluation through mutual scrutiny in which families, as a pledge of their respectability, enforced the obedience of their household to a social code. Honour was lost through scandal, which was nothing other than public knowledge of the transgression, rather than the actual fault itself. Scandal was an affront to those aware of breaches of the customary order or of common opinion. Thus the Protestant preacher caused scandal through his doctrine, the drunkard by his roistering, women through gaudy apparel, and unmarried girls by becoming pregnant.[51] The community itself was assaulted by the transgression and demanded a reparation of the breach of the rules defining it. Indeed, until the second half of the nineteenth century, the church took upon itself a ritual treatment of scandal, in which the sinner must make a public declaration of repentance, accept a period of exclusion from the church, which in extreme cases might amount to perpetual ostracism, and go through a phase of reintegration into the community. While time might erase the stigma of less serious infractions, a grave offence could besmirch family honour for many years, for in these rural communities the collective memory was itself woven out of the record of these transgressions, while the obverse side of the fabric highlighted the consensual rules.

The parish priest was thus trapped between two competing requirements, a situation particularly evident when *curés* denounced the private conduct of some of their parishioners from the pulpit. In the small society of the parish, where nothing could be private or kept private for very long, and where a transgression, once made public, could not be covered up, the *curé* was always acutely aware of the vital role that he exercised within the process of community self-regulation, particularly in resolving the crises caused by these offences. However, the institution that he represented had begun to detach itself from this community culture to join a general movement of privatization which placed the interest of families above the direct judgment of others in the community.

Beyond the articulation of an idealized social order based on the family in the sight of God and the administration of a communal system of normalization more or less integrated with the institutional ritual, another process was at work in the church nave. This was the all-important matter of the construction of sexual identity, for, as all were aware, the honour of the family rested, in the final analysis, upon the shoulders of women. As Furetière observed, "honour flows particularly from two types of virtue, valour for men, and chastity for women" (*l'honneur s'applique plus particulièrement à deux sortes de vertus, à la vaillance pour les hommes, et à la chasteté pour les femmes*).[52] Women, far more than men, were the first objects of public scrutiny, because the inquisitorial gaze of the assembled community was always alert to signs of illegitimate pregnancy, the visible testimony of sin. Thus the first concern of families was to protect women from scandal. This was precisely what the church intended through the special mechanism of legislation concerning "reserved cases," those sins that were so serious that absolution could only be granted by the bishop. As the *Rituel de Québec* made clear, "children below the age of puberty, which is 12 for girls and 14 for boys, are not included under the rubric of reserved Cases. Nor are women or girls who cannot be sent to the Superior without scandal."[53] A woman was likewise subject to the scrutiny of the community because her body was believed to be saturated with sexuality and thus an occasion for sin. The exaggerated prudery of Quebec's early bishops on this score is well known. What it reveals, however, is that women were considered the prime agents of adultery by their conduct and outward appearance, a view ratified by the civil law, which interpreted seduction as something consciously worked by designing women upon unwitting male victims.[54] So well established was this trope in Quebec that nineteenth-century preaching constantly reiterated the same rhetoric that had been introduced in to Canada at the end of the seventeeth century.[55]

There is nothing surprising about this discourse, for in Catholic thought, women and sex were the root of all evil. *Mandements*, sermons, and reports by parish priests on the subject of women invariably emphasized scandalous immodesty, the baring of shoulders and necks, curled hair, overly transparent fabrics, superfluous body ornaments, and shameless apparel. The only conclusion to be drawn from this litany is that it indicates that many women took no account of it and came to church dressed with all the elegance which their age and social status permitted. However, at the same time the ideal of female participation in church rituals sought to establish a standard of behaviour: clothing must be sober and hide the body as much as possible. Indeed, according to these prescriptions, the female body must be completely immobile in church, kneeling over a rosary or a missal in a posture of submission and humility. At Communion, women must keep their heads veiled, their breasts and shoulders completely covered, and their dress "restrained, without allowing themselves the appearance of anything hinting at vanity, sensuality, or luxury."[56] Whatever small degree of participation the church permitted women was conditional upon their desexualization, as clerical discourse worked from the premise that the nun was the ideal woman. In Canada this archetypal female model seems to have emerged at the end of the seventeenth century in an urban and bourgeois environment in which women in comfortable social circumstances were the primary targets of clerical admonitions against luxury. At the same time the church articulated a notion of the Christian mother which was nearly indistinguishable from the image of the nun.[57] Here, undoubtedly, was one of the sources of the ideal of the "domesticated" woman so widely diffused during the second half of the nineteenth century.[58]

However, within the context of the parish, the clergy had to live with women "of the world" (*du monde*), who could not simply be categorized as "worldly" (*mondaines*). Ecclesiastical commentary divided them into three groups: widows, mothers, and unmarried girls. Widows were, on the whole, regarded most favourably, because they were reputed to be asexual. The archetype of the widow-nun, epitomized in Canada by Marie de l'Incarnation, can also be traced in the figure of the converted Aboriginal woman, who symbolized missionary endeavour. Bishop Saint-Vallier offered the following description of a young widow aged twenty-nine: "one hour after her husband's funeral, [she] cut her hair, not to afford greater display of her affliction, but to devote herself more perfectly to God, by completely renouncing the world and keeping her chastity."[59] He was equally laudatory of the governor's wife, who, not satisfied with attending mass every day and devoting her life to pious works, "spends a portion of her life in convents for girls, where she has been given free entry ... the rest of her time she spends at home raising her family and performing daily tasks with her own hands."[60] However, the mother, although protected by her married status, was always compromised by her sexual activities. It was to her that the parish priest primarily addressed his efforts to regulate the sex life of married couples.[61] For example, after giving birth, the mother would have to go through a period when she was considered impure and thus excluded from the sacred space of the church. The ritual of churching would permit her to reintegrate with the parish community by purifying her "of sins [that she may] have committed in the state of Marriage."[62] More significantly, wives must abstain from all sexual relations at Easter and on feast days and Sundays.[63]

However, the real object of clerical concern was, without doubt, the unmarried adolescent girl. For her, the church proposed a series of rituals that entailed the complete sublimation of amorous feelings and budding sensuality in a mystical union with the Saviour. This was centred around consuming the body of Christ during mass, as illustrated by the prayer before Holy Communion suggested to girls boarding at the Ursuline convent: "Oh my Saviour, I have a great desire to receive you, it is this that fills my heart day and night, it is the object of all my thoughts, after which I sigh after having received such a great gift." After taking Communion, the girls were advised to say, "I pray that I never act against your wishes, that I do not abandon myself like the animals to sensual pleasures, but that my entire spirit be occupied by you and that my sole pleasure be to fill my heart with your holy love."[64] In the case of these young women, religion was intended to serve as a kind of bell jar that protected the family.

Although Bishop Henri-Marie de Pontbriand praised Canadian females in 1751 as "pious women above reproach" and "young girls who are good, chaste, and modest, despite the corruption of the century,"[65] the episcopal archives tell a different story, one of insubordinate young women determined to parade seductively whenever they could. The church, of course, was one of those places and the mass one of those times when this desire was most in evidence. A 1732 ordinance prohibited the wearing of "hooded capes," which were

particularly widespread among young women, "less for their usefulness than to be considered fashionable and noticed." Young women
who felt cold sitting in church were advised to wear a "skullcap" or a
wig.[66] It can certainly be assumed that such a regulation caused much
pouting among young women. A century later a priest felt compelled
to intervene in order to defend the reputation of his pew. "My dear
Emilie," he wrote to his niece, "in allowing you to use my pew, I did
not permit you to daub your face with rouge; it is against my wishes.
Wearing cosmetics does not suit tanned complexions such as ours.
Besides, it is offering a reproach to God in wishing to change the appearance of his handiwork and in doing so, you sin more seriously
than you are aware."[67]

What this letter illustrates is that the church, as well as being the
scene of ritual, was a place where one gauged, judged, and desired
the opposite sex. Despite all attempts to limit this phenomenon, it
could not be contained. Above all, the clergy absolutely barred all
women from the holy precincts of the choir, the centre of the liturgical
spectacle. Even in the nave, movements were tightly regulated, with
the intention of curbing as far as possible any kind of social performance. Women were exhorted to approach the "Holy Table" with
"modesty and respect"and to kneel, with their heads to the front and
eyes lowered at all times, looking neither to the right nor to the left,
and to open their mouths in a restrained manner. After communion,
women were directed to pray in a corner of the church "without looking about them," to thank God, and to meditate upon Christ's Passion.[68] The parish clergy was expressly instructed to exclude
immodest women and girls from the sacraments (communion, marriage, bringing children to be baptized) and authorized to refuse
them absolution and prohibit them from taking up the collection,
bringing the offerings, or distributing bread that had been blessed.[69]

Through this exclusion of women and the suspicion directed at
unmarried girls, the clergy hoped to adumbrate a principle of order
applicable to the internal management of the household. This was to
be achieved through the construction of social roles, a process apparent in the iconography of the heavenly and earthly trinities, the one
impressed upon the other. The tripartite and hierarchical division of
the world (God, church, family) enjoined, in its turn, a clearly defined family hierarchy ordered around father, mother, and children.
Was it not, then, in the name of paternal authority, especially the father's power to choose a husband for his daughter, that the clergy
sought to control the activities of women and girls? Here was a
power that was at once effective yet contested, which left a most revealing record of youthful strategies that sought to counter parental

opposition. One tactic was for a pregnant daughter to confront her father with a *fait accompli* and thus compel a marriage to which he would unwillingly give his consent.[70] Herein lay the reason why the clergy so vigorously sought to control the young people of the parish, developing an impressive apparatus of rules concerning the management of "courtship" (*fréquentations*); it was a social duty that tied the *curé* to the father of the family. In the diocese of Quebec, ritual engagements were prohibited by the end of the seventeenth century,[71] with the aim of eradicating the premarital sexual permissiveness associated with this custom. If one is to believe Bishop Briand's denunciation of 1771 that no one "finds anything especially shameful or criminal in the weaknesses that precede marriage,"[72] it would appear that the earlier proscription was entirely ineffectual. What Briand viewed as a degradation of morals was in fact the persistence of an older custom.[73]

In 1843 Bishop Bourget promulgated a formula for courting, intended for the information of clergy and parishioners: no nocturnal or prolonged encounters, no unchaperoned or "unlighted"meetings, no mutual touching, no meeting without the permission of parents, no indecent words or "incitements to unchaste acts," no outings together, "either in their parish or elsewhere, and especially not in town."[74] If the young people had been so imprudent as to exchange promises, all courting was to be prohibited. This circular was accompanied by a set of recommendations governing balls and dances, which in effect both recognized the prelude to courting and enclosed it within very strict boundaries. However, these marriages, which cleverly negotiated the space between the sacramental efficacy of the mass and the maintenance of a communal cultural system – the group's witness validated the act – became progressively more rare as they ran up against the privatizing imperatives of patriarchal power. By the nineteenth century, marriage *à la gaumine* had disappeared, a process in which the church, by defending the authority of fathers, asserted its own right to control marriages.[75] But what needs to be underscored here is that marriage *à la gaumine* illustrated an ambiguous conjunction that lay at the heart of parish communities, in which institutional regulation and the promotion of family structure and the devaluing of individual desire and the workings of communal legitimation were inextricably mingled.

In the final analysis, however, it is difficult to seize upon instances of youthful disobedience outside of the clerical discourse that reprobated it. In the case of the charivari, historians have shown that there was in fact a social and moral order that lay beyond the actual conduct which the clergy disparaged.[76] These events were no longer simply evidence of licentiousness but an illustration of the power of custom that stood in opposition to the regulatory strategies of institutions. In the same way, the subtle positioning through clothing by young women and the attitudes and words of young men, as well as their attempt to turn the official procedures of marriage to their own purposes, expressed a desire for integration, rather than lawlessness or marginalization. Such activities occurred during the ritual of mass because it was the venue where one affirmed one's own status and attempted to have it recognized by others. As well, young people sought to capitalize on the general and consensual legitimacy that encompassed all facets of liturgical activity. However, these attempts at integration drew the ire of the clergy because they were situated outside the established framework of families arranged in order before the Blessed Sacrament. The young person, neither a child nor married, was by his or her very nature considered the bearer of social instability, whose sexuality, as well as position in the parish, was illegitimate because, although physically an adult, he or she was single and had no independent household. In other words, adolescents, in the eyes of the church, occupied a risky stage of life, at the very moment when they were attempting to escape the constraints of their family, but had not yet founded a family of their own.

Escaping from one's family also carried the connotation of leaving the family pew and the church itself during mass. Here again, the ritual afforded an opportunity to express a type of behaviour that not only proclaimed sexual difference but was highly charged with values of self-affirmation. For it was men who left the church during mass; widows, mothers, and girls remained seated in the nave. This behaviour stimulated an unquenchable outpouring of prescriptive literature, evident in the early days of the colony and even more insistent in the nineteenth century. In 1697 Bishop Saint-Vallier advised the *curé* of Charlesbourg to "refuse absolution and communion to those who leave during the sermon."[77] In 1732 the people of Bon-Secours left during the sermon, behaviour that was roundly denounced as giving a bad example to young children.[78] During his parish visits in 1792–93, Bishop Briand frequently observed the habit of leaving during mass as "unnecessarily and with scandal."[79] A few reports drawn up by eighteenth-century rural *curés* for their episcopal visitors mentioned this "failing" in their congregations: habitants went outside "under the pretext of heeding the call of nature or to see to their horses."[80] Despite the fact that the clergy frequently condemned and the bishops repeatedly prohibited this conduct, it would appear that this discourse met a fate similar to that regarding women's behaviour: it became lost in a redundant and inoffensive echo. The parish clergy made note of such action as an abuse, but they did so without illusion and largely pro forma. The wishes of the institutional church once again encountered a solid resistance anchored upon established custom.

But what was the underlying meaning of this custom? As I have previously argued, social division was defined by status and sex. Women and little girls did not leave church during mass, nor did young boys. What this pattern indicates is that an unexpected rite of passage occurred the first time that an adolescent boy left church, a rite that employed the official ritual, but in an astonishing diversion of its actual meaning and purpose. The transgression that in this case lent force to the rite of initiation did not directly depend upon the reservoir of sacredness manipulated by the church, as in the case of First Communion or confirmation. Rather, it involved a repeated attempt to establish limits to the norms decreed by the institution. The significant element, however, was that the phenomenon was directed mainly at the sermon, the only part of the mass spoken in the vulgar tongue. Men left as soon as the Sunday sermon began, as the priest left the sanctuary to mount the pulpit. This was, strictly speaking, not part of the ritual performance, for the sermon entailed mainly an "instruction," the transmission of organized knowledge (what one must believed, how one must pray to God) and moral teachings, the announcement of forthcoming events, and the reading of episcopal edicts. However, I do not believe that one can deduce from their behaviour that men, by leaving, were "contesting" all this. First, not all the men left, a fact that exposed another series of fault lines in parish society, divisions that are more difficult to grasp. Second, one must not exaggerate the scope of the action or over-interpret it. The general image conveyed by the sermon is one of a boring moment in church, a recurring theme of the Voltairian literature of the late eighteen century and one indirectly underscored by the church itself. Priests were instructed to adopt a dynamic tone, to make their preaching simple, and not to drone on interminably. It would seem that men left, first and foremost, to escape numbness. But at the same time, it was important for they to defy the priest's authority, to transgress his prohibitions every Sunday, and thus to lay claim to a certain independence from him,[81] in the full knowledge that however the *curé* might regard their conduct, what he had to say would never directly impinge upon them.

As well, other forms of knowledge and standards of value were elaborated by parish men who congregated outside the church during the sermon, smoking, laughing, and comparing the merits of their horses standing next to one another in the "field of posts" (*champ de poteaux*) where they had left their carriages.[82] While women remained inside, seated in silence, passively receiving the normative wisdom of the church, a male sociability was expressed outside and useful information exchanged; but more tellingly, other hierarchies were articulated, hierarchies founded upon age and the value of horses and land. At times, men affirmed these gradations through fisticuffs, often as the result of strong drink, another mark of masculinity. Herein lies the explanation for the clerical struggle against taverns and Sunday tippling, one waged in the hope of establishing a clear boundary between such eateries and the sacred space of the church.[83] It was a replaying of the old Christian opposition, admirably portrayed in Pieter Bruegel's *The Warfare of Carnival and Lent* (1559), in which the church and the tavern constituted two antinomian polarities in the community incarnating two opposed value systems. Indeed, the tavern (*cabaret*) was the prime venue for the elaboration of representations that not only diverged from those purveyed by the clergy but were ideologically subversive. From the clergy's standpoint, the inn was the place where men of the parish became irrational under the twofold influence of alcohol and exposure to the dubious promptings of corrupt and libertine "hearts and minds," who sought to "entrap" the "innocent"[84]. Under the British regime the parish priest secured the right to oversee what went on within the precincts of the inn. What he especially sought to bring to end, through the scrutiny of the confessional and the enforcement of legal regulations, was the practice of selling and consuming liquor on Sundays and religious holidays.[85] In 1817 the *curé* of L'Assomption fulminated: "There are seven or eight public houses in this village, where a great deal of liquor is sold even [on Christmas Eve], and there is a steady procession of drunkards, quarrelling and fighting, and I have even seen men drunk in the church."[86]

Drunkenness was the rubric around which the whole clerical critique of male behaviour was centred. In Quebec there existed an abundant clerical discourse, backed by concrete legal prohibitions that attempted to repress this masculine activity. In this scheme the alcoholic was considered a habitual sinner, one whom the parish priest might attempt to reform, but who would, if he died under the influence, be denied a religious burial, to the abiding shame of his family.[87] But beyond these pathological cases, the clear association the clergy drew between the sinfulness of drinking and more general forms of male behaviour was similar to their linking of female apparel and adultery. From the unceasing clerical carping against what were indeed common practices, it is possible to discern what constituted unacceptable conduct for men and women. The clergy's intent for both sexes was to bring individuals back to the family as the bedrock of social order, as the setting where they fulfilled their primary social responsibilities. It accounts for why the clergy maintained that drink ultimately eroded the family structure and allowed "all other crimes" into the domestic sphere, most notably adultery, "impure behaviour," marital discord, the language of insult, and much unhappiness, described as the "temporal chastisements visited by God, the grim foretelling of the sinner's eternal damnation." In such dysfunctional households, especially those of Quebec's urban areas, children would be brought up "naked, without education, religion, or fear of God," and would ultimately grow up to be insubordinate subjects.[88]

In one respect, the customary behaviour of parish men who absented themselves from the sermon worked to affirm the clerical ideal of the wife and mother, because women and children were left inside the ritual space that had become the setting for instruction. Men escaped the catechism, which they perceived as reducing them to a childish state, and affirmed their masculinity through a "virile" insubordination and by positioning themselves "outside" – that is, beyond – the sphere of women. For the church, however, masculinity was indistinguishable from paternity and the fulfillment of fatherly responsibilities. The privatization of society, impelled not only by the policies of the state but by the regulations of the church, identified the patriarchal, nuclear family as the essential structure of its organization and conferred rights and powers upon men, but also saddled them with responsibilities. The father, as the principal channel of power that descended from state to local community, was invested with unprecedented authority, which tended to remove men from the old networks of solidarity, status, and the exercise of power. Their resistance to this process was massive and protracted. Men continued to leave the church, but the parish priest's intent was to keep them in their pews, as the ones responsible for the good order of the families they headed and to whom they must give an example of good conduct.[89] Because the reproduction, and thus the continuity, of the family as a social institution ultimately rested upon the father, the church insisted that he be sober and present for all aspects of the ritual.

This essay has attempted to demonstrate the usefulness of an approach that centres upon ritual as performance. By examining social practice through a grille provided by texts and representations which privileges neither the views of clerical elites nor those of popular culture, it has sought to offer a multi-layered understanding of ritual events. In the first place, it offers a dual critique of Bossy's notion of the function of ritual as assuring social peace and his view that this function eventually sank into disuse. The evidence presented in this paper suggests that this was not the dominant function of Catholic ritual in colonial Quebec. Many other social practices were at work in the parish ritual, especially a game of positioning, the elaboration of hierarchy, and the search for status both within the family and outside it. Seen in this light, Bossy's view that a radical individualization occurred in ritual practice as the immediate consequence of the Council of Trent is difficult to accept. Although in the practices decreed by and the representations diffused by the council, there certainly was an intent to interiorize belief, it must be recognized that outside an elite circle of *dévots*, the strategies employed to inculcate these practices, either through ritual or teaching, always relied upon the family as the primary medium. Ordinary believers participated in the ritual in the context of sitting in a family pew and engaged in collective family devotions within the household,[90] and parents saw to the religious instruction of their children.

If "privatization" occurred, it certainly had little effect on individuals, who seem, more firmly than ever, to have been enclosed within a web of collective structures. Bossy is certainly correct in asserting that the church's institutional power became more overt, but there was no complete and total rupture with older patterns of local and customary authority. In this respect, the *mandements* of parish visits, in both the eighteen-[90] and the nineteenth centuries, spoke of the bishop's primary function in visiting the parishes as "removing the cloud of scandal" (*d'ôter les scandales*). No better testimony could be provided for the fact that the church still functioned within a social universe in which community pressure formed the primary element. It firmly reproved scandal because, in its own definition of the term, knowledge of sin was itself an occasion *of* sin. In the eyes of the church, scandal was not only the consequence of the transgression of the rules of local society but also in itself an evil. What the clergy took aim at was not the actual sin, but the knowledge of the sin: clerical authority pronounced only in the wake of rumour.

This was a concept of scandal which, when joined to the desire of families to protect their honour, impelled secrecy as people engaged in desperate attempts to ensure that sins did not travel beyond the family circle. In such struggles we can discern the dim outlines of those family secrets which, in the name of private honour and public morality, would frequently stifle the freedom of the individual. The post-Tridentine sacrament of confession, strictly regulated by the code of secrecy, was intended by the church as the means of substituting its own scrutiny for that of the community. However, in rural Quebec the full force of this change in ritual practice appeared very late, only in the second half of the nineteenth century. It thus became one of the central pillars of a privatized society that increasingly sealed the nuclear family off from the public gaze and ensured that, within its precincts, the rules of morality could be violated through public ignorance and the complicity of church and state.

NOTES

The research that formed the basis for this essay was undertaken with the financial support of the Social Sciences and Humanities Research Council of Canada. The essay was translated by Michael Gauvreau.

1 John Bossy, "The Counter-Reformation and the People of Catholic Europe," *Past and Present* 47 (May 1970): 51–70.
2 See, in particular, the work of Philippe Ariès and Michel Foucault.
3 John Bossy, "Essai de sociographie de la messe, 1200–1700," *Annales: Économies, sociétés, civilisations* 36 (1981): 64: "individualiste et a-sociale."
4 The use of the legal title to auction is attested to at the beginning of the eighteenth century: Archives nationales, Paris (AN-P), Colonies, série C11A, 39, 257–8v, Arrêt du Conseil supérieur, 2 mai 1718. During the 1840s the bishop required a notarized document in order to prove title.
5 AN-P, Colonies, série C11A, 44, 430–2v, Saint Vallier au Conseil de la Marine, 28 avril 1722: "jouissent du revenu des bancs et du droit de les faire crier après la mort de ceux qui les possèdent en donnant préférence aux veuves et enfants." The bishop, who sought to make the parish the principal axis of his policy of institutional development, insisted from the moment of his consecration that this rule be made general practice. See Saint-Vallier, "Statuts publiés dans le troisième synode tenu à Québec le vingt-septième février de l'année 1698," 28 février 1698, in *Mandements, lettres pastorales et circulaires des évêques de Québec, publiés par Mgr Têtu et l'abbé C.-O. Gagnon* (Québec: Côté, 1887; henceforth cited as MEQ), 1: 373. The visitation books from the end of the eighteenth century reveal that some parishes carried on a lengthy resistance to episcopal wishes. For example, in 1773 there were thirty-four hereditary pews at Longueuil and fifty at Varennes. See Archives de l'Archidiocèse de Québec (AAQ), 69, CD, 1, Ordonnances de visites, 1773.
6 The king's regulation governing the conceding of pews in the Canadian churches was handed down on 9 June 1723. It stipulated: "In the matter of children whose mother and father have died, the pews conceded to the said mother and father shall be auctioned in the usual manner, and title given to the person offering the highest bid over the asking price. The children will, however, have a preferential right to secure the pew by paying the former asking price." (À l'égard des enfants dont les père et mère

seront décédés, les bancs concédés aux dits père et mère seront criés en la manière ordinaire, et adjugés au plus offrant et dernier enchérisseur, sur lequel ils auront cependant préférence en payant les sommes portées par la dernière enchère.) In the nineteenth century the church vestries often resorted to the courts to recover ownership of pews whose rents remained unpaid, notably in cases of inheritance. See René Hardy, "À propos du réveil religieux dans le Québec du xixᵉ siècle: Le recours aux tribunaux dans les rapports entre le clergé et les fidèles," *Revue d'histoire de l'Amérique française* 48 (automne 1994): 207–9.

7 Lucien Lemieux, *Histoire du catholicisme québécois, 2,1, Les années difficiles (1760–1839)* (Montréal: Boréal, 1989), 179.

8 The religious authorities played upon this situation when they imposed an interdiction against entering the church as a sanction against recalcitrant individuals, which came to the fore when these parishioners sought to have their children baptized. See, for example, Laval, "Ordonnance contre Jean Dumets sur le refus de baptiser son enfant," 21 octobre 1681, MEQ, 1: 104; Laval, "Ordonnance pour l'administration du sacrement du baptême," 5 février 1677, MEQ, 1: 100–1. This penalty fell into disuse at the beginning of the nineteenth century; see AAQ, 90, CD, 2, 6, Anonymous, "Observations sur le précis," ca. 1814; ibid., 90 CD, 2, 1, Panet, "Observations sur le Précis des ordonnances du diocèse de Québec," ca. 1814.

9 Lemieux, *Histoire du catholicisme québécois*, 181.

10 Ollivier Hubert, *Sur la terre comme au ciel: La gestion des rites par l'Église catholique du Québec (fin xviiᵉ – mi-xixᵉ siècle)* (Sainte-Foy: Les Presses de l'Université Laval, 2000), 246.

11 These issues occupied a large place in the correspondence between colonial administrators and metropolitan authorities. What the petitioners sought was confirmation of their status or improvement of their station in the colonial hierarchy; see AN-P, Colonies, série C11A, which contain approximately twenty letters written between 1668 and 1747 on the question of rank in liturgical ceremonies. The dossiers of parish correspondence and visitation books preserved in diocesan archives also bear witness to the fact that in both the eighteen and nineteenth centuries the same competition for social position was carried on in rural parishes. See Auguste Gosselin, *L'Église du Canada depuis Monseigneur de Laval jusqu'à la Conquête*, 1 (Québec: Laflamme et Proulx, 1911), 311–17; Lemieux, *Histoire du catholicisme québécois*, 182–4.

12 Briand, "Lettre circulaire faisant connaître aux curés les intentions du gouverneur au sujet des cabarets, sur l'union entre les anciens et nouveaux sujets du Roi et sur le premier banc à être accordé aux baillifs," 15 octobre 1768, MEQ, 2: 214.

13 AAQ, 69 CD, 1, "Ordonnances de visites" (Saint-Jean-Baptiste-de-Nicolet), 1772: "a pris le bras du fils de Louis Beaubien et l'a fait sortir du banc parce que le jeune homme montrait quelque résistance."

14 Archives de la Chancellerie de l'Archevêché de Montréal (ACAM), 355.114.807.1 (L'Assomption), Mr de Saint-Ours à Plessis, n.d. (ca. 1807): "le bancs seigneurial [visiblement vacant] qui est a présent occupé par les domestiques de M. Roy [le curé], sur lesqu'elles je ne me permettrer aucunes reflextions le seroit san doutes d'une manière bien plus convenables par les officiers de l'État major de l'assomption et aussi du major de celui de Lavaltrie."

15 Saint-Vallier, "Statuts publiés ...," 28 février 1698, MEQ, 1: 373: "crier [les bancs] à la porte de l'église, pour les accorder à ceux qui en feront le plus grand avantage de l'Église."

16 Cited in Joseph Desautels, *Manuel des curés pour le bon gouvernement temporel des paroisses et des fabriques dans le Bas-Canada* (Montréal: John Lovell, 1864), 54.

17 AAQ, 69 CD, 1, "Ordonnances de visites" (Saint-Étienne-de-Beaumont), 1790: "le premier banc apres celui du curé."

18 Allan Greer, *Habitants et Patriotes: La Rébellion de 1837 dans les campagnes du Bas-Canada* (Montréal, Boréal, 1997), 67–8.

19 This movement is also illustrated by the increasing recourse, beginning in the 1830s, of parish vestries in the Diocese of Trois-Rivières to the courts to recover arrears of pew rents. See René Hardy, *Contrôle social et mutation de la culture religieuse au Québec (1830–1930)* (Montréal: Boréal, 1999), 167–9.

20 Quoted in Auguste Gosselin, *L'Église du Canada apres la Conquête*, 1 (Québec: Laflamme, 1916), 243: "réceptacle de tous les libertins et tous les indévots, ou pour mieux dire, des impies."

21 AAQ, 69 CD 3, "Ordonnances de visites" (Pointe-Olivier), 1809; Greer, *Habitants et Patriotes*, 64–5.

22 This parallel was employed in many *mandements* issued during parish visitations. Two examples are offered, one from each of the chronological limits of this paper: "The people must be persuaded that Jesus Christ visits them in the person of their Bishop, to shower them with blessings" (Les Peuples doivent être persuadés que Jésus-Christ les visite en la personne de leur Évêque, pour les combler de bénédictions), in *Rituel du diocèse de Québec, publié par l'ordre de Monseigneur de Saint Valier, Évêque de Québec* (Paris: Simon Langlois, 1703), 375; and Bourget, "Mandement de la visite pastorale," 19 mars 1842, *Mandements, lettres pastorales, circulaires et autres documents publiés dans le diocèse de Montréal depuis son érection jusqu'à l'année 1869* (Montréal: J. Chapleau et fils, 1869; henceforth cited as MEM), 1: 200; Bourget, "Mandement de visite," 1850, MEM, 2: 128–41.

23 "The confessors named for the visit will have the power, so long as the bishop's party remains in the parish, to absolve those who have been censured or whose cases have been reserved, and they will possess the widest possible latitude in reconciling penitents" (Les Confesseurs nommés pour la visite auront, tant qu'elle durera dans chaque Paroisse, le pouvoir d'absoudre des censures et des cas réservés, avec les facultés les plus

 amples pour la réconciliation des pénitents); see Lartigue, "Mandement de visite pastorale," 1 avril 1837, MEM, 1: 9.

24 ACAM, 355.114.767.1 (L'Assomption), Degeay, curé, à Briand, 1 mai 1767: "Onze cents personnes ont communié avec beaucoup d'édification; souvent les cinq heures du matin me voyaient entrer au confessional et les 10 à 11 heures du soir m'en voyaient sortir … Les fruits du jubilé durent encore, à ce que je me suis apercu dans cette quinzaine de Pâques. Il y eut beacoup de restitutions et de réconciliations qui m'ont paru sincères."

25 Lemieux, *Histoire du catholicisme québécois*, 265–6.

26 One can find a good deal of evidence, especially in the visitation books, as the "abuses" were one of the primary targets of episcopal vigilance, and in dossiers of parish correspondence: "médisances," "calomnies."

27 ACAM, 355.103.792.1 (Saint-Anges-de-Lachine), Keller, curé, à Plessis, 23 février 1792: "Si j'avais l'indécence de conduire des filles dans ma voiture, ce ne serait pas à la chine, encore moins en ville."

28 ACAM, 355.118.791.4 (Sainte-Rose), collectif à Hubert, ca. juillet 1792: "Joseph filliatreau, francois quenneville, andré Nadon anciens Marguilliers, michel Desjardins sindic, michel marié, amable Desjardins, jean-marie morriseau tous demeurants à la paroisse de Ste Rose isle jesus ont l'honneur de vous exposer que Depuis plus de cinq ans Monsieur galet leur curé auroit à la connaissance de toute la paroisse entière fréquente la maison de joseph giroux un des chantres de l'endroit sans discontinuation et que ledit giroux auroit avec lui marie giroux sa soeur, et que depuis quelque temps le dit sieur Curé auroit à la grande surprise de toute ladite paroisse fait enlever la dite giroux de nuit et l'auroit faite menee chez le nommé joseph Bargue chirurgien a terrebonne où depuis quelques jours elle seroit accouchée."

29 ACAM, 355.114.809.2 (Saint-Pierre-du-Portage), Roy, curé, à Plessis, 4 décembre 1809.

30 See, for example, ACAM, 355.118.804.1 (Sainte-Rose), cultivateurs de la paroisse à Denaux, reçu le 20 août 1804. See also Lemieux, *Histoire du catholicisme québécois*, 133–4.

31 On this "work" that priests engaged in, see Serge Gagnon, *Plaisir d'amour et crainte de Dieu: Sexualité et confession au Bas-Canada* (Sainte-Foy: Les Presses de l'Université Laval, 1990); and *Mariage et famille au temps des Papineau* (Québec: Les Presses de l'Université Laval, 1993).

32 ACAM, 355.103.825.2 (Saints-Anges-de-Lachine), P. Finchley à Lartigue, 22 septembre 1825: "jusque dans ses prônes ou sermons des sorties ou remarques qui quoique faites d'une manière indirecte et sans me nommer, ne laissent pas d'être considérées par les personnes présentes comme s'appliquant à moi individuellement ou réfléchissant sur mon caractère et sur ma conduite privée"; "dans la crainte d'éprouver encore de pareilles mortifications."

33 ACAM, 355.106.852.3 (Saint-François-de-Sales), Giroux, curé, à Bourget, 12 avril 1852: "de manière que les personnes qui pouvoient être coupables de tel ou tel vice, ou être les auteurs de tel ou tel désordre, comprissent que ce n'étoit pas leur voisin qui avoit commis ou qui commettoit la faute contre laquelle je parlois; pour rendre la chose plus claire, j'entrois dans quelques détails."

34 Underlined in the original: "beaucoup d'ascendant et d'empire."

35 ACAM, 355.113.825.1 (Sainte-Rose), collectif (15 signatures) à Lartigue, 14 septembre 1825: "ce qui fait qu'agissant par la sorte par *ouï-dire*, le coupable prévaut souvent sur l'innocent."

36 See Gagnon, *Plaisir d'amour; Mariage et famille;* and *Mourir hier et aujourd'hui* (Québec: Les Presses de l'Université Laval, 1987).

37 *Rituel du diocèse de Quebec*, 110: "ouï quelque chose de la Confession pendant que le Pénitent se confessoit: ce qui doit engager les Confesseurs … de prendre garde que les personnes se tiennent dans une distance raisonnable du Confessionnal, et avertir les Pénitens quand il parlent trop haut."

38 Ibid., 119: "Si le Confesseur est obligé de refuser, ou de différer l'absolution, il se conduira de telle sorte, que ce refus, ou delay n'apporte aucun scandale au Pénitent, et afin qu'il ne vienne point a la connoissance de ceux qui sont présens, il recitera sur celui qui a confessé ses pechez cette prière"; "afin que ceux qui sont presens ne puissent connoître que [le prêtre] luy refuse, ou diffère l'absolution."

39 Ibid., 141. See also Saint-Vallier, "Circulaire avant départ pour la France," 1691, MEQ, 1: 285: "[Le lieu destiné pour entendre les confessions] doit toujours être l'Eglise, et non pas la Sacristie, si ce n'est pour les Ecclesiastiques. Que si on y confesse quelquefois d'autres personnes à cause du grand froid, ou autres raisons de nécessité, on ne doit autant qu'on peut ne point y confesser de femmes, mais des hommes, et jamais les femmes quand elles sont seules. [Le prêtre] s'assoira dans un Confessional qui doit être dans la Nef, au lieu le plus en vûë, garni de fenêtres treillisées, pour entendre les Confessions, qui se doivent faire durant le jour autant qu'il est possible."

40 Hubert, *Sur la terre*, 227–31.

41 In the middle of the eighteenth century the bishop expressed his outrage that people were "confessing outside the confessional or in confessionals lacking screens or trellises" (confesse hors du confessionnal ou dans des confessionnaux sans grilles et jalousies); see Pontbriand, "Avis au confesseurs à l'occasion du jubilé de l'année sainte accordée par Notre Saint Père le Pape Benoît XIV," 22 novembre 1751, MEQ, 2: 82. The visitation books confirm the imperfect state of church confessionals in the first part of the nineteenth century.

42 *Mandement*, 28 octobre 1793, cited in Panet, "Mandement sur les rubriques et la discipline," ca. 1830, MEQ, 3: 262–8: "juridiction ecclesiastique."

43 This woman did not hesitate a few years later to write a number of letters
to the bishop, some anonymously, accusing her parish priest of a whole
range of misconduct: kissing the beadle's daughter, lying, and being dead
drunk in the presbytery; see ACAM, 344.117.834.25 (Saint-Vincent-de-
Paul), M.J. Quévillon à Lartigue, 4 octobre 1834; ibid., lettre anonyme à
Signay, s.d.

44 ACAM, 355.117.827.2 (Saint-Vincent-de-Paul), M.J. Quévillon à Panet,
29 juillet 1829: "maniere de vivre"; "connue"; "Monseigneur ayer pitie de
moi, je su a cablé de peine. Je me jette entre vos brapaternelle, se couré
moi, car rien ne m'est plus sencible que d'être privé de la Ste Communion
... je ne pourré jamais m'y présenter sans que je sois sure par vous même
que je suis libre de le faire, sans m'exposer a voir de nouvos la communion refuser. Car si cela marivoit une troisieme foy, je croy que j'en moure-
roit de peine paraport au scandale qui en a déjà résulter ... j'ai communier
plusieurs fois sans qu'il me pass la communion parce que je madonnoit
toujour a communier avec quelqu'un et le 21 de l'octave du St Sacrement,
me voyant a l'église il ne confessat personne quoi que plusieurs désireroit
et le fire demander pour le confessionale et je le vit souvant paroitre der-
riere l'autelle qui avoit laire a observer si j'etoit encor ou non ... comme il
pensoit que je me présenteroit a la communion a la messe il dit au enfant
de coeur qu'il n'avoit confesser personnes et que s'il semprésentoit de na
pas dire le Confiteor ... ne le sachant pas je me suis présenter sans pouvoir communier et il a dit a un des servant que si ge de mandoit pour quoi
in n'a pas dit le Confiteor de me dire que j'aitoit une folle ... le dix de ce
mois metant presenter a la communion avec un autre personne qui s'etoit
presenter avec moi et il me la passer en précense de cantité de monde
parce quil y avoit ce jour la un service anyversaire qui a causer un grand
scandale ... a présent je le crois aussi capable de calomni que de me passer
la communion en publique."

45 Antoine Furetière, "Honneur," in his *Dictionnaire universel*, vol. 2 (La Haye
et Rotterdam: Arnout et Reinier Leers 1690).

46 Brigitte Caulier, "Les confréries de dévotion à Montréal, 17ᵉ–19ᵉ siècles"
(PhD thesis, history, Université de Montréal, 1986); Marie-Aimée Cliche,
Les pratiques de dévotion en Nouvelle-France (Sainte-Foy: Les Presses de
l'Université Laval, 1988); Denise Lemieux, *Les petits innocents: L'enfance en
Nouvelle-France* (Québec: Institut québécois de recherche sur la culture,
1985); John R. Porter, "La dévotion à la Sainte-Famille," in *Le grand héri-
tage: L'Église catholique et les arts au Québec* (Québec: Musée du Québec,
1984), 55–72: "témoignage d'estime ou de soumission qu'on rend à
quelqu'un"; "il faut rendre honneur et respect premierement à Dieu et
aux choses saintes, aux Rois et aux Magistrats, à ses parents et à la vertu."

47 Specific worship ceremonies dedicated to the Holy Family were inaugu-
rated in the diocese in 1684. On the multiplication of ritual manifestations

involving members of the Holy Family, see Ollivier Hubert, "La dispa-
rition des fêtes d'obligation au Québec, xviie–xixe siècle," *Studies in
Religion/Sciences religieuses* 23 (automne 1994): 410–11.

48 Gerard Bouchard, "L'historiographie du Québec rural et la problématique
nord-américaine avant la révolution tranquille: Études d'un refus," *Revue
d'histoire de l'Amérique française* 44 (automne 1990): 199–222. Montreal was
placed under the patronage of the Holy Family. Further, the confraternities of the Holy Family proposed, from their earliest inauguration, not
only to establish a domestic piety through their members but to promote
the vision of a harmonious daily family existence lived under the inspir-
ing image of the terrestrial trinity. The female founder of the Montreal
branch of the confraternity declared her intention to "reform Christian
families along the lines of the Holy Family" (réformer les familles ché-
tiennes sur le modèle de la Sainte Famille); cited in Cliche, *Les pratiques de
dévotion*, 158. Their manual of 1675 was explicit: "They will have in their
houses an image of the Holy Family before whom they will pray on their
knees evening and morning, and will renew every day the gift and consecration that they have made of themselves, their husband, their children,
and all their family, and will urge their husbands as far as they are able to
do the same" (Elles auront dans leurs maisons quelque image de la Saint-
Famille devant laquelle elles feront leur prières soir et matin à genoux, et
renouvelleront tous les jours la donation et consécration qu'elles luy ont
fait d'elles-mesmes, de leur mary, de leur enfans, et de toutes leur Famille,
et porteront tant qu'elles pourront leur mary à faire de mesme), from *La
solide dévotion à la très sainte famille, de jésus, marie et joseph avec un
catéchisme qui enseigne à pratiquer leurs vertus* (1675), cited in Caulier, "Les
confréries de dévotion," 201.

49 Women would imitate the Blessed Virgin, the husband Saint Joseph, and
the children the Infant Jesus. See Cliche, *Les pratiques de dévotion*, 161–4.

50 It is revealing in this context to note how clerical discourse was permeated
with notions of family hierarchy. The family was at once the basis of society and the model of the entire social organization. Thus, if the church
was the "mother" because it was under the authority of the Father-God
and the believers were "children," the paternal image was a general archetype of authority. It evoked the top of a hierarchy, a power that was
protective and just, but powerful and severe; the government was thus
the father of the people, the king of his subjects, the *curé* of his parish, and
the bishop of his clergy, while the pope was the holy father. See Bourget,
"Lettre pastorale de Monseigneur l'Évêque de Montréal, pour encourager
l'association des établissements canadiens des Townships," 17 juin 1848,
MEM, 1: 482.

51 They "make a public display of their crime" (affichent publiquement leur
crime); "l'estime due à la vertu et au mérite."

52 Furetière, "Honneur."

53 *Rituel du diocèse de Québec*, 106: "on ne comprend point dans les Cas réservés les enfants jusqu'à l'âge de puberté, qui est à 12 pour les filles, et à 14 pour les garcons: ny les femmes, ny les filles, lors qu'elles ne peuvent être envoyées au Superieur sans scandale."

54 Collectif Clio, *L'histoire des femmes au Québec depuis quatre siècles* (s.1.: Le Jour éditeur, 1992), 103.

55 Hubert, *Sur la terre*, 283–5.

56 *Rituel du diocèse de Québec*, 166: "abattue, sans rien faire paroître en elles qui ressente la vanité, la sensualité et le luxe."

57 Women's confraternities, comprising devout and aristocratic women, were drawn largely from the upper strata of colonial society. They played a key role in the formulation of the image of the mother, and the members of these organizations were clearly identified as a spiritual "avant-garde." See Caulier, "Les confréries de dévotion"; Cliche, *Les pratiques de dévotion*. On this theme, it would be interesting to consider the development of Marian devotions in New France.

58 Denise Lemieux, "La socialisation des filles dans la famille," in Nadia Fahmy-Eid and Micheline Dumont, eds., *Maîtresses de maison, maîtresses d'école: Femmes, famille et éducation dans l'histoire du Québec* (Montréal: Boréal Express, 1983), 240.

59 Saint-Vallier, "Lettre de Monseigneur l'Évêque de Québec où il rend compte à un de ses amis de son premier voyage au Canada, et de l'état où il a laissé l'Église et la colonie," ca. 1686, MEQ, 1: 233–4: "une heure après les funérailles de son mari, [elle] se coupa les cheveux, non pas pour marquer plus sensiblement son affliction, mais pour se dévouer désormais plus parfaitement à Dieu, en renonçant tout-a-fait au monde, et en gardant la continence."

60 Ibid., 256: "passe une partie de sa vie dans les Monastères des filles, où on a cru lui devoir accorder une libre entrée … le reste du temps se passe dans la maison à élever sa famille et à travailler de ses mains."

61 Gagnon, *Plaisir d'amour.*

62 This ritual was described in *Rituel du diocèse de Québec*, 313–17: "des fautes [qu'elle peut] avoir commises dans l'état du Mariage." See also Hélène Laforce, *Histoire de la sage-femme dans la région de Québec* (Québec: IQRC, 1985), 45.

63 "Instruction à faire aux personnes le jour de leur mariage"; extract from "Explication des cas réservés dans le diocèse de Québec," anonymous manuscript from the first half of the nineteenth century, cited in Gagnon, *Plaisir d'amour*, 89.

64 *Formulaire de prières, à l'usage des pensionnaires des religieuses ursulines* (Québec: Nouvelle imprimerie, 1799), 38–40: "J'ai un grand désir, Ô mon sauveur, de vous recevoir, c'est ce qui occupe mon coeur jour et nuit, c'est

l'objet de mes pensées, c'est après quoi je soupire comme un très grand avantage"; "Que je n'aille point, je vous prie contre vos intentions, m'abandonner comme les bêtes aux plaisirs des sens, mais que tout mon esprit soit occupé de vous et que tout mon plaisir soit de remplir mon coeur de votre saint amour."

65 Briand, "Mandement du jubilé pour la ville de Québec," 5 mars 1771, MEQ, 2: 226: "femmes pieuses et édifiantes"; "filles sages, pudiques et modestes, malgré la corruption du siècle."

66 De Lotbinière, "Ordonnance au sujet de ceux qui sortent de l'église pendant le sermon, ainsi que de ceux qui portent le camail pendant les offices," 10 fevrier 1732, MEQ, 1: 540: "bonnet à manteau"; "camail"; "plutôt pour se faire remarquer et introduire des modes que pour l'utilité qu'on en retire"; "quelque calotte."

67 ACAM, 355.113.833.2 (Rivière des Prairies), Jh. Boissonault à Emélie, 18 septembre 1833: "Ma chère emélie, en te permettant d'user de mon banc, je n'a pas prétendu autoriser le rouge dont tu te barbouilles le visage; c'est contre mon devoir. le fard n'est pas compatible avec les peaux jaûnes et basanées comme les nôtres. C'est faire un reproche à Dieu en voulant réformer son ouvrage et on pèche plus qu'on ne pense."

68 Catéchisme à l'usage du diocèse de Québec, imprimé par l'ordre de Monseigneur Jean Olivier Briand, Éveque de Québec. 4ᵉ éd. (Québec: Nouvelle imprimerie, 1796), 53; Rituel du diocèse de Québec, 166: "Sainte Table"; "modestie et respect"; "sans regarder d'un côté et d'un autre."

69 Laval, "Mandement contre le luxe et vanité des femmes et des filles dans l'église," 26 février 1682, MEQ, 1: 107; Saint-Vallier, "Ordonnance de Monseigneur l'Évêque de Québec, touchant la vénération due aux églises," 22 octobre 1686, MEQ, 1: 185–6.

70 Unmarried girls, stated the bishop, "allow themselves to be taken advantage of, in the hope that they [the young men] will marry them, for they are under the impression that the misdeeds and accidents that can occur in this respect will lend weight to convincing their parents in favour of pursuing the aforementioned marriages" (laissent souvent abuser, sous l'espérance de les [les jeunes gens] épouser, dans la persuasion qu'elles ont que les fautes et les accidents qui leur peuvent arriver en ce sujet, seront autant de motifs à leurs parents de poursuivre leurs dit mariages); see Saint-Vallier, "Ordonnance touchant le sacrement du mariage," 7 juillet 1693, MEQ, 1: 300. At the other end of our period, the parish priest of Saint-Joseph lamented: "Within the space of only a year, five young girls have publicly displayed their crime … And the shameless marriages that occurred have outraged the entire parish!!" (Dans l'espace d'un an seulement, cinq filles ont affiché le crime publiquement … Et que de mariages impudiques qui ont scandalisé la paroisse!!); see ACAM, 355.113. 852.1 (Sainte-Rose), Leblond, curé, à Bourget, 25 avril 1852. On this subject, see

Marie-Aimée Cliche, "Filles-mères, familles et société sous le Régime français," *Histoire sociale/Social History*, 21 (mai 1988): 39–69.

71 Saint-Vallier, "Statuts publiés," 28 février 1698, MEQ, 1: 376.

72 Briand, "Mandement du jubilé," 5 mars 1771, MEQ, 2: 226.

73 On this point, see André Burguière, "Le rituel du mariage en France: Pratiques ecclésiastiques et pratiques populaires (XVIe–XVIIIe siècles), *Annales ÉSC* 33 (mai-juin 1978): 637–49.

74 Bourget, "Circulaire au clergé du diocèse de Montréal," 16 février 1843, MEQ, 1: 228–31: "sans lumiere"; "sollicitations a des actes impudiques"; "dans leur paroisse ou ailleurs, et surtout en ville."

75 On the legal context, see Gagnon, *Mariage et famille*, 91–110. The church progressively abandoned its own authority over regulating marriage in favour of the state and fathers.

76 See, for Quebec, René Hardy, "Le charivari dans la sociabilité rurale québécoise au XIXe siècle," in Roger Levasseur, ed., *De la sociablité: Spécificités et mutations* (Montréal: Boréal, 1990), 59–72; and Greer, *Habitants et Patriotes*, 71–85.

77 "Lettre aux habitants de Charlesbourg," 20 décembre 1697; cited in Guy Plante, *Le rigorisme au XVIIe siècle: Mgr. de Saint-Vallier et le sacrement de pénitence (1685–1727)* (Gembloux: Duculot, 1971), 77: "refuser l'absolution et la communion à ceux qui sortent au prône." See also Saint-Vallier, "Statuts publiés," 28 février 1698, MEQ, 1: 370.

78 Chartier de Lotbinière, "Ordonnance au sujet," 10 février 1732, MEQ, 1: 540.

79 See, for example, AAQ, 69 CD 1, Briand, "Ordonnances de visites" (Saint-Denis-sur-Richelieu), 1772: "sans necessité et avec scandale."

80 AAQ, 69 CD, 1, 88, "Abus et scandales principaux," s.d.: "sous pretexte de besoins naturels ou pour voir leurs chevaux"; and "The blasphemies, the immodesties in our churches are nearly always the same and especially the habit of leaving during divine service" (Les impiétés, les immodesties dans nos églises sont presque toujours les mêmes et surtout les sorties pendant le service divin); see ACAM, 355.114.742.1 (L'Assomption), Degeay, curé, à Pontbriand, ca. 1742. For the end of the period, see Serge Gagnon and René Hardy, eds., *L'Église et le village au Québec, 1850–1930: L'enseignement des cahiers de prones* (Montréal: Leméac, 1979), 93–4.

81 This pattern reveals, very prosaically but continuously, a fundamental trait that was expressed overtly at times of heightened socio-political tension and precisely in the context of an opposition to clerical authority, coupled with a remarkable distancing of women. See, on this subject, Jean-Paul Bernard, *Les Rouges: Libéralisme, nationalisme et anticlericalisme au milieu du XIXe siècle* (Montréal: Presses de l'Université du Québec, 1971); and Allan Greer, *The Patriots and the People: The Rebellion of 1837 in Rural Lower Canada* (Toronto: University of Toronto Press, 1993).

82 AAQ, 69 CD, 1, 87, "abus de paroisse," s.d. At the end of the eighteenth
   century certain inhabitants of Montreal left Notre-Dame Church during
   mass, lit their pipes, and "jabbered at the door" (bavassent à la porte).
   This behaviour is noted in Louis Rousseau, *La prédication à Montréal de
   1800 à 1830, approche religiologique* (Montréal: Fides, 1976), 103. At Quebec
   in 1810 crowds of three or four hundred people were reported at the
   church door by *curé* Doucet during Sunday masses and feast days, "playing, quarrelling, engaged in unspeakable debauchery" (y jouant, s'y que-
   rellant, y formant des parties d'infâmes débauchés). Cited in Lemieux,
   Histoire du catholicisme québécois, 283.
83 See the particularly vivid example of Saint-Vincent-de-Paul in the 1830s,
   when the parish was rocked by a complex struggle that polarized tensions
   and divisions around the erection of a wall which was designed to "protect" (*protéger*) the churchyard from the close proximity of an inn. See
   ACAM, 355.117: "cantines."
84 Briand, "Mandement du jubilé," 5 mars 1771, MEQ, 2: 230: "d'esprit et de
   coeur"; "piège"; "innocence."
85 Edouard-Z. Massicotte, "De l'observance du dimanche et des jours
   fériés," *Bulletin de recherches historiques* 36 (décembre 1930): 709–12; and
   "Ordonnances de Jacques Raudot, 1706" and "L'intendant Hocquart,
   1730," AN-P, Colonies, serie C11A, 24, 368–9v, et 53, 343–3v; Saint-Vallier,
   "Circulaire avant départ pour la France," ca. 1691, MEQ, 1: 282. In 1706
   Intendant Jacques Raudot, following the reports of several incidents that
   had occured in churches and in their doorways, prohibited the sale of liquor on Sunday and decreed a fine of ten livres for breaches of this regulation; he "was persuaded that all these disorders flow from the fact
   that people sell strong drink on Sundays and religious holidays. No one
   in possession of their faculties would be so impudent as to engage in
   such scandalous conduct" (étant persuadé que tous ces désordres ne
   viennent que de la liberté qu'on se donne de vendre des boissons les
   jours de fête et les dimanches, n'y ayant personne assez hardie qui, de
   sang froid, put causer de pareils scandales). For good measure, Raudot
   explicitly "forbade quarrelling or even conversation in the church"
   (défense de se quereller et même de s'entretenir dans les églises) and the
   practice of smoking at the church door, under penalty of a fine of ten
   livres. See *Arrêts et règlements du Conseil supérieur du Québec et ordonnances et jugements des intendants du Canada* (Québec: E.-P. Fréchette,
   1855), 425. A series of municipal regulations attempted to control liquor
   outlets in urban areas. In 1808 a general law was passed regarding rural
   parishes. See Lemieux, *Histoire du catholicisme québécois*, 282–3, 356–8. In
   a more general way, this issue was related to that of the observance of
   Sundays and holidays.

86 ACAM, 355.114.817.1 (L'Assomption), Roy, curé, à Plessis, 10 octobre 1817: "Il y a dans le village sept ou huit cantines. C'est à qui [le soir de Noël] vendra le mieux de là il arrive des yvrognes, des querelles et des batailles, souvent même on a vû des gens yvrent dans l'Église."

87 For example, the case of Louis Fontaine, a former chorister of the parish of Riviere-des-Prairies, who was dismissed from his position "because of excessive drinking" (à cause de ses excès de boisson) and died, "asphyxiated from drink" (étouffé dans la boisson), according to the medical report. His family attempted many times to persuade the bishop to allow a church burial. See ACAM, 355.113.857.1 (Sainte-Rose), Martel, curé, à Bourget, 23 septembre 1857; ibid., 355.113.857.2 (Sainte-Rose), Marien, medecin, à Bourget, s.d.; ibid., 355.113.857.3 (Sainte-Rose), Martel à Bourget, 25 septembre 1857.

88 Briand, "Mandement du jubilé," 5 mars 1771, MEQ, 2: 226: "tous les autres crimes"; "impuretés"; "malédictions temporelles de Dieu, présages funestes de sa malédiction éternelle"; "nus, sans éducation, sans religion, sans crainte de Dieu."

89 In New France, children were raised to fear God, which paved the way for fear of the father. See Lemieux, *Les petits innocents*, 137–41.

90 Further research into this aspect would have a great deal to say concerning domestic ritual practices: prayers, amulets, various benedictions, rituals of birth and death, and the presence of books of devotion.

91 See, for example, Pontbriand, "Mandement pour la visite de la paroisse de Notre-Dame de Québec," 2 décembre 1741, MEQ, 2: 13.

The Fireside Kingdom:
A Mid-Nineteenth-Century
Anglican Perspective on
Marriage and Parenthood

J.I. LITTLE

In the New England of the 1820s and 1830s, according to Nancy Cott, "[e]ssays, sermons, novels, poems and manuals offering advice and philosophy on family life, child rearing, and women's role began to flood the literary market."[1] Few historians have examined the impact of this phenomenon on the Canadian side of the border, where the concept of republican motherhood was obviously much weaker,[2] but in one interesting case, a resident of Lower Canada's Eastern Townships made his own small contribution to the "cult of domesticity." Though he was an Anglican clergyman of orthodox High Church principles, the Reverend James Reid of St Armand East on the Vermont border shared the emphasis on private prayer, meditation, diary keeping, and Bible study that made Anglican Evangelicalism a religion of the home.[3] But emotional revivalism was another matter, and we shall see that Reid's hostility to the concept of sudden conversion intensified his insistence on the crucial role played by parents in moulding future generations.

Reid's sixty-four essays on religion and the family appeared in the *Missiskoui Standard* between January 1837 and April 1838, the Rebellion period when this Tory-sympathizing newspaper hammered persistently and intemperately at Lower Canada's Patriotes and all who would compromise with them.[4] Presumably, the "fireside" essays offered respite from the disturbing political news of the day, but their style was far from lighthearted and their message anything but trivial. In Reid's view, the family was the very foundation of a peaceable Christian society, and the role of parent was the most important one that any individual could assume. And while historians have become increasingly skeptical about the value of didactic literature as a reflection of social reality,[5] Reid's personal diary reveals a strong preoccupation with his own family throughout his long life. The journals from the period of his children's youth were destroyed, but the surviving volumes suggest strongly that he practised what he preached as far as the male parenting role was concerned.[6]

The shift away from the sacraments and priestly authority after the Protestant Reformation placed more onus on the household to provide a framework for Christian discipline. Consequently, the idealization of the family, with a focus on companionate marriage and parental nurturing, was already evident in seventeenth-century England.[7] But referring to New England, John Demos claims that an inclusive image of the family as community began to give way to an exclusive image of family as refuge only in the early nineteenth century.[8] Gender historians assume that this cult of domesticity was greatly intensified by the rise of industrial capitalism because the middle-class home was increasingly seen as a haven from the pressures and anxieties of the market and as a morally superior alternative to "both the 'vain' and fashionable sociability of the rich and the promiscuous sociability of the poor."[9] Referring to Oneida County, New York, at mid-century, Mary Ryan stresses the enlargement, remoteness, and increasing formality of the public sphere, the economic uncertainty for small producers and retailers, and the increasingly individualized nature of middle-class occupations themselves.[10]

Such an analysis is somewhat premature as far as James Reid's essays are concerned, for they were directed at a pre-industrial society of farmers, village merchants, and tradesmen.[11] Still lying a few years in the future was the era of railroad construction and modern "state formation," when community voluntarism would be eclipsed by municipal government, school commissions, and bureaucratic regulation.[12] As an educated clergyman in touch with a wider institutional and intellectual world, Reid was obviously reflecting ideas and values disseminating from more economically and culturally advanced areas, but his newspaper series must have found a receptive audience or it would not have continued as long as it did. The economic crisis and political conflict of the late 1830s in Lower Canada would create its own, more immediate sense of anxiety and alienation in the Eastern Townships. In addition, the diminishing supply of arable wild land in longer-established areas such as St Armand may have increased concerns about the independence of offspring from their parents. Certainly, Reid's diary reveals that he worried constantly about his four sons, two of whom migrated to distant places in the United States, where they died early deaths.

James Reid's essays in the *Missiskoui Standard* stress the importance of public worship and regular church attendance, but the primary emphasis is on parental guidance and love, with a particular focus on family prayer at the evening fireside. These essays are worth examining, not because Reid was a brilliant or original thinker who influenced the intellectual currents of his day, but because little is known beyond the obvious about the social values and teachings of ordinary clergymen in nineteenth-century Canada. And, in this churchgoing era, who would have had more influence on the outlook and behaviour of the general public? As William Westfall has noted of nineteenth-century Ontario, "Protestantism not only shaped how people saw God, it also shaped the culture through which that society interpreted the world."[13]

Born in 1780, the son of a small tenant farmer in Perthshire, Scotland, James Reid experienced religious conversion at the hands of an itinerant preacher at the age of twenty-one.[14] A year later, in 1802, he entered the Haldane Seminary in Edinburgh, remaining for three and a half years. He was then sent to a Perthshire parish, where he was ordained a Congregational minister, but soon afterward he was strongly encouraged by Robert Haldane to become a missionary in Glengarry County, Upper Canada. Here disillusionment soon set in, for the Glengarry Highlanders were already well served by the Presbyterian and Roman Catholic churches, and the Haldane family's Society for the Propagation of the Gospel at Home and Abroad terminated its financial support six months after Reid's arrival. Unable to move because of the debts he had contracted, he managed to survive by supplementing his preaching with teaching school.

The last straw came in 1810, when Reid learned that the Haldanes had switched their allegiance from the Congregationalists to the Baptists.[15] He refused to follow their example, instead counselling his congregation to sell their church to the Presbyterians. He then took a teaching position in the county town of Cornwall, where he fell under the influence of John Strachan, the forceful Scottish-born cleric and teacher who had himself converted from the Church of Scotland to the Church of England. In 1812 Reid poured out his grievances against the Haldanes in a preface to Strachan's lengthy polemic entitled *Hypocrisy Detected*.[16] A year later, through Strachan's influence, Reid was put in charge of the new Royal Institution school in the parish of St Armand, stretching eastward along the Vermont border from Lake Champlain's Missisquoi Bay. Here he formed a lifelong friendship with Charles James Stewart, the wealthy Scottish missionary who was largely responsible for establishing the Church of England in the Eastern Townships.[17] When ordained as a priest in 1816, Reid had already replaced Stewart as the minister for St Armand; he held this position in the small village of Frelighsburg until he died in 1865, at the ripe old age of eighty-five.[18]

Reid played an active role in the community, establishing a temperance society during the 1830s, serving as an official of the local school district for over thirty years,[19] and speaking out in the press against the Reformers. Never forgetting his humble origins and unorthodox education, he appears not to have aspired to the church hierarchy, though his diary reveals that he was a diligent and critical reader of theological works, and that he was sensitive to slights from his religious superiors.[20] Not surprisingly, then, Reid sought out a measure of recognition through publication. In addition to his brief autobiography in the anti-Haldane tract, in 1836 he criticized the Episcopal bishop of Vermont's attack on the temperance movement, and in 1841 he took on the Baptists with his lengthy *Discourse on Infant Baptism*.[21]

He also attempted to publish a biography of Charles Stewart and may have wished to publish the series of eighteen carefully transcribed sermons that are to be found among his papers at Frelighsburg.[22] Based on Genesis and first delivered during the 1820s, these sermons also reflect his belief in the fundamental religious role of the family through his theological defence of infant baptism. After discussing how circumcision became a token of God's covenant with Abraham that his descendants were to be the chosen people, Reid argues that baptism became the same initiating token for Christians. In both cases, children inherited this right from their parents. Not only were children "always, from the beginning of the world, included in every covenant which God made with their parents," but Jesus had commanded that they "be brought unto him, before they could come, either in body or in mind, of their own accord."[23]

Reid does not actually state that infant baptism has a regenerative power or represents the washing away of original sin, as High Church Anglicans insisted,[24] but the implications for the family are clear:

Much is said, and much is printed about the conversion of the world; but if ever the world shall be converted, those who are called Christians must begin to allow their children the enjoyment and benefits of their own divine privileges, and bring them up in the "nurture and admonition of the Lord," and not as the children of heathens or infidels, left to their own choice. As matters are now conducted, the children are left out of the Church, as tender, helpless lambs outside the fold, to be torn and devoured by ravenous beasts. They are left to themselves, in the belief that they have nothing to do with a Gospel ordinance, or a Gospel ordinance with them, until it shall please God to convert them after they have come to the years of maturity. While thus wandering outside of the fold of Christ, purposely and systematically set loose, until they arrive at full stature, not only in body, but also in sin, the preacher is sent to reclaim and convert them.[25]

Reid's focus on baptism was not theological hairsplitting, for it represented a profound division in outlook between radical evangelical Christianity and the more established churches. George Rawlyk has argued that adult baptism was "a ritual permeated not only by religious meaning but also by folk belief and by a sense of almost medieval magic." According to him, at the turn of the nineteenth century a number of radical evangelicals in the Maritime colonies began to regard "believer's baptism" as being at least as important as the actual instant of conversion.[26] While the baptism issue also divided High Church members from Anglican Evangelicals, since the latter believed in the need for subsequent regeneration and justification, this would not necessarily involve a sudden and dramatic conversion experience.[27] Reid did not spell out a position on these internal doctrinal issues, but he certainly envisioned the church as a family-based institution in which emphasis would be placed, not on converting adults, but on raising children and youths to be devout and sober-minded Christians.[28]

While Reid's theological attacks on adult baptism glossed over the social implications, which were greater independence from the patriarchal household and the sense of establishing a new society,[29] his ideas on the family are expressed clearly and comprehensively in his fireside essays, which were written for a general audience. Reid's first essay summarized his argument: "The fireside is a kingdom on a humble scale, which has customs, usages, privileges and Laws peculiar to itself. Here are the nurseries which raise all the plants which flourish in a nation ... Hence the domestic circle is the most important of all societies and governments, because it is the foundation of all the virtues, and of all the vices, that may adorn, or disgrace, the moral face of the world." As in his defence of infant baptism, Reid argued that "the seeds of virtue, religion, truth, justice, honor and charity" had to be sown at the fireside; otherwise "it is, generally speaking, out of question [sic] to expect that they shall grow or flourish, when we come to act on the theatre of the world."[30]

Having established the fundamental importance of the family, Reid in his next essay turned to the initial step in its formation: courtship and marriage. Like the *Extrait du rituel* published by the Catholic Diocese of Quebec a year earlier in 1836, he emphasized the teaching of St Paul that husband and wife should be "united together in mutual love, affection and esteem."[31] He went so far as to state that there should be "an agreement in principles, inclinations, tastes and pursuits." But Reid was not refering to romantic love, for he warned against succumbing to superficial attractions:

"Love" that has respect only to personal appearance, figure, complexion, a pleasant voice, agreeable manners in company, without knowing that they are equally agreeable at the fireside; or to dress, color of the hair, roseate hue of the cheek, or to the expectation of property, without sufficient regard to moral principles and qualities, the temper and disposition of the heart, education, character and connexions, will soon be in danger of losing its ardor, and then for want of something more precious and lasting than mere beauty and superficial qualities, any other result may be expected than a settling down into the quiet, placid contentment of mutual affection and esteem.[32]

Reid repeated this message in later essays, writing, "Young people, when they are about to marry the object of their mutual love and choice, are in most cases, however harsh the phrase may sound, idolators, with respect to each other. Each one is sure there is no fault in the other. All is perfection. One is an angel, the other is a sun."[33] To counter this delusion, he advised that particular attention be paid to how the prospective partners "demean themselves toward their parents, their brothers and their sisters." Prospective marriage partners should always remember, "In making the choice of a husband or a wife, a confidential, kind friend, a prudent, discreet and pious mother is wanted, on the one hand; and on the other, the same qualities are wanted in the kind, industrious and pious father."[34]

Like a modern-day advice columnist, James Reid published and replied to a letter purported to be from a young woman seeking courtship advice on behalf of herself and two female friends. "Fanny Cautious" wrote that her current suitor "is very agreeable as to person. In his manners he is modest and intelligent, but I have my doubts about the propriety of consenting to give him my hand, because he is careless about religion." Likewise, Miranda's suitor "is not without some good and agreeable qualities. He is a very agreeable talker – a good companion, and kind in his disposition; but she laments that he is too fond of spending his evenings in public places, where strong drinks are sold, though he is not yet any thing like a drunkard." Finally, "Fidelia has attracted the attentions of a young man who seems never to be happy unless he can be where his eye can see her: or be so near to her side as to be able to whisper something in her ear." Fidelia remained concerned, however, that her doting suitor "loves his own dear self beyond all."

Protesting that he had not been given much information on which to base his advice, Reid nevertheless warned Fanny Cautious "to remain cautious a little longer in single blessedness. To make the marriage state what it should be, it is indispensable that, besides personal attachment, there must be agreement in principles, similarity of tastes, feelings, and pursuits, between the parties." As for Miranda, the teetotalling Reid dismissed her suitor out of hand, suggesting that if she "is not cautious let her borrow a little of that virtue from Fanny." Finally, Fidelia was advised not to "commit your happiness to the keeping of a man so absorbed in himself." Perhaps it is not surprising that Reid's own two daughters never married, though one lived only to be twenty-seven, but his words of caution were worth considering in light of the sad fate facing unwed mothers and wives in abusive marriages during this era.[35] And he actually challenged the feminine stereotype when he closed his column with the advice that, when men "flatter you for your beauty depend upon it that, either they lack in understanding, or they mean to treat you as babes. Look to something more solid than pride of beauty, fashion or dress. Shew that you have intellects, morals and religion, and that you expect to find the same in them."[36]

That a clergyman would promote the long-standing companionate view of marriage while remaining suspicious of the less stable romantic love should not be surprising,[37] though Reid's attitude was in sharp contrast to that expressed in the popular conduct books of early modern England. The Puritan clerics who wrote these books stressed the importance of mutual physical attraction and sexual pleasure as the basis of a happy marriage, while also insisting on the subordinate status of the wife to the husband.[38] Reid's emphasis on family prayer and religious reading by the evening hearth clearly reflected a patriarchal view of the household, but his fireside essays did stress that both parents must serve as an example to their children and keep a close eye on their activities.[39] And while New England sermons in the 1830s apparently continued to give precedence to the theme of order in family and society, "vividly emphasizing the necessity for women to be subordinate to and dependent on their husbands,"[40] Reid presented a more balanced and nurturing vision of marriage.

Because the religious role of the family was so important to him, Reid argued that married couples should share the same religious principles; otherwise, "union cannot be expected except only in name," and there would be constant dissension about the raising of their children.[41] A mismatched couple would mean that, "instead of maintaining one uniform government at the fire side," there would be two, "each striving to be uppermost." The married couple should "be as much as possible of ONE MIND, in all their pursuits, to promote the comfort and happiness of each other, their mutual respectability and prosperity, as the heads of a family." Mutual compatibility was all the more essential because the husband and wife were united for life: "They cannot separate, without a flagrant breach of the law of God."[42]

To ensure that the "marriage connexion" would be "the happiest state which this sinful, transitory life can afford," the husband was to fulfill his engagement, "not as [a] matter of necessity, or of legal obligation, which he would gladly shun if he could, but willingly, cheerfully, and affectionately, as to one whom he truly loves, and whom he truly delights to please, to succor and to honor." The wife had reciprocal obligations. She was not to assume that, "if she do nothing, her husband is bound to provide for her. She has promised to 'serve him' not indeed as a slave serving a master or a tyrant, but as her husband, her best friend, and her lover."[43]

Dispensing advice that was traditionally directed at wives, but which he clearly meant for husbands as well, Reid wrote: "Guard against the temptations of unnecessary contradiction. If ever allowed, do it in a friendly manner. Never let your words be 'like the piercing of a sword.' When one, under some excitement, is hasty, and speaks unadvisedly, let the other be patient. When one emits sparks of anger, let the other spread over them the extinguishing mantle of love, and remain gentle and meek."[44] To drive home the same point in a later essay, he instructed, "From the time of their coming together as 'one flesh,' they ought to remember that there is a number of smart terms, in their vernacular tongue, with which, in their conversation, they have no longer any business."[45] Reid's idea of spousal companionship may have been "hierarchically arranged," to use Jane Errington's phrase, but it was a surprisingly attenuated hierarchy.[46]

Ryan attributes the dominance of the patriarchy theme in early American domestic writing largely to the fact that the household was the main place of production: "For the family economy to function efficiently, it had to employ discipline and regulation rather than rely on automatic harmony and love."[47] But Keith Wrightson has demonstrated for seventeenth-century England that the patriarchal "ideal" promoted in advice literature was often quite different from the more egalitarian "reality" reflected in diaries, and Amanda

Vickery makes the same point based on a variety of non-didactic sources from the eighteenth century.[48] Unfortunately, it is difficult to judge how compatible Reid felt with his own barely literate wife, Isabella, for she is a rather shadowy figure in a diary filled with musings about their offspring. But neither does he ever criticize her, and he becomes particularly solicitous about her welfare in his later years.[49]

Historians of domesticity have focused largely on the marital couple, but it is clear that, in dispensing his advice, Reid's was not concerned mainly with what Peter Ward has called "the holiest grail which matrimony offered," the happiness of the married partners themselves.[50] Rather, his chief preoccupation was with the role of the married couple as parents to the succeeding generation.[51] Of that role he wrote: "The position in which parents, then, are placed is of far greater importance, in all views that can be taken of it, than any mind can conceive, or the pen of the readiest writer can describe. They have, under God, the very making of the men and women of posterity in charge. For, from them the children not only derive their being but, generally, even their temper, dispositions, feelings, prejudices and sentiments; their industry or negligence, their moral worth or their vicious follies." If there had been a "nature versus nurture" debate in this pre-Darwinian era, Reid would have been in the latter camp (though his reasoning was not always consistent, as we shall see). He argued that children "have derived your nature from, not only their birth, but they have also imbibed your peculiar habits, and manifestations of temper with their food and drink, and drew them in from your very looks and voice & manners."[52]

Repeated many times in the fireside series was the basic argument that, for good or evil, individuals were products of their family upbringing: "When the fountains which supply the world with inhabitants are impure, what can we expect the streams to be? Can an impure fountain send forth sweet water? From such families the preaching of the Gospel may call an individual here and there to the knowledge of the truth, but for want of proper training at the fire side, while the mind was tender, such individuals will always labour under great disadvantages."[53]

For all the power that parents had to do good or ill, there was a strong deterministic cast to Reid's sociological musings, for they left relatively little scope for free will or spiritual conversion.[54] He warned, "The young feel, and think, and act, after the example set before them by their parents, until their habits are formed, & then they are set, set!! It is therefore in vain that we look for much good to arise from the families that are brought up without respect for the word of

God." In fact, Reid came close to contradicting his thesis concerning the benefits of the nurturing family when, in pointing to the royal house of Stuart, he went so far as to argue, "One single error, especially in the fundamental articles of religious belief, received into the mind, and practically acted upon, may put a family, through successive generations, into a new and dangerous channel."[55] And "nature" was given even more status than "nurture" in his column of two weeks later when he wrote: "Tribes and nations are found to this day, after the lapse of thousands of years, to be governed by the principles and maxims of a very remote progenitor ... It is so with families, who from generation to generation are noted for some peculiar habits and propensities, which vitiate their course and mar their happiness."[56] There were only three ways that such a "hereditary curse" could be lifted: "First, the influence of pious, discreet teachers, both in day and Sunday Schools. Secondly, the preaching of the Gospel; the means of grace, where they can be had; and thirdly; any advice, warning, example or admonition, that may lead them to the Bible."[57]

As fatalistic as Reid's more enthusiastic arguments may have been, parental influence remained so strong in his mind that he claimed that one should not be discouraged when, occasionally, "children who had been brought up at the very best firesides are found astray, or even reprobates." The sons of Jacob had conspired to get rid of their brother, Joseph, by selling him into slavery, but "the good seed which had been sown in their hearts, revived and produced good fruit, many years afterwards in Egypt."[58] It is unfortunate that the earlier volumes of Reid's diary have not survived, but those that remain from his later years reveal a concern for his offspring's emotional life that runs counter to the popular stereotype of the cold and aloof pre-industrial father.[59] Even as adults, Reid's four sons remained a constant preoccupation with him, and he maintained close contact with all of them at considerable expense to his pocketbook. In 1849, after all his sons had moved out of the household, Reid wrote in his diary:

Charles is continually writing to me of every admirable quality that he sees in his son. In his last letter, he seems to take shame to himself at the thought that I was a more punctual correspondent than himself, as if the fact was a new discovery. I wrote to him and told him the reason which made the difference in our punctuality. The reason I gave was that children's love to their parents was not equal to the love of parents to their children. I told him that he loved his little boy as he ought to do, and that if he had more boys his love would be no less to one than it would be to each of the rest – that when they came to the age of men and women, merit or good conduct would necessarily cause a preference to take place. I told him not to suppose that his boy's love to him would equal his when he grew to a man's estate; for if he did, he would find himself disappointed ... I do not know but that my sons are as dutiful as any other, but they do not shew it in the way I think they ought, and I think I deserve.[60]

After the death of his infant son, the taciturn Charles succumbed to occasional fits of depression, and his marriage became unstable, much to the elder Reid's concern.[61] Meanwhile, Malcolm, with whom Reid had a stronger bond, was suffering from a wasting disease in faraway Mississippi. Tellingly enough, Malcolm wrote to his father shortly before his death in 1850: "I am extremely thankful to you for your Letter as you wrote as if you considered me more of a man, and less a child than formerly."[62] Reid confided to his diary a few days later: "I cannot get the dear boy out of my mind for hardly a moment. I cannot cease to mourn and weep, and perhaps I do not wish to cease."[63]

Domineering as he may have been, James Reid's devotion to his sons was rewarded even in the case of John, the black sheep of the family, for he became a regular correspondent after marrying and moving with his very capable young wife to the western frontier of the United States during the early 1850s. Unfortunately, after enlisting in the Iowa cavalry during the American Civil War and fighting in many battles, John would die in the infamous Andersonville prisoner-of-war camp in 1864. Then in 1866 Reid's youngest son, James, who had become a local farmer, would in turn succumb to a lingering illness.[64] By this time, Charles and Jane were the only offspring left, but their father had himself finally died the previous year.

Tosh claims, "In preparing sons for their place in a man's world the father's own manhood was at stake, mortgaged to the future."[65] This was clearly true of Reid. Even though his essays did not distinguish between the raising of boys and of girls, he felt freer to praise his daughters, "whom I love as my own Soul ... They are dutiful and loving to us, and live together themselves in the Sweetest love."[66] Their domestic charms and dependence could be enjoyed without reservation because they were intended for marriage,[67] but a stronger restraint also had to be maintained on their social lives. Thus Reid fretted when, in their twenties, the two young women attended social gatherings at which there were dances, though his anger was directed entirely at the hosts for their moral laxity.[68] Indeed, it appears that none of the young men in the community could measure up to Reid's standards for his daughters. Even when a promising Montreal lawyer sent Jane a letter "containing certain proposals," Reid confided to his diary: "The young man has great assurance and much presumption when he would think of such a thing. I hope she will give him no encouragement. I will not oppose, but assuredly will not give consent."[69] His attitude is rather ironic, given his insistence on the moral superiority of marriage and parenthood, but unmarried women who cared for their aging parents, as Jane did, were presumably worthy exceptions.[70] And if Jane was resentful of her status and burden, her father's diary gives no hint that he was aware of it.[71]

Reid was clearly overly protective of his daughters, though it should not be forgotten that a young man could sow his wild oats and then redeem himself through marriage by assuming the respectable role of breadwinner, but a young woman, "once fallen, could never be redeemed."[72] Tellingly enough, the first time that Reid saw his youngest son's intended wife, who was from a neighbouring township, was when he performed their marriage ceremony. He was quick to take offence, however, when women in the village hinted that James had rushed into marriage with someone beneath his social status: "A farmer's daughter in his own vicinity who knows well what kind of home he is bringing her to – who sees what she has to expect, & cannot naturally look for any thing different from, or much better than what she was used to, is more likely to ... exert herself to make it a more comfortable home. Be it ... a matter of mere *convenience* [it] is all the better for that, for if [it] has less of what romancers call *love* it has more reason."[73]

As a clergyman whose daily routine seldom took him far from the household, Reid had a greater opportunity than most men to play an active part in raising his family.[74] According to Cott, however, New England ministers of the early nineteenth century "fervently reiterated their consensus that mothers were more important than fathers in forming 'the tastes, sentiments, and habits of children,' and more effective in instructing them."[75] Errington has found the same theme in the newspapers of Upper Canada,[76] but Reid clearly disagreed, though he assumed that mothers would play the dominant role in early childhood. In his first essay on the family, he wrote, "To teach the art of reading & writing or book learning to any extent, small or great is not the education which I mean, but that which the mother must begin as soon as her child is able to lisp, and which afterwards must be carried on by the father and mother conjointly, when he is able to comprehend the nature of truth; of governing life's passions; of restraining his desires; of obeying their commands; and of doing to his brothers and sisters as he would like to be done by."[77]

Ever the insecure worrier, Reid sometimes felt that he had been too accommodating to his family. He confided to his diary in one of his moments of self-pity: "I never was master as I ought to have been in my own family, and as I yielded and surrendered the authority which God has given to every husband and father, I am mostly punished. I did it for the sake of peace, but I find when too late that a dereliction of duty and right never bring peace."[78] Many gender historians have nevertheless been rather quick to assume that "the idea of fatherhood itself" began to wither away with the rise of domesticity.[79] Patriarchy was slowly being replaced by a more equal partnership, but the father certainly did not relinquish his moral authority over the family.[80]

Reid's concept of family was largely restricted to parents and children, and his journalistic essays refer only briefly to relatives and servants in the household, stressing that they "are the members that compose your fireside society, and that are to join with you in prayer to your common Creator, Preserver and Lord."[81] In a later essay he insisted that, like others in the household, servants should be allowed rest from their labours on Sundays in order to participate in religious rituals. He admitted, however, that "such is the dilapidation of the fire side government in our unhappy days" that most domestics would consider efforts to interfere in their Sabbath leisure time to be "an unwarrantable attempt to control their liberty."[82]

While Reid showed considerable tolerance and affection towards his farmhand, a Scottish pensioner from the British army who was inclined to go on the occasional spree with his drunken wife, he was less patient with the succession of young females who helped in the house, generally not deigning to use their names in his diary entries. Even in his seventies, Reid would do the farm chores without much complaint when left alone by "Auld Sandy," but he became quite irritated whenever "the girl" left Isabella and Jane for a few days to visit her own family.[83] Servants may have been part of the household (though Sandy lived in his own home), but they were hardly members of the family.

What explains the crucially important role that the nuclear family played in Reid's public and private life? To begin with, as an Anglican priest, he had adopted the view that the surest route to spiritual salvation lay through the established church, the bulwark of a peaceful and civilized society. But the rather formal and hierarchical Church of England was never entirely a comfortable fit with the American settlement frontier where he lived, for here society was essentially simplified to a loose collection of independent farmers and villagers in which the nuclear family was by far the most important institution.[84] Reid's emphasis on the religious role of the family was less a product of Evangelical sympathies than an accommodation to his social environment, one in which the ideal family would become the church in microcosm, with parents fulfilling much of the role normally assumed by the clergy.

One should not underestimate the sense of community created by such institutions as the school, the temperance society, and the church itself, in all of which Reid played a leading role.[85] But, while the line between family and outside community was far from distinct in early New England, it is quite sharply delineated in Reid's writing. His diary reveals that, even after four decades in St Armand, he felt somewhat of an outsider in what was clearly a fractious society. In 1849 he complained: "How few people we have with whom I can spend a profitable hour! What a bar my position has been to my improvement! But I cannot help it. This Slab City has been my lot and here I must remain, how ever much soever I may dislike it."[86] Four years later he wrote: "I don't know that they would agree to any thing. They are so divided, and so jealous of one another. It is a wonderful neighbourhood. Where is there one of such intelligence and such conversational, agreeable social manners as to make an evening or an hour with them profitable or interesting to me?"[87]

Since his wife was from Upper Canada, Reid had no in-laws in the area, which may have been just as well for him, given his anxieties about social status. Certainly, he never forgot the public humiliation brought by his own brother and sister after they arrived from Scotland in 1818. The former ran up considerable debts before absconding, and the latter moved to Upper Canada after becoming pregnant and marrying (in Reid's words) "a low Irish Roman Catholic who was many years her junior."[88] When a young woman rejected his son James's offer of marriage in 1850, a humiliated Reid blamed this old scandal: "Seeing how it has hitherto been with us, it may be a blessing that God has taken to himself my dear grandson [Charles's son], in order that my posterity may not increase. In my own family, in my brother and Sister I have been unfortunate."[89]

Aside from the social situation Reid found himself in, one might speculate that his fireside essays, written when he was nearly fifty-seven years old, were a lament for an idealized family relationship that he would have wished to enjoy. Certainly, he may have blamed himself as a father for the failures of his sons, but the evidence from his surviving diaries suggests that his family remained a refuge from his own rather disappointing career. His sensitive and introverted personality also helps to explain why he remained focused on his own family long after his sons had left home. At one point he even questioned whether his obsession with his children was sinful: "I fail most grievously in casting my care respecting them on the

Lord ... Why cannot I believe that he careth for them? Why do I act and feel, as if he did [not] but had all to do myself?"[90]

The focus of family historians of the pre-industrial era has largely been on the Puritans, followed by the evangelicals, and Lawrence Stone argues, "There seems to have been an uninterrupted connection between the caring but authoritarian discipline of the Puritan bourgeois parent of the seventeenth century and the caring but authoritarian discipline of the Evangelical bourgeois parent of the late eighteenth and early nineteenth centuries."[91] Certainly, Wesley advised parents to "break the will if you would not damn the child," and Philip Greven claims that the "aggressively repressive methods" of the evangelical mode of child rearing persisted into nineteenth-century America.[92] As late as the turn of the twentieth century, the official stance of the Canadian Methodist Church was that, even though young children did not commit sin, lacking responsibility, they nevertheless "possessed an evil nature which would lead them to sin when they matured."[93]

But Neil Semple claims that the trend among the more liberal Methodist spokesmen had long been towards the Romantic belief that children were both innocent and naturally moral creatures: "With supervision, discipline and a sound environment, conversion would not be necessary and the safety of childhood could be extended for all children at least into adolescence."[94] Reid appears to have arrived at the same position concerning the lack of need for conversion even while the rather pessimistic tone of his discourse suggests that he adhered to the doctrine of original sin. The essence of his teaching was not the Romantic notion that children were naturally good, but that only nurturing, God-fearing parents could ensure that they did not stray from the narrow path of religion and morality. He wrote in his column of 30 May 1837: "Never think it enough that you pray for them. Exhort them. Explain as much as you can of the Scriptures to them. Teach them their duty. Show them that they are sinners and need repentance, and the pardoning mercy of God through the merits and intercession of Jesus Christ. Give them line upon line and precept upon precept."[95]

Reid nevertheless expressed too much love and concern for his children to conform to Greven's evangelical mode of child rearing.[96] While we have no direct evidence of how he interacted with his sons and daughters while they were infants, we can discern in his diary the intensity of emotion that Greven associates with the genteel parental temperament. One recent study states categorically that Reid's earlier mentor, John Strachan, promoted this genteel mode of child rearing in early-nineteenth-century Upper Canada, with the unintended result that

Strachan's own sons and those of the local gentry became self-centred and independent-spirited young men.[97] But Strachan had exhibited the same rebellious attitude towards his own father a generation earlier,[98] and his sons might well have attempted to escape his suffocating authority no matter what the nature of their early upbringing.

While Reid's sons (some more than others) also exhibited a certain degree of independence as young adults, their behaviour was quite clearly a reaction against paternal dominance, rather than a product of the easygoing indulgence that Greven claims characterized the genteel temperament.[99] Reid most closely conforms to a third category, the moderate temperament, which Greven claims "tried to be authoritative, respectful toward legitimate and essential authority within the family, yet aware of the need to limit the exercise of authority within certain established boundaries."[100] Reid shared Strachan's appreciation of order, balance, harmony, and temperance, but he was too isolated from the colonial elite to indulge in the Upper Canadian clergyman's desire to raise the new generation as a privileged gentry class.

Only further research will reveal how representative Reid's ideas on the family were of the Canadian Protestant clergy and the members of their congregations, but he was certainly not an extremist in his religious beliefs, and Westfall argues that by mid-century the religion of order and the religion of experience had merged into a moderate new Protestant culture in Upper Canada.[101] Whether or not this was true in the Eastern Townships, where the Anglicans and Methodists accounted for well over half the Protestant population in 1851, remains to be seen. But the family letters of Stanstead's Marcus Child, a leading Methodist who became an Anglican in the 1840s, clearly reflect the moderate sensibility described by Greven.[102] And if Child, like Reid and Strachan, was more intimately concerned with the raising of his children than the separate-spheres model of gender roles would lead us to expect, it was because he, like them, believed that fathers should not be excluded from the crucial spiritual role that parenthood played, a role more important than any other in society.[103]

NOTES

This essay is part of a larger project on Protestantism in the Eastern Townships funded by a grant from the Social Sciences and Humanities Research Council of Canada. I wish to thank Professors Richard Vaudry, Marguerite Van Die, and John Craig for their helpful comments.

1 Nancy Cott, *The Bonds of Womanhood: "Women's Sphere" in New England, 1780–1835* (New Haven: Yale University Press, 1977), 63.

2 The most notable exceptions are Elizabeth Jane Errington, *Wives and Mothers, School Mistresses and Scullery Maids: Working Women in Upper Canada, 1790–1840* (Montreal and Kingston: McGill-Queen's University Press, 1995); Katherine McKenna, *A Life of Propriety: Anne Murray Powell and Her Family, 1775–1849* (Kingston and Montreal: McGill-Queen's University Press, 1994); and Cecilia Morgan, *Public Men and Virtuous Women* (Toronto: University of Toronto Press, 1996).

3 John Tosh, *A Man's Place: Masculinity and the Middle-Class Home in Victorian England* (New Haven and London: Yale University Press, 1999), 36. See also David Newsome, *The Parting of Friends: A Study of the Wilberforces and Henry Manning* (London: John Murray, 1966), 10–16.

4 The series began as "Reflections on the Season" on 13 December 1836, but soon changed its title and theme. The focus shifted again from the family after the twenty-fourth essay.

5 See, for example, Amanda Vickery, "Golden Age to Separate Spheres? A Review of the Categories and Chronology of English Women's History," *Historical Journal* 36 (1993): 385–6, 390–1.

6 Four of the thirty-six volumes have survived and are to be found in the Montreal Diocesan Archives of the Anglican Church. They cover the years 1848–54 and 1863–64. A carefully edited transcript of the first two volumes has been produced as a doctoral dissertation by Mary-Ellen Bacon-Reisner as "The Diaries of James Reid (1848–1851): Works and Days of a Country Clergyman" (PhD thesis, Université Laval, 1990), recently published as *The Diary of a Country Clergyman, 1848–1851: James Reid* (Montreal and Kingston: McGill-Queen's University Press, 2000).

7 Tosh, *A Man's Place*, 34; Keith Wrightson, *English Society, 1580–1680* (New Brunswick, NJ: Rutgers University Press, 1984; reprint 1995), chap. 4.

8 John Demos, "Images of the American Family, Then and Now," in Virginia Tufte and Barbara Myerhoff, eds., *Changing Images of the Family* (New Haven: Yale University Press, 1979), 45–55.

9 Cott, *The Bonds of Womanhood*, 92. See also ibid., 64–7, 97; Leonore Davidoff and Catherine Hall, *Family Fortunes: Men and Women of the English Middle Class, 1780–1850* (Chicago: University of Chicago Press, 1987), 20, 28; Tosh, *A Man's Place*, 17–34.

10 Mary Ryan, *Cradle of the Middle Class: The Family in Oneida County, New York, 1790–1865* (Cambridge: Cambridge University Press, 1981), 147–53.

11 St Armand clearly had a sizable village population, for 98 of 252 households occupied less than ten acres in 1842. It was also one of the most progressive agricultural areas in Lower Canada, with the average farmer

in the 1842 manuscript census (defined broadly as all those householders occupying more than ten acres) owning seventy improved acres, seventeen cattle, three horses, twenty-one sheep, and four hogs.

12 See J.I. Little, *State and Society in Transition: The Politics of Institutional Reform in the Eastern Townships, 1838–1852* (Montreal and Kingston: McGill-Queen's University Press, 1997).

13 William Westfall, *Two Worlds: The Protestant Culture of Nineteenth-Century Ontario* (Kingston and Montreal: McGill-Queen's University Press, 1989), 13.

14 The following summary of Reid's early life is based on H.D. MacDermid, "The Rev. James Reid," *Missisquoi Historical Society Reports* 18 (1984): 104–10; Reid's own narrative in *Hypocrisy Detected: in a Letter to the Late Firm of Haldane, Ewing, and Co. with a Preface, Containing the Narrative of Mr. James Reid, a Missionary Sent by These Gentlemen to Upper Canada* (Aberdeen: J. Booth, Jun., 1812), ix–xxviii; and Bacon-Reisner, "The Diaries," 43–96. Reid claims that he was nineteen at the time of his conversion, but he also writes that the missionary who was responsible arrived in his community in 1801.

15 The Haldanes apparently became Baptists in 1808, not 1810 as Reid's narrative states. See Donald E. Meek, "Evangelical Missionaries in the Early Nineteenth-Century Highlands," *Scottish Studies* 28 (1987): 1–2, 8–9.

16 The pamphlet was published anonymously, but the main author was clearly Strachan. See Bacon-Reisner, "The Diaries," 48–9; Anglican Church of Canada Montreal Diocesan Archives (MDA), James Reid Papers, John Strachan to James Reid, Cornwall, 5 March 1814.

17 See Thomas R. Millman, *The Life of the Right Reverend, the Honourable Charles James Stewart, D.D., Oxon., Second Anglican Bishop of Quebec* (London: Huron College, 1953).

18 A second minister was appointed to take over the western part of the parish in 1826, though St Armand was not formally divided into two parishes until 1834. See Bacon-Reisner, "The Diaries," 75–8.

19 See J.I. Little, "A Moral Engine of Such Incalculable Power: The Temperance Movement in the Eastern Townships," *Journal of Eastern Townships Studies* 11 (fall 1997): 11–12; MDA, James Reid Papers, Parish Report, 31 December 1857.

20 Reid did become one of the honorary canons of the cathedral church of the newly erected Diocese of Montreal in 1854, and the following year he was awarded an honorary doctorate of divinity from the University of Bishop's College. See Bacon-Reisner, "The Diaries," 78–9.

21 Rev. James Reid, *Remarks on the Lecture of the Rt. Rev. Bishop Hopkins, against the Temperance Society* (Frelighsburg: Standard Office, 1836); and Rev. James Reid, *A Discourse on Infant Baptism* (Montreal: Armour and Ramsay, 1841). Daniel C. Goodwin suggests that in Nova Scotia "the treatises about baptism may have been on the cutting edge of indigenous

popular and scholarly writing"; see " 'The Very Vitals of Christianity'; The Baptismal Controversy and the Intellectual Awakening in Nova Scotia, 1811–1848," *Nova Scotia Historical Review* 15 (1995): 87.

22 On Reid's aspirations and career as a writer, see Bacon-Reisner, "The Diaries," 97–120. For a comprehensive list of his publications, see ibid., 605–13.

23 Archives of the Parish of St Armand East, "Eighteen Sermons by Rev. James Reid," 182–4; Reid, *A Discourse*, 110. Reid fails to discuss the implications of the fact that the initiation ceremony was confined to males in the Jewish faith, but not in that of Christians.

24 Anglican Evangelicals claimed that regeneration could subsequently be forfeited through sin. See Richard A. Vaudry, "Anglicans and the Atlantic World: Evangelicals, High Churchmen and the Quebec Connection" (unpublished MS), 146–51; Newsome, *The Parting of Friends*, 48.

25 Reid, *A Discourse*, vii.

26 G.A. Rawlyk, "The Rage for Dipping: Joseph Crandall, Elijah Estabrooks, and Believer's Baptism, 1795–1800," in Rawlyk, ed., *The Canada Fire: Radical Evangelicalism in British North America, 1775–1812* (Kingston and Montreal: McGill-Queen's University Press, 1994), 163–4.

27 Tosh, *A Man's Place*, 36, 42.

28 On the baptism issue in the Canadian Methodist Church, see Neil Semple, "'The Nurture and Admonition of the Lord': Nineteenth-Century Canadian Methodism's Response to 'Childhood,' " *Histoire sociale/Social History* 14 (1981): 165–6; and Marguerite Van Die, *An Evangelical Mind: Nathanael Burwash and the Methodist Tradition in Canada, 1839–1918* (Kingston, Montreal, London: McGill-Queen's University Press, 1989), 25–37.

29 Ryan, *Cradle of the Middle Class*, 66–7.

30 *Missiskoui Standard*, 10 January 1837.

31 Ibid., 17 January 1837; Serge Gagnon, *Mariage et famille au temps du Papineau* (Sainte-Foy: Les Presses de l'Université Laval, 1993), 189–90. On St Paul's concept of marriage, see Anthony Fletcher, "The Protestant Idea of Marriage in Early Modern England," in Fletcher and Peter Roberts, eds., *Religion, Culture and Society in Early Modern Britain: Essays in Honour of Patrick Collinson* (Cambridge: Cambridge University Press, 1994), 173–5.

32 *Missiskoui Standard*, 17 January 1837.

33 Ibid., 7 February 1837.

34 Ibid., 31 January 1837.

35 See Errington, *Wives and Mothers*, 39–51, 55–8.

36 *Missiskoui Standard*, 21 February 1837. Errington (*Wives and Mothers*, 36) claims that "colonial leaders told women to cultivate modesty, humility, and chastity," but the newspaper citations she provides as evidence focus, like Reid, on the value of wisdom and knowledge over beauty, wit, and delicacy. On the critique of fashion, see Morgan, *Public Men*, 158–62.

37 Alan Macfarlane states that the companionate view of marriage was accepted in England at least as early as the fourteenth century, while the
concept of the love marriage evolved slowly from that time forward.
Lawrence Stone, on the other hand, claims that romantic love first became
a respectable motive for marriage among the English propertied classes in
the late eighteenth century. See Alan Macfarlane, *Marriage and Love in
England: Modes of Reproduction, 1300–1840* (Oxford, Basil Blackwell, 1986),
331–4; and Lawrence Stone, *The Family, Sex, and Marriage in England,
1500–1800* (New York: Harper and Row, 1977), 7–8, 284–6.

38 Fletcher, "The Protestant Idea of Marriage," 171, 176–9. Wrightson (*English Society*, 91) argues, however, that while "mutuality in marriage is a
less dramatic aspect of moralistic advice than their assertions of male authority, … it was of equal importance to the writers of conduct books and
it should never be ignored."

39 Stone (*The Family, Sex, and Marriage*, 245–6) argues that the re-emergence
of regular, daily family prayer illustrates how patriarchy was strengthened in nineteenth-century England, but Tosh (*A Man's Place*, 73) states,
"It was an open question whether the bedtime prayer of mother and child
was not more important than the family prayers led by father." Van Die's
biography of Nathanael Burwash stresses the religious role played by his
mother; see *An Evangelical Mind*, 20–5.

40 Cott, *The Bonds of Womanhood*, 158. Similarly, Morgan (*Public Men*, 126–8,
147–53) stresses the patriarchal preoccupation of Upper Canada's Methodist
press, though she describes more diverse views in the secular newspapers.

41 *Missiskoui Standard*, 31 January 1837.

42 Ibid., 17 January 1837.

43 *Missiskoui Standard*, 17 January 1837.

44 Ibid., 24 January 1837.

45 Ibid., 7 February 1837.

46 Errington, *Wives and Mothers*, 34.

47 Ryan, *Cradle of the Middle Class*, 32. In his examination of the leading New
England magazines between 1741 and 1794, Stone (*The Family, Sex, and
Marriage*, 387) discovered "a very great deal of discussion of the companionate marriage," but he insists that, as in England, "the double sexual
standard remained as firmly rooted as ever."

48 Wrightson, *English Society*, 92–104; Vickery, "Golden Age," 409–14.

49 Isabella Reid survived her husband by three years. Bacon-Reisner ("The
Diaries," 587) notes that Reid avoided signing the parish register with her
husband as a sponsor, and that her signature was barely legible on the one
occasion that she did sign. But she fails to note that inability to write did not
necessarily mean an inability to read. The book given as a gift to Isabella
Reid by the wife of a neighbouring clergyman was therefore not necessarily
the mistake that Bacon-Reisner suggests.

50 Peter Ward, *Courtship, Love and Marriage in Nineteenth-Century English Canada* (Montreal and Kingston: McGill-Queen's University Press, 1990), 156.

51 Macfarlane (*Marriage and Love*, 174) notes that, outside industrial Western societies, "the relationships that are most important are often those between parents and children, with the marital bond a poor second."

52 *Missiskoui Standard*, 14 February 1837.

53 Ibid., 28 March 1837.

54 Calvin and the Puritans had also believed that "parents must educate and discipline their children in order to give them every chance for salvation." See Mary Cable, *The Little Darlings: A History of Child-Rearing in America* (New York: Charles Scribner's Sons, 1972, reprint 1975), 6.

55 *Missiskoui Standard*, 28 February 1837.

56 Ibid., 14 March 1837.

57 Ibid., 7 March 1837.

58 Ibid.

59 See, for example, Neil Sutherland, *Children in English-Canadian Society: Making the Twentieth-Century Consensus* (Toronto: University of Toronto Press, 1976), 11. Closer to that stereotype is the diary of Nova Scotia's Reverend John Seccombe, written in the 1760s, which was more fixated on his meals than on his family. See Gwendolyn Davies, "'Gendered Responses': The Seccombe Diaries," in Margaret Conrad, ed., *Intimate Relations: Family and Community in Planter Nova Scotia, 1759–1800* (Fredericton: Acadiensis Press, 1995).

60 14 January 1849, in Bacon-Reisner, "The Diaries," 139.

61 See, for example, 30 June 1850, ibid., 339.

62 Quoted 27 September 1850, ibid., 352.

63 2 October 1850, ibid., 356.

64 Though only forty-two at the time of his death, James Reid junior was predeceased by three wives. See Bacon-Reisner, "The Diaries," 84–6, 588–90.

65 Tosh, *A Man's Place*, 115.

66 13 July 1849, in Bacon-Reisner, "The Diaries," 165.

67 Tosh, *A Man's Place*, 115. While Reid made more provision for the formal education of his sons than of his daughters, he was also concerned that the costs he had incurred to establish Malcolm and James would not leave enough money to provide for Jane and Nancy after his death. See Bacon-Reisner, "The Diaries," 86; 15 January 1849, ibid., 140.

68 See, for example, 17 January 1849, in Bacon-Reisner, "The Diaries," 140–1.

69 13 March 1851, ibid., 399, 524–5, 563.

70 On this theme, see Errington, *Wives and Mothers*, 25, 31.

71 Echoing Carroll Smith-Rosenberg, Ryan (*Cradle of the Middle Class*, 193–4) suggests that the essential middle-class family bond was between mother and daughter, but Davidoff and Hall (*Family Fortunes*, 346–7) posit an equally strong tie between father and daughter. Certainly, this was the

case for the family of Reid's contemporary and fellow Eastern Townships resident Marcus Child. See J.I. Little, ed., *The Child Letters: Public and Private Life in a Canadian Merchant-Politician's Family, 1841–1845* (Montreal and Kingston: McGill-Queen's University Press, 1995), 34–5.

72 Lynne Marks, *Revivals and Roller Rinks: Religion, Leisure, and Identity in Late-Nineteenth-Century Small-Town Ontario* (Toronto: University of Toronto Press, 1996), 214. See also, Ryan, *Cradle of the Middle Class*, 193; and Davidoff and Hall, *Family Fortunes*, 332, 404–8.

73 MDA, Reid, "Diary," vol. 25, 4531, 19 December 1852.

74 Parish clergymen with mission responsibilities could, nevertheless, be absent for extended periods of time. See, for example, J.I. Little, "Serving 'the North East Corner of Creation': The Community Role of a Rural Clergyman in the Eastern Townships of Quebec, 1829–1870," *Histoire sociale/Social History* 30 (1997): 21–54.

75 Cott, *The Bonds of Womanhood*, 86.

76 Errington, *Wives and Mothers*, 36, 53–4, 66–7. Morgan (*Public Men*, 153–5) is more ambiguous, but Tosh (*A Man's Place*, 113) makes the same point for England by the 1830s.

77 *Missiskoui Standard*, 10 January 1837.

78 19 March 1850, in Bacon-Reisner, "The Diaries," 319.

79 Ryan, *Cradle of the Middle Class*, 232. See also Robert L. Griswold, *Fatherhood in America: A History* (New York: Basic Books, 1993), 12–14.

80 See Tosh, *A Man's Place*, chap. 4.

81 *Missiskoui Standard*, 21 March 1837.

82 Ibid., 2 May 1837.

83 See, for example, MDA, Reid, "Diary," vol. 36, 6287, 28 March 1864. On the difficulties of finding and keeping female servants in early nineteenth-century New England, see Cott, *The Bonds of Womanhood*, 29–30, 49. For an examination of domestic servants in Upper Canada, see Errington, *Wives and Mothers*, chap. 5.

84 On this concept, see R.C. Harris, "The Historical Geography of North American Regions," *American Behavioral Scientist* 22 (1978): 115–30.

85 On Reid's community role and status, see Bacon-Reisner, "The Diaries," 86–9. For a useful survey of the American literature on family and community, see Philip Greven, "Family and Community in Early America," in Conrad, ed., *Intimate Relations*.

86 18 January 1849, in Bacon-Reisner, "The Diaries," 141.

87 MDA, Reid, "Diary," vol. 25, 4562, 14 February 1853. See also Bacon-Reisner, "The Diaries," 17–20.

88 Bacon-Reisner, "The Diaries," 81–2, 461–2; MDA, Reid, "Diary," vol. 25, 4603, 25 June 1853.

89 24 February 1850, in Bacon-Reisner, "The Diaries," 311–12.

90 14 October 1850, ibid., 359.

91 Stone, *Family, Sex, and Marriage*, 466–7.
92 Philip Greven, *The Protestant Temperament: Patterns of Child-Rearing, Religious Experience, and the Self in Early America* (New York: Alfred A. Knopf, 1980). Linda Pollock also rejects the evolutionary view of child rearing, arguing that changes in attitudes to children reflected in the advice literature were not accompanied by parallel changes in parental behaviour. See Linda Pollock, *Forgotten Children: Parent-Child Relations from 1500 to 1900* (Cambridge: Cambridge University Press, 1983), 270–1. See also Pollock, *A Lasting Relationship: Parents and Children over Three Centuries* (Hanover, NH: University Press of New England, 1987). Contrast the more historical perspective of Tosh (*A Man's Place*, 39–43, 93–100), with its four types of Victorian father. Wesley is quoted in John Cleverly and D.C. Philips, *Visions of Childhood: Influential Models from Locke to Spock* (New York: Teachers College Press, 1986), 29.
93 Semple, "The Nurture and Admonition," 160.
94 Ibid., 159, 164. Van Die (*An Evangelical Mind*, 25–37) places more emphasis than Semple on the ambivalent moral status of the Canadian Methodist child in the nineteenth century.
95 *Missiskoui Standard*, 30 May 1837.
96 Nor did the wealthy and influential Anglican Evangelicals, such as the Wilberforces, who settled at Clapham Common in the 1790s. See Tosh, *A Man's Place*, 36, 41; Newsome, *The Parting of Friends*, 27–56.
97 Paul Anthony Bamfield, "The Well-Regulated Family: John Strachan and the Role of the Family in Early Upper Canada, 1800–1812" (MA thesis, Queen's University, 1985). Errington (*Wives and Mothers*, 285 n117) suggests that the Upper Canadian rhetoric of child rearing generally conformed to Greven's "genteel" model, but her judgment may have been influenced by the fact that most of her case studies were members of the gentry. On French Canada, see Lorraine Gadoury, *La famille dans son intimité: Échanges épistolaires au sein de l'élite canadienne du XVIIe siècle* (Montréal: Hurtubise HMH, 1999).
98 Bamfield, "The Well-Regulated Family," 71.
99 Greven, *The Protestant Temperament*, 265.
100 Ibid., 151.
101 Westfall, *Two Worlds*, chap. 3.
102 Françoise Noël, *Competing for Souls: Missionary Activity and Settlement in the Eastern Townships, 1784–1851* (Sherbrooke: Département d'Histoire, Université de Sherbrooke, 1988), 235; Little, *The Child Letters*.
103 Similarily, the evangelical middle-class fathers examined by Davidoff and Hall (*Family Fortunes*, 329) in early-nineteenth-century England were intensely involved with their families, and Tosh (*A Man's Place*, 77) states that "the doctrine of separate spheres ... is particularly misleading here because it loses sight of the distinctively masculine privilege of

enjoying access to both the public *and* the private sphere." William Dummer Powell, a member of the Upper Canadian Family Compact, was rather indifferent to his children, but he appears not to have been particularly religious. See McKenna, *A Life of Propriety,* 94, 128.

Popular Religion
and Family Strategies

Tribalism, Proselytism, and Pluralism: Protestants, Family, and Denominational Identity in Mid-Nineteenth-Century St Stephen, New Brunswick

HANNAH M. LANE

The daughter of pre-Loyalists, Charlotte Hill Thompson was an early convert to Methodism, the first organized denomination in south-western New Brunswick.[1] When she died in 1864, seven of her surviving children still lived within the parish of St Stephen. Although both she and her husband had been early converts, only four of these seven children were still Methodists. In the first provincial census of religion, taken in 1861, two sons were listed as Episcopalian (Anglican[2] in modern usage). A third son was listed as a Universalist, the denominational tradition that asserted a metaphorical hell and an ultimately universal salvation, although his first wife had been a Methodist church member. In the 1860s he became an Anglican, and where he remarried, it was to a Congregationalist. Charlotte's two daughters were Methodists, but only one was an actual church member. Married to an Anglican, the other was listed in 1861 as a Methodist, as was Charlotte's youngest son; neither, however, was a Methodist church member. The oldest son, William, had married an Anglican, but his wife's religious obituary appears to have been written by a Methodist minister. William was almost sixty when he finally joined a Methodist class meeting, in the words of his obituary, "the church of his choice."[3]

Such denominational fluidity was one hallmark of late-eighteenth- and early-nineteenth-century Protestantism on both sides of the Atlantic. Historians have suggested that denominational boundaries became less fluid over the century, and that the growth of older evangelical denominations increasingly reflected tribalism rather than proselytism.[4] In other words, churches relied more and more on keeping the children of the founders within the fold, rather than on gaining new supporters from outside the denomination. While the cultural significance of tribalism has been analyzed from texts and denominational institutions,[5] its demographic significance is less studied. The social history of religion in particular communities is a relatively recent development in the historiography of British North America, and in general, demographic sources are weakest for the decades of early settlement. Part of a larger project on religion, gender, and class in St Stephen, New Brunswick,[6] this paper explores the demographic significance of tribalism, proselytism, and denominational pluralism among Protestants after the founding generations.[7]

How representative of lay Protestants in mid-nineteenth-century St Stephen were Charlotte Thompson's children and their spouses? The importance of family in maintaining religious tradition is a cross-cultural phenomenon,[8] and tribalism indeed best describes how the majority of men and women in St Stephen formed their denominational identities. However, patterns of denominational identity and evangelical church membership also suggest the persistence and significance beyond the early settler stage of both proselytism and what can be called denominational pluralism: the maintenance of multiple denominational affiliations, whether through nominal adherence reported on census returns, church membership, lay leadership, or other kinds of less clearly "denominational" affiliations, such as pew rental. Proselytism and pluralism – these alternatives to tribalism – thus suggest an element of choice in the decisions of those, such as Charlotte Thompson's oldest son, who stayed within their parents' denominational tradition. The limits to the cultural influence of tribalism can also be seen in the social composition of evangelical church members. While many individuals followed relations who had joined earlier or joined churches along with other family members, not all individuals within evangelical families did so. Evangelical church membership was primarily an adult decision made by a minority of adherents, and most members were women.

The historical vocabulary of the following analysis requires some explication. Denominational identity is a problematic construct, above all because of theoretical debates over the concept of "identity" itself,[9] more familiar to most readers than "subjectivity" or "subject position." Furthermore, the major sources reporting the denominational identities of most St Stephen Protestants – membership records and census returns[10] – were recorded by others, whether enumerators or ministers. These sources, not surprisingly, used prevailing denominational discourse to establish categories.

However, there were exceptions, such as the entries for St Stephen's lone Deist in 1861 or the interrelated Swedenborgians in 1871 (former Methodists and Presbyterians who presumably identified in some way with the teachings of the eighteenth-century philosopher and mystic Emanuel Swedenborg). As this example illustrates, the patterns derived from linking census returns and membership records do show that denominational identity was not always either fixed or coherent, and that it was, moreover, often interwoven with or shaped by other forms of identity, such as family or ethnicity. Yet this very instability was constructed by much more than record keepers. Enumerators might well have preferred the reduced labour of simpler denominational distinctions, and ministers indeed regretted denominational divisions within families and the loss of adherents to other denominations. Denominational identity and identities were ultimately constructed by adult individuals who, if not exercised the autonomy only found in abstract models, certainly exercised the agency required to generate the sheer denominational variety among nineteenth-century Protestants.

Moreover, while membership or lay leadership can legitimately be called involvement in a particular church, census returns referred only to the denominational equivalent of ethnic identity – the answer by an individual or by a parent or spouse on behalf of another individual to the question on nominal religious adherence,[11] not necessarily related to any form of church involvement. Similarly, although membership or lay leadership are forms of church involvement, they may not always be statements of denominational identity. Another difficulty concerns the distinction between proselytism and denominational pluralism. Proselytism here refers to the process by which individuals changed or added to their denominational identities (not to the active recruiting by churches of people from other denominations). Of Charlotte Thompson's two Anglican sons in 1861, the married son was a vestryman and had an Anglican wife, and they both were still Anglican in the 1871 census. He appears to have genuinely ceased to be a Methodist. However, Charlotte Thompson's other non-Methodist children, identified as such only on the census – some still living with her – and her Methodist children with non-Methodist spouses might be better classified as denominationally pluralist individuals or families.

The eighteenth-century settlers of St Stephen brought with them the social diversity that would remain characteristic of the most densely populated parish in the province outside Saint John. In 1791 the then-largest sawmill in the province was built on the St Croix River, and by mid-century the villages along the border with Maine contained retail and artisanal shops, wholesale mercantile businesses linked to wharfs, and a few machine shops.[12] By the 1850s, Methodists, Congregationalists, Baptists, Catholics, and Anglicans had organized churches on both sides of the river. Presbyterians and, until 1870, Universalists worshiped in St Stephen; Unitarians[13] in Calais, Maine. Methodism along the St Croix River had a common origin and shared many forms of Methodist piety and organization. However, this paper focuses on Methodists on the New Brunswick side, who were affiliated with Wesleyan Methodism, and it will use "Methodist" as shorthand for "Wesleyan Methodist." Two Methodist "circuits" of preaching services and class meetings connected the villages and the parish's back settlements, which contained both subsistence and commercial farming.

By 1861 Methodists constituted the single largest denominational group in the parish of St Stephen, at roughly one-quarter the reported population of 5,160. As table 1 shows, Methodists would increase their share of the population to 30 per cent by 1881, despite out-migration. After the Methodists, the next largest groups were Catholics and Anglicans, each a little over one-fifth of the population in 1861, followed by Presbyterians and Baptists. Although Baptists were the largest evangelical group in the province, in St Stephen they had effectively been pre-empted by Methodism's early success. Until 1870 Baptists in the parish of St Stephen attended either a "Regular Baptist" church in the smallest village, a farming and shipbuilding community at the Ledge, or Baptist churches in the Maine villages. All these churches were affiliated with the New Brunswick and Maine Calvinist Baptist denominations, whose official theologies denied the role of free will in an individual's salvation and whose piety involved closed communion – in other words, offered only to their own members. Non-Calvinist open-communion Baptists used both Maine and New Brunswick denominational titles to identify themselves as "Free Will" or "Free Christian" Baptists, and they organized a small church in Calais in the late 1860s. Only a minority of local Congregationalists lived on the St Stephen side of the river, along with a smaller number of Universalists. By 1871 the parish also included a few Adventists, part of the post–Civil War resurgence of millenarianism in New England.[14]

The 1861 census was the first to record nominal religious adherence in New Brunswick. In both 1861 and 1871[15] enumerators were required to visit each house and personally record the inhabitants' own answers to questions. However, in contrast with the more obviously culturally constructed enumeration of economic information, the few references to religion in enumerators' correspondence concern the failure of some enumerators or respondents to distinguish branches of the same

Table 1
Nominal religious adherence, St Stephen, 1861–1881

Religion	1861		1871		1881	
Methodists	1,319	26%	1,813	28%	1,766	30%
Catholics	1,166	23%	1,536	24%	1,235	21%
Anglicans	1,122	22%	1,196	18%	1,116	19%
Presbyterians	708	14%	902	14%	759	13%
Baptists Free	390	7%	376	6%	458	8%
Free Christian/Will Baptists			120	2%	10	<1%
Congregationalists	259	5%	313	5%	410	7%
Universalists	181	3%	175	3%	80	1%
Adventists	0	0	44	<1%	39	<1%
Other	15	<1%	40	<1%	26	<1%
Total Population	5,160		6,515		5,899	

Sources: *Census of the Province of New Brunswick* (Saint John: George W. Day, 1861); *Census of Canada*, 1871 (Ottawa: I.B. Taylor, 1873); 1881 (Ottawa: MacLean, Roger & Co., 1882).

denominational tradition.[16] This problem in fact occurred with regard to divisions within Presbyterians and Baptists in St Stephen in 1861, but since only one Presbyterian church – in St Stephen – served both sides of the river, the tables subsume various kinds of Presbyterians in both census years. Calvinist and non-Calvinist Baptists were distinguished in 1871; in that year only one wholly Baptist family suggested doctrinal differences: the husband was listed as a "Baptist," but the wife as a "Free Will Baptist." Although St Stephen's enumerators were active laymen in their own congregations,[17] this fact did not hinder them from recognizing the parish's overall denominational pluralism.

While one can assume that parents spoke for young children, it is more difficult to determine to what extent enumerators relied on household heads or parents speaking for other members of their families. For example, Universalist Mary Todd appears to have reported her oldest son as a Universalist living at home in Milltown. This same son was also enumerated as an Anglican boarding with a Catholic family in the village of St Stephen, where he worked and where there was no Universalist church. Theologically he may have been both.

The denominational variety reported within families suggests that, where possible, enumerators tried to ascertain these distinctions. Of

701 Protestant or partly Protestant families (two or more related individuals in the same household) in the 1861 census for St Stephen, one-tenth recorded different adherences. A similar analysis of relations in the 1871 census showed that at least 18 per cent of 919 Protestant families reported different adherences. Though larger than that in 1861, the 1871 proportion underestimates denominational differences within families: as the 1871 census had no question on relationships, the analysis is only of relations of the same last name.

The clearest representation of continuity and change in denominational identities can be found by analyzing individuals listed in census returns in both 1861 and 1871 who were old enough by the latter year to have likely reported their own adherence. Of 1,455 Protestant or Protestant-Catholic adults linked to both census returns, 24 per cent reported different adherences.[18] As tables 2 and 3 show, several denominations benefited from both tribalism and proselytism. Methodism retained the highest proportion of adherents and gained a significant proportion of new adherents: 84 per cent of Methodists in 1861 found in the 1871 census were still Methodists; 22 per cent of Methodists in 1871 found in the 1861 census had been listed in 1861 with another adherence. The next largest Protestant group, the Anglicans, gained roughly the same proportion of adherents as they lost.

Ethnic solidarity accounted for the Presbyterians' high rate of retention, but it did not prevent losses to other denominations. Despite several attempts, beginning in the 1830s, the Presbyterians were late in formally organizing a permanent local church, and not surprisingly, many affiliated with other denominations. In 1836 the first and short-lived Presbyterian minister stationed in St Stephen described local Methodists as "a sly sneaking sect" who "compass land and sea to make proselytes."[19] Family histories suggest that some new Presbyterians in 1871 were, in fact, finally returning to the fold; it is impossible to tell how much this phenomenon may have been true for other groups. The Baptists were the most denominationally fluid, reflecting their local conflicts and reorganization in the 1860s.[20] Overall, most changes in adherence were within logical "limits" of theology or style of worship: for example, within a Calvinist range. Offering both revivalism and monthly open communion, Methodism was most likely to "make converts indiscriminately."[21]

Not surprisingly, Protestant-Catholic affiliations within the same family or for the same individual were rare. Only 5 per cent of Catholic or partly Catholic families in 1861 included family members who were Protestant, and this proportion appears to be representative of the Catholic pattern as a whole.[22] Of Catholic spouses listed in the

Table 2
Individuals age >14 in 1861 or age >24 in 1871, linked to both the 1861 and the 1871 St Stephen, New Brunswick, parish census returns

		Denomination in 1871 as a percentage of 1861 totals								
Denomination in 1861	Totals in 1861	Meth.	Angl.	Presb.	Cong.	Regular Baptists	Free Will/ Christian Baptists	Univ.	Cath.	Other
Methodists	540	84	7	3	<1	2	<1	1	1	2
Anglicans	360	13	78	4	<1	1		<1	2	1
Presbyterians	233	9	9	75	3	3		<1	<1	
Congregationalists	110	9	3	4	75	5		4		
Baptists	131	32	6	2	7	43	8	2		1
Universalists	65	5	3	5	3	1		77	1	5
Catholics	361	<1	1		<1			<1	97	<1
Other	7	14	29			29		14		14
Total linked 1807										

Table 3
Individuals age >14 in 1861 or age >24 in 1871, linked to both the 1861 and the 1871 St Stephen, New Brunswick, parish census returns

Denomination in 1871	Totals in 1871	Denomination in 1861 as a percentage of 1871 totals							
		Meth.	Angl.	Presb.	Cong.	Baptists	Univ.	Cath.	Other
Methodists	579	78	8	4	2	7	<1	<1	<1
Anglicans	355	10	79	6	1	2	<1	1	<1
Presbyterians	211	7	6	83	2	1	1		
Congregationalists	108	4	2	6	77	8	2	1	
Regular Baptists	88	14	6	7	7	64	1		1
Free Will/Christian Baptists	13	23				77			
Universalists	66	8	3	1.5	6	3	75	1.5	1.5
Catholics	363	<1	2				<1	97	
Other	24	50	21			8	13	4	4

St Stephen census in 1861 or 1871 with marriages found in Charlotte County records between 1845 and 1870, only 5 per cent had been married by a Protestant clergyman, compared with only 1 per cent of Protestant spouses who had been married by a Catholic clergyman. Of Catholics linked to both the 1861 and 1871 census returns, only 6 per cent reported different adherences. Few sources describe these families,[23] and they represent two extremes. One of the earliest Catholic settlers in St Stephen, Robert Bunten, was married to a Methodist church member who hosted a class meeting in their home. Bunten bequeathed most of his estate to his "beloved wife Sarah," also his executrix, but left roughly one-tenth of his personal property to the local Catholic church.[24] In another family, a Catholic groom and a Baptist bride had to elope and were "disowned" by the bride's Baptist family.[25]

Individual changes in reported adherence are a better measure of proselytism than tribalism: for older adults, the two census years were simply snapshots of two moments in their overall life course, and the earlier adherence may not have been that of their parents or their childhood. In the absence of literary sources for most families, it is almost impossible to determine why people changed denominations. Some may have simply chosen to attend the nearest church. Others may have wished to identify themselves with a more socially prestigious denomination. The Milltown Congregational church had formed as a result of Methodist schism in 1844, and thirty years later a Methodist minister claimed that newcomers to Milltown became Congregationalists because the latter had "social position, wealth and show."[26] While some changes in denomination probably represented the appeal of the new, others may have represented dissatisfaction with the old. The flow of Anglicans to and from other denominations probably reflected tensions within the Church of England in New Brunswick (and elsewhere) between evangelicals and Tractarians (in the modern sense, the "high church" wing of the denomination). These tensions led to a schism in Christ Church, St Stephen, in 1870. Some changes were perhaps responses to personal crises: one can speculate that the suicide-murder of two siblings[27] may have led an Anglican mother and her son to Universalism, the denomination whose theology included the ultimate redemption of all humanity.

As this particular family illustrates, proselytism itself could also be a familial process. Many individuals reporting different adherences in the 1861 and 1871 censuses represented changes in the adherence of entire families, while other individuals appear to have changed to the adherence of the families with whom they resided by the 1871 census. Expanding the group shown in tables 2 and 3 to include children identifies changes in the reported denominational adherences of families. Of 576 Protestants of any age living in families in 1861 who were also listed in 1871, but with a different adherence from that recorded in 1861, 64 per cent appear to have made the same change along with two or more members of their 1861 family, and another 14 per cent along with one member of their 1861 family. Of the remainder and those who were not living in families in 1861, at least one-quarter married between 1861 and 1871 and may have changed to the new spouse's denomination. A few denominational mavericks within their 1861 families appear to have conformed to the family's overall denominational adherence in 1871, or at least to have been reported by their family as having done so.

The persistence of proselytism and denominational pluralism reflected two broader tendencies within nineteenth-century Protestantism, one cultural – latitudinarianism – and the other social – the fluidity of local congregations. In contrast with the narrower and more exclusive theological understanding of the "church" within the early high-church tradition and later within Tractarianism, the ecclesiology of much of eighteenth- and nineteenth-century Anglicanism was latitudinarian.[28] A retrospective of Methodism in the Atlantic colonies noted that early Methodists had retained "Episcopal predilections," and that, in turn, many Anglicans had rented pews in Methodist chapels.[29] Given Methodism's origins as a movement within the Church of England, it is not surprising that Methodist writers expressed an ambiguous ecclesiology, sometimes referring to "church" in the sectarian sense as the body of church members, sometimes to the congregation of hearers, and sometimes to the church universal.[30] Evangelical writers exhorted their readers to family prayer and family conversion, but this language was not denominational. Obituaries in particular represented their subjects as urging the conversion or continued piety of their surviving relations.[31] Yet as one minister observed, because Methodism "frowns upon bigotry, exclusiveness, and isolation," parents were "less anxious than they ought to be that their children should cherish a discriminating but deep and abiding attachment to Methodism and early and permanently identify themselves with it."[32]

Similarly, some Universalists complained that many who doctrinally were Universalists were content to remain members or adherents of "orthodox" churches.[33] This practice may also explain why Methodist ministers perceived Universalism as a more dangerous threat in New Brunswick[34] than its rare presence in the form of organized churches would suggest.[35] Apart from formal doctrine, mid-nineteenth-century Universalism outside cities such as Boston was still evangelical in much of its cultural style. In fact, a former Baptist minister in Calais who became editor of the New Brunswick Regular Baptist newspaper claimed that the Universalism espoused by a member of the legislative assembly from Charlotte County "so closely resembled the anti-universalism of Methodists, Baptists, churchmen and others, that it would be difficult to distinguish the one from the other."[36] One Universalist Sabbath school exhibition in Milltown included recitations such as "The Happy Christian Family," which reportedly confused some of the non-Universalists in attendance: "we heard a fellow remark, 'that were it not that he knew he was in a Universalist House, he should have thought he was in a Christian church.'" The children "'must have Christian parents, who must have set them Christian examples, but they had by some means got into the wrong house.'"[37]

Methodist clergy represented Universalism as a potentially divisive force within families, and not without some reason. Among the founders of the local Universalist Society were a group of former Methodists, including two sons of the senior Methodist class leader.[38] In the early 1850s another minister described local Universalism as a "serious" obstacle "because its influence is distributed through social and domestic channels among our own people."[39] A third Methodist minister wrote, "Scarcely a family of our Zion, but has some member directly or indirectly influenced" by Universalism. Yet some lay Protestants may not have perceived Universalism and Methodism as incompatible. The third minister cited above memorialized two men in the 1850s, intending to show "the weakness of Universalism to give support in the dying hour." But their reportedly fervent deathbed language and praise of Methodism as a source of conversion and consolation did not actually disavow the key doctrines of Universalism. In fact, one of the men, whose religious obituary appeared in the Methodist newspaper, was also memorialized in a local newspaper in clearly Universalist language.[40] Another minister also memorialized two local Universalists as devout evangelicals, but did not claim that they had recanted their Universalism: though Methodist converts "may not all live and die in connection with us, yet we will give thanks for their ultimate and eternal salvation."[41]

The latitudinarian tradition within nineteenth-century Protestantism was matched by the social fluidity of nineteenth-century congregations. Two bishops visiting St Stephen a decade apart remarked on this characteristic: the first wrote in 1836 that many had yet "to choose their religious profession"; the second noted "the multitude of conflicting sects" and "the difficulty of keeping steady congregations."[42] Even late in the nineteenth century, attending a variety of churches was a form of recreation and not necessarily a commitment to a particular denomination.[43] Churches usually offered more than one Sunday service, and evangelical churches offered weeknight prayer meetings. Finally, the high level of transiency within nineteenth-century communities also contributed to congregational fluidity.

For these reasons, organizational ascendancy could alternate between rival denominations in small communities. In 1832 forty men and women at the Ledge formed a Baptist Society, whose first minister was ordained at the home of a Methodist family. In 1837, membership peaked at 145, but the majority transferred in the following year to the Methodists, who had just built their own chapel. Moreover, the Methodists had the advantage of a nearby and externally subsidized minister.[44] One Methodist church member and trustee held pews in both the Methodist and the Baptist chapels; his wife was probably Baptist, since he bequeathed the Baptist pew to her.[45] At Upper Mills, New Brunswick, and its opposite, Baring, Maine, the Baptists were also initially strong, but they declined when the Methodists began holding more regular services in Upper Mills. However, even as their numbers declined, enrolment increased in the Baptist Sunday school, at that time the only one available locally.[46]

Children appear to have been the point of both conflict and cooperation for lay Methodists and Baptists. In 1871 one Methodist minister implied that lay Baptists at the Ledge had gone "from house to house whispering in the ears of our children that they have not been baptized." However, a local editorial "endorsed by the leading christian [sic] men on this river" claimed that "clergy" were chiefly responsible for denominational conflicts. The writer later denied that Methodists and Baptists "at the Ledge would not speak to each other," citing a joint Sunday school concert.[47] At Upper Mills and Baring the local Sunday school appears to have alternated between Baptist and Methodist sponsorship, at one point converging into the "Sons of Temperance Union Sabbath School."[48]

Another response to latitudinarianism was the denominational pluralism exemplified by the chapel built at the rural settlement of Old Ridge in 1851. Of thirty-five pew-holding families in the Old Ridge chapel during the 1850s and 1860s, only two could not be assigned a denominational affiliation based on the 1861 census and records of church membership or lay leadership. Five families contained individuals with different affiliations or individuals who had changed affiliations by 1861. Twelve families appear to have been entirely Anglican, and sixteen families entirely Methodist. Of the twelve male trustees or financial officers at Old Ridge in 1851, only half were clearly identifiably Methodist members or adherents. Legally Methodist, the chapel and its Sunday school would become known as the "Union" church.[49]

In the context of St Stephen's denominational pluralism and fluidity, some ministers attempted to clarify denominational distinctions. In response to requests, ministers preached on subjects such as "wherein do we differ and why from our brethren."[50] Though few in number, the Adventists stirred up considerable controversy in St Stephen, where they were almost entirely composed of converts from other denominations. At the end of a two-day debate by Methodist and Adventist ministers on the nature of immortality, the question was decided by a "vote of the crowd."[51] Ministers delineated denominational boundaries, but lay Protestants could choose their responses to them.

Thus far the discussion has focused on denominational identity as reported on census returns, rather than actual church involvement. No surviving records list the names of those who attended church regularly, but evangelical denominations kept lists of church members – the smaller group within their congregations of those who actually joined the church. Wesleyan Methodist records date from the 1840s; Congregationalist records are complete from the founding of the Calais church in 1825 and the Milltown church in 1846. The records of the Presbyterian church, which served both sides of the river, identify all new members from its organization in 1854 to 1862; records for the following years are erratic but complete again from 1872 on.[52]

As the most ethnically based Protestant group, Presbyterian church members not surprisingly best illustrate the model of tribalism. As late as 1871 some, including the leading elder of St Stephen's Free Church, called themselves adherents of the Church of Scotland, which had no local congregation, while others called themselves Reformed Presbyterian, the Scots-Irish descendants of the Covenanters. Of 123 Presbyterian church members with a known birthplace from census returns or death records, over two-thirds were British immigrants, mostly Irish. Of a smaller group of Presbyterian church members linked to the 1861 or 1871 census, only 8 per cent reported another denomination on either census.

In contrast, proselytism and denominational pluralism played a more significant role in local Methodism and Congregationalism. Compared to Presbyterians, Methodist and Congregationalist church members included a much higher proportion of sometime adherents of other denominations before, after, or during their membership. As the oldest organized Protestant denominations in the area, they were the only local options for formal church membership until the 1830s. Both denominations experienced recurring revivalism and continued to attract adherents from other denominations (and lose some to others) well into the 1870s. Of 652 Methodist church members linked to the 1861 or 1871 census, 30 per cent were listed at least once as adherents of another denomination; of 158 Congregationalist church members, 39 per cent were listed at least once as adherents of another denomination. In fact, one could argue that, since Congregational churches determined their own doctrine and polity and owned their own property, Congregationalism in St Stephen (or, indeed, anywhere) was never really a denomination. Although many Congregationalists were descended from nominally Congregationalist pre-Loyalists, so were other Protestants in the area. Moreover, the nine founders of the Calais church in 1825 included one Methodist and one Baptist, and half the founders of the Milltown church in 1846 were former Methodists.[53]

Some church members maintained more than one denominational affiliation at the same time. Of current church members in the 1861 census, 14 per cent of the Congregationalists and 12 per cent of the Methodists were listed as adherents of a denomination other than that of their membership. Lydia Hill's obituary conveys both the resistance to proselytism offered by some churches and the rival claims of old and new family denominational loyalties. A Baptist from Maine, she married a Methodist church member in Milltown in 1829. She wished "to obtain a release from the Baptist Church in order to join the Church to which her partner belonged, and to accomplish this, she undertook a journey of several miles, and presented her request for a dismission to the proper Church Court, believing, that as there was a Baptist Church in Milltown, she would most readily obtain her request." However, her home church learned that she actually intended to join the Methodists, and it "refused" her "application, and that not in the most gracious manner." Nevertheless, she joined a class meeting and remained a "consistent" Methodist member until her death in 1863.[54] Yet either her personal religious beliefs or the fact that she had not obtained a formal "dismission" from the church of her youth may explain why she reported herself as a Baptist in the 1861 census.

The application of the concept of tribalism to voluntarist church growth originated in studies of New England Puritanism and concerned the efforts of Congregational churches to bring the descendants of the founders into the church membership by either recruitment or redefining the basis of membership. Nineteenth-century evangelicals voiced similar concerns, and several studies have explored the place of the family in evangelical discourse.[55] However, the demography of evangelical church membership has shown both the force of tribalism in explaining membership growth and its limits as a cultural influence within evangelical families with regard to actual church membership.

As a simple reference to kinship, tribalism describes one dimension of the social composition of Congregationalist and Methodist church memberships. The following analysis uses kinship groups consisting of immediate family members residing together (parents, children, siblings, and spouses) and, for those not linked to the database, of individuals with the same last name who joined within a few years of each other. Roughly 70 per cent of Congregationalist and Methodist church members were related to one or more members of the same denomination, and given the flow between the two denominations, a number had family members in the other denomination. However, these patterns may not be particularly distinctive to churches; temperance groups or other voluntarist or fraternal associations may have had the same kinship patterns.

Historians have also noted that many evangelicals joined churches at the same time as other family members, and this was also true of local Congregationalists and Methodists.[56] Of all members of the two Congregational churches between 1825 and 1881, 4 per cent were identified as founders, 40 per cent transferred their membership from other evangelical churches, and 56 per cent were received as first-time church members. At least 35 per cent of the transfer members and 26 per cent of the first-time members joined with at least one other family member. Of new Methodist church members between 1850 and 1881 (members not present in 1849, the first complete year for both circuits), at least 39 per cent joined along with one or more members of their immediate families.[57]

An analysis of the limits to tribalism as a cultural influence within evangelical families with regard to actual church membership must consider both commonalities and differences in the nature of church membership within denominations. In all three denominations, church members were only a proportion of the larger congregation of regular or casual churchgoers. Methodist, Congregational, and Presbyterian churches all required from new members some expression of religious experience and their acceptance by the existing membership and lay leadership. All three denominations expected regular church attendance from new members. However, the nature of this religious experience and the terms of continued church membership varied.

Most Methodist and many Congregationalist church members joined during revivals. This distinction reflected both different cultural understandings of "revival" which influenced the use of the term by observers and the fact that Methodist church members consisted of those individuals who joined a class meeting. Thus Methodist members included both those who had been converted and those who were still seeking conversion; moreover, surviving conversion accounts portrayed both gradual and sudden conversion experiences.

Congregationalism in New England was so varied that it is difficult to generalize about whether Maine and New Brunswick Congregationalist church members considered themselves fully converted or not and how they might have portrayed that conversion experience. Studies of earlier Congregationalism have shown that many delayed church membership from religious scruples concerning the genuineness or finality of their conversions.[58] In contrast with this Calvinist understanding of conversion, Methodist theology and piety allowed for the possibility of falling from and returning to a converted state. The Calais Congregational church was both "Calvinist" and orthodox enough to inspire the formation of a Unitarian Society in 1831, as in other New England communities in the same years. However, subsequent Congregationalist creeds suggest the liberalization of official theologies. The 1846 creed of the Milltown Congregational church, founded in part by former Methodists, asserted that all who believed in God and repented of their sins could be saved; the revised 1855 creed of the Calais church asserted both "man's free agency" and God's knowledge from the beginning of time of who would be saved.[59]

The three denominations also differed in the terms of continued church membership. Continued Methodist church membership in these decades involved attendance at a weekly or monthly class meeting. This devotional subgroup was still at the centre of local Methodism, though some ministers waited up to two years after an individual had ceased to attend class before dropping them from the membership. Presbyterian church members consisted of those who had been admitted to communion at least once a year. With an understanding of church membership as a covenant between members and church that could only be mutually dissolved, Congregational churches even maintained a category of non-resident members.

These denominational differences concerning the nature of church membership not surprisingly shaped the differing rates of church membership among Congregationalists, Methodists, and Presbyterians listed in the 1861 census. Few evangelical church members joined before age fifteen,[60] and most of these did so in the 1870s, when a few ministers actively recruited younger members. For this reason, those over the age of fourteen were defined as the constituency for determining overall rates of church membership. With the longest run of extant records and the least demanding requirements for continued church membership, Congregationalists not surprisingly had the highest rate of overall church membership: 50 per cent of Congregationalist adherents over fourteen in 1861 were church members sometime between 1825 and 1881, and 40 per cent were current church members. A more extensive revision of the Milltown church roll in 1870 to those still resident in the community and attending the Milltown church (again, only part of the congregation as a whole) brought the figure for current members in 1871 down to 28 per cent of adherents over fourteen in 1871. Of Methodist adherents over fourteen in 1861, at least 41 per cent[61] were church members sometime between 1840 and 1881, but only 25 per cent were current church members. The proportions of Congregationalist and Methodist adherents in 1861 who were ever members in the surrounding decades – 49 and 41 per cent respectively – are close to the overall proportion (44 per cent) of evangelical adherents in the same age group in Brantford, Canada West, in 1852 who were ever members in a similar length of time.[62]

The low proportion of church members among Presbyterians linked to census returns can be explained both by the nature of surviving sources and by the denomination's religious culture. The Presbyterian church was not organized until 1854, and though the records are complete for the years before the 1861 census and the years after the 1871 census, these are obviously much narrower windows of time within which adherents could have joined, when compared to the decades of Methodist and Congregationalist records. Quite apart from the counter-factual question of how many Presbyterian adherents might have been sometime church members if their church had organized earlier, the missing records mean that the overall rate of church membership among adherents listed in census returns excludes those who might have joined in the 1860s but had ceased to be church members by 1872. Fortunately, rates of current church membership among adherents listed in census returns can be calculated with greater confidence. Of Presbyterian adherents over the age of fourteen in 1861, only 12 per cent were members from the church's organization in 1854 to 1861. Only 6 per cent of Presbyterian adherents in the 1871 census could be clearly linked to a complete 1872 membership list, and this even lower rate may reflect the possibility that adherents listed in the April 1871 census had left by the time of the May 1872 list. However, these low rates of membership can also be explained by the denomination's religious culture. Like Congregationalists, Presbyterians sometimes delayed church membership from scruples concerning the genuineness or finality of their conversions.[63] In other words, tribalism defined solely by ethnicity and the virtual absence of proselytism can describe the Presbyterian church membership, but not tribalism defined as the recruitment of adherents and families to church membership.

By modern standards, church membership rates among adherents of these three denominations in St Stephen may seem high, particularly among Congregationalists, but contemporary clergy tended to see the glass as half-empty. The transience of nineteenth-century communities meant that many adherents listed in a census did not stay long enough to join a church, and indeed, their awareness of this transience may have deterred many from joining. This pattern, in turn, limited the likelihood of all family members uniting in a single church. Those who did join were also transient: of all Methodist members between 1840 and 1881, only 27 per cent were still members in 1881, and another 15 per cent disappeared from the records without a clear explanation. Of the remainder, 40 per cent were listed as having left St Stephen (some of these moved to Calais, where they may have joined other churches). Contemporary or later comments on the records of nearly all Congregationalist members between 1825 and 1881 show that at least 35 per cent had left Calais and St Stephen.

Concern for family prayer and religious education was a key part of early Congregationalism and Methodism. However, nineteenth-century denominational publications and the Sunday school movement showed an increased interest in the conversion and church membership of the young. This was a major concern of evangelical Maternal Associations, founded in 1815 at Portland, Maine, by the wife of a Congregationalist minister and spread throughout the northeast.[64] A few Congregationalist and Methodist women formed one at Milltown in 1836. Members read from evangelical publications, sang hymns, and prayed "that God would glorify himself – in the early conversion of the children of the Association, that they may become eminently useful in the church of God."[65]

Historians have argued that these concerns did not reflect the transformation of church membership into a rite of passage. Instead, such concerns were a response to the resistance of many ministers and laity to the idea that children could or should convert and join churches, a resistance that was only overcome late in the century.[66] For example, only three ministers' reports from Methodist-sponsored Sabbath schools in St Stephen between 1826 and 1855 noted the "conversion" of children.[67] The argument that public discourse did not reflect behaviour and indeed took decades to shape it is supported by the findings of demographic studies of church membership. Studies of New England Congregationalism have shown that, while most church members were adult and married, ages at first church membership varied too much to be linked to any one stage of the life course.[68] These same two patterns – a predominantly adult church membership and varied ages at first church membership – also characterized Congregationalist and Methodist church memberships in St Stephen.

This fact is evident, first, from the fact that most Congregationalist, Methodist, and Presbyterian church members were already married when they joined local churches. Of 1,767 church members with a known marital status at the time they joined locally, roughly two-thirds were married or widowed. Identifying the ages at which individuals joined the church requires distinguishing those who were probably joining an evangelical church for the first-time from those who could have been members elsewhere. Congregationalist records clearly identified first-time evangelical church members as constituting a little over half its membership between 1825 and 1881, and roughly three-quarters of this group could be linked to census returns or death records. Methodist church members were more numerous, but their records are incomplete before 1849 and lack the same detail on new members. Of 749 new Methodist church members from 1850 to 1881, the ages and previous residency in St Stephen of at least three-fifths could be determined. Comparing this group of Methodists, who could have joined a class meeting at an earlier age, with Congregationalists identified as first-time church members shows a wide range of ages at first membership. However, a majority of the Methodists and almost half the Congregationalists joined as adults, not youths: 30 per cent of both the Congregationalists and the Methodists were aged twenty-five to thirty-nine when they joined; 19 per cent of the Methodists were aged forty to fifty-four when they joined, compared with 11 per cent of the Congregationalists; 9 per cent of Methodists and 6 per cent of the Congregationalists were aged fifty-five or over.

As this range in ages suggests, Methodist and Congregationalist church membership was not a pervasive and socially timed rite of passage. Nevertheless, as in Brantford in roughly the same period, the Congregationalists showed greater and earlier recruitment of youth to church membership. While only roughly 6 per cent of both groups of new members were under the age of fifteen when they joined, 47 per cent of the Congregationalists were aged fifteen to twenty-four, compared with 36 per cent of the Methodists. Not until the mid-1870s did Methodists in St Stephen begin organizing class meetings that were not entirely adult, and these were short-lived: a class meeting for girls led by young women and a class meeting for young men led by the clergyman were organized in the newly incorporated town of St Stephen. These and other signs of increased institutional concern with recruiting the young reflected the international Sunday school movement and the optimism and institutional expansion of denominations in the postbellum and post-Confederation decades. In St Stephen, however, the decline of shipbuilding and the depression in the lumber industry after 1874 accelerated the out-migration of the young, limiting the numbers who appeared and stayed in membership records.

Because of the time span of surviving records, rates of church membership among differing age groups in the 1861 census best show the differences between all three denominations. As table 4 indicates, rates of church membership were highest among those aged forty or over. Among those under twenty-five, Congregationalist adherents had the highest rate of church membership and Presbyterians the lowest. As noted earlier, for many Presbyterians, the sin in taking communion if one had not been genuinely converted was so great that it deterred many from seeking church membership until late in life.[69]

Not only were rates of church membership highest among older evangelical adherents, but among older members the proportions of men and women were much closer than among youthful members, who were predominantly female.[70] This pattern points to the major counterforce to the influence of tribalism on families: the cultural construction of gender identity and the social situation of men and women. The greater involvement of women in churches has been documented for both Protestants and Catholics in a number of contexts.[71] In societies in which women are more socialized to caring and cooperation and men are more socialized to accumulation and aggression, however disguised as economic ambition or service to the state, a religious culture that values the former and is deeply ambivalent and often critical of the latter will be more attractive to women than to men. Since the Reformation, women have formed the majority of voluntarist church members in churches that often offered women opportunities for expression, association, or leadership not available elsewhere. Women were excluded from formal politics, and in communities such as St Stephen they had few equivalents to quasi-religious fraternal associations such as the Masons or the Orange Order until later in the century.[72]

For Methodists, the nature of men's work was often a significant deterrent to church membership. Men who worked in lumbering or seafaring away from the parish for many months of the year could not regularly attend class meetings, on which membership depended.

Table 4
Church membership as a percentage of age groups in the 1861 census

	Ages 15–24	Ages 25–39	Ages 40–54	Ages 55+
CONGREGATIONALISTS (N=163)				
Current members 1860–61	20	36	61	91
Past members 1825–59	1	4	2	
Future members 1862–81	13	4	7	
Never members 1825–81	66	56	30	9
METHODISTS (N=686)				
Current members 1860–61	13	24	36	42
Past members 1840/49–59	<1	2	8	11
Future members 1862–81	13	14	14	3
Never members 1825–81	74	60	42	44
PRESBYTERIANS (N=412)				
Members 1854–61	2	15	21	21
Future members 1862–81	1	6	7	5
Not in surviving records 1862+	97	79	72	74

While some local men were self-employed or still worked in pre-industrial time discipline, many – particularly in the sawmills – worked up to fifteen-hour days six days a week. This employment conflicted with the times of prayer meetings and most class meetings, and undoubtedly left men of any denomination in need of simple rest on Sunday. For these reasons, evangelical clergy supported the periodic early-closing movements in the communities along the St Croix River from the 1840s throughout the century. In general, the poor were somewhat underrepresented among evangelical church members,[73] but in the poorest villages and in the back settlements, Methodist ministers and lay leaders opted out of the denomination's traditional methods of church finance, reducing the cultural pressure on members to contribute.[74]

In St Stephen roughly two-thirds of evangelical church members were women: 69 per cent of the Congregationalists, 68 per cent of the Methodists, and 63 per cent of the Presbyterians. Women joined these churches at all stages of the life course, whereas most men did so while married. Presbyterians appear to have had the highest proportion of single women – 46 per cent of the women whose marital status at the time of joining is known, compared with 6 per cent of the men

– but this pattern may reflect the fact that the Presbyterian records tended to use "Miss" more often. Of the comparable group of Congregationalists, 42 per cent of the women members were single, compared with 22 per cent of the men; similarly, 39 per cent of Methodist women members were single, compared with 21 per cent of the men.

Most single men were also young, and in explaining why "the duty of joining the fellowship of the church is delayed and neglected to a greater extent on the part of our young men than among the young of the other sex," evangelical writers identified several factors. Young men were more geographically mobile, were more preoccupied with establishing themselves in an occupation, and were represented as more exposed to worldly temptations arising from both work and leisure.[75] Writers also represented some young men as parading in their communities on Sundays as overt non-churchgoers or as harassing those who were churchgoers, though accounts from smaller communities portrayed this behaviour more as nuisance courtship.[76] Local observers even claimed that many such young men in St Stephen and Calais were from churchgoing families.[77] That this was a wide spread perception or at least construction of a social problem[78] is indicated by a religious obituary written elsewhere but copied to local papers. The oldest son of a Congregationalist family in Calais, Henry Weymouth had moved to South Carolina in the disappointed hope for a cure from consumption: "On the first Sabbath of his stay, it was noticed that instead of being seen about the tavern door, or the corner of the street, the place and company which attracted him was early Sabbath School and the Church."[79] Weymouth's mother had joined the church before she was married, and his two sisters joined in the early 1850s while in their teens. His own increased church involvement was undoubtedly a response to the prospect of death, but he had not joined the church while he lived in Calais, perhaps following the example of his father, who did not join until 1864.

Analysis of the married couples in the 1861 census who headed families containing Methodist or Congregationalist church members shows that Weymouth's father was not untypical. In 35 per cent of 191 families containing Methodist church members and 45 per cent of 56 families containing Congregationalist church members, the wife joined the church in the surrounding decades, but not the husband. Another 19 per cent of the Methodist couples and 16 per cent of the Congregationalist couples joined the church in the same year. In 15 per cent of the Methodist and 13 per cent of the Congregationalist families, the wife joined, followed by the husband, but in only 6 per cent of the former and 11 per cent of the latter was the reverse true. In roughly 6 per cent of both groups, the wife did not join the church. In the remainder, neither the household head nor his wife joined: the church members were their children, siblings, or parents.

Family played a role in the timing of male church membership, both in the reasons for delaying membership and in the eventual decision to join. The memoirs of Mark Trafton, a Methodist Episcopal minister stationed in Calais, suggest that a young man's definition of male identity in contrast with female identity in his family meant resisting female religiosity. After portraying his father as a depressed alcoholic, Trafton wrote that his mother joined a Maine Methodist church first, followed by his sisters: "this created in me most violent feelings of opposition, and I made all possible efforts to shake off her convictions." Only later did the friendship of an older male Methodist lead Trafton into the church.[80] However, other young men believed they needed to be in a "settled" and married state before taking "the solemn step" of church membership.[81] Religious obituaries often stressed the role of a wife or mother in leading men to conversion. One man's tormented and prolonged conversion experience lasted several weeks; it was finally resolved one night when he and his wife rose in the middle of the night to pray together until dawn. The obituary of a Presbyterian doctor written for the Methodist paper began with his "pious mother" in Scotland and stated that, even after he had emigrated (and married an Anglican), "that good mother did not forget her son, for many were her religious epistles to him, and more the prayers presented for him." Though he had not joined the Presbyterian church at its organization in 1854, he had felt fully converted before his death in 1856: " 'My mother's prayers,' he exclaimed, 'are answered!' "[82]

In a family descended from the parish's pre-Loyalist migrants from Maine, membership in a Methodist class meeting both united and divided married couples. Baptized in 1840 at the age of fifty-one, Levina Libby was listed among the members of a village Methodist class meeting that met at the home of her brother-in-law and his wife, both members. Yet next to Levina Libby's name was a note that she "was not allowed by her husband to meet," and her name does not appear again in the membership records. In contrast, two of the class leaders in the back settlements were married women whose husbands attended their meetings.[83]

The experiences of parents and children in the same class meeting could also vary. Thomas Hannah was the leader of a class meeting that his daughters attended, and he was concerned that one daughter in particular would become discouraged when he became ill: " 'I fear my poor child will lose her good impressions in the absence of class meetings while I am sick." However, some Methodist writers were careful not to idealize families and the class meeting, and used the gulf between reality and the ideal as a point of exhortation. A minister's daughter was roughly seventeen years old when she joined her mother's class meeting, and her obituary, written by another minister, described her experience critically: "She was somewhat disappointed. There was not that cordiality and fervour which she anticipated. She left almost unnoticed. It seemed as though her first entrance into that social means of grace, which had cost her so much feeling, and which formed such an event in her own life, were to others a matter of indifference. 'It was hard' she said a few days before her death, 'that no one took me by the hand.'" The writer argued that Methodism would be more successful in recruiting "the children of the church" if churches were "more careful in cherishing the first unfoldings of religious life, throwing around these youthful ones the bonds of tenderest Christian sympathy." The obituary also implied that the woman's parents were later forced to drop her from the membership for some unspecified reason, but that the family had survived this "test" of "love and loyalty."

Robert Hitchings and his middle-aged daughter attended the same Methodist class meeting and died within hours of each other. In the words of the minister who eulogized them, "Truly in life they were as one, and in earth they were not divided ... I pray all his children may be converted to God, and at last meet their dear father and beloved sister [in heaven]."[84] But the Hitchings family as a whole had weathered a serious conflict a decade earlier, when father and son had divided in the Milltown schism. This schism provides the most extreme example of family conflict connected with denominational identities, that which occurred in the family of the senior class leader, Abner Hill Sr, in the Milltown Methodist church. Hill married three times, and the full narrative of this intricate family and church conflict is documented elsewhere.[85] The narrative's dramatic highlights included an elopement, the schism of the Milltown Methodists and the formation of a rival Congregational church, and the destruction by arson of the Methodist chapel, reputedly instigated by Abner Hill's son-in-law and perhaps also the son of Robert Hitchings. Even after Hill's death, his Congregationalist and Universalist children unsuccessfully challenged his will, claiming "imbecility" dating from the Methodism schism and accusing Hill's widow and other unnamed Methodists of having coerced him into making it.

A much milder suggestion of the conflict that could be created by denominational differences appears in a letter reportedly from

"Maryanne" sent to the *Presbyterian Witness* and reprinted in the *Wesleyan*. Maryanne was a Presbyterian married to a Baptist: "Before marriage we talked the matter over and couldn't agree ... like hundreds of others, we 'agreed to disagree' ... Such agreements never bring that oneness of mind and heart that married Christians are entitled to ... We can't talk of religion without ... controversy, so religion is almost a forbidden subject." Maryanne saw her troubles as partly due to her husband's unwillingness to attend her church on occasion and his church's practice of closed communion, which excluded her (though it was also Presbyterian practice). While acknowledging the attitude of some that "it is the woman's place to yield as far as possible all points of difference and be a member of the same church as her husband," she declined to deny the validity of her baptism.[86]

These examples of how families might have experienced patterns of shared or differing denominational identities suggest that these identities were not the idealized glue that bound families together in evangelical discourse. However, assuming that most families perceived differences of denominational identity or church involvement in terms of conflict is also problematic. The experience of most families is undocumented, but one can speculate that the extremes of idealized family religion or serious conflict were exceptional. As Maryanne's account of a less-than-cooperative husband suggests, families had some choice over whether denominational differences became a major point of conflict.

Published accounts of two evangelical family reunions represented the ideal of the religiously united family, untroubled by actual denominational differences. Both exemplify what one study of twentieth-century evangelical reunions has called the foundation narratives of such reunions: rituals of reading certain biblical passages and recounting a family history of pilgrimage into wilderness and passage through various adversities.[87] Beginning in 1839, a family of Scottish immigrants had held an annual reunion at which they "read the Scriptures, sang and prayed together": "Great peace and unanimity prevailed, and all felt "how good and how pleasant it was for brethren to dwell together in unity.' The chapter read on that occasion and at every anniversary since was the 24th of Joshua, in which are recounted the assembling of the tribes at Shechem and God's gracious dealings with them. They adopted the motto 'As for me and my house we will serve the Lord.' " By the time this account was written in the 1870s, the families of those listed as attending this reunion were Presbyterian, Baptist, and Methodist.[88] On the occasion of the golden wedding anniversary of William and Esther Boardman, their family of businessmen and professionals not only held a reunion but published a four-page newspaper.[89]

In addition to lists of marriages and deaths and an account of the re-union itself, the newspaper included religious obituaries or poetry on the various members of the family who had died in the previous fifty years, particularly those who had died while children. The unknown writers also included prose reflections or poems on family religion and on Civil War themes. Some family members had left the St Croix region, but most resided in St Stephen or Calais, and the children, grand-children, and their spouses represented at least four denominations: Congregationalists, Baptists, Universalists, and Methodists. The narra-tive of the original move from Massachusetts to the St Croix was pre-sented in the style of the first chapter of 1st Chronicles in the King James Version, and an account of "the tribes that came up" for the re-union in 1865 was given as the last chapter. The Boardman descendants had indeed reconciled tribalism and proselytism.

In sum, most Protestants in mid-nineteenth-century St Stephen did form their denominational identities and church involvement within a familial setting, but with varying dynamics. Tribalism describes how the majority of men and women in St Stephen formed their de-nominational identities as reported on census returns, and even those who changed denominational identities often did so as part of a fa-milial process. However, tribalism only partly describes patterns of church membership within evangelical families. Less than half of evangelical adherents formally joined local churches as members, and while women joined at all stages of the life course, most men joined while married.

The persistence of proselytism and denominational fluidity among Protestants in St Stephen raises a number of questions concerning the significance of denominationalism in nineteenth-century Canada. To begin with, only similar studies can determine whether the commu-nity itself was typical or atypical. In a sense, these demographic pat-terns also suggest a paradox. On the one hand, the fluidity of a sizable minority of Protestants, particularly evangelicals, suggests that the significance of denominational identities among lay Protestants may be overstated. Nevertheless, these identities must have signified something for so many individuals and families to have troubled to change them. Local Methodism and Congregationalism fit one writer's description of Methodism in the Maritimes as "eclectic; hav-ing gathered largely from other denominations,"[90] and the broader in-fluence of proselytism on the history of denominationalism needs to be explored further. Voluntary societies and the early Sunday school movement are the most obvious nineteenth-century forerunners of the modern ecumenical movement. Yet the fluid denominational identities of many lay Protestants were also significant in sustaining interdenominational cooperation. Those families who were able to live with denominational differences without serious conflict may also have laid the foundations for this cooperation.[91] And in the case of the rural church at Old Ridge, lay Anglicans and Presbyterians along with Methodists had made the decision for church union decades before 1925.

NOTE

The database analyzed in this essay includes the complete manuscript census returns for St Stephen, New Brunswick, 1851–71; St Stephen parish assessments, 1860–62; and the following church records, all on microfilm at the Provincial Archives of New Brunswick, Frederiction: pew, baptismal, marriage, membership, and Quarterly Official Board records for the St Stephen and Milltown Methodist circuits; vestry minutes, Christ Church, St Stephen; records of the Congregational Church, Milltown, New Brunswick, and of the Presbyterian Church, St Stephen. Some Methodist deeds and early pew records are located in the Ganong Collection at the New Brunswick Museum, Saint John. A copy of the membership records of the Congregational Church, Calais, Maine, is at the Maine State Historical Society, Portland; see also *Historical Sketch of the First Congregational Church, Calais, Maine, with Confession of Faith, Covenant, Rules and Catalogue of members to May, 1877* (Boston: Thomas Todd, 1877). Calais and St Stephen members of the Maine Universalist Mission, Education, and Tract Societies are listed in *Proceedings of the Maine Convention of Universalists* (Augusta, 1851), on microfilm at the Harvard Divinity School.

St Stephen rural cemetery records; the marriage register kept by George Stillman Hill; Charlotte County marriage records, 1835–44; Charlotte County probate records, 1835–61; and vital statistics from newspapers also aided record linkage. I am also indebted to Gail Campbell for access to her data for other Charlotte County parishes, 1851–71, and the Charlotte County marriage records, 1845–71. Marriage records kept by the town of Calais and the Calais census returns for 1850–60 are on microfilm at the Maine State Archives, Augusta. Directories and family histories were also used and are listed in Lane, "Methodism and Economic Life" (see note 6 below). Correspondence to the Wesleyan Missionary Society Committee is available on microfilm at the Provincial Archives of New Brunswick and at many other institutions in Canada.

1 See T.W. Acheson, "Methodism and the Problem of Methodist Identity in Nineteenth-Century New Brunswick," in Charles H.H. Scobie and John Webster Grant, eds., *The Contribution of Methodism to Atlantic Canada* (Montreal and Kingston: McGill-Queen's University Press, 1992), 107–23.

2 "Episcopalian" was the common usage, but "Anglican," though anachronistic, is more familiar to modern readers and avoids confusion with adherents of the American Methodist Episcopal Church, sometimes called Episcopal Methodists.

3 *Calais Advertiser*, 13 September 1860; *St. Croix Courier*, 9 October 1873. The Thompson family profile is drawn from I.C. Knowlton, *Annals of Calais, Maine, and St. Stephen, New Brunswick* (1875; repr. St Stephen) and from the database described in the note on sources above.

4 John Webster Grant, *A Profusion of Spires: Religion in Nineteenth-Century Ontario* (Toronto: University of Toronto Press, 1988), 52–3, 165, 222, 225; William Westfall, *Two Worlds: The Protestant Culture of Nineteenth-Century Ontario* (Kingston and Montreal: McGill-Queen's University Press, 1989), 46–7, 72.

5 For Methodism, see Neil Semple, "'The Nurture and Admonition of the Lord': Nineteenth Century Canadian Methodism's Response to "Childhood,'" *Histoire sociale/Social History* 14 (1981): 157–75.

6 See Hannah M. Lane, "Re-Numbering Souls: Lay Methodism and Church Growth in St. Stephen, New Brunswick, 1861–1881" (MA thesis, University of New Brunswick, 1993), and "Methodism and Economic Life in Mid-Nineteenth Century St. Stephen, New Brunswick" (PhD thesis, University of New Brunswik, in progress). I would like to acknowledge the financial support of the Social Sciences and Humanities Research Council of Canada for this research.

7 An earlier version of this essay was presented at the 10th Annual Church History Workshop (Anglican Diocese of Fredericton, University of New Brunswick, and Provincial Archives of New Brunswick), May 1997.

8 See Gerald R. Moran and Maris A. Vinovskis, "The Puritan Family and Religion," in *Religion, Family, and the Life Course: Explorations in the Social History of Early America* (Ann Arbor: University of Michigan Press, 1992), 14–15.

9 See Joy Parr, "Gender History and Historical Practice," *Canadian Historical Review*, 76 (1995): 361; and William Katerberg, "History as Identity: The Possibilities and Dilemmas of Subjectivity in North American Religious History," President's Address, Canadian Society of Church History, *Historical Papers 1997*, 136–40.

10 In St Stephen, marriage records and, for the Church of England and Wesleyan Methodism, also baptismal records documented the rites of passage sought by the general Protestant population, rather than a particular denominational group.

11 The terms "adherent" or "adherence" in this paper follow nineteenth-century usage and refer to what was recorded on census returns, which was not always a specific denomination. Published census totals for 1861 used the term "religious profession", and for 1871 and 1881 "religion."

However, the former is ambiguous, since profession had a more specific meaning for voluntarist churches, and the latter is misleading in the modern sense of the word.

12 Graeme Wynn, *Timber Colony* (Toronto: University of Toronto Press, 1981), 150, 162, 96. The key modern sources for nineteenth-century St Stephen are Harold A. Davis, *An International Community on the St. Croix (1604–1930)* (1950; repr., Orono: University of Maine, 1974), and T.W. Acheson, "Denominationalism in a Loyalist County: A Social History of Charlotte County, N.B." (MA thesis, University of New Brunswick, 1964).

13 By definition, Unitarians denied the Trinity – the divinity of Christ and the Holy Spirit. However, local Unitarianism originated more in a critique of Calvinism, and the "carefully worded" Unitarian covenant "ignores all the vexed questions of theology"; see Knowlton, *Annals of Calais*, 69–72.

14 Jonathan M. Butler, "Adventism and the American Experience," in Edwin S. Gaustad, ed., *The Rise of Adventism: Religion and Society in Mid-Nineteenth-Century America* (New York: Harper & Row, 1974), 174.

15 In 1871 enumerators received both oral instructions and a manual stressing that religion, ethnicity, and occupation were to be recorded as given by the respondent; see *Census of Canada, 1870–71*, vol. 1 (Ottawa: I.B. Taylor, 1873), xii, xxii; Department of Agriculture, *Manual containing 'The Census Act' and the Instructions to the Officers Employed in the Taking of the First Census of Canada (1871)* (Ottawa: Brown Chamberlin, 1871), 22–3.

16 See Alan A. Brookes, " 'Doing the Best I Can': The Taking of the 1861 New Brunswick Census," *Histoire sociale/Social History* 9 (May 1976): 70–91; Provincial Archives of New Brunswick (PANB), RS266-C no. 7, Provincial Secretary, Census Returns, Correspondence, 1861.

17 Two merchants – Anglican and Roman Catholic – in 1861, and these two, as well as a Presbyterian mason, in 1871. In addition to the database described above, see *St. Croix Courier*, 7 June 1867.

18 I have used age twenty-four as the upper boundary of youth, because by age twenty-five or over the majority of both men and women were married.

19 Cited in F.E. Archibald, "Contribution of the Scottish Church to New Brunswick Presbyterianism from Its Earliest Beginnings until the Time of the Disruption, and Afterwards, 1784–1852" (PhD thesis, University of Edinburgh, 1932), 82.

20 *St. Croix Courier*, 8 September 1866, 14 December 1866; Knowlton, *Annals of Calais*, 117–18.

21 John Webster Grant, *The Church in the Canadian Era* (Burlington, Ont.: Welch Publishing Co., 1988), 13.

22 Analysis of relations of the same last name as the household head in St Stephen in 1871 found 4 per cent of Catholic families with Protestant relations. A study of Irish Catholic husbands from a national sample of

the 1871 census found between 2 and 3 per cent with Protestant wives. See Madeline A. Richard, *Ethnic Groups and Marital Choices: Ethnic History and Marital Assimilation, Canada, 1871 and 1971* (Vancouver: University of British Columbia Press, 1991, calculated from tables 14 and 16; see also Nanciellen Davis, "French-British Marriages, Gender and Cultural Orientation: An Example from Nineteenth Century New Brunswick," *Canadian Ethnic Studies* 27 (1995): 125.

23 For the ecclesiastical barriers to Protestant-Catholic marriages, see Peter Ward, *Courtship, Love, and Marriage in Nineteenth-Century English Canada* (Montreal and Kingston: McGill-Queen's University Press, 1990), 23–5. Though Protestant missionaries tended to portray newly converted francophone Protestants as ostracized by their families, such families in South Ely, Quebec, did not break altogether from their Catholic relations; moreover, francophone Protestants continued to demonstrate denominational fluidity, some returning to Catholicism or taking a Catholic spouse, and others moving to another Protestant denomination (see essay by Christine Hudon elsewhere in this volume).

24 This profile is drawn from the database and George Boardman, "Early Days on the St. Croix" (series), *St. Croix Courier*, 24 October 1895.

25 D.M.L. Dougherty, *A History of Getchell Settlement-Mayfield* (N.p.: Privately printed, 1988), 24.

26 *Provincial Wesleyan*, 20 April 1874.

27 *St. Croix Courier*, 28 January 1869.

28 T.W. Acheson, *Saint John: The Making of a Colonial Urban Community* (Toronto: University of Toronto Press, 1985), 116–18.

29 T. Watson Smith, *History of Methodism in Eastern British North America* (Halifax: Methodist Book Room, 1877), 2: 348, 423, 426.

30 Lane, "Re-numbering Souls," 89–90.

31 See, for example, the obituaries of St Stephen Methodists and Congregationalists published in the *Provincial Wesleyan*, 15 February 1855, 19 November 1857; *Calais Advertiser*, 21 October 1846; and Lane, "Re-numbering Souls," chap. 10, "Spiritual History and 'Holy Dying' in Local Methodism."

32 *Provincial Wesleyan*, 1 May 1872.

33 See the letter from sea captain John Irving, Dover, NB, in the Maine Universalist newspaper the *Gospel Banner*, 17 July 1858; see also 24 September 1859, 14 and 21 January 1860, 18 March 1860, 11 April 1860, and 26 July 1862.

34 See, for example, William Temple to Wesleyan Missionary Society Committee (WMSC), 9 March 1838; George Johnson to WMSC, 12 August 1834; "Spiritual Report," St David Circuit, 1830.

35 For both affinity and conflict between Methodism and Universalism, see also Heather M. Watts, " 'Soul-Chearing Doctrines': Universalism in Nineteenth-Century Nova Scotia," *Nova Scotia Historical Review* 7 (1987): 48–63.

36 Reprinted in the *Gospel Banner*, 2 November 1859.

37 *Calais Advertiser*, 1 January 1851.

38 *Provincial Wesleyan*, 3 February 1864; Knowlton, *Annals of Calais*, 88.

39 "Spiritual Report," Milltown Circuit, 1854; see also reports in 1850 and 1852 from another minister.

40 *Provincial Wesleyan*, 3 May 1855; St Andrew's *Standard*, 21 February 1855.

41 Knowlton, *Annals of Calais*, 88; *Provincial Wesleyan*, 3 February 1864.

42 John Inglis cited in Davis, *An International Community*, 137; see also John Medley, *Notes of a Visitation Tour through Parts of the Diocese of Fredericton, New Brunswick, in 1846* (London: Society for the Propagation of the Gospel, 1846), 5.

43 The grandson of a Methodist class leader, George F. Hill appears to have attended almost every Protestant church in St Stephen and Calais, commenting both on his social life and occasionally on the sermon (I am indebted to Gail Campbell for her transcription of the diary of George F. Hill, 1850–54, PANB, MS6/34. See also the diary of Ida J. Harding, Saint John, NB 1877–80, in Elizabeth W. McGahan ed., *Whispers from the Past: Selections from the Writings of New Brunswick Women* (Fredericton: Goose Lane Editions, 1986).

44 Knowlton, *Annals of Calais*, 79; *Christian Visitor*, 6 October 1870; New Brunswick Association of Baptists, *Minutes*, 1834–44; Western New Brunswick Association of Baptists, *Minutes*, 1845–47 (various publishers); *Christian Visitor*, 1 March 1848.

45 For the legal intricacies of family pew ownership and its role as social capital, see also the essay by Ollivier Hubert elsewhere in this volume.

46 Rev. Joshua Millet, *History of the Baptists in Maine* (Portland: Charles Day & Co., 1845), 369–70; Washington Baptist Association, *Minutes*, 1843–56 (various publishers); Clifford G. Chase, *A History of Baring* (compiled for the Centenary Celebration, 4 July 1925; repr. 1950).

47 Edited by a Presbyterian church member, the *St. Croix Courier* published weekly instalments or commentary on the baptism debate at the Ledge from January to June 1871; a similar local debate had occurred in the 1850s.

48 *Provincial Wesleyan*, 15 May 1856.

49 Schedule 2, Manuscript Census, St Stephen, 1871; *St. Croix Courier*, 29 July 1880; for another "Union" church in a neighbouring parish, see also 1 July 1869.

50 See *St. Croix Courier*, 2 July 1868, 3 September 1868, 19 January 1870, 15 December 1870.

51 *St. Croix Courier*, 10 September 1868, 10 October 1868, 31 March 1870; Knowlton, *Annals of Calais*, 118–19, unfortunately for modern scholars, the *Courier*'s reporter left before the vote was counted, see *St. Croix Courier*, 1 December 1870.

52 Wesleyan Methodist records for the St Stephen circuit survive from 1840 and for the Milltown circuit from 1849. The demographic analysis of

church members includes Maine residents, but the analysis of rates of church membership is based on members linked to St Stephen census returns.

53 For the influence of denominational diversity on Congregationalism elsewhere in British North America, see J.I. Little, "Serving 'the North East Corner of Creation': The Community Role of a Rural Clergyman in the Eastern Townships of Quebec, 1829–1870," *Histoire sociale/Social History* 30 (May 1997): 28–33.

54 *Provincial Wesleyan*, 27 May 1863.

55 In *The Christian Home in Victorian America, 1840–1900* (Bloomington: Indiana University Press, 1986), Colleen McDannell situates evangelical discourse within the larger cultural setting of Protestant and Catholic family religion.

56 Marguerite Van Die, " 'The Marks of a Genuine Revival': Religion, Social Change, Gender, and Community in Mid-Victorian Brantford, Ontario," *Canadian Historical Review* 79 (September 1998): 534.

57 Multi-generational and more impressionistic criteria for kinship used in Hannah M. Lane, " 'Wife, Mother, Sister, Friend' Methodist Women in St. Stephen, New Brunswick, 1861–1881," in Janet Guildford and Suzanne Morton, eds., *Separate Spheres: Women's Worlds in the 19th Century Maritimes* (Fredericton: Acadiensis Press, 1994) suggested that a majority of new and returning members in the 1860s and 1870s joined along with a member of the larger kin group.

58 William T. Young, *The Congregationalists* (Westport, Conn.: Greenwood Press, 1990), 62–3, 58–9.

59 In addition to sources listed in the data base, see Knowlton, *Annals of Calais*, 69, 62–3.

60 See the analysis of ages at first membership and the minutes of the Milltown- St Stephen Maternal Association, (PANB).

61 Membership records for the Milltown circuit are missing before 1849; this calculation excludes members and adherents living at the Ledge, which was part of the neighbouring parish's circuit after 1855.

62 Van Die, " 'The Marks of a Genuine Revival,' " 529 and 533.

63 Laurie Stanley-Blackwell, " 'Tabernacles in the Wilderness': The Open-Air Communion Tradition in Nineteenth- and Twentieth-Century Cape Breton," in Charles H.H. Scobie and G.A. Rawlyk, eds., *The Contribution of Presbyterianism to the Maritime Provinces of Canada* (Montreal and Kingston: McGill-Queen's University Press, 1997), 104–5. However, in "Church and Community: The Presbyterian Kirk-Session in the District of Bathurst, Upper Canada" (MA thesis, University of Western Ontario, 1979), Duff Willis Crerar argues that "Presbyterians did not consider children (though baptized) full communicants until they made profession of their faith themselves, usually in adolescence" (88). This question is further compli-

cated by the Presbyterian distinction between eligibility for and the actually taking of communion.

64 See Richard A. Meckel, "Educating a Ministry of Mothers: Evangelical Maternal Associations, 1815–1860," *Journal of the Early Republic* 2 (winter 1982): 403–23.

65 PANB, Maternal Association of Milltown- St Stephen, Constitution, article 5. Surviving records date from 1836–38 and 1844–46.

66 For Congregationalism, see Ann M. Boylan, *Sunday School: The Formation of an American Institution, 1790–1880* (New Haven: Yale University Press, 1988), 142–51; for Methodism, see Neil Semple, *The Lord's Dominion: The History of Canadian Methodism* (Montreal and Kingston: McGill-Queen's University Press, 1996), chap. 14, "Young People and the Methodist Moral Order", and Lane, " 'Re-numbering Souls," chap. 8, "The Demography of Church Growth (2): Youth."

67 "Sabbath School Reports," St Stephen and Milltown Circuits, 1836, 1840, and 1843; reports for the years after 1855 have not survived.

68 See Stephen R. Grossbart, "Seeking the Divine Favour: Conversion and Church Admission in Eastern Connecticut, 1711–1832," *William and Mary Quarterly*, 3rd ser., 48 (1989): 696–740; and Richard D. Shiels, "The Scope of the Second Great Awakening: Andover, Massachusetts, as a Case Study," *Journal of the Early Republic*, 5 (summer 1985): 223–46.

69 Stanley-Blackwell, " 'Tabernacles in the Wilderness,' " 105.

70 For similar demographic patterns, see Lynne Marks, *Revivals and Roller Rinks: Religion, Leisure, and Identity in Late-Nineteenth-Century Small-Town Ontario* (Toronto: University of Toronto Press, 1996), 31.

71 See Ann Braude, "Women's History Is American Religious History," in Thomas Tweed, ed., *Retelling U.S. Religious History* (Berkeley: University of California Press, 1997), 87–107, and Hugh McLeod, *Piety and Poverty: Working-Class Religion in Berlin, London and New York 1870–1914* (New York: Holmes & Meier, 1996), chap. 7, "Male and Female."

72 See Lane, " 'Wife, Mother, Sister, Friend,' " 93–117, and the essay by Marguerite Van Die elsewhere in this volume.

73 Preliminary analysis for the larger study from which this paper is drawn suggests that rates of church membership among married men and women from poor families were lower than among married men and women from wealthier families. However, rates of membership among single men and women from poorer families were higher than among single men and women from wealthier families. This pattern may have reflected a greater tendency among the latter to keep young adults at home; in other words, the constituency of single adherents from wealthier families might be inflated because their counterparts in poorer families were more likely to have left the parish.

74 See Hannah M. Lane, "'The Pence of the Poor and the Pounds of the Rich': Methodist Church Finance and Wealth-Holding in Mid-Nineteenth Century St. Stephen, New Brunswick," Canadian Methodist Historical Society, *Papers, 1997 and 1998* (Toronto, 1999), 90–116.

75 *Provincial Wesleyan,* 1 November 1851, 7 December 1854, 3 and 10 January 1856. See also Cecilia Morgan, *Public Men and Virtuous Women: The Gendered Languages of Religion and Politics in Upper Canada, 1791–1850* (Toronto: University of Toronto Press, 1996), 153–8; for similar concerns in a later period, see the essay by Patricia Dirks elsewhere in this volume.

76 "Letter," *Morning News* (Saint John), 24 January 1855; a week later the paper copied a similar article from a Boston newspaper. See also the *Provincial Wesleyan,* 24 November 1853; and *Maine Farmer,* 27 May 1836, cited in Richard P. Horwitz, *Anthropology towards History: Culture and Work in a 19th Century Maine Town* (Middleton, Conn.: Wesleyan University Press, 1977), 95. For complaints later in the century, see Peter McGahan, *Killers, Thieves, Tramps & Sinners* (Fredericton: Goose Lane Editions, 1989), 22–4.

77 *Calais Advertiser,* 18 March 1847, 8 October 1851. These local complaints also implied that some young men went to church meetings only to check out who was there and then left. For an interesting comparison, see the essay by Ollivier Hubert (elsewhere in this volume) on late-eighteenth-century Catholic concerns over men who left before the service was over.

78 To observers and participants, the distinction between courtship, flirtation, and harassment was not always clear; see Marks, *Revivals and Roller Rinks,* 36–7, 81–5; and Karen Dubinsky, *Improper Advances: Rape and Heterosexual Conflict in Ontario, 1880–1929* (Chicago and London: University of Chicago Press, 1993), 116.

79 *Calais Advertiser,* 4 March 1858.

80 Mark Trafton, *Scenes of My Life* (New York: Nelson & Phillips, 1878), 35–7.

81 *Provincial Wesleyan,* 1 November 1851.

82 Ibid., 1 April 1858, 1 April 1856.

83 The letters and reports of Methodist ministers in New Brunswick suggest that, as in Upper Canada, early writers identified conversion or church membership as both uniting and divisive forces within families; see Morgan, *Public Men and Virtuous Women,* 112–15, and for Baptists and Presbyterians, see Lynne Marks, "Christian Harmony: Family, Neighbours, and Community in Upper Canadian Church Discipline Records," in Franca Iacovetta and Wendy Mitchinson, eds., *On the Case: Explorations in Social History* (Toronto: University of Toronto Press, 1998), 123.

84 *Provincial Wesleyan,* 15 February 1855, 23 December 1863, 7 July 1858.

85 See Lane, "Methodism and Economy," chap. 5–6.

86 *Provincial Wesleyan,* 8 September 1877.

87 Gwen Kennedy Neville, *Kinship and Pilgrimage: Rituals of Reunion in American Protestant Culture* (New York: Oxford University Press, 1987), 61.

88 *St. Croix Courier*, 13 November 1873.
89 A photocopy of the family of William Boardman's *Golden Wedding and Family Gazette* (Calais, Maine, April 1865), is in the Maine State Library, Augusta.
90 *Provincial Wesleyan*, 1 February 1879.
91 I am indebted to Nancy Christie for this insight.

Family Fortunes and Religious Identity: The French-Canadian Protestants of South Ely, Quebec, 1850–1901

CHRISTINE HUDON

The study of the relations between religion and family comprises a number of dimensions, which can be elucidated by a sociology of religious behaviour attentive to differing practices and levels of intensity among men and women and to intergenerational differences. Historical anthropology affords another approach to illuminating religious sociability and the way in which religious texts and clerical discourse constructed gender and family roles. As well, social history offers many possibilities for exploring the dynamic of the nexus between religion and family. This essay adopts a social-historical perspective and examines the demographic and social dimensions of religious membership and identity through a local community study of French-speaking Protestants in Quebec. The purpose is to shed light on the experience of a religious minority whose existence has for many years been erased from collective memory and only recently rediscovered by historians.[1]

Through a detailed analysis of the correspondence of missionaries and their reports, the testimony of early converts and their pastors,[2] and the writings of late-nineteenth- and early-twentieth-century hagiographers,[3] recent scholarship has precisely identified the exact chronology of the Protestant missionary impulse in French Canada and outlined its results. It is evident that the missionaries achieved their greatest success during the 1840s and 1850s, when many people converted to Protestantism. However, conversions were far less numerous in the succeeding decades. Historians have advanced two main reasons to account for the failure of this religious proselytism:

first, the fierce opposition of the Roman Catholic Church, which was quick to denounce the travelling *colporteurs* who purveyed Bibles to prospective converts, Protestant teachers and pastors, and anyone who dared to have any dealings with them; second, the competition between Protestant churches and missionary societies, which weakened the overall effectiveness of the work. On another level, following the lead of Protestant missionaries who depicted the departure of the first families of converts to the Eastern Townships of Quebec, the United States, and Upper Canada as an exodus, historians have linked this emigration to a pervasive ostracism and social pressure.

Although the sources used in these various historical treatments remain valuable for an understanding of the history of Quebec's French-speaking Protestants, much can be gained by a careful reading of other types of historical documents, which provide another window into the experience of this religious minority. Because they have until now mined sources that are mainly literary, historians have cast into the background certain aspects of the lives of the converts and their kin. Consequently, there remain many unexplored questions. In what circumstances did these families actually embrace Protestantism? What were the consequences of their religious choice? How did these men and women live? To what extent were they affected by emigration? How did their family fortunes differ from those of their Catholic counterparts, and to what extent did the two groups resemble each other?

In answering these questions, this study relies upon the manuscript censuses from 1851 to 1901, as well as the registers of baptisms, marriages, and burials of a large number of Catholic and Protestant parishes[4] in the Richelieu-Yamaska region and in the Eastern Townships.[5] An analysis of newspapers, especially *L'Aurore*, published in Montreal from 1866, also enables the historian to trace the movements of a number of families. Obituaries and social columns provide information vital to any reconstitution of family migration within Quebec's Protestant community.

For the purposes of this essay, I have limited the scope to South Ely, a Protestant community situated in the Eastern Townships southeast of Montreal. Three criteria dictated the choice of this locality: the quality of the sources, the abundance of information, and the relative longevity of this particular community. In what follows, I first examine the beginning of the South Ely community, not through the eyes of the missionaries, as many previous historians have done, but through the lens provided by the experience of the converts themselves, in order to discern the circumstances of their conversion and the characteristics of their family religious strategies. Then, through another approach, this study seeks to trace the evolution of the community as a whole over a time span of fifty years by highlighting its demographic character. Finally, the essay concludes with a study of the phenomenon of migration and attempts to analyze its main outlines and implications for the South Ely congregation. However, before we explore in greater depth the fate of individual converts, it is necessary to provide in the bold brush strokes the history of Protestantism in French-Canadian parishes.

FRENCH-LANGUAGE PROTESTANTS
IN QUEBEC

From tentative and largely fruitless beginnings in the early nineteenth century, proselytism directed to French Canadians by Protestant organizations intensified during the 1830s and 1840s.[6] Animated by the theology of the "Réveil," the Swiss missionaries Henriette Feller and Louis Roussy established themselves in Montreal in 1834 and 1835, and then at Grande-Ligne on Montreal's south shore, where they were able to make a number of converts. By the summer of 1836 sixteen adults had joined this congregation, and this centre rapidly became the headquarters of further missionary activities. Grande-Ligne was the name given to the small mission station formed around Feller and Roussy. Initially free of any denominational links, the Swiss leaders of this mission affiliated with the Baptist Home Society in 1850, which guaranteed them regular and stable funding, and thus they were able to inaugurate a number of other mission stations during the following years. One was opened at Saint-Pie in 1844, and a chapel was erected at Marieville in 1852. Missionaries were also active in townships situated further east, such as Milton, Granby, Roxton, and Ely, where they succeeded in converting a number of individuals. A chapel at Roxton was established in 1862, and six years later Protestants in Ely founded a place of worship. The pastor, François-Xavier Smith, the son of one of the first converts at Saint-Pie, had resided at Ely since October 1864. Other Protestant churches and missionary societies rapidly followed suit and entered the French-language mission field. In Montreal in 1839, English-speaking clergy and laity belonging to a number of denominations founded the French Canadian Missionary Society (FCMS), which directed its apostolic activity towards the north shore of the St Lawrence. In 1841 the Presbyterian Church of Canada established itself in Montreal, without noteworthy success. In 1846 the Anglicans opened a church at Sabrevois, not far from Grande-Ligne. Finally, the Methodists founded a few missions in the Eastern Townships.

When French-speaking preachers and Bible *colporteurs* arrived in Quebec, English-speaking Protestant missionaries had been firmly rooted in the Eastern Townships for several decades.[7] American Methodist preachers had been the first to work there at the end of the eighteenth century, visiting the townships in an attempt to convert American immigrants drawn to this area by the abundance of land. Missionaries affiliated with other denominations and religious movements, notably the Baptists, Congregationalists, Presbyterians, Quakers, Adventists, and Universalists, followed in the Methodist wake. With less success, the Anglicans also threw themselves into the mission enterprise. These efforts, aimed solely at English-speaking settlers, had made the Eastern Townships into a welter of competing local congregations, a true religious mosaic, a characteristic that distinguished it from the rest of Quebec, where the Catholic Church dominated the social landscape. Thus it was within a region strongly imprinted with ethnic and religious diversity and heavily marked by evangelicalism that French-speaking Protestant missionaries in the middle decades of the nineteenth century sought to build their churches.

But what was the result of all this missionary activity? The data offered by the missionaries in their annual reports provide only approximate and frequently contradictory figures. Anxious to convince their financial backers that their work was not in vain and deserved continuing support, they spoke eagerly of "encouraging results" produced by their activity and counted not only actual church members, but those they believed were sympathetic to their message and attended their meetings and sermons. However, on many other occasions the missionaries pointed to a stagnation or a decrease in their membership and complained bitterly of the disastrous consequences of emigration from the province. Thus the numerical data that the missionaries provided remain partial and ultimately unreliable. In tallying the numbers of their congregations, they often omitted to explain how they defined church membership and which persons were actually part of their calculations. Did they consider only baptized members? Did they count only adults? Or did they include children of a certain age in their statistics?

The imprecise nature of missionary statistics does not enable the historian to know exactly how many French Canadians converted to Protestantism. In this respect, we have only very divergent estiments, some conservative, others so speculative as to verge on fantasy. According to René Hardy, the Grande-Ligne mission comprised about 700 members in 1860, and at the same period the effectives of the

FCMS numbered about 117.[8] In 1886 the newspaper *L'Aurore* presented a far more optimistic account of conversion efforts among French Canadians. It estimated at twenty-five thousand "the number of French-speaking Protestants on this continent" and claimed that about six thousand of these were attached to Grande-Ligne.[9] The same source affirmed that this pioneer mission already had fifteen hundred members in 1845. In 1891 one Protestant went so far as to assert that forty thousand French Canadians had abandoned the Catholic Church "to follow the gospel" (*pour suivre l'Évangile*),[10] although he also noted that many of these had already emigrated to the United States. Nowhere, however, did the author explain how he had arrived at these figures.

Of all the churches and missionary societies, Grande-Ligne, linked to the Baptists, was indubitably the most successful during the early decades of Protestant missionary activity. However, this situation changed radically during the 1880s, as Methodist and Presbyterian missions enjoyed considerable growth, the Presbyterians even luring into their ranks a number of workers from the FCMS. This latter organization declined and finally disappeared. The Grande-Ligne mission itself experienced a series of persistent troubles, and while a number of established congregations were able to survive, efforts to create new mission stations were nugatory.

THE BEGINNINGS OF SOUTH ELY

The Franco-Protestant community of South Ely (now known as Valcourt) was born in the 1850s, during the era that witnessed the greatest vitality of the Grande-Ligne parent mission, which extended its territory and built new mission stations. As previously noted, Ely was located in one of the regions of Quebec that had been most intensively visited by preachers and *colporteurs* of French-language Bibles, and there were a number of local conditions that favoured proselytism in this area. The seigneurial parishes situated a few kilometres to the west had been hard hit by the insurrections of 1837–38. The Catholic Church and clergy were closely associated with the counter-revolutionary forces and had suffered a corresponding loss of prestige. Moreover, the area was new and thinly settled, and it thus slipped outside the control of the established churches, leaving a free field for travelling evangelists. Settlement in Ely, as in the neighbouring townships, had barely begun when the first French-speaking missionaries arrived. The first settler, an American immigrant from Bethel, Vermont, took up land in Ely township in 1830,[11] and others soon followed. In 1831 the township had 25 inhabitants;[12] twenty years later 1,018 people lived in Ely. Of this number, 584 (57 per cent) were of French origin.[13] In 1861 the relative weight of the French-Canadian element had slightly increased, now comprising 62 per cent of the population, or 1,094 of 1,743 inhabitants. Beginning about 1850, Catholic clergy made periodic visitations to the faithful in this area, but its institutional presence was quite limited, and consequently, its influence was far less than in older-settled parishes. At South Ely the Catholic Church slowly began to lay its institutional groundwork in the 1850s, roughly twenty years after the arrival of the first French-Canadian settlers. St Joseph parish (Valcourt) was founded in 1854, and Father Julien Leblanc, its first *curé*, began the construction of a Catholic chapel, which was largely completed by 1856. This building stood close by other structures, just to the north of it at around the same time, used for Protestant worship services. Like neighbouring townships, Ely numbered many Anglo-Protestant settlers, divided among Presbyterians, Methodists, and Anglicans, a denominational diversity that actually served to lessen the social pressures that the Catholic clergy could bring to bear on francophone converts to Protestantism.

Well before the opening of the Baptist chapel in 1868, Ely township was home to a small group of French-speaking Protestants who had settled there a few years earlier. In the summer of 1854 three French-Canadian families recently converted to Protestantism had moved there from L'Ange-Gardien, a parish located about fifty kilometres south west of South Ely.[14] In 1852 they still attended the Catholic Church, where several of their children had been baptized,[15] but in May 1854, though they continued to live at L'Ange-Gardien, they had severed their ties with the Catholic Church and become Protestants. A few months later they left their parish to settle at Ely. Let us pause to consider the history of these three families before their conversion.

THE EARLY NUCLEUS

Arriving at the same time in this township of recent settlement, the families of Simon Malboeuf, Joseph Commeau, and Isaac Casgrain were close kin relations. Flavie Malboeuf, the wife of Joseph Com-meau, and Olive Malboeuf, the wife of Isaac Casgrain, were sisters of Simon Malboeuf.[16] A variety of common experiences had undoubtedly further cemented the bonds between the families. Before coming to Ely, they had together lived the hardship of a first migration. Like many others, they had left to settle in the back-settlement *rangs* of Saint-Césaire, which had been newly opened to the wave of settlement that formed the Catholic parishes of Saint-Paul d'Abbotsford and L'Ange-Gardien. In 1846 Simon Malboeuf, still a bachelor, and Isaac Casgrain and Joseph Commeau and their wives and young children left Saint-Mathias, which was located on the Richelieu River. A few months later, Simon married Isabelle Gélineau, *dite* Daniel, of Saint-Césaire. In their new parish the three families all lived in the Casimir *rang* in close proximity to one another. In 1851 they occupied very humble wooden houses and worked about sixty arpents of land. One-third of Joseph Commeau's farm was cultivated. In the census year he produced about forty bushels of wheat, fifty bushels of oats, six bushels of corn, and twelve bushels of potatoes. His brothers-in-law, Simon Malboeuf and Isaac Casgrain, each farmed about ten arpents. Simon harvested about twenty-five bushels of wheat, ten bushels of peas, and thirty-six bushels of oats. Isaac's farm produced fifteen bushels of wheat, eleven bushels of peas, fifty bushels of oats, twenty bushels of corn, and sixty bushels of potatoes. These harvests were rather paltry, although not out of line with those of other settlers in the area. It should be stated that the land in these *rangs* posed serious difficulties for the cultivation of grain, as its clayey soil was particularly difficult to clear and drain.

At the beginning of the 1850s, the parish of Saint-Césaire was shaken by a fundamental conflict.[17] As early as 1848, the *curé* and many inhabitants had sought to divide the parish in order to give parishioners in the back settlements easier access to a place of worship. Since the inhabitants could not agree on the boundaries to be assigned to the new parish, their request was refused by Mgr Ignace Bourget, the bishop of Montreal. The project surfaced again in 1851, and this time it obtained the approval of the bishop, who constituted the parish of L'Ange-Gardien on 21 October 1851. However, this decision quickly caused discontent, as one group of parishioners contested the boundaries of the parish and demanded a further division, hoping that two entities could be formed rather than the one sanctioned by Bourget. Even those who were pleased with the episcopal decree and said that they were satisfied with the new boundaries could not agree on a site where the new church should be built: some wanted it erected at the Seraphine *rang*; others lobbied the bishop to choose a site on the Grande-Ligne road.[18] Mgr Bourget chose the Seraphine *rang*, much to the displeasure of those who had promoted the other location. Indeed, the site selected by the bishop was difficult for many of the settlers to reach easily, and in order to attend church, they were forced to build a new road, thus placing additional financial obligations on already limited budgets. To one request that recounted the difficulties and the "immense expenses that will be necessary to build this road and a number of bridges," the bishop retorted with a categorical negative, qualifying their petition as "useless" and "null and void."[19]

The families of Simon Malboeuf, Isaac Casgrain, and Joseph Commeau were among those who opposed the choice made by Mgr Bourget, a decision reaffirmed by Mgr Jean-Charles Prince, the first bishop of the newly constituted diocese of Saint-Hyacinthe, to which the parish of L'Ange-Gardien was attached. In January 1853 Father J.-A. Provençal, *curé* of Saint-Césaire, warned his superior that these people were likely to take their discontent to greater extremes, writing, "I fear that these people will go too far."[20] His assistant, Father J.-S. Singer, was far more explicit in a letter written a few months later: "From what we see ... and hear, we are correct in fearing for the future of these poor folk. The spirit that directs them ... and the efforts that are being made for their perdition worry and alarm us ... Twice a week, one of these miserable Swiss impostors visits a body of the settlers on the mountain and invites all the Canadians of the neighbourhood to his meetings, in order to win them over to his side ... We believe, in the sincerity of our heart, that the erection of two churches would be the way of removing this evil and preserving the faith of our dear Canadians."[21]

The missionary to whom Father Singer referred was none other than Louis Roussy of Grande-Ligne, who had been visiting the parishes of the region for a number of years. A pioneer of proselytization among French Canadians, he became a quasi-legendary figure for many Protestants, an exceptional individual with whom they claimed a spiritual kinship. At the beginning of the twentieth century the obituaries of Isabelle Gélineau, *dite* Daniel (the wife of Malboeuf) and Flavie Malboeuf (the wife of Commeau) underscored with pride the role of the Swiss missionary in the conversion of the two women and their families.[22] According to Protestant sources, the Commeau, Casgrain, and Malboeuf families were baptized at Marieville, "at the beginnings of Protestantism in that place."[23]

It is difficult to determine what was the compelling motive in the decision of these families to sever their ties with the Catholic Church. These converts left no autobiographies or direct or indirect testimonies about their conversion. But even if they had done so, it would be problematic to separate the genuine elements of the story from the discourse they would have used to justify their decision. This said, the connection between their conversion and the conflict that shook L'Ange-Gardien parish was surely more than coincidental. One might wonder if the evangelistic efforts of Louis Roussy would have been sufficient, under other circumstances, to shake their faith. The Malboeuf, Casgrain, and Commeau families would perhaps not have given so much attention to the teachings of the missionary if they had not already been frustrated by the decisions of a bishop apparently little disposed to consider their aspirations and difficult material circumstances. At L'Ange-Gardien Protestant preaching found fertile ground among families sorely disappointed with their church. Far from being an isolated case, this situation occurred over and over again in other places. Some parishes where conversions occurred in the nineteenth century were, in effect, the scenes of conflit between the Catholic clergy and parts of the population. In 1843 several families of Saint-Pie, a neighbouring parish of L'Ange-Gardien, abjured Catholicism at the same time as an ongoing conflict raged over the construction of a new church. At the same time, at Marieville, the churchwarden Alexis Brouillet converted to Protestantism after quarrelling with his *curé* over the construction of a new presbytery. In 1866–67 about ten families of Saint-Valerien-de-Milton, disagreeing with a plan of church construction, became Protestants. Three years later a similar quarrel encouraged twenty-six heads in families in Saint-Ephrem-d'Upton to send a letter of apostasy to the Catholic authorities.[24] Finally, at the end of the century the parishioners of Maskinonge, in Mauricie, noisily and publicly abjured their Catholicism and joined the ranks of Grande-Ligne converts. All these inhabitants were strongly opposed to moving the parish church, which had been authorized by the ecclesiastical authorities.[25] Some of their kin joined them in their new religious identity. Significantly, many of these small francophone Protestant communities were largely composed of interrelated families, a fact that illustrates the importance of the family in the process of conversion.[26]

In her study of French-speaking Protestant communities in Quebec, Dominique Vogt-Raguy casts doubt on the depth of the conversions that occurred during this period of conflict, arguing that they "did not occur out of conviction, but as a rejection in order to challenge the authority of the priest and to take public issue with his decisions."[27] In her estimation, the spectacular apostasies were ephemeral and their protagonists were sooner or later reintegrated into the Catholic fold. This seems to have been the case in a number of the parishes mentioned earlier. Many inhabitants of Saint-Valérien-de-Milton and Saint-Ephrem-d'Upton returned to Catholicism a few months or years after their noisy exit. But a significant number of converts, notably the Malboeuf, Casgrain, and Commeau families, remained committed to their new faith. These examples thus enjoin a certain prudence when we seek to know the reasons for conversion. It is better not to judge the quality of the motives that drove people to modify their religious allegiance. Certain factors and reasons that at first sight might appear superficial do not exclude a more durable and sincere engagement. In each case, the motives of the individuals and families in question might be varied and, more tellingly, difficult to evaluate.

CHAIN MIGRATION

Shortly after their conversion to Protestantism, Malboeuf, Casgrain, Commeau, and their families left L'Ange-Gardien, after having lived in the Casimir *rang* for less than ten years. Upon arrival in Ely township, they took up land close to one another, as they had done a number of years before when they settled in Saint-Césaire. Protestant sources, especially the obituaries of Flavie Malboeuf, Isabelle Gélineau, *dite* Daniel, and some of their descendants, stated that these three families migrated because of their conversion and the subsequent persecution that they suffered at the hands of their former Catholic co-religionists. However, upon closer examination, this factor does not appear to have been the compelling one in their decision to leave their old parish and settle at South Ely. Indeed, their experience was similar to that of many other Catholic family groups, since the majority of French Canadians who moved to Ely township came from the Richelieu and Yamaska regions, mainly from the parishes of Saint-Athanase, Saint-Césaire, and L'Ange-Gardien.[28] In fact, two brothers, three sisters, and the father and mother of Isabelle Gélineau, *dite* Daniel, all of whom remained Catholic, were among the migrants who came from the latter two parishes. Louis Daniel, the father of Isabelle, who died at Valcourt in 1855 and was interred in the Catholic cemetery, lived in the same dwelling with his Protestant daughter and son-in-law.[29] Many families were involved in a similar pattern of settling in one township and then pulling up stakes after a few years to try their luck in a new area; for example, many members of the Bombardier family, related to the Gélineau, *dite* Daniel family, left L'Ange-Gardien or Saint-Césaire, where they had settled only a few years earlier, and moved to Ely.

A disaster that occurred in the summer of 1854 probably induced a number of residents of Saint-Césaire and L'Ange-Gardien to migrate. During the month of August a forest fire ravaged parts of these parishes, burning crops, decimating herds, and destroying farmhouses and outbuildings.[30] While there is no direct evidence that this catastrophe forced the three Protestant families in question to move, it can be inferred that their experience and subsequent choice to migrate was probably no different from that made by their Catholic neighbours. Indeed, it is likely that the Malboeuf, Casgrain, and Commeau families chose South Ely over other neighbourhoods precisely because many of their friends and acquaintances had already moved there. Catholic parish registers attest to the fact that members of the Daniel family had located in the area as early as 1845. In light of this evidence, one must therefore seriously qualify the notion that migration was the consequence of persecution. If the converts from L'Ange-Gardien were solely preoccupied with escaping ostracism and social pressure, is it reasonable to suppose that they would have picked a township where many of their former Catholic neighbours already lived? As the experience of these three Baptist families demonstrates, here is a classic case of chain migration, where kin and relatives played a key role in the initial decision and land selection.[31] What this example indicates is that family solidarities transcended denominational boundaries and that conversion to Protestantism did not necessarily imply the severing of relations with family and kin who remained Catholic. Here again, lived experience of nineteenth-century French-Canadian families offers insights that nuance and qualify the testimony of missionaries,[32] which have been simply echoed in the work of present-day historians.[33]

THE DEVELOPMENT OF A COMMUNITY

Once settled in South Ely, the three Protestant families grew rapidly as a result of many births.[34] At the time of their arrival in the township, Simon Malboeuf (age twenty-seven) and Isabelle Gélineau, *dite* Daniel (age twenty-four) already had five children. In the following years Isabelle gave birth to two girls and five boys; one of these children died before reaching puberty, but the others survived. The couple never left the community, and many of their children settled in the neighbouring *rangs*. At the time of the 1901 census, six of them still resided at South Ely. In announcing the couple's golden wedding anniversary in 1896, the newspaper *L'Aurore* stated that "two-thirds of the congregation was related to them" (*les deux tiers de la congrégation leur était apparenté*). Isabelle died aged sixty-eight in March 1898, and her obituary observed that "through her children, Mme Malboeuf was linked with all the families of the congregation. She was like a mother in Israel" among us.[35] The two other couples who came to South Ely were older, and they already had many children: the Commeaus had seven, and the Casgrains eight, with two more born after their migration. Like the Malboeufs, Olive and Isaac Casgrain spent the rest of their lives in South Ely, and a number of their children also settled in the community. Four still lived there in 1901. However, the family experience of the Commeaus was different. Most of the children of this family left Quebec during the 1880s to settle in New England. Only one of the Commeau daughters, Appoline, aged sixty, still lived in South Ely in 1901.

During the 1850s and 1860s a number of other families joined the Malboeufs, Casgrains, and Commeaus. In 1859 Benjamin Boisvert and his wife and three children arrived to swell the numbers of the small French Protestant community of South Ely. Their itinerary was similar to that of the three founding families. A few years earlier Benjamin had left his home parish of Saint-Léon, located on the north shore of the St Lawrence, to settle in Farnham township, just south of L'Ange-Gardien parish. He and his family came to South Ely a few years after their conversion to Protestantism. According to *L'Aurore*, it was the presence of a small group of converts that persuaded them to immigrate to this area.[36] In turn, Boisvert drew other French-speaking Protestants to Ely. At the beginning of the 1860s, his parents, Toussaint and Julie Ferron, aged sixty and fifty respectively, selected land in the township, along with many of their grown-up children. This family had lived in the United States for a number of years; indeed, one daughter, Mathilde, who was born there, married Pierre Casgrain, son of Isaac, around 1875. Other marriages linked the Boisverts to the Malboeufs, Casgrains, and Commeaus. Toussaint junior and Joseph, the brothers of Mathilde and Benjamin, married Philomène Casgrain and Alphonsine Commeau respectively. In 1873 Benjamin's daughter, Célina, married Jean-Baptiste Malboeuf. During the 1870s Isaac Casgrain, having become a widower, married Julie Ferron, the widow of Toussaint Boisvert. Indeed, all these families displayed a remarkable cohesion, as none of their children became Catholic. In their case, adherence to Protestantism was a lifelong commitment, although matters were certainly different for some other Franco-Protestant settlers at South Ely.

AN AMBIGUOUS SITUATION

Several families who came to South Ely during the same era, among them the Dugreniers, differed from those we have previously examined by their more ambiguous pattern of religious commitment. In 1829 the father, Jean-Baptiste Dugrenier, married Françoise Gaudreau at the Catholic church of Saint-Denis-sur-Richelieu. During the 1840s this couple moved to settle in the newly opened *rangs* of Saint-Césaire, and towards the middle of the following decade they moved again. Like many of their former neighbours, the choice was Ely, where a number of Dugrenier families, all Catholic, already lived. It is possible that these households were related to Jean-Baptiste and that their presence affected his choice in settling in this particular spot. In the 1861 census, only Jean-Baptiste and one of his daughters, Marie, a servant to a shingle maker named Murray Fisk, stated that they were

Baptists. The other members of their family declared to the census taker that they were Catholics. Ten years earlier the census disclosed a similar pattern of religious identity: the husband was Protestant, but the wife and children were Catholic. In 1851 Jean-Baptiste owned over two hundred arpents of land, which placed him among the fifteen most substantial landowners in the vicinity. As far as he was concerned, membership in a Protestant church did not mean that he was ostracized from the local economic network. However, we do not know to what extent he was an active participant in the religious life of the small Baptist congregation. Jean-Baptiste Dugrenier died at Ely during the 1870s, aged in his sixties.

But what became of his children? Did they follow in his footsteps, or did they, like their mother, remain faithful to Catholicism? From what we can glean from parish registers and the census, the religious itineraries of a number of members of this family resemble nothing less than a kind of musical chairs alternating between Baptist and Catholic. Take, for example, Jean-Baptiste's son Charles. In 1868, a few years before the death of his father, he married Henriette Gauthier, a Catholic. Three children issued from this marriage, all baptized in the Catholic church, though each time their father was absent from the ceremony. Henriette died in May 1879 and was buried in the Baptist cemetery. Six months later Charles remarried, this time to a Protestant, Esther Boisvert, daughter of Toussaint, and they had three children, all raised in the Baptist communion. As for the daughter and two sons of Charles's first marriage, they seemed to have subsequently joined the Protestant church. The family of Charles Dugrenier left Quebec during the 1890s, and by 1906 all were discovered living in New Hampshire, the two sons at Lebanon and Candia and the others at Manchester, where they were members of the Methodist church.[37] Two daughters remained single, while the other two had wed Americans.

However, what is significant is that at least three of Charles's six brothers and sisters married a Catholic spouse. One of them, Antoine-Luc, married Mathilde Duranleau in a ceremony officiated by a priest. His eldest daughter was baptized as a Catholic, but Antoine-Luc did not attend the ceremony. In 1906, like his brother Charles, he lived in Manchester, New Hampshire. At that time only one of Jean-Baptiste Dugrenier's children still lived in Quebec: his son Joseph, who had established himself at Stukely, just south of Ely township. According to all available evidence from census and parish registers, Joseph was a Catholic.

Like the Dugreniers, the families of Simon Dussault, Damase Daigneau, and Narcisse Daigneau present a series of ambiguous religious itineraries. Simon Dussault arrived at Ely during the 1850s and married Lucie Roch, a marriage celebrated by a Catholic priest. In 1861 all members of his family were listed as Catholic. Ten years later Dussault, now a widower, married Adèle Massé in the Baptist church of Saint-Pie. The couple had at least four children, all baptized in the Catholic church in the absence of their father, sometimes many months after their birth, a circumstance that definitely contravened Catholicism's regulations, which prescribed the speedy baptism of newborn children. For example, Adèle-Joséphine was nearly three and a half months old when she was baptized, and her brother, Trefflé, was almost a year old. In 1871 all members of the Dussault family, with the exception of Simon, declared that they belonged to the Catholic church. Ten years later, the final census in which the family was present in South Ely, Simon himself was listed in the census as a Catholic.

In the case of the two Daigneau households, they arrived at Ely during the 1860s. In 1871 only the heads of family stated that they belonged to the Baptist church, and in subsequent censuses they offered divergent statements of their religious identity. In 1881 Narcisse, his wife, and all their children declared that they were Catholic. They left the township during the following years and apparently moved to New England. In 1905 one of the sons of Narcisse Daigneau married Sadie Lachance at the Baptist church in Salem, Massachusetts. The stay of Damase Daigneau and his family at Ely was even shorter. Already in 1881 they had moved elsewhere, but they were found by the census taker at Waterloo, a village just to the south where there were many places of worship. All members of the family professed to be Methodists.

How are we to interpret these different examples? One thing is sure: we cannot explain these interdenominational comings and goings as the result of error or the initiative of the census takers. If this had been the case, we could expect to find similar "errors" occurring in the records pertaining to the Malboeuf, Casgrain, and Commeau families and other households strongly identified with Protestantism. This was never the case, as these families were always listed in the census as Protestant. As well, the census was not alone in testifying to the religious ambivalence of certain families and individuals. As we have seen, registers of baptisms, marriages, and burials describe the same pattern of musical chairs played out by many family groups between the two religions. So what does all this mean? Is it possible that it indicates that some converts were uneasy about openly declaring their religious membership? Does it illustrate that within particular households, religion was a source of tension between a husband who had converted to Protestantism and a wife who wanted to remain, out of either conviction or social pressure, with Catholicism? Indeed, in the families where one person became Protestant, it was always the husband. While their husbands converted to Protestantism, wives maintained their ties to the Catholic church and continued to have their children baptized there. But what then is the significance of interfaith marriages between Protestants and Catholics? Do they invariably indicate the difficulty that some Protestants experienced in finding a spouse who shared their faith?[38] Or are they rather a sign of simple opportunism or religious indifference? Unfortunately, the sources do not permit further insight into the motives that underlie the behaviour of these families. But it should be remembered that households, in the course of their daily existence, experienced internal tensions as a result of a public ambiguity in which all family members did not share the same faith or denominational allegiance.

EFFERVESCENCE, STAGNATION, AND DECLINE IN SOUTH ELY

As we have seen, the beginnings of the Franco-Protestant community in South Ely can be traced to the arrival of a handful of young families who migrated from the adjoining seigneurial parishes and townships. A close analysis of the censuses reveals that, with the arrival of new recruits and the emigration of many individuals and families, the community's demographic profile underwent a gradual alteration during the ensuing years. At the beginning of the 1860s the future of South Ely appeared promising. Louis Pasche, the itinerant missionary whose charge included Roxton, Granby, and Ely, decided to concentrate his activities at the last site, abandoning his circuit in Roxton and limiting his visits to Granby to once a month.[39] The headquarters of Grande-Ligne had high hopes for the young community of South Ely, expecting to create there a dynamic mission centre anchored around a flourishing, ever-expanding congregation. The arrival of a number of families raised these expectations. In 1861 South Ely's French-speaking Protestant community comprised fifty-five people, all Baptist (see table 1). Only one anglophone, Caroline Woodward, the wife of Joseph Bérard, was a member of the Baptist church. Significantly, marriage between French-speaking and English-speaking Protestants was rare throughout the period covered by this study: other than the Bérard-Woodward couple, the community contained only four other households where one spouse was a French-speaking Baptist and the other was English-speaking. These were Olive Casgrain and George Dexter, married in 1859; Isabelle Casgrain and Nathan Scott, married at the beginning of the 1860s; Melina Malboeuf and John Greenwood, united in October 1878; and Emma Racicot and Homer Lay, married in November 1878. The last couple moved to Stukely, where they had a son less than seven months later. The common thread running through all these marriages was that they involved in each case a French-speaking wife. At Ely only Joseph Bérard married an English-speaking woman. However, it is possible that other men did marry English-speaking Protestant spouses, but they would have done so elsewhere, outside the congregation, where their union would not have been recorded in the South Ely register or in those of any of the other French Protestant churches of the region.

In 1861 South Ely was a youthful community whose average age was 18.9 years, a statistic that reflects the fact that over half the community (thirty individuals) was under age 15. Only two people, Jean-Baptiste Malboeuf, the father of Simon, and Joseph Commeau, were over 60. In terms of numbers, this Franco-Protestant community reached its apogee in 1871, numbering seventy-eight people, of whom seventy-three declared that they were Baptist, while five others – Toussaint Boisvert, his wife Julie, and their three children – listed themselves as "Evangelical." The average age of the group had, however, risen to 23.9 years. Those under 15 made up 54.2 per cent of the congregation: in absolute terms, thirty-nine individuals. As to those 60 and over, there were now four. Although two Franco-Protestant families had left the community during the intevening decade, the arrival of six new households had more than compensated for this loss.

In the 1870s and 1880s the community remained relatively stable. In both 1881 and 1891 the census recorded seventy-six Franco-Protestants at South Ely (table 1). However, by 1881 Baptist numbers had markedly declined, totalling only thirty-seven, while thirty-nine others were members of the Methodist church, the latter including many individuals of the Malboeuf, Casgrain, and Commeau families. With the exception of Isaac Casgrain senior and his second wife, Julie Ferron, South Ely's Methodist congregation was largely composed of the sons and daughters of the first converts, although Simon Malboeuf, Joseph Commeau, their spouses, and many of their children remained pillars of the Baptist church. The precise motives that compelled this shift in denominational identities remain obscure, but it is known that Ely and the adjoining townships experienced a lively competition between churches and missionary societies during the late nineteenth century. Methodists and Baptists both tried to extend their scope of activity, making no attempts at sharing the mission field or coordinating their efforts.[40]

The Methodists were well established at Roxton and Waterloo, and it would appear that Amand Parent, the pastor of the Waterloo congregation, visited the South Ely Protestants. According to Dominique Vogt-Raguy, this interdenominational rivalry did a disservice to the cause of French-speaking Protestantism in the long run, because it dispersed energies by needlessly perpetuating quarrels. However, in the case of Ely, this struggle for adherents seems not to have seriously hampered the development of the community. It is possible that, in the short run, the fact that some individuals converted to Methodism may have engendered tensions, but there is no basis for interpreting these as profound or lasting dissensions. Indeed, those families who adhered to Methodism in 1881 had reverted to the Baptist faith ten years later. Only one family had left the township. One might well argue that the single lingering negative effect wrought by this competition was to give Protestants a public image of quarrelling, disunited sectarians, which might have dissuaded Catholics from allowing a favourable hearing to the preaching of *colporteurs* and missionaries. However, on this score, there were more powerful determining factors at work, such as the growing influence of the Catholic Church and the social pressure that it could bring to bear.

Other aspects of the Protestant community's demographic profile emerge from the 1881 census. Taking both Baptist and Methodist groups together, the average age was similar to that of the previous decade, standing at 23.3 years. Children under the age of 15 represented 42 per cent of the community, and four persons were over the age of 60. Apart from Methodists and Baptists, there were four French-Canadian families affiliated with the Church of England. This particular segment of the community evinced a pattern of closer relations with the village's anglophone community than with other Franco-Protestants; indeed, they had no kinship ties and contracted no marriage alliances with the latter. Their stay in South Ely was very brief: by 1891 all four of these families had left the township. Subsequent censuses, however, always turned up a few individuals of French-Canadian origin who had become Protestant, generally identifying themselves as Anglican after marrying an English-speaking spouse. Although their numbers were small, their presence in South Ely testifies to the attraction for certain French Canadians exerted by Protestantism and English culture in this part of Quebec. In effect, in this township and in many villages of the region, every census listed a number of economically well situated families and individuals, especially those who enjoyed close social relations with anglophones, who had joined the ranks of Protestantism. For these French Canadians, speaking English and attending Anglican, Presbyterian, or Methodist services was a route to employment and business opportunities.[41] Religion thus provided a means for certain French Canadians to secure entry to anglophone society, and more importantly, it enabled them to alter their cultural identity and gradually integrate themselves into this community.

During the last two decades of the nineteenth century the South Ely community continued to age. Between 1881 and 1891, population numbers remained stable, but the average age had increased to 26.7 years, reflecting the fact that within the Baptist group only 34.2 per cent were children under 15, and those over 60 had increased to six individuals. At the end of the nineteenth century the congregation began to diminish in terms of absolute numbers, falling from seventy-six in 1891 to sixty in the 1901 census. The portrait was now of an aging community experiencing a loss of vitality. The average age had climbed to 31.7 years, and only eighteen persons, representing 31 per cent of the congregation, were under 15. Two francophone Protestants, Benjamin Boisvert and his wife, had joined the Seventh-day Adventist church.[42] In addition to this shifting demographic balance, the South Ely community also began to experience religious difficulties, symbolized by troubles in holding on to resident pastors.[43] In order to retain their school, the French Baptists were compelled to admit anglophone pupils and to provide instruction in English.[44] These difficulties were paralleled in the other Franco-Protestant communities of the Eastern Townships. For example, the Baptist parish of Saint-Pie disappeared at the beginning of the twentieth century and reverted to what it had been in the 1840s, a circuit served by itinerant *colporteurs*. After 1910 the Baptist congregation at Roxton Pond also declined, although the churches at Grande-Ligne and Marieville were able to maintain their numbers. The former, according to Dominique Vogt-Raguy, numbered about one hundred "resident" members, which excluded children, and there were fifty-seven Baptists at Marieville.[45] On the Methodist side, a decline in membership was also evident, with Waterloo abandoned in 1885 and Roxton Pond in 1899. French Protestantism, which in the 1860s and 1870s had apparently carved out a niche in Shefford County,[46] had by 1900 entered a terminal decline.

In the final analysis, South Ely's francophone Protestant community always remained numerically small. However, it displayed a cohesiveness and a homogeneity, characteristics that reflected the group's origin in a nucleus of interrelated families. In 1861 the three founding families, the Casgrains, the Commeaus, and the Malboeufs, alone comprised two-thirds of the membership of the community. These households and their direct descendants made up 60 per cent of the group in 1871, 77 per cent in 1881, 59 per cent in 1891, and 55 per cent in 1901. If, throughout this period, a few new families came from neighbouring townships such as Farnham and Granby and from older Baptist communities such as Marieville, South Ely ultimately was unable to renew its numbers through immigration from outside. Conversions of individual Catholics resident in Valcourt parish were extremely rare. South Ely succeeded in maintaining itself only through the number of births. However, the departure of many households to other communities in Quebec and emigration to the United States and Upper Canada/Ontario, particularly after 1871, only accelerated the aging of the community.

MIGRATION AND EMIGRATION

The foregoing analysis has touched upon the issue of migration and emigration in the context of examining the itinerary of the founding families who left the seigneurial lands to establish themselves in the Eastern Townships. As well, in the late nineteenth century many of South Ely's Franco-Protestants left the community to settle elsewhere. But what was the significance of this process for these families?

The reports of the evangelical missionaries who provided religious services at South Ely often mentioned that emigration siphoned church members away from the community.[47] In 1870 the Reverend François-Xavier Smith deplored the exodus of at least forty-five potential members and expressed sadness at the imminent departure of the thirty-five remaining adults: "Our best families and friends have left us; it is truly discouraging," he wrote.[48] But does the census corroborate this bleak assessment? If it actually describes the movements of the South Ely families over a ten-year period, the enumeration does not reveal a phenomenon of the magnitude that Smith described. In 1871 the principal families still resided in the community. Of course, some individuals had left, but globally, the congregation had grown in numbers. How many Protestants actually left the community? Because of the practice that census takers had of assigning married women their husbands' names, rather than their maiden names, we can offer no precise figure of the number of women who left the community, especially after 1881.[49] The data regarding men is more certain. Table 2 reveals the results of a balance sheet of departures of men and male children from the community. As it demonstrates, the census does not reveal a massive exodus of

South Ely's French-speaking Protestants. How, then, to explain the divergence between the missionary's testimony and the census data? Two explanations can be advanced. It is possible that the community contained particularly large numbers for a short period of time during the 1860s. Because this thriving condition occurred in the interval between two censuses, it is impossible to measure the actual extent of out-migration. The other explanation relates to the relative credibility to be assigned to the minister. To what extent did he accurately depict reality? It is possible that to his Anglo-Protestant financial backers he exaggerated the importance of emigration in order to justify his own rather mediocre success in attracting new converts.

While one might debate its actual magnitude, the phenomenon of out-migration was evident in South Ely in the years after 1870, particularly affecting a group of small landowners who in 1871 were recorded as owning less than 60 arpents. This category included George Dexter, the husband of Olive Casgrain, Joseph Commeau junior, Hubert Boucher, and Joseph Bérard. More substantial farmers, such as Isaac Casgrain and Joseph Commeau senior, who each owned 100 arpents, Simon Malboeuf, who had 150, and Jean-Baptiste Dugrenier with 220, undoubtedly felt less pressure to move elsewhere. The situation of these four landowners, especially the latter two, compared favourably with that of many of South Ely's inhabitants. In 1871 roughly half of these owned less than 90 arpents, with the average size of farm listed at 101 arpents.

The individuals and families who left the community all opted for different destinations. Parish registers, Protestant newspapers, and other sources confirm that some stayed in Quebec. For example, Damase Daigneau and Isaïe Malboeuf both settled in Waterloo, the former between 1871 and 1881 and the latter in the following decade.[50] Isabelle Casgrain, who in 1887 became a travelling evangelist and *colporteur* for the Bible Society in Montreal and subsequently for the Grande-Ligne church, also remained within the borders of the province.[51] She had, in the middle of the 1860s, married Nathan Scott, an unskilled labourer, and it was probably to provide for her own and her family's sustenance that she undertook this form of employment. Indeed, the 1871 census listed Nathan Scott as absent, as did the South Ely Baptist register in 1878. In 1881 Isabelle was living in a house adjoining that of the now-elderly Isaac Casgrain, her father. She declared that she was a widow caring for her two sons, John and Louis, fourteen and twelve years old respectively. It is certainly possible that it was the death of her husband which induced her to leave the community and take up missionary work, a task that she fulfilled until her death in 1922. However, the course adopted by Isabelle Casgrain was rather unusual by comparison with that chosen by other members of South Ely's Franco-Protestant community. The community, in fact, produced very few missionaries, or *colporteurs*. In contrast with Baptist missions in other French-Canadian communities, there were no leading families of pastors, missionaries or teachers in South Ely.[52] To my knowledge, only one other inhabitant of South Ely ever engaged in missionary work. This was Samuel Casgrain, Isabelle's nephew, a Bible *colporteur* who in 1903 was working for the Grande-Ligne church. The following year he entered the service of the Methodist church,[53] and he died at Lac-Long in 1910, aged thirty-one.

Rather than settling in Quebec, other inhabitants of South Ely chose to migrate to New England. The widow of Joseph Commeau and a number of his children moved to Middleboro, Massachusetts.[54] The attraction of the industrial cities of the American northeast was also evident in the fate of Hubert Boucher and his family, drawn to Fall River in the 1880s and still residing there at the time of his death in 1906.[55] Other former inhabitants of South Ely seem to have chosen this Massachusetts town. For example, Sarah Rivard, who died a few months before Boucher,[56] was the daughter of Olive Casgrain and George Dexter, who had left during the 1870s. It is possible that at the end of the nineteenth century there was a network linking migrants from South Ely to Fall River, but examples are too few to conclude that there had been a chain migration and long-standing close connections between the two communities. However, the presence in Fall River of François-Xavier Smith, the former pastor at South Ely, undoubtedly drew certain members of his old congregation. In 1873 Smith published an advertisement in *L'Aurore*, which stated, "Those of our Protestant brethren who wish to enjoy, for themselves and their families, the advantages of Protestant worship in the French language can do no better than to look for work in Fall River, where they can expect a warm welcome at the hands of their co-religionists."[57]

The emigration of South Ely's inhabitants continued after 1901. In 1907 a pastor living in New England announced in *L'Aurore* that "many families [have] recently arrived from South Ely."[58] The image of emigration conveyed by these missionary accounts was one of a final, definitive choice in which each departure further drained Quebec's Protestant congregations of their meagre numbers.[59] Once again, however, examination of the census compels some qualification of this assessment. At least five men of South Ely left the community temporarily and then returned, some for a brief sojourn, others permanently. This was the experience of Benjamin Boisvert, who lived in the United States with his family for a few years between 1862 and 1876 and subsequently returned to Ely, where they were still living in 1901. This was also the course chosen by Isaac Casgrain junior, who was absent in 1871 and 1881, but listed in the census in 1891 and 1901. At the time of his return, Isaac was married and had two children. As young adults, Cleophas Malboeuf, Charles Dugrenier, and Joseph Casgrain also left South Ely for a time, before returning. While it is likely that this was a pattern followed by a number of the community's young men, the ten-year interval between censuses prevents a complete assessment of the phenomenon of temporary out-migration. But it is certain that many departures were not definitive: in 1907 Lina Dugrenier, whose family had left South Ely during the 1890s, returned from Manchester, New Hampshire, to marry Adhemar Bourbeau.[60] This example gives credence to the notion that there were continuing contacts between Franco-Protestants of the diaspora and their co-religionists who remained in Quebec.

Once in the United States, many francophone Protestant families joined the ranks of French Baptist churches, while others became Methodists or Congregationalists. The latter denomination was chosen by Catherine Boisvert and Hubert Boucher. Others became members of English-speaking congregations.[61] However, the arrival of these reinforcements from Quebec did not ensure the prosperity of the Protestant congregations of New England, themselves touched by out-migration in the 1880s. Like their Catholic compatriots, many Franco-Protestants were often forced to move from city to city to find work or in the expectation of improving their living conditions.[62] What is certain is that the migrations of French-Canadian Protestant families were more complex than recorded in Protestant missionary accounts. In many respects, their experience resembles that of thousands of French-Canadian Catholics who left at the same time to establish themselves, either temporarily or permanently, in the United States.[63]

CONCLUSION

This essay, based on parish registers, censuses and newspapers, has attempted to trace the life course of three generations of francophone Protestants established at South Ely, a small community in Quebec's Eastern Townships. By using hitherto untapped sources, this particular example has attempted to illuminate the experience of a minority group and to determine to what extent it differed from that of Quebec's Catholics. In this study, missionaries and the clergy have been deliberately left out, as I have wanted above all to highlight the fortunes of the Protestant converts and their families. A number of conclusions emerge from the study.

First, the Protestant community of South Ely was composed of a small nucleus of men and women, converted during the 1850s, who came from the neighbouring seigneurial parishes. The Catholics who lived in the area do not seem to have been particularly receptive to the Protestant message, even though, at first sight, this area of recent colonization was characterized by a denominational diversity and a relatively weak presence on the part of the Catholic clergy, two conditions favourable to evangelism.

Second, this study has demonstrated that family was a determining factor, a key element in understanding the French-Canadian Protestant experience. The South Ely community was formed by three families who were closely related even before their conversion. As we have seen, adoption of Protestantism did not mean, for these converts, the severing of all links with family members. The Malboeufs, Commeaus, and Casgrains all settled in close proximity to their kin, who remained Catholic. Indeed, this study has also shown that, in some cases, Catholics and Protestants lived together in the same household. Without denying that as a result of the conversion to Protestantism of certain families and individuals in rural parishes, these converts would have been subject to a certain amount of social pressure, we can question the extent to which the converts experienced a full-scale ostracization. Once the initial shock of conversion was over, would these families have lived completely cut off from their neighbours and kin who remained in the Catholic faith? This study has cast considerable doubt on this view.

While it must be admitted that the religious choice made by the converts undoubtedly had a decisive impact on their lives and those of their children, it must be recognized that other decisions, especially one to migrate, could have also been motivated by factors other than religion. Indeed, the migratory trajectory of these converts displayed considerable similarity to that of many Catholic families who, in this period, left their home parishes to settle in the Eastern Townships or the United States. Like the Catholics, many French-speaking Protestants departed for a time in search of work opportunities and then returned after a few years, often to marry and farm at Ely. Some of these individuals later moved on after

Table 1
Numbers and average age of French-Canadian Protestants in South Ely,
1861–1901

	1861	1871	1881	1891	1901
French-Canadian Protestant heads of families	9	17	18[2]	15	13
French-Canadian Protestants	55	78	76[2]	76	60
Average age of Protestants	18.9[1]	23.9	23.3	26.7	30.4

1 The 1861 census does not give the actual age of persons enumerated but, rather, the age that they would be on their next birthday.
2 Four Anglican families of French-Canadian origin have been excluded from this table.

Table 2
Balance sheet of numbers of males leaving South Ely from one census to the next

1861–71	1871–81	1881–91	1891–1901
7	23	18	19

Note: These figures exclude all those individuals whose death can be ascertained either from parish registers or from newspaper obituaries.

varying periods of residence. Thus migration and emigration acted as a formative experience for the Protestant community, one full of consequences for its eventual shape and development.

This case study has been based on a close analysis of the experience of a few families, and it does not claim to be an exhaustive treatment of the issues facing Quebec's French-speaking Protestant community in the nineteenth century. However, it has demonstrated that missionary records alone do not allow the historian insight into the complexity of the experience of the converts or their families. Although these sources are extremely rich, they present a generally stereotypical account of the tenacity of the converts and tend to insist on the unique character of their experience. This essay, in the final analysis, insists upon the need for other studies that use the documents and methods of the social historian to go beyond the writings produced by missionaries, which have confined historians to analysis of discourse and studies of representations and perceptions.

NOTES

This essay has been translated by Michael Gauvreau.

1 See Philippe Sylvain, "Aperçu sur le prosélytisme au Canada français de
   1760 à 1860," *Mémoire de la Société Royale du Canada* 55 (1961), section 1:
   65–76; David-Thiery Ruddel, *Le protestantisme français au Québec, 1840–
   1919: 'Images' et témoignages* (Ottawa: Musée national de L'Homme, 1983);
   René Hardy, "Le prosélytisme protestant et la réaction de l'Église
   catholique," dans *Contrôle social et mutation de la culture religieuse au Québec,
   1830–1930* (Montréal: Boréal, 1999), 17–66; Sandrine Bellier, "Le schisme
   de Maskinongé, 1892–1920" (mémoire de maîtrise, études québécoises,
   Université du Québec à Trois-Rivières, 1994); Benoit Lavigne, "Les Canadiens français protestants de la Rive sud de Montréal: Étude socio-
   économique (1839–1871)" (mémoire de maîtrise, histoire, Université de
   Montréal, 1995); Marie-Claude Rocher, "Les protestants francophones au
   Québec au XIXe siècle: Une expérience de communication de l'histoire par
   l'exposition en musée" (mémoire de maîtrise, histoire, Université Laval,
   1993); Dominique Vogt-Raguy, "Les communautés protestantes francophones au Québec, 1834–1925" (thèse de doctorat, histoire, Université
   Michel de Montaigne Bordeaux III, 1996).
2 Many of these works have been published in English. See N. Cyr, *Memoir of
   the Rev. C.H.O. Cote, M.D., with a Memoir of Mrs. M.Y. Cote and a History of the
   Grande Ligne Mission, Canada East* (Philadelphia: American Baptist Publication Society, 1853); Amand Parent, *The Life of Rev. Amand Parent, the first
   French-Canadian Ordained by the Methodist Church* (Toronto: William Briggs,
   1887); A.A. Ayers, *A Historical Sketch of the Grande-Ligne Mission* (n.p., 1898).
3 Many of them were the children or grandchildren of the first converts, and
   their writings aimed to perpetuate the memory of the evangelists. See
   R.-P. Duclos, *Histoire du protestantisme français au Canada et aux États-Unis,*
   2 vols. (Montréal: Librairie evangélique, 1913); Paul Villard, *Up to the Light:
   The Story of French Protestantism in Canada* (Toronto: Ryerson Press, 1928).
4 I have consulted copies of Protestant registers held at the Archives Nationales du Québec à Montréal (ANQM, specifically those of South Ely
   (1878–79), Grande-Ligne (1839–99), Marieville (1853–73), Saint-Pie (1845–
   73), and Roxton (1871–99). Unfortunately, these records do not cover the
   entire period in question, although they remain extremely useful.
5 It should be noted in this context that both Bellier, "Le schisme de
   Maskinongé," and Lavigne, "Les Canadiens français protestants," have
   used census data and parish registers in their work.
6 On the beginnings of Protestant proselytization, see Hardy, "Le prosélytisme protestant"; Lavigne, "Les Canadiens français protestants"; et
   Vogt-Raguy, "Les communautés."

7 On the process of settlement and religious life in the Eastern Townships, consult Jean-Pierre Kesteman, Peter Southam, and Diane Saint-Pierre, *Histoire des Cantons de l'Est* (Ste Foy: Les Presses de l'Université Laval/IQRC, 1998); and Françoise Noël, *Competing for Souls: Missionary Activity and Settlement in the Eastern Townships, 1784–1851* (Sherbrooke: Université de Sherbrooke, 1988).

8 René Hardy, "La Rébellion de 1837–1838 et l'essor du protestantisme canadien-français," *Revue d'histoire de l'Amérique française* 29 (septembre 1975): n105.

9 *L'Aurore*, 25 février 1886, 4. The newspaper offered a similarly rosy assessment of the future prospects of this group: it predicted that in 1916 there would be 300,000 francophone Protestants in America, in a total francophone population of 4 million; for 1951 it raised the number of French Protestants in a total French-speaking population of 8 million; and for 1985 it assured its reader that there would be 16 million French Protestants and that there would be "no place for any Catholics" (*aurait plus de place pour un seul catholique*).

10 *Maskinongé: Lettres de deux prêtres, d'un avocat, et d'une nonne, et les réponses à ces lettres par des missionnaires protestants* (Montréal: Société missionnaire de la Mission de la Grande-Ligne, 1892), 86.

11 Kesteman, Southam and Saint-Pierre, *Histoire*, 113.

12 Manuscript census of 1831.

13 Manuscript census of 1851. These figures are also provided in Albert Gravel, *À travers les cantons de Stukely, Shefford et Ely* (Sherbrooke: n.p., 1967), 23.

14 The date of arrival of these families has been determined from the Protestant registers of Grande-Ligne, which record the places of residence of those parents who sought to register their newborn children. It should be noted that the church members of Grande-Ligne did not baptize infant children.

15 ANQM, Registre de la paroisse catholique de Saint-Césaire. The latest date at which they appeared in Catholic registers is 29 January 1852.

16 The history of these families has been reconstituted from the manuscript census of 1851 and the Catholic registers of the parishes of Saint-Mathias and Saint-Césaire.

17 Archives de l'Évêché de Saint-Hyacinthe (AESH), Abbé Isidore Desnoyers, "Histoire de la paroisse de L'Ange Gardien" (manuscript account written ca. 1885).

18 Grande-Ligne road must not be confused with the Grande-Ligne that gave its name to the French Baptist mission. These are two different places located many kilometres apart.

19 AESH, Desnoyers, "Histoire de la paroisse de L'Ange Gardien," 21: "dépenses immenses qu'il faudrait faire pour établir ce chemin et construire les ponts"; "inutile, non avenue."

20 AESH, XVII, c. 18, J.-A. Provençal à Mgr Prince, 31 janvier 1853: "Je crains quelques excès de la part de ces gens-là."

21 AESH, XVII, c. 18, J.-A. Singer à Mgr. Prince, 5 août 1853: "D'après ce que nous voyons ... et ce que nous entendons, nous éprouvons justement de vives craintes pour l'avenir de ces pauvres gens. L'esprit qui les anime ... et les efforts que l'on fait pour leur perte, tout nous inquiète et nous alarme. ... Deux fois par semaine, un de ces misérables imposteurs Suisses visite une partie des habitants à la montagne et il invite tous les Canadiens de l'endroit à ses meetings, afin de les gagner dans son parti. ... Nous croyons donc, dans la sincérité de notre coeur, que l'érection de deux églises serait le moyen de remédier au mal et de conserver la foi de nos chers Canadiens."

22 "Nécrologie d'Isabelle Malboeuf," L'Aurore, 19 mars 1898, 13; "Nécrologie de Flavie Commeau," L'Aurore, 27 septembre 1902, 11.

23 "Nécrologie de Flavie Commeau," 11: "au début du protestantisme dans cet endroit."

24 On the examples cited above, see C. Hudon, "Le prêtre, le ministre et l'apostat: Les stratégies pastorales face au protestantisme canadien-français au xixe siècle," Études d'histoire religieuse, 1995, 85–6.

25 Bellier, "Le schisme."

26 Vogt-Raguy, "Les communautés," 379–80.

27 Ibid., 348: "ces conversions ne se [firent] pas par conviction, mais par rejet pour braver l'autorité du prêtre et s'opposer avec éclat à ses décisions."

28 Alphonse-Raymond Bombardier, Valcourt et sa région avant le vingtième siècle (n.p., 1976), 40, 76.

29 AESH, Registre catholique des baptêmes, des mariages et des sépultures de Saint-Joseph-d'Ely (Valcourt).

30 AESH, Desnoyers, "Histoire de la paroisse de L'Ange Gardien," 33.

31 On the importance of chain migration and the role of kin networks, consult France Gagnon, "Parenté et migration: Le cas des Canadiens français à Montréal entre 1845 et 1875," Canadian Historical Association/Société historique du Canada, Historical Papers/Communications historiques, 1988, 63–85.

32 See, for example, Cyr, Memoir. See also the many conversion narratives contained in missionary reports and Protestant newspapers.

33 See, among others, Vogt-Raguy, "Les communautés," 345.

34 The reconstruction of these families has been based on manuscript censuses, Protestant parish registers, and L'Aurore.

35 L'Aurore, 19 mars 1898, 13: "par ses enfants, Mme Malboeuf était unie avec toutes les familles de la congrégation. Elle était comme une mère en Israel."

36 Ibid., 5 mai 1887, 4.

37 Ibid., 30 mars 1906, 9.

38 One Protestant source, written a little later than the period covered in this study, described the difficulties experienced by some French-Canadian

Protestants in finding a spouse. See ANQM, United Church of Canada, Personal Papers, C.E. Amaron 5/AMA/9, Camille Chazeaud to C.E. Amaron, 18 septembre 1911.

39 Vogt-Raguy, "Les communautés," 136.

40 Ibid., 272.

41 See C. Hudon, *Prêtres et fidèles dans le diocèse de Saint-Hyacinthe, 1820–1875* (Sillery: Septentrion, 1996), 40–1.

42 On the origins of Millerism and Seventh-day Adventism in the Eastern Townships, see Denis Fortin, " 'The World Turned Upside Down': Millerism in the Eastern Townships, 1835–1845," *Revue d'études des Cantons de l'Est* 11 (automne 1997): 39–59.

43 Vogt-Raguy, "Les communautés," 596–7.

44 Ibid., 602.

45 Ibid., 606; see also the tables in appendices 30–3 of this thesis.

46 Lavigne, "Les Canadiens français protestants," 80.

47 *The Register of the Evangelical Society of la Grande-Ligne*, March 1864, 7.

48 Ibid., March 1870, 2.

49 Before 1881 many women were enumerated under their maiden names, but after 1881 they were listed under their husband's names. The marriage acts contained in Protestant registers enable the identification of some wives, but efforts to trace them through this source have been fruitless. Some of the marriage acts cannot be located.

50 For the purposes of this study, I have consulted the manuscript census records not only for South Ely but also for Waterloo, Granby, North Ely, Roxton Falls, and Roxton Pond.

51 Vogt-Raguy, "Les communautés," appendix 25.

52 Ibid., 470.

53 Ibid., appendix 25.

54 *L'Aurore*, 17 septembre 1902, 11.

55 Ibid., 15 mars 1907, 7.

56 Ibid.

57 Ibid., 6 juin 1873: "Ceux de nos frères protestants qui désirent jouir pour eux-mêmes et pour leurs familles, des avantages d'un culte protestant en langue française, ne pourront faire mieux que de chercher l'ouvrage dans Fall River où ils auraient un bon accueil de la part de leurs coreligionnaires." At this time, the preaching of the Fall River pastor was attended by about sixty or seventy people. François-Xavier Smith retired from the ministry in 1898, after a career of forty-nine years in the cause of evangelism.

58 *L'Aurore*, 11 janvier 1907: "plusieurs familles [étaient] dernièrement arrivées de South Ely."

59 On this subject, see Vogt-Raguy, "Les communautés," 364.

60 *L'Aurore*, 3 décembre 1907.

61 *L'Aurore* contains many personal accounts of this process.

62 On the geographical mobility of Franco-Americans, see Yves Roby, *Les Franco-Américains de la Nouvelle-Angleterre, 1776–1930* (Sillery: Septentrion, 1990), 77–8. On francophone Protestants, see the missionary accounts and the obituary notices in *L'Aurore*.
63 See Bruno Ramirez, *On the Move: French-Canadian and Italian Migrants in the North Atlantic Economy, 1860–1914* (Toronto: McClelland and Stewart, 1991).

Contested Family: Navigating Kin and Culture in Protestant Missions to the Tsimshian, 1857–1896

SUSAN NEYLAN

The family was a key tool and target of Protestant missionaries who worked among the aboriginal peoples of the North Pacific Coast during the second half of the nineteenth century.[1] Combining notions of the family as the foundation of Christianity society with the contemporary vision of it as a refuge from the influences of industrial capitalism and secularism, missionaries to British Columbia attempted to remake the Aboriginal family according to Western ideals. As a concept, however, the family was a contested one, infused with very different meanings by Euro-Canadian missionary and Tsimshian.[2] Intricately and intimately connected to social status, to property and resource rights, and even to spiritual power itself, Tsimshian definitions of the family were both challenged and utilized by Euro-Canadian and Native missionaries for the purposes of proselytization. This essay is a brief exploration of the family as a contested site in the religious encounter between Native and missionary. Using discursive and practical modes to challenge notions of the family, missionaries exalted the role of the Native Christian family in the colonial discourse, attempted to alter marriage customs among Tsimshian converts, and introduced a patrilineal naming system. Similarly, the Tsimshian had their own agendas and used the emerging mission and church organizations to maintain older clan and village relations and, to some extent, traditional spiritual leadership.

Christian missionization of British Columbia's First Nations began in the mid-nineteenth century. Much of the historiography has defined it as an imposed, colonial process that sought to utterly transform

Native cultures, societies, and world views.[3] However, this perspective undermines the extent to which missionization was a process in which Native peoples determined outcomes too. Christianity is an aspect of Native history, not simply a force acting upon it. Accordingly, Native Christianization is more accurately understood as a hegemonic experience.[4] Just as colonial forces were heterogeneous, so the myriad of responses to those forces cannot be encapsulated by a single term such as "resistance" or "colonized." Colonial successes were never total or uncontested.[5] They begin with a notion, as Raymond Williams suggests, of domination rather than dominance – in other words, as an ongoing process and a lived experience.[6] In this respect, colonial hegemony, including missionization, does not follow a top-down model of social control. The resulting forged relationship between colonizer and colonized was dialogic – a "clearing out of a space of mutual intelligibility," "constant negotiation and change of the meaning elements in discourse"– but not necessarily a mutually beneficial one.[7]

First Nations actively took part in missions and shaped and defined the processes of their own Christianization, but they could not entirely direct or control them. Christianity necessitated a reordering of one's sense of self and subsequent relationship with one's community. Yet the Christian idea of spiritual power derived through the transformative experience was not new to the Tsimshian. It resonated with conventional Tsimshian notions of power acquisition. Even after missionization, the Tsimshian sense of self was never predicated on Christian or colonial culture alone. For Tsimshian and Euro-Canadian alike, the family was a key site in the struggle for cultural domination during the mission era, as the following examples will demonstrate. Navigating these new religious identities in the mission context reveals colonial hegemony at work.

TSIMSHIAN FAMILY AND SPIRITUAL POWER

The region of the North Pacific Coast of British Columbia, including the Lower Nass and Skeena River watersheds, was a socio-economic and cultural zone in the Aboriginal or pre-European period and the homeland of approximately 10–12,000 Tsimshianic-speaking peoples (divided into three or four major cultural-linguistic groups: Coast and Southern Tsimshian, Nisga'a, and Gitxsan) for thousands of years prior to the arrival of Europeans.[8] Tsimshianic societies were hierarchical, and the maintenance of authority and power depended an extensive system of trade, exchange, and redistribution of material resources, which frequently extended over long distances and even outside the immediate North Coast area. Scholars often describe the continued importance of the region after the arrival of Europeans in the eighteenth century for these same reasons. The peoples of this area remained intermediaries in a trade that came to include Europeans. This intensive and central involvement in trade facilitated variety and cross-cultural understanding and fostered the adaptive growth of their own traditions. When new religious ideas accompanied the arrival of various Protestant denominations in the 1850s and 1860s, the Tsimshian, Nisga'a, and Gitksan were geographically situated in the middle of the mission field and subsequently involved in Christian evangelism, dominating the dissemination of information concerning Christianity.

The Tsimshian concept of family was a matrilineal collective that resided in a single or cluster of longhouses, rather than the patrilineal and patriarchal nuclear family idealized by missionaries. Furthermore, familial relations have broad application and significance in Tsimshian culture, manifested in a regional as well as in localized forms because of a highly developed clan, crest, and house system among all Tsimshianic-speaking nations. The Coast Tsimshian clan system, part of a much larger and centuries-old international kinship system, is represented by two sets of paired crests (*pteex*), each with reciprocal obligations to their counterpart in the pair: Killerwhale (called locally Blackfish) Wolf (*Gispwudwada/Laxgibuu*), and Raven/Eagle (*Ganhada/Laxsgiik*). Clan membership is determined matrilineally and represents a shared ancestry, regardless of blood kinship. Each clan is further subdivided into various ranked crests, which are composed of clusterings of groups that share a common place of origin. This structure accounts for the existence of subsidiary crests within each clan and the ranked positions of each within the broad Tsimshian classes (royalty, nobility, commoner, and slave).[9]

The Tsimshian organize themselves by household within these larger familial groupings. Hence the core social unit of the Tsimshian – in essence, *the family* – is the house, representing a membership, a territory, and a repository, as well as a building.[10] In the Coast Tsimshian language (*Sm'algyax*) the same word, *walp* or *waap*, used for family also means house or dwelling.[11] The Tsimshian house (*walp*) was symbolically a box or container filled with food, wealth, and "real" people. However, not all people residing in the longhouse were considered family members. For example, slaves existed outside the social structure, except as property or labour within a particular lineage. As Margaret Seguin Anderson explains, "Lineage members were not 'in a waab'; they *were* the *waab* ... Becoming 'real' depended on lifelong participation in the property distributions of the *yaokw* [*yaawk*, or Tsimshian potlatch]. The 'members' of a *waab* were actually the ranked names, not the individuals who filled the names at any point in time."[12] This collection of immortal names is passed through the matriline, and the house chief assumes the leading name, a social system that remains in place today. The Tsimshian potlatch (*yaawk*) or feast, in which names and positions are assumed and given authority through public recognition, "empties" the house (*walp*) as it simultaneously fills it through the incarnation of new name-holders.[13] Hence the matrilineal household was the key component in Tsimshian social structure, around which all resource use, production, consumption, political power, property relations, and material life revolved. Each conjugal unit existed only as part of the collective group, which worked for the benefit of all members and where lineage heads or chiefs demanded absolute loyalty.[14]

Furthermore, in pre-Christian Tsimshian culture, certain types of spiritual power and religious leadership were intimately linked to this social system of a matrilineal household. The acquisition of spiritual power and protection was requisite for all free Tsimshian individuals.[15] Guardian helpers were important to Tsimshian culture and were accessed by individuals to assist them in any and all aspects of their daily lives. However, aside from shamanic encounters and personal vision quests, most powers were obtained or consulted through a much more formal, ritualized structure, where hereditary sources were paramount. This "formalized" spiritual leadership in Tsimshian culture was wielded by chiefs (*smhalaayt*) and shamans (*swansk halaayt*).[16] First contact with supernatural powers took place during childhood, through a series of dances and ceremonies at which children received their first "power name." These powers were similar to crests in that they remained within the matrilineage and were inherited. At the time of contact with Europeans, membership of all high-ranking Tsimshian in at least one of the four dancing or secret societies (*wut'aahalaayt*) was also socially mandatory and included components of power acquisition.

Of the two basic types of specialist spiritual power available to men and women in Tsimshian society – chiefly and shamanic – the former was closely linked to kinship. Chiefly power could be activated by particular chiefs who directly received power and "threw" it into others.[17] The fact that chiefs and their powers were the basis of Tsimshian social organization would have significant implications for the roles they would assume after mission Christianity appeared. Chiefs "put on" names or crests and mainly utilized spiritual powers in the service of their house (*walp*).[18] The power names they received as recognition of this spiritual service thus belonged to the house. In this capacity, empowerment of chiefs and, in turn, all whom they initiated in throwing ceremonies or secret societies was contingent upon which gifts of power they were entitled to receive from their house or lineage or because of their social rank. In this respect, spirituality and the family were interconnected in pre-Christian Tsimshian culture.

Given that access to power was largely placed in the hands of the house and clan chiefs, the personal quest to gain assistance or a guardian spirit and the lifelong process of shamanic power acquisition were left firmly outside the kin-group framework.[19] While shamanic powers could be accessed anytime (or whenever contacted by non-human helpers), the chiefs' roles as religious leaders were limited to the winter months. The seasonal movements from summer to winter village locations were paralleled by a shift from an economic to a spiritual focus. Accordingly, during the summer months chiefs were known as *smgigyet*, ("real people"), but in the winter they became *smhalaayt* ("real *halaayt*") through their function as priests.[20] The implications for the reception of Christian power within this religious system of passive and active encounters with power were far-reaching. Conversion to Protestant Christianity, especially the type offered by evangelical denominations, broadened the possibilities of transformative experience to more people, who were neither shamans nor *smhalaayt*. Paradoxically, it allowed the empowered shamans and chiefs potentially another mode of retaining their roles of spiritual leadership and specialization, something that historically was more true for chiefs than for shamans.

In the mid-nineteenth century, Christian missionaries sought to alter this complex system by attempting to replace both the social structure and the religious culture of the Tsimshianic nations. The reformulation of the family became the missionaries' key tool to accomplish this goal. For the Euro-Canadian missionary, the nuclear family not only represented the ideal social unit necessarily to provide stability in the emergent Christian community, but it also reflected the moral order they sought to enforce through mechanisms of discipline, social control, and cultural replacement. Missionaries failed to recognize, however, that the Tsimshian would use Christian power to reinforce their age-old concept of the family. When chiefs acquired a new power through their conversion to Christianity, it reflected on the status of the entire house (*walp*). Family members frequently followed their chiefs in becoming Christians in support of this spiritual power acquisition, while missionaries preferred to believe mass conversions were due to their own persuasiveness.

MISSIONS TO THE TSIMSHIAN

The Coast Tsimshian word for European or Caucasian is k'amsiiwa, which means "driftwood."[21] Secular interests of the interior fur trade in the nineteenth century brought Christian beliefs and instructors into the region in a more sustained way than had the fleeting contacts of the earlier naval explorers and the coastal ship-to-shore maritime fur trade of the eighteenth century. Only then did the driftwood begin piling up on Tsimshian shores. Despite some interest in the North Coast as a potential missionary field in the early nineteenth century, it was not until the 1850s that permanent Protestant mission work began directly in Tsimshian territory.

William Duncan was one of British Columbia's best-known missionaries to First Nations peoples. A lay preacher sponsored by the Church Missionary Society (CMS), he established the first Anglican mission among the Tsimshian at the Hudson's Bay Company's Fort Simpson in 1857. Five years later he moved to the recently abandoned Tsimshian site of Metlakatla, taking with him about fifty Native converts. Duncan's intention was to isolate Native Christians not only from their "traditional" culture but also from the negative influences of Euro-Canadian settlements. From 1862 until 1887 Metlakatla, with a population of over nine hundred Tsimshian Christians and other First Nations people from the region, encouraged nothing short of a sweeping reformation of Tsimshian society.[22] As an industrial endeavour, it was designed to promote Victorian "progress" and the merits of European civilization. Victorian-style homes, gardens, and a seawall attempted to convert Tsimshian space as well as souls. Both as a model of practice and as a physical base from which to launch new missionary endeavours and regular itinerant circuits, Metlakatla lay at the heart of Anglican activity for the region, and after 1878 it became the centre of the Diocese of Caledonia. Anglican missions at Kincolith, Aiyansh, Kitwanga, Kitwancool, Hazelton, and Kitkatla emerged by the end of the nineteenth century to attend Tsimshian, Nisga'a, and Gitxsan Christians.

Other Protestant groups found acceptance among the Tsimshian and likewise expanded mission work throughout the entire North Coast region. The high-ranking and chiefly Tsimshian family of Elizabeth "Diex" Lawson (Diiks) and her son and daughter-in-law, Alfred and Mary Catherine "Kate" Dudoward, established Methodism among the Tsimshian. Originally converted to the Methodist church in Victoria, this family carried its new faith home to Fort Simpson. For several years the Dudowards conducted church services of their own and were instrumental in securing a permanent

Methodist mission for Fort Simpson in 1874. The Reverend Thomas Crosby and his wife, Emma Crosby (née Douse), arrived that year, and for the next twenty-five years they were key figures in the spread of Methodist missions to coastal communities and to villages along the Nass and Skeena Rivers. The church also made extensive use of Native missionaries, catechists, and mission assistants, as Euro-Canadian mission workers were always in short supply. By the close of the century Methodist missions were thriving at Fort Simpson (renamed Port Simpson in 1880), Greenville (Laxgalts'ap), Port Essington, Kitamaat, Kispiox, and Kitseguecla.

The introduction of the Salvation Army among the Tsimshian followed a similar pattern as the establishment of Methodism. By 1890 Native peoples had converted to this variant of evangelical Christianity in Victoria and established their own version of the Army on the North Coast. Official Salvation Army involvement did not begin until 1896, when a representative was sent to Port Simpson. By the end of the nineteenth century the Army had also founded missions at Metlakatla and Port Essington and established a new village, Glen Vowell, as its centre of operations in the region.

With a wide variety of not only denominations but variations within each mission (e.g., the Anglican church had a Church Army and Red and White Cross groups; and the Methodists had Epworth Leagues and Bands of Christian Workers) competing for Tsimshian souls, Tsimshian Christians had a choice in Christian forms, which gave them greater ability to retain those aspects of their pre-Christian cultures that they felt were vital. The presence of the Roman Catholics in Gitksan-Wet'suwet'en territory presented competition for Protestant missions that were active on the Upper Skeena River. While Hazelton and Moricetown were major Catholic mission sites, the former itself becoming an important distribution centre following the Omineca gold rush (1870s), nearby New Kitseguecla, Meanskinisht (Cedarvale), and Glen Vowell were new villages established later and under Protestant influence.[23]

MISSIONARIES AND THE RECONCEPTUALIZATION OF THE TSIMSHIAN FAMILY

The vision of the family that Euro-Canadian missionaries encouraged their Tsimshian converts to adopt was predicated on the belief that a Christian society could only be built on and sustained by a stable, nuclear family. This concept is particularly obvious in the missionary discourse about their work. Missionaries deemed the nuclear family household the "natural" and God-given foundation of any civil society, and hence it became the crucial site in which devoted Christians and "civilized Indians" were to be made. In other words, missionaries thought that their program of conversion and cultural replacement would be most effectively achieved at the level of the family, which was also the social unit they believed could be most easily controlled and manipulated.

For the majority of Euro-Canadian missionaries, only church-sanctioned matrimony and the patriarchal nuclear family formed the true moral and social centre of any Christian community. This conceptualization of the family also delineated the ideal division of labour between the sexes, which placed adult male Tsimshian in the role of household heads and family breadwinners, while Tsimshian women were relegated to the private realm of home and motherhood. One missionary identified some of the key traits associated with male roles in the new mission order as being as hard work, industry, respectability, and "civilized" living. Writing about the famous Tsimshian chief Paul Ligeex after his conversion to Christianity, he noted, "He is industrious, and gains a good livelihood, and lives in a comfortable house of his own building."[24] Archetypal Native catechists appear through the Northwest Coast mission propaganda to both celebrate and promote missionary ideals of loyalty, duty, obedience, and leadership in their male converts. Native women who became Christians were conceptualized according to Victorian models of femininity and domestic and maternal duty, and as morally and sexually vulnerable beings.[25] Young female converts attending the industrial school at Metlakatla were described by the visiting Anglican bishop as "devout," "well-behaved," and "tender plants," whom the missionary "guards ... from too early or ill-advised exposure to the blasts and storms of the voyages of life."[26] Upon marriage, Native women's schooling ceased, and they assumed their role as wives and especially as "the future mothers of a new generation."[27] These gender roles proscribed by Euro-Canadians in the missionary discourse were, of course, also strongly shaped by the broad image of the missionary's "Indian" and the tendency to portray Native culture in opposition to supposedly "superior" mission life.[28]

Two significant post-contact challenges to "traditional" Tsimshian culture brought on by intensive missionization which directly threatened Tsimshian concepts of the family were the introduction of Western patriarchy and patrilineage and the nature of Christian power acquisition.[29] First, missionaries encouraged a masculinization of all social relations. They expected a patrilineal genealogy to replace the matrilineal clan system. This change involved substantiating Christian baptismal surnames following the male line of families. The social foundation of Christian Tsimshian society was encouraged to be a patriarchal nuclear family. Adherence to different notions of the "family" among First Nations proved to be problematic for Euro-Canadians because these did not conform to Victorian definitions. Membership in specific Christian denominations or church organizations of Christianity were conceptualized by missionaries as an alternative to matrilineal clan affiliation. Clearly, many Euro-Canadians did not understand how the Tsimshian system of semi-moieties functioned, particularly with respect to how nuclear families were divided among two clans, whereby husbands and wives were always from different crests, and children adopted the clan affiliation of their mother. Under the new church membership model, missionaries hoped that entire families would belong to the same congregation. Another patriarchal aspect of missionary intent towards Tsimshian Christian culture was that many positions of leadership and authority were male-dominated. While female Christians could become teachers, interpreters, and lay leaders within the mission or, in the one exceptional case, officers of the Salvation Army, the majority of spiritual leaders were, at least nominally, men.

Secondly, under the missionary model of a Christianized Tsimshian culture, powers were not to be inherited. According to missionaries, there was only one true source of spiritual power (the Christian God), and individuals did not travel interdimensionally or acquire Christian power by having it thrown into them by a chief-priest (*smhalaayt*). Christian power was awakened by God, and individuals were "saved" through Christ. The pinnacle of spiritual power could not be achieved in life and was assured only after death, when all "deserving" Christian souls would "dwell in the house of the Lord for ever." This notion was at variance with the fundamental Tsimshian belief that individuals acquired powers throughout their lifetime to realize their potential of becoming more than human. Likewise, Christian power was not disseminated and activated through *yaawk* (potlatch), *adawx* (sacred house and crest histories), or *naxnox* ("wonders") performances. Instead, key church rituals marked the acquisition of Christian spirituality and demarcated the individual's position within the church (e.g., baptism, confession/testimony, confirmation, or communion). This patriarchal and mission-centric conception of religion had profound implications for Tsimshian families and their roles in society.

Even the Euro-Canadian perceptions of mission work itself stressed the significance of family structure. A scholar of Christian colonialism, Nicholas Thomas, discusses the contradictory character of European missionary objectives as defined in the colonial discourse in terms of familial hierarchy.[30] His ideas serve to demonstrate how concepts of the family were interwoven into mission leadership and can, I believe, be applied to the Tsimshian experience. Thomas argues that non-Native missionaries aimed to distance, hierarchize, and incorporate indigenous groups through their mission work. This process was manifested in both the actions of missionaries in the field and the rhetoric they produced describing their mission work. First, distance was established between the European missionary and his or her charges through an emphasis on difference and the creation of an apparent boundary between indigenous culture and Western culture.[31] This dichotomy was universally described in the colonial discourse as one between "savagery" and "civilization." Consequently, much of the written record has encouraged the writing of mission histories built on Euro-Canadian categories and criteria that emphasized a contrast between what they viewed as opposites – Native and Christian – the "before" and "after" conversion story so popular throughout missionary propaganda. Next, missionaries tried to define and enforce a social hierarchy in the mission environment itself to facilitate conversion to Christianity, but in a way that reflected their perceived cultural hierarchy, in which Western societies were deemed superior to Native ones. Lastly, they attempted incorporate the "other" by transforming their followers from "Natives" into "Christians." One strategy that missionaries employed to achieve these goals was to mimic the structure of the family by representing themselves as adult parents of Native "children." Indeed, Thomas concludes "that missionary work employed and enacted the notions of infantalization and quasi-familial hierarchy in a far more thorough way than any other colonial project: The construction of difference in terms of familial relation was not a static condition but articulated with an attempt to implement social change on the colonial periphery in a particular way."[32] As parental figures, European missionaries viewed themselves as natural supervisors for Native children (a category that included adults and children alike), and through this unequal relationship, they empowered themselves as agents of change.[33]

Thomas's notion of the uses of missionary paternal authority is applicable to the North Pacific Coast of British Columbia. It was manifested in the duties that Protestant missionaries assumed in the daily functioning of the mission villages, roles that extended far beyond those of religious leader and instructor. Missionaries were social engineers, work supervisors, teachers, and disciplinarians who justified their authority on the grounds that their followers were "child like" and required parental guidance. The generational aspect of the "before" and "after" conversion story was staged in photographs portraying mission-raised "civilized" Native children alongside their still "heathen" parents. It is also seen in the rationale behind the introduction of residential schools for First Nations children. Ideally, the Euro-Canadian missionary or teacher assumed the role of parental authority over Native children. In practice, however, many of these missionary "parents" were anything but loving and nurturing. Over the long term, the residential school system was destructively effective at creating dysfunctional Tsimshian families and it scarred generations of Aboriginal Canadians.[34]

Backing the missionaries' religious and social reforms was colonial authority. The mission village itself functioned as a microcosm of the huge plethora of colonial infrastructures that weighed heavily upon the province's First Nations after British Columbia joined Canada in 1871, including the Indian Act, reserve allotments, and a Euro-Canadian education system. The body of late-nineteenth-century legislation known as the Indian Act, which pervasively governed the lives of Aboriginal peoples within Canada (and continues to do so), mirrored this familial hierarchy through laws that deemed all Natives societies still in their infancy and designated Native individuals as minors and wards of the state. Moreover, this legislation had built into it gender discrimination that deprived Aboriginal women of their "Indian" status (and that of their child) if they married a man who was not a status Indian.[35] This rule had potentially devastating effects on matrilineal social structures, especially over the long term.

A VIEW FROM THE MISSION FIELD
ON THE IMPORTANCE OF FAMILY

Clearly, the view from the mission field on the family reveals specific missionary interests and agendas. A few examples of the contested nature of the family under missionization to the Tsimshian will serve to highlight how both Natives and non-Natives defined the concept. Missionaries created a quasi-familial hierarchy whereby they attempted to assume the role as family patriarch. They also saw the structure of the family as important to the conversion of Native peoples and to the stability of Native Christian villages. The Aboriginal family (like its Euro-Canadian counterpart) was (and is) the smallest unit of society, and thus the base from which the missionary could build up a new social order. As Anglican bishop George Hills wrote in 1860, observing the true potential for salvation through mission work among British Columbia's Aboriginal people, "they are fallen from nature. Their habits are unnatural & it is Christian civilization which alone can bring them back to true nature & to teach them to live for the true object of human existence & to show forth the true graces of cultured & redeemed manhood."[36] The "true graces of cultured & redeemed manhood" were precisely what the missionaries believed could be accomplished through their programs of "civilizing," "uplifting," and "saving." Christianity may have been spread through encounters with "other" religious specialists (e.g., indigenous shamans and prophets who utilized "traditional" and Christian sources of power) and through popular revivals, but it had always been maintained at the family level, regardless of how the family was defined.

Therefore missionaries were acutely aware of the importance of kinship in the process of change they sought to bring about. They were attuned to how the family of an individual Native Christian responded to the conversion of one of her or his members. They often used narratives of the reaction of Native families to converts as a gauge to measure the success or failure of their missions. For example, after witnessing a recent convert's confession at baptism, Hills commented: "Nayahk, the wife of Lipplighcumlee, a sorcerer ... suffered much from the mockery of her husband. At her earnest demand he gave up devilry. Under eighteen months regular instruction. Been consistent in the midst of opposition; adhered to the Mission when many were against. Has a blessing of her family, all of whom have renounced heathenism. Her husband, the sorcerer, laments his past life, and would be the first to put his foot upon the evil system."[37] Here one family represents both the impediment to conversion (i.e., the shaman's mockery, the environment of an unconverted community) and the perseverance and eventual triumph of the faithful (i.e., Nayahk convinced her husband to convert; her family remained supportive). Another clergyman, the Reverend R. Dundas, wrote of hearing an elderly Native woman's testimony: "This woman, who cannot be less than fifty, has had no instruction, save what she has heard in the church. It has come chiefly from her own daughter of fifteen, who is one of the Mission-house inmates, and has been with Mr. Duncan for four years, his best and most promising young convert. She has been baptized by the Bishop, and has now been the instructoress of her parents, both of whom will be baptized by me tomorrow."[38] Thus the influence of family clearly had the potential to be the Euro-Canadian missionary's greatest ally.

Missionaries also saw the family as their most effective tool in spreading the gospel beyond the mission's reach and maintaining Christianity on the North Coast. Family connections would remain important after individuals became particularly devout members of the church and active missionaries themselves. Many of the best-known Native mission workers on the North Coast were related by blood or marriage as well as denominational affiliation. Hence entire families became leaders of the church, not simply individuals. Methodist Native missionaries provide good examples of this phenomenon. Arthur Wellington Clah was the uncle of the Reverend William Henry Pierce (through adoption) and Franz Boas's collaborator, Henry W. Tate, and all were noted Christians within their communities. The Haida mission family of Amos (Gedanst) and Agnes Russ and their son-in-law, the Reverend Peter Kelly, likewise, used family connections to promote Christianity.[39] However, the best example of the significance of family, both as a mission strategy and as a story exploited in the missionary discourse as a triumph of Christian hegemony, is the history of the founding of the Methodist mission on the North Coast by the Tsimshian Dudoward family.

Thomas Crosby recounts with pride in several publications, the so-called Great Revival experienced by British Columbia's coastal First Nations in the 1860s and 1870s.[40] On the North Coast this event was repeatedly the result of the initiative of Native families. The founding of the Methodist mission at Fort Simpson in 1874 figures prominently in the Euro-Canadian missionary discourse as an example of the role of family evangelization and the importance of the conversion of high-ranking families to the work of Christianization. In March 1873 in Victoria an evangelical revival occurred that led to the conversion of many First Nations people from all over the province, including a number of Tsimshian, Nisga'a, Heiltsuk, and Haida people from the North Coast area. It began in a mission hall that had been made over from an old barroom. The recently converted disseminated Christian teachings rapidly. Missionary books and pamphlets are littered with references to the story of the barroom mission and the central role played by its Native converts in spreading Christianity throughout the colony/province.

The principal figures in this narrative were the Coast Tsimshian woman Diex (Diiks), or Mrs Elizabeth Lawson, whom the Reverend C.M. Tate called "the mother of Methodism among the Tsimpshean tribes," and her son, Alfred Dudoward.[41]

On the night of her conversion she commenced to pray for her son, Alfred Dudoire [Dudoward], one of the chiefs at Port Simpson, six hundred miles north. In three weeks he arrived in Victoria in a large war canoe capable of carrying three or four tons. He was not at all pleased with the state of affairs, and set about testing the new converts, but in the operation he himself was converted, and the next morning wanted to take brother Tate in his canoe, and start home to tell his people the glad tidings of salvation. But, as Brother Tate could not leave the work, he advised Alfred to go himself, which he did, taking some of the new converts with him, and instead of carrying a cargo of rum, which he intended, he took Bibles and hymn-books, wherewith to carry on the work of God among his people.[42]

In his personal reminiscences, Tate remarked: "Can you picture a canoe load of painted savages coming to Victoria, in order to procure a thousand dollars worth of the white man's rum, wherewith to make more devilish, a projected heathen feast, and that same canoe filled with converted baptized Indian people, singing the songs of salvation, which had filled their hearts with joy and gladness, thus becoming the first missionaries to the tribes of the far north, under the auspices of the Canadian Methodist Church?"[43] The visual imagery that Tate used recalls the marked physical and behavioural changes which Euro-Canadian missionaries in general ascribed to individual converts. Just as the missionaries' texts abound with evidence of "true conversion," so they also expected (and represented in their discourse) changed attitudes, especially the turning away from "traditional" Native culture (i.e., "painted savages" and "devilish feasts") towards Christian behaviour (i.e. "singing songs of salvation" and with hearts "filled with joy" at "becoming missionaries").

According to Tate, the conversion of Diex and her son Alfred (Chief Sgagweet) was the direct result of the Methodist missionaries who had conducted revival meetings in the converted bar in Victoria. Tate emphasized how he attempted to get Alfred to join his mother in services but had made little headway until "he finally landed one night in the mission and was brought under conviction that his life was wrong."[44] Clearly, the assumption is that, by converting to Christianity, Alfred had changed his behaviour and forsaken his Tsimshian obligations, such as supplying alcohol for feasting. The description of a canoe loaded with Bibles instead of a "cargo of rum" was a powerful metaphor for what successful mission work could achieve.

This pattern of self-proselytizing preceding formal denominational involvement seems to have been the rule rather than the exception on the North Coast. Missions at Port Simpson, Kitamaat, Kitkatla, and China Hat were "founded" by First Nations families, and several were in fact staffed in their formative years by Native missionaries and teachers. The establishment of Methodist missions on the North Coast, with its origins in a revival in Victoria, was echoed twenty years later with the entry of the Salvation Army into the region.[45] Once again, the mission was able to get its start through enthusiasm generated by Native revivals in Victoria and Native peoples, frequently family groups, who carried the message northward. The missionaries, however, preferred to see themselves as the impetus behind mission establishment, and their narratives reflect their egocentric view of the process (such as was the case for the Dudowards' role in founding the mission at Port Simpson).

Native oral traditions of the event provide contrasting evidence and points of detail. Moreover, they illuminate differences between how the family was viewed by Euro-Canadians and by Tsimshian and the diverse discourses on conversion that were produced as a result. Further biographical information on the Tsimshian involved reveal that the "conversion" of the Dudowards did not occur as the unified work of a nuclear family. Alfred Dudoward was most likely converted to Christianity well prior to his attendance at Victoria's barroom services. William Duncan's own school registry for Fort Simpson in 1857 listed an Alfred Dudoire as one of his pupils.[46] Archibald Greenaway's graduate thesis on the Port Simpson mission gives a little more background on Kate Dudoward, based on the oral history of the Dudoward family.[47] Kate was the daughter of a Tsimshian mother and a non-Native customs officer named Holmes, although apparently her parents parted company. Her mother was employed as a domestic servant, and for a time Kate lived in Victoria. In 1870 her mother was called back to Fort Simpson to assume the title and rank in her family, as there was no clear male heir. Kate was left behind in the care of Catholic nuns. However, her mother and the delegation who had been sent to bring her back to the North Coast were attacked en route and killed. The fourteen-year-old Kate was installed as chief instead. She began teaching other Tsimshian (particularly her kinswomen and slaves) what she knew of Christianity, although her shift from Catholicism to Protestantism may have been influenced by the nearby Anglican mission at Metlakatla. She married Alfred Dudoward in 1871.

Tsimshian oral history also provides some different details about the couple's eventful conversion at the Victoria revivals in 1873.[48] Like his wife, Alfred had a mixed Native and European heritage.[49] He too had lived for a time in Victoria while his mother, Elizabeth Lawson, was employed as a domestic. He assumed a chieftainship, necessitating his return to the North Coast, while his mother remained in Victoria. When the couple visited the city in 1872 with their first child, Alfred's mother had already been converted to Methodism. Thus contrary to Euro-Canadian narratives, Kate and Alfred Dudoward had clearly been exposed to Christianity as children. Kate in particular had already begun evangelizing on her own before and after her marriage. The couple continued to increase their familiarity with Christian teachings and with the Methodist denomination during their ten-month stay in the city, before returning home to Fort Simpson in 1873 with Bibles and hymnals.

Over the next year Kate organized and led classes in Christian instruction, in addition to conducting worship services every Sunday.[50] However, an "urgent" invitation was sent to the Methodists to request formal missionary involvement only after a rival Tsimshian group, composed of those who had converted to Anglicanism, had left to live in Metlakatla. Catherine's evangelism then sparked widespread interest.[51] These sudden and mass conversions of entire communities are understandable, given the "traditional" Tsimshian methods of power acquisition discussed earlier. The realization of one's superhuman potential through spiritual transformation commonly belonged within the framework of lineage organization. With the exception of shamanic powers, power acquisition was controlled by house and clan traditions. While many of these powers were derived from house ancestors, new powers, such as Christianity, could be added to the storehouse of powers already owned by the family.[52] As lineage chiefs, both Alfred and Kate Dudoward added Christian power to their respective houses.

Kate worked for decades as an interpreter, teacher, and even preacher for several missions in the North Coast region. In the early years her position was quite influential, but she remained active in Christian organizations throughout her life, and the Dudowards were considered anchors of the Methodist church in Port Simpson.[53] Because she was from a high-ranking family in the community and had been designated a chief before she had married, she already held a socially powerful position. Her husband sat on the village council, and both of them were class leaders for the weekly study meetings in the early 1870s. However, their status as Christians, at least as defined by missionary Thomas Crosby, was repeatedly questioned. He removed and reinstated both Kate and Alfred Dudoward from the membership rolls several times in the 1880s, often relieving them of their posts as class leaders because their standing in the Methodist church was "on trial."[54] In 1892 they threatened to leave the church, and by 1895 Alfred had joined the Salvation Army.[55] Hence, at the very height of their most active involvement in mission work, the Dudowards' "official" status within the church was in doubt. Clearly, the missionary discourse on Native Christians desired a specific code of conduct, and even the most active and motivated Native Christian families altered, challenged, and defied these expectations.

The emphases on differing roles for Elizabeth, Alfred, and Kate in the missionary narrative and in Native oral accounts of the founding of the Methodist mission on the North Coast illuminate the family as a contested concept. While acknowledging the contributions of the mother, the missionary narrative ultimately attributes the actual transmission of Methodist Christianity to Port Simpson to the heroic Alfred, who defies his original obligations to secure feasting supplies, bringing back "Christian faith" instead. However, the emphasis on the unified family transformation – mother, son, and wife – conforms with the mission model of the family and its function for the church. In contrast, the Native accounts attribute far greater independent action and initiative to Kate Dudoward, both before and after her marriage to Alfred, and to the continuing Tsimshian social structure. Such breadth of activity did not conform to the wifely role that the Euro-Canadian discourse ascribed to Kate, whereas her supportive role after the establishment of an official Methodist mission in the region (as translator, interpreter, and class leader) was more in line with a proscribed European gender model. Yet the idea of the missionary playing the part of family patriarch (or less commonly, matriarch), imposing European conceptions of family on Native Christians, and of these converts passively acquiescing to these models is erroneous. The Dudowards and other Native converts themselves had a perspective on what it meant to be Christian and what meaning they ascribed to their own conversions. Furthermore, the missionary stance on particular aspects of the family could be contradictory and inconsistent. The example of missionary attitudes towards Tsimshian marriages will illustrate this point forcefully.

DEFINING MARRIAGE

One of the most crucial indices of community values is marriage practices. As Kenelm Burridge writes, "nothing can so alter the textures of community life as change in the form of marriage," because marriages give the society its "character and form; introduce alliances, allegiances, and opposition; set the continuities and entail responsibilities for the nurture and protection of children so that, in time, they in their turn may become full members of the community prepared to meet their responsibilities in relation to future generations."[56] Christian missionaries were potentially intrusive agents of radical social change precisely because of their narrow view of what constituted marriage and their attempts to impose this view on indigenous populations. Conversion to Christianity, at least for Euro-Canadian missionaries, also entailed changes in behaviour and social practices. Monogamous and patrilineal, Christian marriages formed the basis of the nuclear family. In the nineteenth century they were intended to be a lifelong union between a non-related, adult couple, formally sanctioned through a church ceremony. From the missionary perspective, sexual relations between men and women were permitted only within this context, even if the realities of frontier environments belied this ideal.[57] Missionaries of all denominations encouraged adherence in principle, and often in practice, to such definitions of marriage. However, working among the Tsimshianic peoples of the North Pacific Coast, Protestant missionaries contested specific characteristics of Native marriages and customs of sexual access.

Anthropologists Marjorie Halpin and Margaret Seguin Anderson observe that, historically, "[t]he Tsimshian are said to have a rule of preference for marriage with a man's mother's brother's daughter [called a cross-cousin marriage], although late twentieth-century research has been unable to verify it."[58] Indeed, this may have been more of a social ideal than a common practice.[59] More apparent was the primary goal of consolidating wealth and position through marriage.[60] Hence marriages were typically arranged among social equals by the matrilineal group of each prospective spouse. The Tsimshian had sophisticated rules regarding who made appropriate marriage partners. Jay Miller recounts a Tsimshian narrative in which the marriage between two high-ranking Tsimshian, planned since childhood, went astray when the feelings of the individuals were placed ahead of those of their community: "Therefore a law was made that marriages would be arranged for the benefit of the crest and family, not according to the whims of individuals. If a couple were to marry, their parents discussed the arrangements. Their uncles also conferred. Then all of the relatives on both sides met and agreed."[61] Hence Tsimshian marriages were a matter between house and lineage groups. Gifts were exchanged among the families of the bride and groom on several occasions, including at a potlatch when the marriage was publicly announced.

Another central characteristic of Coast Tsimshian marriages was the rule of clan exogamy. Not only were the couple to be relatively equal in class, status, and wealth, but they were not to have the same clan/crest (*pteex*) affiliation. Strict exogamy customs determined potential partners from outside one's own clan for marriage and also governed inheritance rights (to names, property, titles, etc.). The matrilineal exogamous groups (clans/crests) extended to all the Tsimshianic-speaking groups and their two closest neighbours, the Tlingit and the Haida. Interethnic marriages, particularly common among high-ranking people, likewise observed the rules that prohibited marriage between "friend clans."[62] While married people continued to perform their important roles and obligations to their own house (*walp*) and crest (*pteex*), they also had responsibilities to their spouse's group.[63] Marriages to clanless groups were "traditionally" not favoured, although these had different ramifications for men and for women. The place of Tsimshian women and their children in the social structure was not profoundly effected by the ethnic origins of the husband or father. However, when a man married into a group without a clan system, his children would have no family ties to Tsimshian society and therefore could not inherit Tsimshian names, property, or resources without first being adopted by a Tsimshian matriline.[64] Adoption in order to create a permissible match was sometimes resorted to for those without a clan affiliation. Individuals of mixed Euro-Canadian and Native heritage continued to derive their clan affiliation and status from their Native mothers. Hence social status, from the Tsimshian perspective, was not diminished because of non-Native patrimony. Indeed, if marriages between non-Native women and Tsimshian men been more common at this time, the clan structure would have been rapidly disrupted, regardless of where the couple resided.[65] After the application of the Indian Act to British Columbia First Nations, Tsimshian women who lost their "Indian" status by marrying non-status "Indian" or non-Native men might still own property and assume names, although they no longer lived in the community.

Cross-cousin marriages were immediately condemned by missionaries as incestuous. Ironically, missionary opposition to exogamous marriages allowed for matches that the Tsimshian would have regarded (and in some communities, continue to regard) as incestuous.[66] From her fieldwork in the Port Simpson area in the early twentieth century, Viola Garfield concludes that missionaries achieved some, but not total, success in breaking down the prejudices against marrying within one's own clan.[67] However, in the nineteenth century this appears to have been an uphill battle for many missionaries. Although they regarded the system as detrimental to the development of a single, cohesive Christian identity, some missionaries were forced to admit that existing social groupings and practices could help maintain a peaceful and cooperative community, even after conversion. Even William Duncan declared, "I have never interferred with the crest business. It was very helpful to me."[68]

Those who did try to alter "traditional" marriage practices, such as Thomas Crosby, failed to discourage the law of clan exogamy among the Coast Tsimshian. The very first Native couple married by him at Port Simpson according to Christian rite met with disapproval from the community's elders when it was revealed that they were of the same clan. After they had directly confronted Crosby about the matter, he was obliged to take greater care before consenting to perform marriage ceremonies, for although he believed the custom was dying out, he also remarked that "if a marriage, arranged without regard to the old prejudices, turned out badly, they [Tsimshian] took care to ascribe the trouble to the fact that the young people were of the same crest." He also admitted that non-Aboriginal influence was to blame for upsetting these customs: "the old clan system worked beneficially before the decimation of the tribes by drink and debauchery; but great demoralization followed the coming of the white race and temporary alliances became common."[69]

As with the endogamy taboo, Crosby was forced to acquiesce to "traditional" Tsimshian marriage practices with respect to distributions of wealth that accompanied them. Good matches were expected to bring property and resources to a couple's respective houses. In one incident in the mid-1870s, a marriage between a young couple was arranged by their families and property had been exchanged. Unaware of these arrangements, the missionary married the young woman to another man in a Christian ceremony. Immediately, there was an uproar when a group of Tsimshian confronted Crosby in the mission house "and said that I had done an awful thing to marry that couple; that another young man had expected to marry the girl, as his friends had given large presents to her friends. Now there would be great trouble if that property was not returned. 'Oh,' I said, 'you are a silly people. Do you think if in my country a young fellow had given presents to a girl, expecting to marry her, that he would kick up a row because of a few paltry presents? No, he would go off and try to get another girl, and be ashamed to say anything about it.' They said, 'Oh sir, you needn't talk about your people. We must have these presents back or there will be trouble.'"[70] Following a council meeting, the matter was resolved by ordering that the "gifts" be returned. Afterwards Crosby claimed to be especially diligent "to find out if more than one party had presents," before he agreed to perform a Christian ceremony of marriage for a Native couple.[71]

What Crosby's wistful Eurocentrism demonstrates is the contrasting Native and non-Native views of the institution of marriage and the ceremonies to announce the partnership. Tsimshian marriages were formal, contractual agreements between lineages, expressing "personal friendships, political exigencies and interests in the maintenance of wealth and social position."[72] Accordingly, they were regarded as permanent arrangements, and relatives attempted to keep the couples together. Yet separation was not impossible.[73] In fact, divorce was both common and uncomplicated in Tsimshianic societies. The relative autonomy and considerable independence of married women from their husbands in these matrilineal societies were anomalous to Euro-Canadian missionaries, who idealized a patriarchal household where women and children were dependents. Tsimshian women were responsible to an entirely different kin group than their husbands, and as the carriers of inheritable property, they were often the first to separate when the marriage proved disadvantageous. Separation was relatively easy: it was simply a matter of the partners going their separate ways by moving into different living quarters.[74]

However, in many mission villages the roles of wife and husband were greatly altered when women were excluded from property ownership and management.[75] The force of Canadian laws eventually had a considerable impact on (physical) property ownership and inheritance rights in a way that highlights the clash between the older matrilineal Tsimshian system and Canadian property statutes favouring patrilineal and patriarchal rights. For example, under the older system a chief's house passed to the nephew who succeeded him in name and position. Under British Columbia law, wives and children had a claim to this inheritance. Over time, this right altered social relationships within Tsimshian families and changed the nature of specific lineage responsibilities (e.g., whether the father's or the mother's lineage prepared a new home site for their grown children, or which lineage members assisted in the construction of houses).[76]

Furthermore, there were different types of marriage among Northwest Coast societies for which there were no Euro-Canadian or Christian equivalents, such as wealth marriages and childhood unions, neither of which were viewed as permanent arrangements.[77] Missionaries repeatedly confused these non-connubial types of marriages with sexual liaisons and, along with slavery, denounced them as immoral and synonymous with prostitution. Among the Tsimshian, polygany (a man married to more than one woman at a time) was practised. While it was reportedly fairly rare and usually confined to only the wealthiest of chiefs, there is evidence that some Native Christians continued the practice even after their conversion. For example, in the 1860s, at the time of his close association with William Duncan and his Anglican missions at Fort/Port Simpson and Metlakatla, Tsimshian evangelist Arthur Wellington Clah had two wives.[78] Missionaries encouraged monogamous alliances, and their pursuit of this form left secondary wives and their children without the system of "traditional" support and provision.

The behaviour of Euro-Canadian missionaries towards marriage must have been truly perplexing for the Tsimshian. While they espoused the married state as the only legitimate one for sexually active adults, missionaries used forced marriages or even forced divorces as disciplinary actions, intent on imposing their views on the matter. A case in point is Duncan's approach to marriage, which in one instance even contradicted the advice of other missionaries in the field.[79] At Metlakatla he married a Native couple against their will and justified the marriage on disciplinary grounds. Mary Jackson, a Native woman whom the missionary had been training as teacher, had become involved in a sexual relationship with Frank Allen. Upon discovering this liaison, Duncan fined Allen $300 and insisted the couple should be promptly married. However, although it was their intention to be married, Allen and Jackson were not yet prepared to hold a "traditional" Tsimshian marriage feast. Another Anglican missionary, the Reverend W.H. Collison, under the advice of the bishop, had refused to marry this couple against their wishes. Nevertheless, Duncan persisted and married them himself. Following the nuptials, he immediately imprisoned Allen in the mission jail for one week. As soon as he was released, his wife was likewise imprisoned for a week, "as punishment for the immorality."[80] Hence this Native couple were penalized for their premartial relationship, although the process of marrying them according to Tsimshian custom may have already been underway. Yet a forced Christian marriage was proposed as the solution for their moral "indiscretion."

This attitude sent very mixed messages to Native people attempting to comprehend what moral position on marriage and sexuality the missionaries espoused. For example, missionaries were quick to point out the corrupting influences of non-Natives in encouraging premarital sex and prostitution. They proposed their own Christian missions and girls' schools as the means to "save" young Native women, "for after the girls were taken into the Homes and Schools, and became bright, clean, and intelligent," noted one Methodist missionary, "they also grew more attractive and were more sought after by these white scoundrels. Some of course married them, which was better."[81] Missionaries seemed to foster the idea that the married state was preferable to sexual relations outside wedlock, even if it meant marriage to men who were "scoundrels." Given the failure of some missionaries to recognize Tsimshian marriages, they also appear to have promoted the idea that Christian marriages were more a valid and appropriate ceremony for all Native Christians to go through. These attitudes may have been borne out in practice. For example, by the early twentieth century, at missions on the Upper Skeena River, couples who had been married in a church ceremony allegedly had a greater say in church organizations than couples who had not been married according to Christian rite.[82] As Margaret Whitehead points out, Aboriginal women, regardless of their status or class, could a expect a sacred ritual and feast as part of their Christian ceremony, which in pre-Christian society would have only been available to those of chiefly class.[83]

THE SIGNIFICANCE OF NAMES

Another related component in the missionary's attempt to impose the patriarchal model of a nuclear family on the Tsimshian was the encouragement of a patrilineal naming system. Like the Euro-Canadians' failure to discourage clan exogamy and the significance of the matrilineage in Native marriage customs, Protestant missionaries also could not displace the "traditional" system of Tsimshian family naming. The historic and contemporary Tsimshian practice of social organization is a complex but flexible system. Adaptability in how kinship structures were defined and maintained, in how naming and inheritance practices were sustained, and in the composition of marriage arrangements allowed the Tsimshian to continue their "traditional" social system long after contact with Europeans. Over the long term, however, there have been shifts in the social body of Tsimshian culture. Numerous pressures provided a powerful impetus for these changes; certainly, missionary activities were central among them.

Personal names, for example, and the practice of naming are a promising way of getting at the politics of the social self in the family context. Transformation had always been a sign of power in both Tsimshian and evangelical Christian culture. Naming frequently signified transformation. With the new Tsimshian name came power and rank dependent on one's station in society and the power associated with the name being received. Baptism was the Christian rite that recognized the transformation of the individual from his or her state of "natural sin" to a new identity as a Christian. The Tsimshian inherited names and, indeed, clan affiliation through the mother's line. Christian names and, later, the government's recording of "Indian names" for band roles were patrilineal. There is no evidence to suggest that at any time did Christian names supersede matrilineal family names. Each name had specific occasions when it was used; each name had "power" in its own particular context.

According to some historians, among many evangelical denominations in the nineteenth century, such as the Methodists, the conversion experience was akin to a rite of adolescence "closely associated with the passage into adulthood."[84] Baptism may have marked the beginning of this progression in youth or recorded the achievement of true conversion in adulthood. The ceremony was commemorated through the giving of a "Christian" name. Similarly, no Tsimshian adult of any significant status would have failed to have gone through several formal naming rites. Names were linked to inheritance, property, and titles and ultimately to status and power. To be without a name (that is, received into the potlatch system, or *yaawk*) was to be "never healed" or *'wa'aayin*.[85] "In the minds of the elders," concludes Marjorie Halpin, "names are of ultimate social value. 'Names make you heavy' ... names *are* wealth." To be without a name, an " 'Unhealed Person,' " "was to be a deviant, essentially someone outside the social order. That is, it was less a social class, as commonly believed, than a moral condition."[86]

In this respect, the Tsimshian received Christian baptism and the conferring of a Christian name as a familiar recognition of belonging to a community. Just as evangelical Christians believed that without a conversion experience a person was unredeemed before God and had not achieved her or his potential for salvation, so the Tsimshian conception of the power in names was all about realizing one's human potential. Houses acquire crests over time, just as the human members of the house accumulate names.[87] As John Cove explains, each new name marks a point of development in an individual's life. "Chiefly names, or real-names, can be seen as starting the ultimate in human potential; their acquisition marks the transition from ordinary to real."[88] Consider the resonance that the missionary's explanation of the significance of baptism and the receipt of a Christian name may have had for Native converts, given prior Tsimshian practices.

This similarity of belief in the power associated with names suggests a point of commonality between Native and Christian spiritual beliefs. However, it also illustrates how the significance of a name, and with it the associations of family, was interpreted very differently by Native and non-Native. For the Euro-Canadian missionaryies, what they thought was the symbolic entry into Christianity – baptism, the beginning of a long education in the new faith – was interpreted by many Tsimshian individuals as a new source of power: an end in itself, rather than a beginning. The missionaries themselves may have inadvertently given this impression. For example, Anglican and Methodist missionaries at Port Simpson, in the earliest days of their missions, gave their schoolchildren Christian names as Christmas gifts.[89] The ceremony of baptism not only paralleled that of Tsimshian acquisition of new names, but it was reminiscent of bestowing extremely important names. Baptism "in the Name of the Father, the Son, and the Holy Ghost" was an opportunity to receive new names associated with heaven, which had traditionally been a very potent quality for Tsimshian power names or "real" names.[90]

Understanding the context in which new names were assumed and used is paramount in fully appreciating the changes they signified. When First Nations still retained control over the social context, "traditional" naming practices prevailed. When Euro-Canadian colonial structures imposed band membership or Christian names, there were some modifications. Indeed, the collection of names used by any one individual to identify him or herself became utterly bewildering to non-Natives.[91] An adult might be familiarly referred to by his or her childhood name, while at formal occasions that same individual went by her or his adult name. However, in other venues, Tsimshian were called by their Christian names or patrilineal surnames. Moreover, children frequently changed their surnames according to the family they lived with, and hence individual children might have two or three different last names.[92] Clearly, the matrilineal moiety system was fully capable of accommodation to post-contact realities, such as massive population reductions as a result of epidemics or Christian missionization, by modifying "traditional" social systems to accord with immediate needs and conditions.[93] Christian names were not hereditary in the lineage, and only Native names remained exclusively in the matrilineal house (*walp*). Hence, despite the introduction of what appears to be a replacement naming system through baptismal names and patrilineal surnames, the older system prevailed parallel to these new ones.

Yet there have been some changes in the use of certain names directly because of missionary activity. One of the most obvious has been the effect on women. Tsimshian women could lose their Christian names when they married, something that was not possible with "traditional" Tsimshian names. Under the pre-Christian system, once names had been assumed and formally sanctioned through a potlatch, they could be discredited, challenged, extinguished, or revived by their holders, or even temporarily "held" by another, but never completely lost from the woman's house upon marriage. Of course, under this new system, women could assume their husbands' Christian names through marriage, something that their male counterparts could not do. In other words, Christian names introduced a new dynamic into naming practices which, on one level at least, realigned the male-female roles within social memberships. Recall that in Tsimshian society "traditionally" human descendants circulated through a series of fixed identities within their matrilineages.[94] While the matrilineages gave names to children, they frequently cross-referenced the father's clan. Jay Miller gives the example of "a child with a father who was a member of the Orca crest might have 'glistening' as part of the name, as in 'Eagle Glistening in the Sunlight.'"[95] Christian names were passed on in a completely different way, creating a named patrilineage into which females entered and left but males did not.

While missionaries may have attempted to discourage certain aspects of arranged marriages and naming practices, even more influential in challenging the power and authority of family names were anti-potlatch attitudes (the very mechanism for filling names), unfilled names because of population loss, and the "statusization" of Native people vis-à-vis the Indian Act and reserve system.[96] Remarkably, Native peoples were not entirely deterred by these obstacles, especially over traditions of family identity. Church organizations, formally sanctioned by mission and colonial officials alike, offered Tsimshian Christians alternatives for the continuance of some of these social customs, albeit in modified form.

TSIMSHIANIC CHRISTIAN SOCIETY

As new Christian social organizations emerged, the Tsimshian and their neighbours utilized them to continue their most important "traditional" social practices, just as European technologies had altered their property and material culture. Euro-Canadian missionaries were frequently drawn into the existing Native kinship systems in complex ways, even as they sought to alter them. For example, Anglican clergyman Robert Tomlinson was adopted into a Nisga'a clan, a decision that stemmed from the identification of the black ink dove with which he had marked all his linen during his travels with the clan's icon, the Raven. To permit a proper match according to Nisga'a customs of marriage and family, Tomlinson's wife and children were adopted by the Eagle clan. Subsequently, when his son Robert junior married, his wife was also incorporated into the Native family system through her joining a clan. With considerable irony, the adoption proceedings were formalized through a potlatch, as a time when missionaries were campaigning for its eradication.[97]

Hence, although missionaries made much of the distinction between Christian and non-Christian, First Nations were more concerned with the cohesion of the group, which could include the missionaries in their midst. There was an awareness among missionaries that older notions of family were still intact and functioning long after the Tsimshian were deemed Christianized. Although they undoubtedly caused some internal tensions, especially if Christian teaching was perceived as "privileged" knowledge from a parent-like missionary, "Christian" and "heathen" were not mutually exclusive categories for Aboriginals.[98] Despite how the Euro-Canadian missionaries rationalized Tsimshian society into Christian and non-Christian parts, historically, these were not insurmountable divisions. It is true that there was a certain degree of exclusiveness in the creation of "Christian villages," but none were entirely isolated from "traditionalist" influences. Furthermore, "traditional" modes of leadership based on house chiefs still existed at many missions themselves. It is well known that one of the two factions which ripped William Duncan's Metlakatla apart after 1882, opposed him, and sided with the bishop was composed of several hereditary chiefs who had seized the opportunity to gain some of the power they had lost under Duncan's egalitarian Christianity. The hereditary system of leadership had not been subverted by conversion to Christianity. "Traditional" chiefs remained highly influential, in spite of Christian village organization and the imposition of Canadian-style systems of local government through the Indian Act. Well into the early twentieth century, for example, village councillors were elected, but hereditary chiefs still retained considerable authority over local affairs. It was customary in many villages, such as Port Simpson, for the head of the council to be a chief.[99] In some Native communities today a socially stratified system still exists, where the leaders of churches are also hereditary nobles.[100]

Just as outsiders (missionaries) living among Tsimshian peoples were socially embraced as insiders, so Native Christians utilized the new forms of organizations to maintain the social solidarity of their cultures. Denominational affiliation and membership in various church organizations such as ladies' auxiliaries, class meeting, Epworth Leagues, and temperance societies could be and were used to continue pre-existing social structures. In this way, the variety of denominations available to the Tsimshianic peoples offered new ways to express "traditional" ideas about family.[101] For example, two fraternal societies – the Firemen and the Soldiers – emerged in Port Simpson in the late nineteenth century.[102] In addition to performing specific duties on behalf of their community, as their names readily suggest, these organizations also developed an outlet for social rivalries between houses and lineages. Each society vied to attract a greater number of chiefs into its membership and to elect the most prestigious chief to act as head of the society. Formerly, the secret societies had been an important source of wealth for the chiefs, providing them with a continual economic income through initiation tributes. When such societies were outlawed by missionaries, their "spirit" remained, as did the power and prestige they brought to chiefs.[103] Likewise, athletic clubs or educational associations that emerged out of the local church organizations assumed, at least in part, many of the social functions formerly performed by the matri-lineage, particularly with regard to arrangements after the death of a member or relative.[104] John Barker points out that, among the Nisga'a, churches frequently encouraged voluntary community orga-nizations, which in turn performed services for funeral feast organiz-ers, particularly the witnessing and thus validating of the inheritance of Nisga'a names and offices.[105] Hence, in some contexts, Christianity could provide the mechanisms for perpetuating "traditional" family names and house leadership.

CONCLUSION

Protestant missionaries to the Tsimshian in the nineteenth century challenged the concept of family and saw its reformulation after Euro-Canadian models as essential to the success of their work. It is ironic that in the end they failed to fully achieve these goals, despite generations of Tsimshian Christians. The clan system, a collective rather than a nuclear group and the central core of the matrilineal household (*walp*) – the "traditional" Tsimshian family – remains in-tact today, when other social structures have been discontinued. Fur-thermore, the missionaries' attempts to enforce patriarchal familial relations by altering marriage customs, naming systems, and male leadership in the majority of religious offices changed the nature of male and female roles, but with unexpected results. Jay Miller observes that, because the missionaries attacked "traditional" Tsimshian spiritual power, specifically the chief-priests' (*smhalaayt*) authority in the displays of masked wonders (*naxnox*) and the secret dancing societies (*wut'aahalaayt*), "the realm of women, the basis for matrilineality, has survived well into the present, while the realm of men, the basis for traditional religious expressions, has not, except as sometimes recast" in Christian ways.[106] Similarly, historian Paul Tennant declared that on British Columbia's North Coast "a full symbiosis between Protestantism and the traditional clan system" was achieved by the twentieth century.[107] Therefore conversion to Christianity arguably was an additive process for the Tsimshianic-speaking peoples, not merely in terms of spirituality but also in terms of social organization and customs. A dialogic relationship be-tween Tsimshian and Euro-Canadian emerged through missioniza-tion. The contested nature of the family, whether in marriage practices, the inheritance of names, or community groups, illustrates Christian hegemony as a dynamic process in which Native peoples as well as missionaries navigated the course.

NOTES

1 This essay draws heavily on sections of my doctoral dissertation: Susan
  Neylan, " 'The Heavens Are Changing': Nineteenth Century Protestant Mis-
  sionization on the North Pacific Coast" (PhD dissertation, University of
  British Columbia, 1999) and my book *The Heavens Are Changing": Nineteenth-
  Century Protestant Missions and Tsimshian Christianity* (McGill-Queen's University Press, forthcoming). I gratefully acknowledge the Social Sciences and
  Humanities Research Council of Canada for providing me with a doctoral
  fellowship to help fund my research. Special thanks are due to to Dr Arthur
  J. Ray and Melinda Jetté for their helpful comments, and to Nancy Christie
  for the invitation to contribute to this collection.
2 Although this essay includes examples from a larger North Coast region
  populated by Tsimshianic-speaking peoples (Tsimshian, Nisga'a, and
  Gitxsan), the term "Tsimshian" refers to the Tsimshian proper (including the
  Canyon Tsimshian), labelled in the older literature "Coast Tsimshian."
  Spelling conventions for words in the Coast Tsimshian language (*Sm'algyax*)
  follow Jay Miller, *Tsimshian Culture: A Light through the Ages* (Lincoln and
  London: Nebraska University Press, 1997); and Wayne Suttles, ed., *Handbook of North American Indians*, vol.7, *The Northwest Coast* (Washington,
  DC: Smithsonian Institution, 1990); and Christopher Roth, personal communication, March 2001.
3 Forrest La Violette, *The Struggle for Survival: Indian Cultures and the Protestant Ethic in British Columbia* (Toronto: University of Toronto Press, 1961);
  and Robin Fisher, *Contact and Conflict: Indian-European Relations in British
  Columbia, 1774–1890* (Vancouver: University of British Columbia Press,
  1977).
4 Cultural hegemony as a theoretical framework is especially useful when
  analyzing encounters between two cultures. Raymond Williams defines it
  as "a complex interlocking of political, social and cultural forces." But
  more than ideology or political rule, hegemony permeates all levels of life,
  becoming "commonsensical" when predominant. It "has continually to
  be renewed, recreated, defended, and modified. It is also continually resisted, limited, altered, challenged by pressures not at all its own." Therefore it exists simultaneously as an external and an internalized process.
  Thus more than a model of resistance-acceptance, as a concept it can be
  applied to identify an active role in historical processes for both colonizer
  and colonized. See Raymond Williams, *Marxism and Literature* (Oxford:
  Oxford University Press, 1977), 108, 112.
5 This perspective owes much to the recent and voluminous scholarship on
  colonial cultures. For example, see Jean and John Comaroff, *Of Revelation
  and Revolution*, vol. 1, *Christianity, Colonialism, and Consciousness in South*

Africa, and vol. 2, *The Dialectics of Modernity on a South African Frontier* (Chicago: Chicago University Press, 1991, 1997); Frederick Cooper and Ann Laura Stoler, eds., *Tensions of Empire: Colonial Cultures in a Bourgeois World* (Berkeley: University of California Press, 1997); and Steven Kaplan, ed., *Indigenous Responses to Western Christianity* (New York: New York University Press, 1995).

6 Williams, *Marxism and Literature*, 112.

7 Michael Harkin, "Power and Progress: The Evangelic Dialogue among the Heiltsuk," *Ethnohistory* 40 (winter 1993): 6. The "dialogic" approach has been utilized by anthropologists, historians, and other social scientists in the process of "doing history" as well as within the final products of their research. Richard White calls it "the middle ground"; see Richard White, *The Middle Ground: Indians, Empires, and Republics in the Great Lakes Region, 1650–1815* (New York: Cambridge University Press, 1991). And Arnold Krupat calls this "ethnocriticism"; see Arnold Krupat, *Ethnocriticism: Ethnography, History, Literature* (Berkeley: University of California Press, 1992).

8 George F. MacDonald, Gary Coupland, and David Archer, "The Coast Tsimshian, ca. 1750," in *Historical Atlas of Canada*, vol. I, *From the Beginning to 1800*, ed. R. Cole Harris and cartographer Geoffrey J. Matthews (Toronto: University of Toronto Press, 1987), plate 13. However, scholars (such as the above) of Tsimshianic-speaking peoples have frequently recognized only three major groupings: Coast Tsimshian, Nisga'a, and Gitxsan.

9 Jay Miller, "Tsimshian Ethno-Ethnohistory: A 'Real' Indigenous Chronology," *Ethnohistory* 45 (fall 1998): 661.

10 Miller, *Tsimshian Culture*, 45.

11 Or *waap* or *waab* in southern villages. See John Asher Dunn, *A Practical Dictionary of the Coast Tsimshian Language*, Canadian Ethnology Service, Mercury Series, Paper no. 42 (Ottawa: National Museums of Canada, 1978), s.v. "family," "house." Instead of the term "family," Viola Garfield uses "household," meaning both or either "belonging to the same kinship group or subdivision of a clan" or "includes all those people who live in a single dwelling ... includ[ing] people belonging to different clans." See Viola E. Garfield, *Tsimshian Clan and Society*, University of Washington Publications in Anthropology, 7, no. 3 (Seattle: University of Washington Press, 1939), 174.

12 Margaret Seguin, "Lest There Be No Salmon: Symbols in Traditional Tsimshian Potlatch," in Seguin, ed., *The Tsimshian: Images of the Past; Views for the Present* (Vancouver: University of British Columbia Press, 1984), 111.

13 Ibid., 125.

14 Clarence Bolt, *Thomas Crosby and the Tsimshian: Small Shoes for Feet Too Large* (Vancouver: University of British Columbia Press, 1992), 24.

15 Viola E. Garfield, "The Tsimshian and Their Neighbors," in Garfield and Paul S. Wingert, *The Tsimshian Indians and Their Arts* (Seattle: University of Washington Press, 1966), 39.

16 Both terms contain the suffix *halaayt,* a difficult word to translate accurately into English but a key concept in Tsimshian spirituality. *Halaayt* means "dance" or "dancer," but it is also the term applied to "shaman" and "initiate" (all the potential participants in dancing). In other words, the term refers to both the manifestation of power (e.g., a particular ritual or an object used in one, such as a mask) and the demonstration of that power (e.g., the empowered individual). See Marie-Françoise Guédon, "An Introduction to Tsimshian Worldview and Its Practitioners," in Seguin, *The Tsimshian,* 138–140.

17 Marjorie Halpin, " 'Seeing' in Stone: Tsimshian Masking and the Twin Stone Masks," in Seguin, *The Tsimshian,* 286.

18 John Cove, *Shattered Images: Dialogues and Meditations on Tsimshian Narratives* (Ottawa: Carleton University Press, 1987), 229, 230.

19 For the purposes of my focus on how spiritual power and family were connected, I do not fully explore the nature of non-hereditary and shamanic power acquisition. Shamans did not seek supernatural power; rather, it sought them. They acquired power through direct contact with supernatural forces (more accurately, non-human or extra-human powers) outside a ritual framework, and they underwent a temporary "death" in so doing. Names derived from these spiritual encounters usually were not passed to other individuals. See Cove, *Shattered Images,* 157–228; Guédon, "An Introduction to Tsimshian Worldview," 137–59; and Marie-Françoise Guédon, "Tsimshian Shamanic Images," in Seguin, *The Tsimshian,* 174–211.

20 Miller, *Tsimshian Culture,* 23.

21 Dunn, *A Practical Dictionary of the Coast Tsimshian Language,* s.v. "European," "Caucasian," "ạmksiwạh." Christopher Roth suggested the current spelling (personal communication, March 2001).

22 As the reserve system was implemented in the North Coast area during the 1880s, Duncan and Tsimshian Metlakatlans also came into conflict with colonial and church authorities over land issues. Unable to resolve them, Duncan and over six hundred Tsimshian left the Canadian province in 1887 to establish New Metlakatla on Annette Island in Alaska.

23 Maureen Cassidy, *The Gathering Place: A History of the Wet'suwet'en Village of Tse-kya* (Hagwilget: Hagwilget Band Council, 1987), 25; R.M. Galois, "The History of the Upper Skeena Region, 1850–1927," *Native Studies Review* 9 (1993–1994): 122.

24 Henry S. Wellcome, *The Story of Metlakahtla* (London and New York: Saxon and Co., 1887), 71–2.

25 Jean Barman, "Taming Aboriginal Sexuality: Gender, Power, and Race in British Columbia, 1850–1900," *BC Studies*, no. 115/116 (autumn/winter 1997–98): 237–66.

26 J.J. Halcombe, "Stranger than Fiction," Reprints from *Mission Life* 3 (1 November 1871): 616.

27 Ibid.

28 See, for example, Robert F. Berkhofer Jr. *The White Man's Indian: Images of the American Indian from Columbus to the Present* (New York: Vintage Books, 1978); Sarah Carter, "The Missionaries' Indian: The Publications of John McDougall, John Maclean, and Egerton Ryerson Young," *Prairie Forum* 9 (1984): 27–44; and Daniel Francis, *The Imaginary Indian: The Image of the Indian in Canadian Culture* (Vancouver: Arsenel Pulp Press, 1992).

29 Of course, these were not the only two post-contact challenges. There were dozens of other colonial challenges to indigenous cultures and a wide array of Native responses to them.

30 Nicholas Thomas, "Colonial Conversions: Difference, Hierarchy, and History in Early Twentieth Century Evangelical Propaganda," *Comparative Studies in Society and History* 34 (April 1992): 366–89.

31 Thomas draws on other scholarly inquiries into colonial discourse and into what Edward Said termed its "codification of difference." See Edward W. Said, *Culture and Imperialism* (New York: Knopf, 1993), 130.

32 Thomas, "Colonial Conversions," 380.

33 Ibid., 383.

34 The legacy of Indian residential schools in Canada is a dark and shameful one. Residential schools at Port Simpson, Metlakatla, and Kitamaat emerged in Tsimshian territories in the nineteenth century, and the Native role as student has been thoroughly and effectively explored by scholars who give this topic the breadth it deserves. See J.R. Miller, *Shingwauk's Vision: A History of Native Residential Schools* (Toronto: University of Toronto Press, 1996); Elizabeth Furniss, *Victims of Benevolence: The Dark Legacy of the Williams Lake Residential School*, 2nd ed. (Vancouver: Arsenal Pulp Press, 1995); Celia Haig-Brown, *Resistance and Renewal: Surviving the Indian Residential School* (Vancouver: Tillacum Library, 1988); and Jean Barman, Yvonne Hébert, and Don McCaskill, eds., *Indian Education in Canada*, Vol. 1, *The Legacy* (Vancouver: Nakoda Institute and University of British Columbia Press, 1986).

35 With the revisions to the Indian Act introduced by Bill C-31 (1985), the rules regarding patrilineal transmission of Indian status have been partially redressed; however, bands are permitted to create local rules regarding band membership whereby the potential exists for matrilineal succession to continue to be ignored.

36 Archives of the Anglican Provincial Synod of British Columbia and Yukon, Vancouver, George Hills, (Anglican) bishop of Columbia, Journals, vol. 1, 23 November 1860, 266–7.

37 Wellcome, *Story of Metlakahtla*, 59.
38 Ibid., 77.
39 Some missionaries encouraged marriages between young women from
    the misson residential schools and young Christian men. See Margaret
    Whitehead, "'A Useful Christian Woman': First Nations Women and
    Protestant Missionary Work in British Columbia," *Atlantis* 18 (fall/
    summer 1992–93): 158.
40 Thomas Crosby, *Among the An-ko-me-nums, or Flathead Tribes of Indians of
    the Pacific Coast* (Toronto: William Briggs, 1907), 17. References to revivals
    and religious awakenings are also common throughout Thomas Crosby,
    Up and Down the North Pacific Coast by Canoe and Mission Ship (Toronto:
    Methodist Mission Rooms for the Missionary Society of the Methodist
    Church, The Young People's Forward Movement, 1914).
41 Rev. C.M. Tate, *Our Indian Missions in British Columbia* (Toronto: Methodist
    Young People's Forward Movement, Methodist Mission Rooms, n.d.
    [1900?]), 4.
42 Ibid., 4–5.
43 British Columbia Archives (BCA), Add. MSS. 303, box 1, file 2, C.M. Tate,
    "Reminiscences, 1852–1933" (typescript), 11.
44 Ibid.
45 John Webster Grant, *Moon of Wintertime: Missionaries and Indians of Canada in
    Encounter since 1534* (Toronto: University of Toronto Press, 1984), 135–6. The
    Salvation Army in the Upper Skeena River region was established by mem-
    bers of a Port Simpson Tsimshian family, William Young and his sister, in
    the 1890s. See R.G. Moyles, *The Blood and Fire in Canada: A History of the
    Salvation Army in the Dominion, 1882–1976* (Toronto: Peter Martin Assoc.,
    1977), 114.
46 R.M. Galois, "Colonial Encounters: The Worlds of Arthur Wellington
    Clah, 1855–1881," *BC Studies*, nos. 115/116 (autumn/winter 1997–98):
    141n133.
47 Archibald McDonald Greenaway, "The Challenge of Port Simpson" (BDiv
    thesis, Vancouver School of Theology, 1955), 24–5.
48 Ibid., 25–6.
49 Alfred was the son of HBC (Fort Simpson) employee Felix Dudoire. See
    Galois, "Colonial Encounters," 141n133.
50 Greenaway, "The Challenge of Port Simpson," 26.
51 Ibid., 28.
52 Guédon, "An Introduction to Tsimshian Worldview," 143.
53 Oliver R. Howard, "Fire in the Belly: A Brief Introduction to a Few of the
    Methodist Men and Women Who Presented the Gospel of Jesus Christ to
    the Natives of British Columbia," *Papers of the Canadian Methodist Histori-
    cal Society* 8 (1990): 237.
54 United Church Archives of British Columbia, Vancouver, Methodist
    Church of Canada, British Columbia Conference, Port Simpson District,

Port Simpson Mission Register, 1874–96; Greenaway, "The Challenge of Port Simpson," 60, 75; and Bolt, *Thomas Crosby*, 48.

55 Bolt, *Thomas Crosby*, 48.

56 Kenelm Burridge, *In the Way: A Study of Christian Missionary Endeavours* (Vancouver: University of British Columbia Press, 1991), 127.

57 For a discussion of this and related themes, see Barman, "Taming Aboriginal Sexuality," 237–66.

58 Marjorie M. Halpin and Margaret Seguin, "Tsimshian Peoples: Southern Tsimshian, Coast Tsimshian, Nishga, and Gitksan," in Suttles, *Handbook of North American Indians, Coast*, 7: 277.

59 Garfield, *Tsimshian Clan and Society*, p. 232.

60 Halpin and Seguin, "Tsimshian Peoples," 277.

61 Miller, *Tsimshian Culture*, 78–9.

62 John A. Dunn, "International Matri-moieties: The North Maritime Province of the North Pacific Coast," in Seguin, *The Tsimshian*, 100.

63 Margaret Seguin Anderson and Tammy Anderson Blumhagen, "Memories and Moments: Conversations and Re-collections," *BC Studies*, no. 104 (winter 1994): 89.

64 Garfield, *Tsimshian Clan and Society*, 231.

65 Ibid.

66 All persons whose mothers were sisters (extending through grandmothers) called one another sister and brother. See Anderson and Blumhagen, "Memories and Moments," 90.

67 Garfield, *Tsimshian Clan and Society*, 232.

68 William Duncan, "Historical and Legendary Statements," in U.S., Congress, Senate, Subcommittee on Indian Affairs, *Survey of the Condition of the Indians in the United States: Part 35, Metlakahtla Indians*, Alaska, 74th Congr., 2nd sess, 1939; quoted in Jean Usher, *William Duncan of Metlakatla* (Ottawa: National Museum of Man, 1974), 153n14.

69 Crosby, *Up and Down the North Pacific Coast*, 311–12.

70 Ibid., 72.

71 Ibid., 73.

72 Garfield, "The Tsimshian and Their Neighbors," 24.

73 Ibid.

74 Carol Cooper notes the existence of more formal ceremonies among some Tsimshianic groups, such as the *Llin* as practised among the Nisga'a, which "dissolved the bonds and obligations between a man and his wife." See Carol Cooper, "Native Women of the Northern Pacific Coast: An Historical Perspective, 1830–1900," *Journal of Canadian Studies* 27 (winter 1992–93): 55.

75 Jo-Anne Fiske, "Colonization and the Decline of Women's Status: The Tsimshian Case," *Feminist Studies* 17 (fall 1991): 525.

76 Garfield, *Tsimshian Clan and Society*, 280, 326.

77 Michael Harkin discusses how missionaries to the Tsimshian's neighbours, the Heiltsuk, denounced child and investment marriages as forms of prostitution when they were actually non-sexual alliances "conducted solely for the purposes of exchanging wealth." See Michael Harkin, "Engendering Discipline: Discourse and Counterdiscourse in the Methodist-Heiltsuk Dialogue," *Ethnohistory* 43 (fall 1996): 646–7.

78 His first and principal wife was the niece of Nis'akx/Martha McNeill, named Adooskw or Dadks (baptized Dorcas Wellington). Clah mentions a second wife, Habbeleken, in 1867, but this marriage appears to have been short-lived. Numerous references to his two wives are found in his journals: see National Archives of Canada (NR), MG 40, F11, no. A-1711, Arthur Wellington Clah, Journals. See also Galois, "Colonial Encounters," 111n22.

79 General Touch and Rev. W.R. Blackett, *Report of the Deputation to Metlakatla* (London: n.p., 1886), 12–13

80 Ibid., 13.

81 Crosby, *Up and Down the North Pacific Coast,* 174.

82 BCA, Add. MSS 1201, A-1415, Northwest Coast Files, Marius Barbeau, Informants: Gamanut and Mrs Cox, B-F-89.14: "discussion of marriage under white law," (n.d., typed copy, 2 p.).

83 Margaret Whitehead, *Now You Are My Brother: Missionaries in British Columbia,* Sound Heritage Series, no. 34 (Victoria: Provincial Archives of British Columbia, 1981), 158–9.

84 Gail Malmgreen, "Domestic Discords: Women and the Family in East Cheshire Methodism, 1750–1830," in Jim Obelkevich, Lyndal Roper, and Raphael Samuel, eds., *Disciplines of Faith: Studies in Religion, Politics, and Patriarchy* (London: Routledge and Kegan Paul, 1987), 59.

85 Marjorie Halpin, "Feast Names of Hartley Bay," in Seguin, *The Tsimshian,* 59.

86 Ibid.

87 Cove, *Shattered Images,* 125.

88 Ibid.

89 Garfield, *Tsimshian Clan and Society,* 225.

90 Halpin, "'Seeing' in Stone," 284–5.

91 Garfield, *Tsimshian Clan and Society,* 225.

92 Ibid.

93 Jay Miller points to an instance, where, after the joining of two tribal groups (Tsimshian and Xaixais) in the village of Klemtu (China Hat), the elite transformed the tribal divisions into exogamous, matrilineal moieties. See Jay Miller, "Moieties and Cultural America: Manipulation of Knowledge in a Pacific Northwest Coast Native Community," *Arctic Anthropology* 18 (1981): 23.

94 Cove, *Shattered Images,* 73–4, 89; and Miller, *Tsimshian Culture,* 129.

95 Miller, *Tsimshian Culture,* 126.

96 For example, see Fisher, *Contact and Conflict*, 206–9, 211; Douglas Cole and Ira Chaikin, *An Iron Hand upon the People: The Law against the Potlatch on the Northwest Coast* (Vancouver: Douglas and McIntyre, 1990); and Christopher Bracken, *The Potlatch Papers: A Colonial Case History* (Chicago: University of Chicago Press, 1997).

97 BCA, no. 1238, Mr Robert Tomlinson Jr., excerpt from interview by Mrs Robert Tomlinson Jr [his second wife] in 1955; and interviewed by Mrs Walter T. Stewart, 1955; cited in Whitehead, *Now You Are My Brother*, 10–11. Dr RG Large also cites an abridged version of this story in R. G. Large, *Skeena: River of Destiny* (Sidney: Gray's Publishing and the Museum of Northern British Columbia, 1981), 80.

98 Palmer Patterson discusses how Nass River missionary R.A.A. Doolan was perceived by the Nisga'a as a chiefly figure introducing a new "privilege" among them, which was consistent with how Nisga'a youth were expected to be given specific knowledge and trained for leadership. See Palmer E. Patterson, "Nishga Perceptions of Their First Resident Missionary, the Reverend R.R.A. Doolan, (1864–1867)," *Anthropologica* 30 (1988): 134.

99 Garfield, *Tsimshian Clan and Society*, 323.

100 Miller, "Moieties and Cultural America," 31.

101 Clah's journals are particularly revealing on the significance of interdenominational antagonism among the Tsimshian as a manifestation of the continuance of older familial and kinship systems. He described, for example, literally years of friction between Native groups within the Methodists and the Salvation Army at Port Simpson, including incidents of violence and a "lock-out" of the Army from the Methodist church building they had been using. See NA, MG 40, F11, no. A-1707, Arthur Wellington Clah, Journals, especially entries December 1892–December 1894.

102 Garfield, *Tsimshian Clan and Society*, 319.

103 University of British Columbia Library, AW 1 R7173, no. 1, William Beynon Manuscript, vol. 2, no. 41, William Beynon, notes to "The Power of haxnᵊjᵊm 'Halait,'" 2–4.

104 Garfield, *Tsimshian Clan and Society*, 320; and William Beynon, "The Tsimshians of Metlakatla, Alaska," *American Anthropologist* 43 (1941): 86.

105 John Barker, "Tangled Reconciliations: The Anglican Church and the Nisga'a of British Columbia," *American Ethnologist* 25 (1998): 443.

106 Miller, "Tsimshian Ethno-Ethnohistory," 659–60.

107 Paul Tennant, *Aboriginal Peoples and Politics: The Indian Land Question in British Columbia, 1849–1989* (Vancouver: University of British Columbia Press, 1990), 78.

Gender, Social Change, and
the Language of Domesticity

Salvation in Indifference: Gendered Expressions of Italian-Canadian Immigrant Catholicity, 1900–1940

ENRICO CARLSON CUMBO

In an endnote to his celebrated "Cult and Occult in Italian-American Culture," Rudolph Vecoli made a passing remark on "the traditional differences in religious practices on the part of Italian men and women." Though a given in this and other studies, the nature and extent of these differences have very rarely been treated.[1] What has been written has depended largely on official, clerical documentation expressing a generally one-sided view of Italian immigrant piety. From the first years of Italian immigration, North American Catholic clerics, oftentimes even those of Italian origin, viewed Italian women generally as theologically ignorant and superstitious, and the men especially as nominal Catholics – anticlerical, indifferent, if not entirely irreligious. These and other views comprised the so-called Italian Problem, a litany of clerical Catholic complaints which was considered a major stumbling block to Canadian Catholic assimilation. The Italians themselves were defined as a home mission field, a latter-day "Italian Indies."[2] Though similarly uncertain, the Protestant home missionaries saw in the Italians' apparent nominalism an opportunity to evangelize them. Many were convinced that a combination of practical outreach, language and civics instruction, and the gospel "simply taught" would result eventually in the immigrants' transformation into "Christian Canadian citizens of the right type." As a Methodist missionary commented in 1915, underscoring the presumably growing prevalence of Italian Catholic nomimalism, "The Romish Church has imposed too many absurdities on the faith of [these] people. The people have thrown off the yoke and many no longer believe in the Roman Church which has reigned imperially for centuries and is destined now to its downfall in the conscience of the present Italian generation."[3]

Preoccupied with their own concerns, the Protestant and Catholic proselytizers misunderstood the depth of the immigrants' folk-cultural religion, the largely familial and communal world of southern Italian popular Catholicism. This essay examines this complex world and the gendered, especially male, expressions of popular piety in the late nineteenth and early twentieth centuries. An important characteristic of this Catholicism was its gendered configuration. Men's relationship to the divine, their spiritual roles and functions, differed in key respects from that of women. While distinct, however, these were also, and necessarily, complementary and interdependent. Familial, communal expectations intersected with gender-specific roles in the New World as in the Old, the *mezzogiorno*. Clerical Catholic and Protestant efforts to reconfigure this universe often resulted in tensions and the re-enforcement of "traditional" beliefs and practices.

The study is divided into two parts. The first examines the manifestations of Catholic belief among Italian male migrants in pre–World War I southern Ontario, a major locus of south Italian migration; and the second, the permutations of male and female Italian Catholicity in the settled immigrant enclaves of pre–World War II southern Ontario, in particular the Toronto-Hamilton area. At issue are central questions of religious, ethnic, and social cultural identity. What were the "traditional differences" in the religious practices of men and women? What world view underlay these distinctive definitions? In what way and to what extent were these traditions maintained in pre-war southern Ontario?[4]

NEW WORLD EXPRESSIONS OF POPULAR CATHOLICISM: THE MALE MIGRANT EXPERIENCE

Until recently, being a "Catholic," a *cristiano*, in southern Italy was synonymous with being human. On first meeting Carlo Levi, the famous anti-fascist exile in Gagliano, Lucania, in the 1930s, the poverty-stricken peasantry of the village informed him: "We're not Christians, we're not human beings; we're not thought of as men but simply as beasts, or even less than beasts, mere creatures of the wild."[5] Catholicism in this context was a way of being – an existential totality and an affirmation of human dignity. Formal creeds, the sacraments, and clerically sanctioned, Tridentine orthodox practices were only a part of this way of being. The religion of the *mezzogiorno* was an admixture of Tridentine orthodoxy and pre-Tridentine and so-called pre-Christian practices. It was also a product of cumulative folk "wisdom" reflecting and rooted in lived experience and folk-cultural traditions, in which notions such as fate and the evil eye – amoral forces, neither holy nor unholy – acted in concert with God and the saints in a complex universe of meaning. Notwithstanding Methodist claims, the migration process did not result in the dissolution of these Old World beliefs. The sacred cosmos did not suddenly change with the Italian discovery of "l'America." The devotional nexus of popular belief remained because it was known, practicable, functional, and immediate.

The mass emigration of Italians to Canada was characterized initially by a large migration of young, male sojourners. They worked seasonally as navvies in lumbering, mining, and railroad camps in the Canadian outback and as "pick and shovel workers" in the large urban centres. Tied to the imperatives of the family economy and in anticipation of upward social mobility in the Old World, they saved what they could from their meagre wages and sent remittances back home. The migrants' expectation was to return to Italy once they had earned enough money to buy a plot of land, secure a dowry, or generally meet the obligations that had sent them overseas.[6]

In their contact with these men, Italian officials and Catholic clerics feared that they would fall away, abandon the faith, and be lured to Protestantism, materialism, or any of a variety of secular ideologies. While there were certainly some who cut their ties with the past, this was not the norm. As Robert Harney points out, even in the rough, brutish culture of the mining camps, the "external and internalized social coercion which guarded the *villagio pettegolo*, the 'gossipy village,'" and the migrants' strong sense "of filial piety, parental duty and morality" served to sustain these ties;[7] the *paese* and its moral order continued to define their priorities. This orientation remained even among long-time sojourners. As Gaspare Cusumano observed of the Sicilian Cinisani in New York in the 1920s, "The town of Cinisi is forever in their minds: 'I wonder if I can get back in time for the next crop? I hope I can get back in time for the *festa*?'"[8] In the absence of familiar saints, surrogates were found. Italian canal workers in the Niagara–western New York area, for example, hung up popular prints of St Lucy and the Holy Family in their otherwise barren, ramshackle boarding houses. Images of this sort were obtained at the points of embarkation or acquired through clerical or lay contacts in the New World.[9]

The retention of the old ways among migrants is perhaps best illustrated in their response to Protestant proselytizing. A Methodist mission to Italians was first opened in the Toronto Ward, the downtown foreign quarter, in the early 1890s. The effort was short-lived, but it was followed in 1905 by a more established mission centre in the same area, where it remained for the next thirty years. The mission combined evangelical outreach and civics instruction with practical, social service; the latter included coal distribution, job contacts, interpretative assistance, and English classes. To the consternation of the city's Catholic hierarchy, the mission's temporal services were utilized, and some converts were made. In the end, however, very little came of these and similar efforts in Ontario and elsewhere. By 1921 the Toronto Methodists could claim only seventy-seven members, less than 1 per cent of the city's total Italian population; the conversion rate outside Toronto was even lower.[10]

This outcome is partly explained by seasonal transiency and the migrants' general lack of commitment to the host country. The core problem, however, was in the content of the Protestant message itself. The proselytizers' civic priorities and "civilizing" mission were largely irrelevant to the migrants' primary objectives. More important was the moral austerity of the evangelical message, the relative starkness of worship, and the proselytizers' complete misreading of popular Catholicism. In their Protestant triumphalism, the Italian missionaries particularly confused the Roman Catholic Church and Catholic devotional practices – "empty ceremonials," "gross ignorance and superstition," "saint worship" – with clerical "fanaticism" and papal control. According to this view, Roman "superstition" was a form of clerical "enslavement," an externally imposed, corrupting influence on an otherwise "intelligent race." This was the reason, presumably, that the majority of Italian men remained "incredulous" and nomimal Catholics. The church's "failure to appeal to reason", its inability "to satisfy their religious cravings," the proselytizers maintained, augered well for the future of Italian Protestantism.[11] Though many immigrants continued to use the missions' resources, few took this message seriously. After years of labour with Italian men, an Italian-Canadian missionary lamented privately, "The men have their habits fixed and cannot be uprooted. We have to deal with [Italian adults] one by one, and perhaps fail in the end."[12] The root of the problem lay in the men's religious consciousness. As an astute commentator, himself an Italian-American Protestant, observed in 1918, "When the peasant leaves his native village, he will forget everything but his patron saint."[13]

In rejecting Protestantism, Italian migrants did not conform to Canadian Catholicism. For many, the New World was a land of hard work and irreligion, a land where emigrant *cristiani* were treated as *bestie* and *turchi* ("pagans"). A popular Calabrian lament, a *villanella*, forewarned prospective migrants of the dangers of "l'America":

"You'll find no church to enter, nor even saints to worship."[14] In the early years of the twentieth century, at least, the warning applied equally to North American Catholicism. The Catholic hierarchy in southern Ontario was relatively late in responding to the Italian presence. Though aware of their growing numbers, the Toronto diocese did very little for them. The immigrants' Catholicism was simply taken for granted. The Catholic hierarchy acted only when compelled by the threat of Protestant proselytizing in the latter 1900s. The first Italian parish in the province, Our Lady of Mount Carmel in Toronto, was consecrated in 1908, three years after the founding of the second Methodist mission in the Ward.[15] The first Italian priest in Ontario, John F. Bonomi, arrived in Hamilton in 1908, but did not head an Italian parish until 1912; by then, three Italian Protestant missions had already been established. The pattern was repeated elsewhere in Ontario.[16]

Even with the churches established, Italian migrants developed an often adverse relationship with the clergy. This was rooted partly in traditional notions of anticlericalism (*mangiapretismo*). Priests in the Old World were often characterized as lazy, privileged, sexually aberrant in their ambiguous masculinity as celibates, and meddling in their capacity as confessors. These views were compounded in the New World by ultramontanist clerics and northern Italian priests unfamiliar with or antagonistic to the folk Catholic practices of the majority southern Italians. Predictably, lay-clerical tensions arose very early. Anticlerical suspicions, for example, resulted in the ouster of the first two pastors from Mount Carmel in Toronto, the first, allegedly, for sexual indiscretion and the second for misappropriating funds.[17] For some, the minimal temporal assistance provided by the church, relative to the Protestant efforts, accentuated their ill will towards the clergy.[18] The clergy's resentment, in turn, was fed by the Italians' "disrespect" of clerical authority, their stinginess in church offerings, and their low church attendance. These and other "traits" were already adumbrated in the "Italian Problem" and reiterated in correspondence and parish reports as examples of the Italians' "inborn indifference."[19] Defining their relationship to the church in Old World terms, however, the men did not see themselves as any less Catholic for their minimal church contributions or anticlerical suspicions. Their relationship to the Canadian church was conditioned by a number of factors, none of them having to do with "indifference."

First of all, the requirements of work and the heavy labouring and industrial work schedule of the New World disallowed any regular association with the church. [20] Among the more fortunate, Sundays were the only time for rest, and attending mass was not their first priority.

The Italian national parishes, moreover, were very different from their Old World prototypes. Like their Protestant equivalents, they were organized explicitly as institutional, social-religious agencies for the eventual assimilation of the newcomers into Canadian Catholic citizenship. Clerics were called upon to "missionize," to "exhort" Italians to "approach the Sacraments," and to join lay organizations such as the Holy Name and St Vincent de Paul societies, so much a part of North American parish life. These societies were largely alien to the migrants' Old World experience; they bore little relationship to the variety of male religious associations in the *mezzogiorno*. These included confraternities and lay brotherhoods (*fratelli*), communal or district *festa* societies, and "class" (*ceto*) or work-based patron-saint associations. Though often affiliated with a church, they espoused a strong sense of lay autonomy and group solidarity and resembled medieval guilds and sick benefit and burial associations more than church societies. The North American parish associations, by contrast, were led by middle-class men attuned to the norms of North American Catholic piety and lay-clerical proprieties. They stressed Christian altruism, personal sanctification, and self-improvement and demanded time and associational commitments that first-generation immigrants and migrants least of all could ill afford.[21] Extant church records indicate small memberships in the Italian parishes comprising long-settled immigrants and *notabili*, the enclave elite; even here, membership levels in the 1910s fluctuated greatly.[22]

For migrants especially, the absence of women – or more specifically, *their* women – compromised the normative Old World practices associated with the church. Regular mass attendance, the fullfilment of sacramental obligations, and other church-related duties were largely women's work in the *mezzogiorno*. Women served as familial intermediaries connecting the institutional church and the numinous to the spiritual needs of their families. As functional members of the household, their obligations included advancing their families' spiritual economy. As several informants explained, "the women bring home the graces" through their ritual devotions and prayers.[23] This is not to say that men were in any way indifferent. Men's religious roles in this context were primarily subsidiary and complementary to their women's; they maintained their personal devotion to their saints and madonnas (among other devotions, as will be seen). In carrying out their familial duties, moreover, the women in the *paese* continued to act as religious proxies for their men. If they kept up the tradition and continued in their prayers and devotions – all the more necessary as protective measures for kin working in dangerous jobs in a land "without saints" – the graces brought "home" transcended the distances separating family members; the individual was subsumed in the family, however dispersed. Thus just as the male migrants worked overseas for the material betterment of the family, so the women at home helped to advance familial interests through their "spiritual labour."[24] Certainly, not everyone thought in these terms. Protestant notions of personal salvation or Catholic clerical exhortations to duty may have led some to question these assumptions. Still, for sojourners functioning primarily within a familial, collectivist framework, minimal church association could still bring maximal spiritual benefits.

If their presence was inadequate by orthodox standards, Italian migrants did attend church en masse in their own terms, in their own time, and in their own way. Large numbers were present at select activities. The 1908 opening of Our Lady of Mount Carmel Church, for example, was greeted with "great enthusiasm" by a "large congregation." The opening of St Anthony's Church in Hamilton in 1912 saw "hundreds line the streets, unable to gain admittance, [the church already] crowded to the very doors."[25] The interest shown in these events was prompted partly by curiosity and by the pomp and entertainment (band music) provided, but also by the solemnity of the occasion. However temporary their sojourn, Italian migrants looked on the church as an integral part of the sacred landscape, the locus of important rites and rituals and of saintly dispensations, a place "where they could give expression to their sacred cosmos"[26] in keeping with traditional (regional and gender-based) expectations. This was a different construction of the church than that of the clergy, whose spiritual and assimilative priorities called on Italians "to bury all Old Country prejudices of locality or politics and work side by side as *good* Catholics in the new land of their adoption."[27] As in the Old World, Christmas, Easter, and especially Good Friday celebrations were everywhere well attended. In the Toronto Ward the Sicilians' annual Good Friday procession and Passion Play had become "neighbourhood events" by the mid-1910s; basic sacramental obligations were met at these times.[28] Not least of all, the churches witnessed a large male presence on special feast days, in particular the early rudimentary *feste*, the quintessential "outside" expressions of male popular piety and *paese* identity (on which more later).

For clerics, it was precisely these "exceptions," the men's selective relationship to the church, that proved their indifference. For the majority of men, however, the exceptions were the rule, at least with regards to church-based obligations. They would have agreed fully with the missionary who exhorted them to follow in the "national religion of their ancestors and the traditions of their fore *fathers*."[29]

Ironically, the affirmation of this Catholicity was in part illustrated in their very antagonism to the clergy in the early tensions concerning their definition of and relationship to the church.

Beyond church-centred definitions, the men's Catholic identity involved the totality of their world view. Informants from Toronto and Hamilton, for example, recalled the ubiquity of *mal occhio* and fate beliefs not as superstitions but as integral parts of their Christian universe. In Canada as in the *mezzogiorno*, men wore charms or used prayers and gestures to ward off the evil eye. The machinations of fate, *il destino*, were as pervasive in the New World as in the Old. Like fate, other supernatural forms and entities could and did migrate with the sojourners. They revealed themselves in dreams and nightmares, and they inhabited shadows and the material world. As Carla Bianco notes in her study of the Roseto diaspora, Rosetans believed that the Old World *munaceddi* were "extremely adaptable little demons" and could be found even in the New York subway system.[30]

Writing of his boyhood in the 1940s, an Italian American of strongly anticlerical views recalled, "our neighbourhood could not conceive of people living among us not being Catholic. If they weren't Catholic, they were [considered] crazy."[31] With the exception of a few Protestants and "atheists" of uncertain identity, this view applied equally to the largely male migrant enclaves of southern Ontario in the early twentieth century.[32] Committed as they were to the old country, the essentialist Catholicity of these men was rooted in and remained intimately connected to the Old World *paese*. Like the *munaceddi*, however, the Italians' world view was "adaptable"; the longer the stay, the greater the adaptation – although not in the sense anticipated by Canadian or Italian Catholic clerics. This pattern became most evident in the case of the first permanent settlers and the increasing number of migrants who began to settle in the years just prior to and following World War I.

NEW WORLD EXPRESSIONS OF POPULAR CATHOLICISM: SETTLEMENT

Though sojourning continued into the 1920s, Italian migration patterns had begun to change by the early 1910s. Increasingly, Italian men arrived with a view to permanent settlement in Canada. The Great War put an end to these hopes, but only temporarily, as the post-war period witnessed a renewed influx characterized by kin and family reunions and a growing parity in the ratio of male to female immigrants. At the same time Italian naturalization rates increased dramatically. Just over 30 per cent of Italian Canadians were citizens in 1921. Within a decade the rate had more than doubled to 63 per cent, and it increased again to 83 per cent by 1941. The major urban centres witnessed even higher rates of Italian naturalization in the interwar period.[33]

While clearly committed to staying in Canada, the majority of the immigrants did not sever their ties with the Old World. They continued to send remittances to remaining family, corresponded with kin and *paesani*, and maintained a strong sense of local identity in their continued association with the *paese*'s patronal feast day. A *divus loci* normally confined to its "territory of grace," the patronal saint crossed the ocean with the immigrants and, in so doing, expanded its territory to the village diaspora. Still rooted in the *mezzogiorno*, however, the saint linked the devotee to a particular place and a particular time, the *paese festa*. Unable to attend the all-important event, the immigrant devotees participated vicariously through the *questue*, the collection of money (and with it of vows and prayers) required for the organization of the *festa* in the home village. As in the Old World, the collection was normally the duty of select men, New World auxillaries to the village organizers. Like the organizers, they served as the New World custodians of the saint's public image and reputation vis-à-vis fellow villagers and regional *paesani*. The money was collected not only for devotional reasons but as an expression of local patriotism and communal solidarity among the *paese* diaspora. The "global village" reaffirmed its local identity and fellow feeling annually in and through the village *festa*; faith and patriotism in this sense were intimately linked. At stake was the realization of vows, the continued protection of the village and diaspora, and the success and status of the village feast vis-à-vis other village feasts.[34]

The importance of the overseas *questue* is examplified in the large sums collected and in the special projects initiated by immigrants for the advancement of the *festa* or the betterment or replacement of sacred statuary in the home village. Hamilton's Racalmutesi, for example – the single largest Italian immigrant group in the city – helped to pay for two gold crowns worn to this day by Racalmuto's patron saint, the Madonna del Monte, and the Christ Child at her side; the crowns were forged in the interwar period and weigh some 1,500 kilograms. Over time, the *paesi* themselves, especially those with heavy out-migration, became more and more dependent on the overseas *questue*. In these cases the immigrants found themselves in the unenviable position of helping to sustain *paese* feasts in order to preserve appearances and the saint's (and *paese*'s) public standing.[35] Whatever the immigrants' relationship to their patronal saints, the former's sustained connection with the *paese* points to a dimension of New World religiosity demanding recognition beyond the national parish or enclave; this requirement applied equally to immigrant men and women and to the private and communal spheres. Italians in Toronto continued to participate in the parish life of their Old World villages – chiefly *festa*-related but also fundraising for new churches, chapels, and other events.[36] Though naturalized Canadians, first-generation Italians remained citizens of their *paese*, and through their annual devotion to the patronal saint, they affirmed their localized identity in conjuction with fellow *paesani* throughout the world.

While rooted in the Old World, the immigrants' Catholicity also adapted to New World conditions. Necessitated in part by the external environment, adaptation was also a product of the internal, inherently adaptive capacities of popular belief. In the case of first-generation women, this "adaptive continuity" is seen in both their home-based and their church-centric devotions.

As in the Old World, the home life of Italian-Canadian women entailed a strong religious dimension, some of it compatible with North American Catholic standards. Mothers acted as the primary moral and religious instructors of the young. Children were taught "the basics of the Catholic faith" and introduced to the panoply of Catholic saints – some encountered for the first time in the New World – and the devotions, prayers, and stories associated with their lives. Italian children were instilled with "the importance of being Catholic," even as they attended Protestant kindergartens. Official Catholic concerns in this regard were ill-founded. Italian parents thought of the kindergartens in practical terms as play and daycare centres, functional programs little affecting theirs or their children's sense of Catholicity.[37] On reaching school age, the vast majority of the children were enrolled in the separate primary schools; by the 1920s the Catholic schools in the larger "Little Italies" in the Toronto-Hamilton area were overwhelmingly Italian.[38]

The Old World ideal of women as spiritual keepers of hearth and home was also in keeping with North American expectations to a large extent. Like Catholics elsewhere, Italian women in southern Ontario lit votive candles in home shrines and displayed a variety of sacred images in their homes. Along with regional icons, these included images of the Virgin Mary, the Sacred Heart of Jesus, the Holy Family, and other standard Catholic depictions of the sacred – rosaries, scapulars, medallions, mission holy cards. These images were often placed next to family photographs and important family heirlooms. The panoply of images, in addition to specialized rites and vows at home – feast-day penances, food rites – functioned as spiritual conduits to the sacred through which family-based problems and concerns were addressed, hence the icons' proximity in particular to familial objects. The immigrant experience allowed for an adaptation of new forms of worship without undermining older constructions of popular belief. The women's exposure to other regional Italian, as well as other immigrant and North American, saints and devotions allowed them to incorporate these devotions syncretically, thus increasing rather than delimiting their contact with the divine in the New World.

The devotional life of women at home was also characterized by less than in clerical terms ideal practices. The Old World relationship of mutual *pietas*, the functional clientilism of saint and devotee, continued and included extra-canonical and magical religious practices sometimes adapting other regional and New World forms. It was commonly believed, for example, that scapular medals were ideal protective devices against sickness, misfortune, and the evil eye. Other scapular forms, *abitini*, were also believed to be powerful sources of protection. The display of an associational membership in the Apostleship of Prayer (unknown to immigrants in the Old World), a scapular of the Virgin around one's neck, or even a broadside or "votive letter" printed with an account of a miracle could serve as a protective talisman and connector to celestial agents. Devotions of this sort involved more than crude, manipulative magic since they assumed a mutual, emotive, and ongoing relationship with celestial entities and an understanding of the complex workings of the immigrants' Christian universe. Far from simply assimilating clerically orthodox standards of belief, many women added to or adapted new forms and practices – saints, medallions, devotions, folk remedies, and charms – incorporating them into older patterns of "spiritual work" for the protection and betterment of their homes and families.[39]

The women's association with the church was also characterized by adaptive continuity. Far more than men, women remained "conspicuous in their piety," attending church services, novenas, rosary recitations, and other church-based devotions. To a point, the spiritual and associational life of the New World parish opened up social opportunities unavailable to women in the *mezzogiorno*. Their involvement in church bazaars, church picnics, choirs, and various sodalities and associations (Sacred Heart League, Christian Mothers, Children of Mary, Altar Society) exposed them to new ways of thinking and new forms of worship and fellowship. Italian prelates, for their part, believed that through church associational life, women at least were better able to conform to standard Catholic practices and influence their families "for the better." This view was reiterated in

Sunday sermons, church missions, and parish bulletins and "alma-nacs."[40] Certain forms of traditional popular devotions associated closely with women were also modified or changed outright. A pre-eminent example was the *lingua strascinnuni*, the devotion of licking the floor as a devotee approached the sanctuary of the saint. The practice was discouraged by the North American clergy and appears to have died out by the 1920s.[41]

In noting these changes, however, we need to be careful not to make too much of the church's impact on the devotional and associational life of first-generation women. First of all, the women's associational membership, so central to North American parish life, was relatively low when compared to Canadian Catholic parishes. In the five Italian national parishes in Toronto and Hamilton, for instance, total member-ship comprised less than 20 per cent of parishioners at any time be-tween the 1910s and the 1940s. Even this figure was too high since the percentage included multiple memberships.[42] The majority of immi-grant women did not join church associations. This absence was due to a variety of reasons, among them time and work constraints. Equally important, as already noted of male sojourners, was the unfa-miliar, North American character of the associations, with sustained membership requiring acculturation on the immigrants' part. Other factors included the "clique" and "exclusive" atmosphere occasion-ally encountered in the associational gatherings, the centrality of home-based spirituality, and the conviviality provided by family, kin, and *paesan* gatherings, in addition to membership in alternative women's circles outside Catholic clerical control (in settlement and even Protestant mission houses).[43]

Secondly, the end of stringent penitences, like the *lingua strascin-nuni*, did not result in the demise of Old World, female-centric no-tions of suffering or generally "unseemly" expressions of popular piety. Italian women continued as the family's "burden bearers" and primary "spiritual labourers" in other ways. They went on carrying heavy candles and walked barefoot in the local *feste*, for example.[44] More problematically, they continued to act as the familial proxies in church devotions. The idea of proxy suffering was not alien to Catho-lic orthodoxy. Christ, the saints, and the Madonna acted in many ways as "burden bearers" for the faithful. The notion of women as bearers of suffering was also in keeping with orthodox traditions (in the mythic prototypes of Eve and Mary). The problem, of course, lay in the women "carrying" the bulk of the burden, to the detriment, presumably, of individual spiritual initiative; and the unseemly pub-lic "excesses" of the women's devotions, an embarrassment to the North American Catholic hierarchy. However heterodox or unseemly their behaviour, first-generation women continued to "carry their cross" and that of others, a conviction held onto by the immigrant women themselves for more than religious reasons.[45]

A third consideration is that, whatever their association with the church, Italian women were "far from priest-ridden." An informant, describing his mother typically as a "strong Catholic, very religious and devoted to the saints," for instance, observed that she "didn't go to [Sunday] mass every week because of the amount of work she had to do at home."[46] Even among regular churchgoers, clerical expectations were far from realized and were on occasion actively sabotaged. In keeping with Old World anticlericalism, for example, priests remained objects of suspicion. In addition to the usual allegations of "laziness" and sexual misconduct, priests in the New World were often thought of as "money hungry" and "money grubbers," "always berating" parishioners for their consistently low church donations throughout the year. Several informants recalled the calculated subterfuge of Italian families who attended St Agnes Church, Toronto, in the interwar period. In what amounted to a weekly ritual, they changed their quarters into nickels and dimes the Saturday before mass so as to have small change for the Sunday mass collection. "When the big nickel came in," one man recalled, "Reverend Truffa [the Salesian pastor at St Agnes in the 1920s] called it the devil's quarter … Every Sunday, he'd say, 'Let's hear the rustle of bills, not those devil's quarters!'" Stories of this sort are legion, with quarter-sized buttons sometimes replacing the nickels and dimes and playing cards masquerading as bills.[47] More important were the consistently low communion-reception rates, even among the women attending regularly. The low rates of the 1910s continued in the interwar period. As late as the 1940s, when the second generation was well into maturity, Italian mass attendance and weekly communion-reception rates remained among the lowest of any Catholic group in urban southern Ontario.[48]

Fourthly, what may have appeared to be orthodox behaviour, reflecting clerical expectations, was not always what it seemed. Italian women appropriated church teachings selectively, imaginatively, and eclectically. At church as at home, popular theology acted as a prism, refracting orthodox light through the filter of lived experience. This "refraction of the orthodox" took a variety of forms. Some perceived the (officially) heterodox as orthodox – for example, the often-expressed belief in the Trinity as the Holy Family (a meaningful, concrete replacement of abstruse theology) or the "practical," magical use of the Pater Noster, the rosary, novena prayers, and evil-eye incantations as mutual extensions of each other. Others experienced new forms of worship through old frames of reference, as in the adaptation of unfamiliar Marian scapular traditions or first-generation affiliation with New World devotions, such as the Sacred Heart League, incorporating them into the familiar clientilism and "religious alchemy" of traditional belief.[49] Yet another form of refraction was the spiritual world of "parallel divergence," the individual-communal coexistence of divergent and even contradictory patterns of belief. The church's official characterization of St Joseph (a meek, mild, resigned old man), for example, differed from the rustic, familiar peasant saint of popular folklore. Sicilian Miloccans in fact "made a sharp distinction" between two feasts: the *festa* of "St Joseph of the church," celebrated in March, and the feast of "St Joseph in the country," held in May. Vows made to the one saint were never paid to the other.[50] Similar distinctions were made in the New World, even as the "different" saints shared an identity and similitude in the church statues representing "them." In short, we need to be careful in assuming that formal, church-based devotions to universally recognizable saints, even among regular churchgoers and church associational members, were "appropriately" orthodox in their form, content, or object of devotion.

Women's church attendance was also a product, oftentimes, of ambiguous or alternative agendas. The primary determinant in attending services had less to do with morals or church regulations than with private and familial needs. An important part of attendance was lighting candles and acquiring holy water for homes shrines and home-based devotions. The church in this sense was an extension of the home. Candle-lighting especially was an important ritual in women's piety; so much so, in fact, that when a parish dispute erupted at St Agnes Church in 1922–23, pitting the pastor against the parish lay committee, among the committee's first actions was the sequestering of eight thousand candles in the expectation that it "should collect the money derived" from their extensive devotional use.[51] The act of candle-lighting connected the devotees in an immediate, practical way to the world of the sacred. The candle flame was a visual representation of and a pervasive, insistent testimony to their prayers and supplications. Perhaps more than in the Old World, candle-lighting in North America took on a special importance, the practice necessarily replacing the panoply of traditional votive and devotional offerings that would have been intolerable in the New World (among them the placement of foods and other materials on church altars and side altars). The varieties of "refraction," religious alchemy, and eclecticism ought not to be seen as a "corruption" or "a poor assimilation of Catholic doctrine." The majority of Italian women did not see themselves as "poor Catholics," but rather simply as Catholics, *cristiani*. They espoused a faith and a way of being rooted practically in the exigencies of daily life.

Like the first-generation women, Italian immigrant men remained Catholics in their own way. They expressed this Catholicity through a similar prism of refraction and adaptive continuity. Traditional ways were not discarded but adapted to the exigencies of lived experience in the New World. This phenomenon can be seen in three important areas of male religious life: in their relationship to the church, in their private, personal devotions, and in the organization of communal, "outdoor" expressions of faith and identity, both encapsulated in the distinctively immigrant Italian *festa*.

As in the pre–World War I period, Italian immigrant and North American clerics continued to view Italian men as "Christian tourists," infrequent or occasional church visitors. As the Reverend Aloysius Scafuro of St Clement's Church, Toronto, commented in 1920, referring especially to Italian men, "a very small percentage of the Italians go to church; but for Baptism, wedding [*sic*] and Funerals, they like to make a big splash. Consequently the almost common saying: These people go to church three times in life." By the mid-1920s Scafuro was despairing of his "missionary work" among Toronto's Italians. "My sole purpose is to try to save at least five per cent of my Italians, either immigrants or born here in the city," he wrote in 1924. "So far, we have not one per cent." In the same year, the pastor of St Agnes Church, the Reverend Joseph Basso, wrote to Toronto's Archbishop Neil McNeil requesting to be relieved of his duties. The only hope for the parish, he said, was for "a young and zealous priest, a more intelligent and patient man than myself [to carry on the work]."[52] A "zealous missionary" himself in his early years, the Reverend John Bonomi appears, similarly, to have grown disenchanted with his work among Hamilton's Italians by the mid-1920s. Though a pastor at both St Anthony's and All Souls Churches, he seems to have "abandoned" the former by the early 1930s. He barely visited the church and allowed the building itself to deteriorate, evidently unconcerned at its increasingly "wretched appearance."[53]

The disenchantment of these and other priests was a product of lay-clerical and personality problems centred primarily on jurisdictional and financial matters. The situation, however, was not as bleak as Scafuro maintained. Even under his tenure, many attended services more than "three times in life." As we have seen, Christmas, Holy Week, and Easter celebrations, in addition to (select) church feasts such as St Anthony's and All Souls' Day, witnessed an increased male attendance. Periodic missions, moreover, saw large numbers of men show up in churches. As early as 1914, for example, the church of Mount Carmel initiated a week-long mission in which "400 to 500" Italians, men and women, crowded the church on weekends, with "many obliged to stand".[54] Missions everywhere were popular events. As in the Old World, parishioners were attracted by "distinguished preachers" and dramatic public orators. Though spiritually defined, the attraction was also in the entertainment provided, a respite from the rigours of work and the grind of daily routine.[55] Male church attendance was also evident at exceptional times, as in the mid-1930s at Mount Carmel when the Reverend Stephen Auad, then pastor, gained a reputation as "the little man of miracles." Auad claimed to heal "the sick and dying" through the intercession of St Anthony and other saints. For a brief time the church became a pilgrimage site, "a rival to that at St. Anne de Beaupre," attracting many thousands, Italian immigrants and Canadians alike.[56]

With the replacement of unpopular clerics such as Scafuro and Basso, the tensions of the early 1920s lessened somewhat. The Salesian takeover of St Agnes in 1924 and the later acquisition of the parish and St Clement's by the Franciscans resulted in a relative improvement in lay-clerical relations, especially male associational contacts with the church. Church social, non-devotional activities increased, involving more men and young people than ever before as participants and observers. These included bowling, theatre, and recreation and sports clubs, in addition to Catholic Youth Organization activities and young peoples' societies. Popular, "forward"-looking priests took the lead in these endeavours, men such as the Reverend Charles Mascari of St Anthony's, Hamilton, and Reverends Patrick Crowley and Riccardo Polticchia at St Agnes, Toronto. Social outreach, they hoped, would result in spiritual "renewal."[57]

The expectation was not met. As we have seen, the associational and spiritual statistics in the national parishes from the 1910s through the 1940s improved only marginally at best; male church attendance remained static and communion reception minimal. Prelates continued to refer to the "Italian Problem" and persistent male "indifference."[58] There is some truth to this view if judged by strictly clerical standards, but there were other standards as well. As in the Old World and in the pre–World War I period, Italian men defined their relationship to the church in the context of personal need, relative sufficiency, and gendered proxy roles. What might have been an insufficient institutional affiliation to clerics was more than sufficient for many men. They attended church at select times for select purposes, beyond which the women were left to "bring home the graces." For many, a cleric's reputation and personality determined the extent of men's personal affiliation with the institutional church.[59]

Yet another factor in appraising the men's apparent "indifference," increasingly important with settlement, was their conception of the church as sacred landscape. The church, as building and sacred site, took on greater importance with settlement, even as formal religious association remained static. It was not only a locus of social gatherings and activities but also the localized "residence" of the saints and an indispensable seat of traditional piety and sacred rites (of passage) – the latter all the more important with long-term settlement in the New World.[60] The larger immigrant (*paese*) communities especially looked to the Italian church as the place to house *their* saints and to affirm *their* way of being. Because of the concentration of fellow *paesani* and the increasing need to cater to their religious needs, the communities took a proprietory interest in the church as a cultural-religious extension of their enclaves. Hamilton's All Souls Church, for example, built in the early 1920s, was constructed with the large-scale assistance in time and labour of the majority Racalmutese Sicilians in the West End enclave. Though male membership and attendance at the church remained low in the years following construction, the city's Racalmutesi thought of the church as "their own." So much so, in fact, that Racalmutese leaders approached Bonomi during the construction requesting that the church be named after their patronal saint, the Madonna del Monte. According to oral testimony, he refused, insisting that the church belonged "to all of the Italians." The name finally chosen – Our Lady of All Souls – though apparently "a compromise decision," reflected his ideal. The name referred to the universal Madonna of "all souls" (that is all the city's Italians) and not the regional Madonna of the majority Racalmutesi. Even so, great uncertainty remained as to the church's "real" name long after its construction. Some continued to refer to it as the church of the Madonna (del Monte), others to Our Lady of All Souls or simply All Souls, and still others to Our Lady of Mount Carmel, an early proposal. As late as 1954, the Hamilton Chancery wrote to the Reverend Remo Rizzatto, then pastor of All Souls, inquiring as to what "the official title of this church" was. Evidently, not all "the old people of this parish," as Rizzatto wrote, acquiesced to Bonomi's ideal.[61]

The national parish, then, served a multiplicity of functions as a social nodal point, a locus of contested sacred space and of Italian Catholic identities – all this even as its orthodox, clerically defined purposes remained secondary. Just as the clerics and Italian elites sought to use the church as an assimilative tool for their own purposes, so first-generation men and women – as members of a *paese* group or society and as individuals or family "representatives" – used it for their own ends, assimilating or adapting it to their own purposes.

The men's identity as Catholics was not restricted to their affiliation with the church. Private devotions to regional saints continued, sustained by Old World contacts, *questue* obligations, and the household placement of old prints and weathered postcards of village saints and madonnas. "The saints are part of your life," an informant observed. "The Madonna [of Montevergine] is the mother of my heart." Devotions of this sort sometimes involved eclectic and "refractive" expressions unique to a devotee's personal experience and world view. A Toronto man, for example, recalled that his "grandfather was not much for churchgoing [in the 1910s and 1920s], but he had his own prayers and his own devotion to his favourite saint, San Silvestro." The devotion involved an annual celebration in which the man, an amateur musician, and a friend regaled the saint with prayers and songs at home, in commemoration of a favour long ago received.[62]

Though unique, the incident is reminiscent of the traditional, public litanies sung to the saints at Christmas, Easter, and the harvest season. Practices of this sort were difficult to maintain in the New World, at least in their original form and removed, as they were, from their original context. Popular and non-church-based to begin with, the chants, *lamenti*, litanies, *cunti* (legends and sacred tales, often sung), and other religious declamations found no place in the North American churches. They were not lost, however, since they were retained in memory and recited occasionally at family gatherings and extended communal functions, such as *feste* or *paese*-based picnics. Occasions like these were also forums for traditional storytelling, which, though compromised by the advent of radio, growing literacy, and the rigours of the North American workweek, still found an immigrant audience.[63]

Personal devotions were not confined to the home or church. Imbued with personal and eclectic meanings, prints, icons, crosses, and makeshift shrines adorned outdoor spaces – doorways, yard entrances, backyards, sheds, and outdoor storage sites. Except by the individuals and families who erected them, in most cases they went unnoticed. On occasion, as in the case of the Rosebank grotto of the Madonna of Mount Carmel on Staten Island, private devotions could develop into public shrines of widespread popularity.[64] More broadly, like the women in the enclaves and their *paesani* in the *mezzogiorno*, immigrant men participated in the magico-spiritual world discussed, a syncretic combination of official, idiosyncretic, and traditional, "superstitious" beliefs. God, fate, folk spirits, demons, and the evil eye pervaded daily life. The simple act of crossing a loaf of bread with a knife, for example, a Sicilian tradition usually conducted by the male head of family, was imbued with ritual significance. The father expressed his authority in the right/rite to bless the fruit of his labour; gave thanks for the food about to be eaten, a benedictory and propitiatory act (addressing the volatility of fate and divine forces); dismissed potential harm in the ritual act of crossing; and – in an interesting case of "refraction" (*that is*, the popular religious apprehension of formal theology) – commemorated the indispensability and "sanctity of bread," recalling Christ's "miracle at the Last Supper" and the miracle of the multiplication of loaves.[65]

An important and fundamentally male expression of Catholicity in the New World, as in the Old, was the organization of the communal *festa*. As we have seen, the Old World feasts associated partly with the church – the *ceti*-based, *fratelli*, and Holy Week and patronal *feste* – shared little in common with the Catholicism of the New World. Neither the *ceti* celebration, with its occupational and specific church affiliations, nor the *paese*-based confraternity and patronal feasts, with their strongly lay associations and territorial and historically rooted identities, had any equivalent in North America. The work-based devotional societies appear to have died out entirely in the New World. Their demise was due in part to insufficient membership and resources. Very few immigrants remained tied to or continued to define themselves as members of their traditional *ceti*; many became involved in other kinds of work in "l'*America*." Similarly, the *fratelli* societies as such had no equivalent in the New World. Though they were superficially similar to church-based Christian confraternities and Third Order societies, the Catholic universality, strong clerical direction, and strictly orthodox foundations of these organizations differentiated them from the strongly lay, regionally distinctive fraternal associations of the *mezzogiorno*. Of the three associations, the *festa* society, or *comitato*, was the only one reconstituted in the New World, usually under the auspices of an immigrant mutual aid or benevolent society, the all-male *mutuo soccorso*.[66] As in the Old World, the *festa* itself consisted typically of a solemn, formal procession with a statue or banner of the saint, accompanied by devotees carrying candles and other votive offerings, High Mass and panegyrics in church, and ancillary private devotions at home. It also involved fireworks, band music, lottery draws, athletic games, picnic outings, and other entertainment. At its grandest, the occasion attracted many thousands of people, as in the case of the Madonna del Monte feast in Hamilton in 1931, when, according to one account, over 30,000 Sicilians "participated in the great [event]."[67]

The *festa* highlights the important role of lay men in the configuration and expression of communal religious sensibilities. This may be seen in a number of ways. Through the *comitato*, first of all, the *paese* community affirmed its traditional lay control of the *festa* celebration. The committee saw itself as the guardian of tradition, responsible for the maintenance and "integrity" of the feast as known. To the consternation of clerics, the priest was hired solely to celebrate High Mass and bestow the virtues of the saint in the panegyrics. The *comitato* retained ultimate control of the *festa's* programming and expenses. This could and sometimes did result in serious conflict. A clerical report in the 1910s, for instance, described a celebration in which clerics and committee members came to blows. In a long tradition of such conflicts, *festa* committees sometimes hid their saints' statues in saloon lofts and warehouses lest the priests get hold of them.[68] Lay-clerical tensions remained a constant in Italian and especially male immigrant relationships with the church. The *festa* was a primary source of that tension.

Secondly, in keeping with tradition, the *festa* was a forum for expressing the "totality" of lay immigrant Catholicity. Combining private and public devotions, admixing sacred and profane, the feast revealed the immigrants' distinctive *cristianeismo* in all of its apparent contradictions. The inclusion of fireworks and band music – major organizational costs – were not "extravagances," not mere diversions, but essential parts of the whole. The very expense, time, and effort taken and the shared public manifestations of these efforts were indicative of the extent of the devotees' respect for, and devotion to their patron saint. In his standing as a fellow *paesano* in the immediacy of the sacred, the saint too "participated" in the events of the *festa*. While there were certainly men for whom the feast was "an occasion [merely] for carousing and merrymaking"[69] or an opportunity for advancing private and business interests, many more participated fully in the public integration of sacred and profane. At a core level, as Robert Orsi writes, the *festa* "shows itself to be the people's claiming of time [and space] for themselves ... within which they could be themselves, affirming their deepest values [as men and women]"[70] and acclaiming their common humanity as "Christians." Though the men were equally devoted to their patron saints, their organizational and proprietary roles in the *festa* differed somewhat from the women's more expressive and overtly "spiritual" participation.

A third factor was that the patronal feast pointed explicitly to the interconnection of *paesan* devotions and *paese* patriotism, of spiritual identity and village or regional consciousness, a linkage rooted in the figure of the saint and devolving on the men especially to preserve and present publicly. As we have seen, the *questue* connected Italian devotees throughout the diaspora to their original *festa*. For those with the resources and population base to "re-enact" the feast as well, the transoceanic link, the connection of *divus loci* and *paese* immigrants, was all the more immediate. *Paese* fellow feeling did not always result in interethnic harmony; provincialism and interethnic suspicions remained. In Toronto, for instance, the feast of San Rocco was contested between two village groups, the Modugnesi and Monteleonesi. The latter celebrated their feast in August and the former in September, the result of different harvest seasons in their respective regions of Puglia. The two groups had little to do with each other. Not only were *paese* pride and *festa* support (financial and otherwise) at stake, but so was the groups' "claim" to San Rocco himself as *their* patron saint, *their divus loci*. At stake also was the committee's, and through it the *paese*'s, pride as "guardians" of the saint's image. Not surprisingly, the two groups fought over ownership of the only statue of San Rocco at Mount Carmel. In Hamilton the very size of the Racalmutese community and the prominence bestowed on its madonna was perceived by others as a form of ethnic "domination," a sort of regional "colonialism" through popular religion; we have already seen an inkling of this attitude in the tensions over the naming of All Souls Church.[71] Still, for all the misunderstandings and controversies – and all the more so *because* of them – the patronal *festa* connected the male immigrant to the *paese* (as village, region, or *patria*, "fatherland") and the Catholicism and traditions of that *paese* to his identity as an Italian-Canadian "Christian."

Fourthly, the *festa* itself, while manifestly ethnic, was also a Canadian celebration, an affirmation of the men's civic identity as "good citizens and Christians."[72] In all such *feste*, intertwined British and Italian flags decorated the immigrant quarters. Bunting in the national colours was dispersed throughout the procession route. Italian musical selections and "operatic airs" were followed by British and Canadian patriotic numbers and renditions of "God Save the King," a prominent part of any *festa* program. English was also spoken formally, as part of a church service or in speeches given by guest celebrities or local *notabili*. In all these displays the organizers and participants affirmed their pride and "heritage" as Italians and their loyalty as British subjects and citizens. These claims to respectability were bound up with and expressed through the *festa*, an unabashedly and unapologetically southern Italian expression of religion and culture. If Protestant missionaries were scandalized and Catholic prelates frustrated and embarrassed by it, the majority of the *festa* participants saw little to concern them. They thought of themselves as no less Canadian for being Catholics in their own way. Far from an embarrassment, the *festa* exhibited "the best" of their culture. For the immigrant men, especially the members of the *comitato*, the feast was a forum for the expression of communal pride. As an informant noted of the Madonna del Monte feast in 1931, himself a member of the *comitato* that year, "We showed them [non-Racalmutese Italians and Canadians alike] what we were capable of doing. We put on a great feast [*una festa proprio mondiale*] … and everyone came."[73]

In filling out an archdiocesan spiritual statistics form in 1946, the Reverend G. McKenna, pastor at Mount Carmel Church, answered the question "Catholics fallen away [?]" with a curt reply: "Very few who would admit it." Answering the same question the following year, he wrote again, "Scarcely any who would admit they have given up their religion."[74] While there were certainly some who "gave up their religion," becoming Protestant or abandoning the faith entirely, there were many more who remained Catholics, lived as Catholics, defined themselves as Catholics – and thus had nothing "to admit." They may not have fit McKenna's criteria of a Catholic, but they did fit and abide by their own conceptions of Catholicism.

The sacramental obligations and formal church practices that defined McKenna's Catholic comprised only a part of the religious world of Italians and Italian immigrants. Of far greater importance, pervading their day-to-day lives, was the existential totality of their folk-cultural universe. This universe was premised on the socio-economic realities of lived experience. The family economy was reflected in the spiritual economy of the sacred, and to that extent, it was highly gendered. In the *mezzogiorno*, women tended largely to "internal," church- and *domus*-centred forms of piety and men to "external," public-associational and communal forms. In both cases, however, they functioned as integrated parts of a whole, dependent on and complementary to each other. Transcending these divisions was the private world of personal and eclectic devotions, a world of "refractive" orthodox and traditional folk practices.

The universe and traditional devotional life of first-generation Italians continued in Canada. Though adapted and inherently adaptive, the familial devotions, gender roles, and generally vibrant religious life of Italians remained a cultural fixture of Italian colonies until well after World War II. In the existential totality of this universe, the first generation remained true to its beliefs because, as Carlo Levi wrote of the peasants of Lucania, "to be a Christian is to be a human being."

NOTES

1 Rudolph Vecoli, "Cult and Occult in Italian-American Culture: The Persistence of a Religious Heritage," in Thomas Marzik, ed., *Immigrants and Religion in Urban America* (Philadelphia, 1977), 47n34. See also Rudolph Vecoli, "Prelates and Peasants: Italian Immigrants and the Catholic Church," *Journal of Social History* 2 (1968–69): 217–68; Silvano Tomasi, *Piety and Power* (Staten Island, 1975); and Robert Orsi, *The Madonna of 115th Street* (New Haven, 1985).

2 On contemporary Catholic clerical definitions of the "Italian Problem," see, for instance, A.R. Bandini, "Concerning the Italian Problem," *Ecclesiastical Review* 62 (March 1920): 278–85; and Henry J. Browne, "The Italian Problem in the Catholic Church of the United States, 1880–1900," United States Catholic Historical Society, *Historical Records and Studies* 35 (1946).

3 J. M. Garbellano, "They of Italy Salute You," *Missionary Outlook* (*MO*), July 1915, 151.

4 This study is based on taped oral interviews and internal ethnic and formal archival and quantitative sources. The orals derive from my dissertation research and comprise 112 interviews and 35 additional interviews from the Hamilton-Toronto area. For details on the former, see Enrico Carlson Cumbo, "As the Twig Bends, the Tree's Inclined: Growing Up Italian in Toronto, 1905–1940" (PhD dissertation, University of Toronto, 1996).

5 Carlo Levi, *Christ Stopped at Eboli* (Harmondsworth, 1948), 1.

6 See Robert Harney, "Men without Women: Italian Migrants in Canada, 1885–1930," in Betty Caroli et al., eds., *The Italian Immigrant Woman in North America* (Toronto, 1978); George Pozzetta, ed., *Pane e lavoro* (Toronto, 1980); and Michael La Sorte, *La America: Images of Italian Greenhorn Experience* (Philadelphia, 1985).

7 Harney, "Men without Women," 80, 84, 89–92.

8 Quoted in R.E. Park and H.A. Miller, *Old World Traits Transplanted* (New York, 1921), 150.

9 Vincenza Scarpaci, *A Portrait of the Italians in America* (New York, 1983), 83; Jacob Riis, "Feast Days in Little Italy," *Century Magazine* 58 (August 1899): 496; Broughton Brandenburg, *Imported Americans* (New York, 1904), 140–1; Orsi, *The Madonna of 115th Street*, 22–3, 164.

10 The 1921 Methodist *Yearbook* lists only two other Italian missions in Ontario: North Bay with a membership of ten and Copper Cliff (no data). The Italian conversion rate among Presbyterians was similarly low. See United Church Archives (*UCA*), Methodist Church, *Minutes of Conferences*, Home Mission reports; Methodist Church, *Yearbook* (1921), 23, 40, 51; Presbyterian Church of Canada, Board of Home Missions and Social Service, series 2, box 3, file 29.

11 *MO*, April 1910, 92; June 1910, 124; July 1915, 151; August 1923, 173–4; Woman's Missionary Society (wms), *Annual Report* (1910–11), cxvii; *Missionary Bulletin*, July–September 1919, 343–6; April–June 1920, 251–2; uca, pamphlets, Rafaelle De Pierro, "Italians in Europe and in Canada" (Toronto, 1917), 10–16; Eva Lake, "Italians and the Simple Gospel" (New York, n.d.), 1–8.

12 uca, Methodist Church Missionary Society, Home Department, Italian Work, M. Trentadue to S.W. Dean, 25 July 1910.

13 Enrico Sartorio, *Social and Religious Life of Italians in America* (Boston, 1918), 103. For an overview of Italian Protestant work in southern Ontario, see Enrico C. Cumbo, "Impediment to the Harvest: The Limitations of the Methodist Proselytization of Italian Canadian Immigrants in Toronto, 1905–25," in M. McGowan and B. Clarke, eds., *Catholics at the Gatheirng Place* (Toronto, 1993), 155–76.

14 Quoted in Anna Chairetakis, "Tears of Blood: The Calabrian *Villanella* and Immigrant Epiphanies," in L. Del Giudice, ed., *Studies in Italian American Folklore* (Logan, 1993), 38, 39–40.

15 Mark McGowan, "We Are All Canadians: A Social, Religious and Cultural Portrait of Toronto's English-Speaking Catholics, 1890–1920" (PhD dissertation, University of Toronto, 1988), 87–9, 349–50; John Zucchi, *Italians in Toronto* (Kingston and Montreal, 1988), 128–29.

16 Protestant missions predated the establishment of Italian-language Catholic parishes in Welland, Niagara Falls, and various sites in northern Ontario. See wms, *Annual Reports* (1907ff), and Methodist Church, *Yearbooks*; Scalabrini House, Toronto (sht), Pietro Pisani, "Per l'assistenza religiosa degli italiani del canada" (1909), 11–12. On J.F. Bonomi, see Archives of the Roman Catholic Diocese of Hamilton (arcdh), Priest files, J. Bonomi, Parish files, St Anthony and All Souls; All Souls Church, Hamilton, J.F. Bonomi, correspondence.

17 *MO*, April 1910, 125; Zucchi, *Italians in Toronto*, 128–9, 132.

18 Interviews with Ralph and Rose Panzine, Toronto, 8 June 1990; Grace and Rocco Volpe, Toronto, 30 July 1992; Archives of the Roman Catholic Archdiocese of Toronto (arcat), Bishop McNeil Papers, Social Welfare, J.P. Bench, Catholic Charities report (ca. 1915); *Catholic Register* (cr), 24 February 1910, 6; 8 August 1912, 4; 14 October 1915, 7.

19 arcat, McNeil Papers, Italian Catholics, Rev. Francesco Fiori to McNeil, 17 December 1917; ibid., Priest files, Revs. A. Scafuro and J. Longo correspondence; sht, Toronto, Historical Correspondence, J.M. Mahoney to Superior-General (Scalabrini), 23 December 1907; Zucchi, *Italians in Toronto*, 121–3, 134–6.

20 See, for instance, arcdh, All Souls Church, Hamilton, correspondence, John Bonomi to P. Vincentini, 29 January 1910.

21 ARCAT, Priest files, Rev. A. Scafuro correspondence; *CR*, 27 January 1910, 10; McGowan, "We Are All Canadians," 217–28. For a discussion of immigrant religious societies, see the second part of this essay.

22 In Toronto, for example, the Holy Name Society at Mount Carmel "held its own" at about seventy (on paper), but the societies at St Agnes and St Clement's, the other Italian parishes in the city, were organized, dissolved, and reorganized throughout the 1910s. See Carlson Cumbo, "As the Twig Bends," 389–404, 439–40, and tables 6B-D; McGowan, "We Are All Canadians," 223–4.

23 Interview with S. Sanella, N. Mancini, and P. Vicari, Toronto, 24 August 1987.

24 Towards the same practical ends in both cases: family health and security.

25 *CR*, 15 October 1908, 8; 12 November 1908, 8; Hamilton *Spectator*, 20 May 1912, 4; Hamilton Public Library, Special Collections, *Herald* Scrapbook, "Churches," vol. 2, 17–18; SHT, Pisani, "Per l'assistenza religiosa," 5.

26 Ferdinando Fasce, "The Italian American Catholic Parish in the Early Twentieth Century: A View From Waterbury, Connecticut," *Studi Emigrazione* 28 (September 1991): 351; Orsi, *The Madonna of 115th Street*, 163–4.

27 *CR*, 12 November 1908, 8, my emphasis; similarly, *Hamilton Spectator*, 20 May 1912, 4; 23 October 1923.

28 For a quantitative discussion of these obligations see Carlson Cumbo, "As the Twig Bends," 400–1, 441. On the Good Friday procession and Passion Play, see St Patrick's, *Annals*, 12 April 1914; *CR*, 6 April 1916, 8; 27 April 1916, 8, 10; Zucchi, *Italians in Toronto*, 138.

29 *CR*, 8 October 1908, 8.

30 Carla Bianco, *The Two Rosetos* (Bloomington, 1974), 85, 90–2; interviews.

31 J. Della Femina and Charles Sopkin, *An Italian Grows in Brooklyn* (Boston, 1978), 148.

32 ARCAT, Revs. Scafuro and Longo correspondence; *CR*, 23 April 1908, 4; SHT, Pisani, "Per l'assistenza religiosa," 8; Fasce, "The Italian American Catholic Parish," 349; Frank Salamone, "Power and Dominance in Sicilian Households in Rochester, NY," *Studi emigrazione* 31 (1994): 85.

33 Canada, Census, 1941, vol. 4, table 8, 165; Carlson Cumbo, "As the Twig Bends," tables 1F, 1G, and appendix 2, "Assessment Tables."

34 Mia di Tota, "Saint Cults and Political Alignments in Southern Italy," *Dialectical Anthropology* 5 (May 1981): 320–4; Zucchi, *Italians in Toronto*, 137–8; Vecoli, "Cult and Occult," 29; interviews.

35 Eugenio N. Messana. *Racalmuto nella storia della Sicilia* (Canicatti, 1969), 95; Mariano Fresta, "La festa di S. Alfio," *La ricerca folklorica* 25 (April 1992): 99–109; W.A. Douglass, *Emigration in a South Italian Town* (New Brunswick, 1984), 127–30.

36 Zucchi, *Italians in Toronto*, 138; Douglass, *Emigration*, 130.

37 Interviews with L. Motta, Toronto, 20, 23 June 1989; P. Zona, Toronto,
    12–18 June 1990; G. and R. Volpe, Toronto, 30 July 1992; UCA, *Minutes* of
    the Missionary Committee of the Toronto Methodist Union, 4 April 1918;
    MO, June 1916, 128.
38 For a quantitative discussion, see Carlson Cumbo, "As the Twig Bends,"
    chap. 3.
39 Orsi, *The Madonna of 115th Street*, 67; Carla Bianco, *Emigrazione/Emigration*
    (Bari, 1980), 141,145–57; interview with G. Grillo, Toronto, 10 November
    1989.
40 ARCAT, St Mary of the Angels Parish, Parrochia di S. Clemente, almanacs,
    1919–20; St Patrick's Parish, Toronto, St Patrick Church, *Annals*, commen-
    tary and "Parish Statistics," 1913–19; Rev. Scafuro correspondence, 1919–
    24; ARCDH, St Anthony Parish, letters and "Summary of Italian Parish
    Situation" (1933); interviews
41 Orsi, *The Madonna of 115th Street*, 11; Fresta, "La festa di S. Alfio," 108.
    None of my informants recalled ever witnessing this penitence in Canada.
42 The largest single membership by far was in the Sacred Heart League, a
    largely private devotion with little actual church attendance. See ARCAT,
    St Patrick's Church, *Annals*, 1913–20, 1935–44; National parish files,
    Mount Carmel, St Agnes, and St Mary of the Angels; ARCDH, Parish files,
    All Souls Church and St Anthony Parish; Carlson Cumbo, "As the Twig
    Bends," chap. 6, table 6.
43 Interviews. On women's alternative membership, see City of Toronto Ar-
    chives (CTA), Central Neighborhood House, monthly and annual reports,
    1911–24; WMS, *Annual Reports*, "Italian Missions," 1905–25. In this context,
    it should be noted that, unlike the Irish-Celtic and North American experi-
    ence, the actual impact of the "devotional revolution" and (clerically di-
    rected) "feminization" of Catholicity in the latter nineteenth century was
    less keenly felt in the Italian South, partly as a result of the limited oppor-
    tunities available for female participation in formal organizational life out-
    side kin and family structures. But a more important factor was the
    diversity of *maddonine* prototypes, which differed substantially from the
    uniform, idealized Mary of church orthodoxy. The peasant's folk universe
    and the uncertainties of lived experience, furthermore, tempered the "gra-
    cious femininity," the moralist, selfless virtue and unquestioned obedience
    fostered in Marian piety. The clerical hierarchy in the *mezzogiorno* proved
    unable, in the end, to redirect popular piety along strictly orthodox, ultra-
    montanist lines. A product of long-held folk-cultural assumptions, the role
    of women in religious life was little affected by clerical prescriptions or
    "revolutionary"change.
44 Orsi, *The Madonna of 115th Street*, chap. 6–8; Jacob A. Riis, "Feast Days in
    Little Italy," *The Century* 58 (August 1899): 498; Joseph Sciorra, "Multivo-

cality and Vernacular Architecture," in Del Giudice, *Studies in Italian American Folklore*, 226–7. The term "burden bearers" is Orsi's.

45 Suffering served, ironically, as a source of women's "empowerment" in the obligations, respect, and deference garnered from family members (for whom they suffered). Interviews, especially Caterina S., Toronto, 27 August 1987.

46 Interview with Joseph C., Toronto, 12. September, 1990. See also Salamone, "Power and Dominance," 85.

47 Interview with C. Bush, Toronto, 14 September 1989. For examples of low-church collections, see ARCAT, McNeil Papers, Addenda, "Church [Collections]," MNAH26.34–35; ARCDH, Diocesan Spiritual Statistics, "Diocesan Collections," 1939ff; St Anthony parish, "Summary."

48 In the 1940s, for instance, the average number of Hamilton diocesan parishioners not fulfilling their Easter duty was about forty per parish; the equivalent number for All Souls and St Anthony's was about four hundred and two hundred respectively; figures calculated from diocesan "Spiritual and Financial Statistics," pastoral visitations, and parish files, 1939–43 (overall figures for Toronto available only for 1942 and 1943).

49 Orsi, *The Madonna of 115th Street*, 203; Michael Carroll, *Veiled Threats: The Logic of Popular Catholicism in Italy* (Baltimore, 1996), 8off; interviews.

50 Charlotte Chapman, *Milocca: A Sicilian Village* (Cambridge, 1971), 177–8; Jerry Mangione, *Mount Allegro* (New York, 1972), 89–93. On popular tales associated with St Joseph and other reconstructed "peasant" saints, see, for example: Giuseppe Pitrè, *Fiabe e leggende popolari siciliane* (Palermo, 1888), 247–51.

51 ARCAT, Parish files, St Agnes, "Parish Meeting," January 1923, 1; interviews.

52 ARCAT, Priest files, Rev. A. Scafuro, Scafuro to J.P. Treacy, 20 January 1920; Scafuro to Archbishop N. McNeil, October 1924; St Agnes Church, correspondence, J. Basso to Archbishop N. McNeil, 4 April 1924.

53 On the "abandonment" of St Anthony Church, see especially ARCDH, St Anthony Church "Summary" (1933), correspondence, petitions, and complaints.

54 ARCAT, St Patrick's, *Annals*, 22 March and 5 April 1914.

55 As several informants recalled, "We got a kick out of them," "they were very good ... the missionaries were a treat to listen to," "the louder their voices the more you liked them" (interviews with P. Zona, C. Bush, and Joseph C.). On Italian church missions, see also (ARCDH, *Catholic Voice*, 2 (September/October 1932): 16; All Souls Church, correspondence, prewar mission cards appended; Jay Dolan, *The American Catholic Experience* (Garden City, 1985), 212–13, 225–7.

56 ARCAT, Priests files, Rev. Stephen Auad, unidentified newspaper clippings, 1935; interviews, especially with L. Motta.

57 On the variety of parish activities, see parish anniversary booklets and ARCAT parish files; V. Dell'Angela, Toronto, Miceli family papers. On Mascari, see ARCDH, Parish files, St Ann's and St Patrick's, clerical biographies; Pauline Mascari, correspondence and scrapbook, Hamilton. On Crowley and Polticchia, see ARCAT, Priest files, St Agnes Parish; interviews, especially Multicultural History Society of Ontario Collection, Toronto R. Polticchia, 15 December 1977.

58 As Crowley noted typically, "We have many coming to church, but there are very many [more] who do not" (ARCAT, St Agnes Church, Rev. P. Crowley to Rev. John Harris, 31 May 1937). See also Carlson Cumbo, "As the Twig Bends", table 30, viii.

59 This was a commonly expressed sentiment in the interviews conducted. Even then, as several informants commented, "You can't separate the people that go to church as Catholic [from] those that don't ... They're all Catholic" (interview with Mancini, Vicari, and Sanella).

60 These rites were important not only for religious reasons but also for the communal and kin network connections made. Lay antagonism resulted when the priests refused to carry out the rites for lack of payment or insufficient parish association.

61 ARCDH, All Souls Church, Rev. R. Rizzatto to Chancery Office, 12 May 1954; Chancery Office to Rev. R. Rizzatto, 14 May 1954; *Catholic Magazine* January 1918; Hamilton *Herald*, 23 May 1931; C. Mattina, "L'emigrazione racalmutese in una comunità del Canada" (unpublished paper, Universita' degli studi di Palermo, 1994), 47–9; interviews.

62 Interview with P. Vicari and P. Zona. For a discussion of Old World chants, litanies, and *cunti* as communal patrimony, see, for instance, Luisa Caico, *Sicilian Ways and Days* (London, 1910), 73–4, 118–27.

63 Interviews; Bianco, *Emigrazione*, 76–83; Chapman, *Milocca*, 239–43; Phyllis Williams, *South Italian Folkways* (New York, 1969 [1938]), chap. 7.

64 Sciorra, "Multivocality and Vernacular Architecture," 203–43.

65 Interviews, especially with R. Carducci and with S. Cumbo, Hamilton, 21 August 1989.

66 If the *fratelli* associations served partly as mutual aids in the Old World, the immigrant mutual aids functioned partly as *fratelli* organizations in the New. On the multi-faceted functions of immigrant mutual aids, see Michael Karni et al., *Records of Ethnic Fratenal Benefit Associations in the United States: Essays and Inventories* (St Paul, Minn., 1981).

67 "La festa della Società recalmutese [*sic*]," *Progresso Italo-Americano*, 28 Agosto 1931, 9; similarly, CTA, Central Neighborhood House, series F, box 1, file 1, F. Fraser, "Italy in the Ward," *Ward Graphic*, 1918, 14; ARCAT, St Patrick's, *Annals*, 16 August, 27 November 1914, 17 September 1916; Archives of Ontario, RC 4–32, Department of the Attorney General, file 1926, no. 1693, "Sunday Celebration by Italians at Port Colborne" (July 1926).

68 P. Mario Francesconi, ed., *Storia della congregazione scalabriniana* (Roma: Centro Studi Emigrazione, 1974), 4: 160; Riis, "Feast Days,"493; Richard Swiderski, *Voices* (Bowling Green, 1986), 40–7, 65; Vecoli, "elates and Peasants," 235; interviews. Many *festa* societies in southern Ontario today keep their saints' statues in warehouses or in members' homes.

69 Vecoli, "Prelates and Peasants," 231.

70 Robert Orsi, "Popular Religion and the Italian Community," *American Catholic Studies Newsletter* 9 (fall 1983): unpaged.

71 Interviews. On the feast of San Rocco, see ARCAT, Church of Mount Carmel, San Rocco controversy correspondence; St Agnes Church, "Statutory Declaration of Josephine Circelli" (1934). The issue is also touched on in Zucchi, *Italians in Toronto*, 139.

72 Hamilton *Spectator*, 2 June 1913.

73 Interview with A. Unelli, Hamilton, 28 May 1983.

74 ARCAT, Church of Mount Carmel, "Spiritual Statistics: Archdiocese of Toronto," 1946, 1947.

Revisiting "Separate Spheres": Women, Religion, and the Family in Mid-Victorian Brantford, Ontario

MARGUERITE VAN DIE

... seeking the spheres to connect them, till the bridge you will need be form'd, till the ductile anchor hold, till the gossamer thread you fling, catch somewhere, O my soul

Convinced that traditional Christian belief and sensibility had lost their cogency at the end of the nineteenth century, Walt Whitman gave expression to the soul's ongoing search for meaning and coherence in the evocative image of a spider casting the strands of a new web.[1] Religious historians have continued to touch upon this insight by adopting secularization as a central paradigm to analyze the effect of modern life upon religion in the Western world. Whitman's trope, of the separation of spheres of life once experienced as connected, has also been extensively used by feminist historians interested in analyzing the increased relegation of middle-class women to the private or domestic sphere in the nineteenth century. The two processes – secularization and the separation of spheres – both aspects of modernity, have been viewed as integrally connected. Under the impact of industrialization and new scientific thought, it has been argued, religion was relocated from the public to the private and domestic sphere, becoming increasingly the domain of women, children, and clergy.[2]

Revisionism is the wheel that turns the historian's mill, and as the concept of modernity has become increasingly problematized, so too have those of secularization and the separation of spheres.[3] Feminist analysis, for example, has for some time critiqued the dichotomy between the public (male) sphere of "work" and the private (female) domestic sphere that figured so prominently in its earlier discourse. A growing body of literature argues that women carved a space in the "social," an area of charitable, political, and associational work that bridged the home and the public sphere.[4] Building on these arguments, Mary Ryan has suggested how we might rethink the term "public" when applied to women by observing that "public life can be cultivated in many democratic spaces where obstinate differences in power, material status, and hence interest, can find expression."[5] Linda Kerber, in turn, has argued that "separate spheres" should be understood not as a pervasive reality but, rather, as a rhetorical device that characterized new power relations in response to economic and social change.[6] Others have taken this criticism further to argue that life was and is infinitely more complex than dualistic categories permit.[7] Seen as narrative fictions that mask as well as clarify aspects of lived experience, such dualisms, as Anne Braude suggests, have profoundly shaped our understanding of the process of secularization. That process, she insists, has been analyzed primarily in terms of male absence in religious activities and institutions, a focus that has ignored the fact that, from the perspective of women's experience, the story is one of increasing vitality and public presence.[8]

Such critiques, part of a broader decentring of modernity and re-examination of earlier secularization theory, call for new directions in analyzing women's role in religion. Though feminist historians have noted the important place that religion has occupied in women's lives, they have taken a largely functionalist approach. Viewing nineteenth-century religion primarily as an oppressive or liberating opportunity for women, they have offered little analysis of the substantive nature of religious practice or its public dimensions in women's lives.[9] Given nineteenth-century women's primary role as caregivers, we need to ask how concerns of gender and family helped to shape their religiosity and if they had an impact on the public expression of religion.

I propose to examine these two important questions through a narrow but informative lens: a detailed study of women, family, and religion in one nineteenth-century town – Brantford, Ontario – from approximately 1825 to 1885, an era of intensive social, economic, and religious change. Whereas a number of studies using a similar community focus have already demonstrated the important place of religion in middle-class formation, here the interest will be not so much on class as on the public role of religion.[10] Rather than assuming that religion inevitably became privatized and part of the fragmentation and "separation of spheres" associated with modernity, this essay will explore the extent to which religion, as experienced and advanced by women, resisted such differentiation. Four broad areas will guide the analysis: the impact of structural change upon religious life in Brantford and upon women's numerical participation; the continuing influence of earlier forms of piety because of immigration; the place of material concerns in religious practice; and women's role in religious nurturing, moral surveillance, and revival. This detailed exploration will lay the groundwork for a brief and more speculative discussion at the end of the essay that reassesses both secularization and the applicability of "separate spheres" as a meaningful category for women's religious life.[11]

Nineteenth-century central Canada offers a particularly interesting field for exploring the extent to which religious belief and practice acted as a bridge between public and private life for women. The social and economic changes of this era, as well as the pervasive presence of evangelical Protestantism and ultramontane Catholicism, have been well documented.[12] Brantford, whose population at this time was primarily Protestant with an active, if contracting, Roman Catholic minority, participated in the structural changes as well as in the growing religiosity of the era. Between 1830 and 1890 the town's population grew from an estimated 350 to 13,000, and its economy gradually shifted from a craft base to one of factory production, with diminishing opportunities for self-employment as economic power shifted to those members of the older generation who were already well established.[13] For women, these changes took a somewhat different form. Census figures show that by 1861, thanks in part to a severe economic downturn in 1857, women, once a minority in town life, had begun to outnumber men. Over the next two decades the number of widows increased dramatically, reflecting the general aging of the population, while young people increasingly lived for longer periods under the parental roof.[14] Home life also underwent considerable change. In 1852, 50 per cent of married households in which the husband was self-employed were also the site of his workplace, and at least 14 per cent of these provided lodging for employees. By 1880, 61 per cent of such households enjoyed the preferred separation of home and business.[15] This change, long considered a cornerstone of the "separate spheres" thesis, was not, however, pervasive. As some married women were able to retreat into the home, others, primarily single, entered the workforce. Though women made up no more than 4 per cent of the business community throughout this period, their participation in the labour force increased from 10.5 per cent in 1851 to 17.5 per cent in 1881.[16]

Though incisive, none of these structural changes appear to have undermined the town's religious life. Far from undergoing a decline in influence, religion in nineteenth-century Brantford was an increasingly thriving concern: church participation grew; male civic leaders invested ever-increasing funds in a growing infrastructure of church buildings and voluntary societies; Sunday school and youth work flourished. While much of this expansion can be measured by an incremental increase in congregational membership, growth was also fuelled by periods of shared revival among the town's evangelical denominations. In the mid-1850s and again in 1875 and 1879, these revivals dramatically boosted the numbers of Brantford's Congregationalists, Methodists, Baptists, and Presbyterians.[17] Although Anglican and Roman Catholic state-church traditions were less favourable to the voluntarism that helped to drive evangelical extension and their population share declined during the period under examination, these two denominations nevertheless followed the general pattern of institutional consolidation through ambitious church-building programs and Sunday school outreach.[18]

The results, at least for the religiously minded, were impressive. In 1830 the infrastructure of organized religion had consisted of only a small Congregational Sunday school and an Anglican chapel. By 1890 the institutional presence of religion consisted of fourteen churches, twenty Sunday schools (including six mission churches) with 4,026 pupils under the supervision of 423 officers and teachers, and such voluntary societies and institutions as a flourishing WCTU, a well-appointed YMCA with a female auxiliary, a Widows' Home, and a Ladies' College under Presbyterian direction.

Religious expansion was not unique to Brantford. Replicated through the villages and towns of central and eastern Canada, it formed the basis for much gratitude and self-congratulation in congregational and denominational histories.[19] Notwithstanding such obvious growth, however, a fear of waning religious influence and vitality lurked beneath the surface. Ministers, dependent for their livelihood on the same lay largesse that underwrote the proliferation of church structures, were aware that the social and economic forces which had helped to establish a strong church presence could just as easily undermine religion. "We cannot see the line which divides the church and the world," read one such jeremiad in a Presbyterian journal in 1868, when surplus funds where beginning to be invested in a flurry of church-building in Brantford and elsewhere.[20] To prevent the secular from crowding out the sacred in the competitive economic world of nineteenth-century Canada, the laity was reminded that all of life was to be informed by religion: The worship of God is to blend with everything. You go to church on the Sabbath you say, to fulfil your public religious duties, but man and woman professing to be Christians, know yet that, on Monday morning you go down from Sabbath attitudes into the world's great scene of traffic, and labor, and strifes, and sorrows, and sins, you go there, too, to your public religious duties."[21]

Although this concern was addressed to both men and women, it was quite clear that when it came to losing salvation on Monday mornings, women were much less at risk than men. It has been well documented that nineteenth-century women were considered the more pious of the sexes, but less note has been taken of the fact that their piety was never seen as solely a private matter. "In every generation, the strong religious convictions of women have been the mainstay of our holy religion," proclaimed Brantford's minister William Cochrane to the assembly gathered in his Zion Presbyterian Church to mark the annual convocation of the Brantford Ladies' College.[22] Similar observations flowed regularly from pulpit and press. It is against this backdrop of dramatic institutional growth, coupled with constant fear of spiritual declension, that we must view women's participation in religious life in Brantford. They were part of a successful enterprise, and church membership rolls underscore their numerical preponderance throughout the period under discussion (see table 1).

Such statistical information, maintained by ministers and church officers, was in itself part of the public world of religion. Women's application for and reception into church membership were public acts, occasions when, first before their respective church disciplinary committees and then before the entire congregation, they were examined and asked to testify to their religious experience. Yet, though it was widely assumed that female piety was the mainstay of religion, once those public acts were performed and recorded, women's voices, unlike those of their menfolk, become largely muted in the official church records detailing the maintenance of congregational and denominational life. Even when women played a role in these activities through their own gender-based benevolent and moral reform societies, which began in Brantford in the early 1830s, no recorded minutes of these appear to have survived for the period under investigation. Nevertheless, by probing census and church records, congregational histories, and a limited number of biographical sources, it is possible to move beyond documenting women's numerical preponderance in religious life and offer some insights into why the public profession of religion was such a vital part of women's experience.

Table 1
Female membership as a percentage of the total of selected congregations

Congregation	Period	Total members	Female % total (number)
Zion Presbyterian	1850–84	389	53 (206)
First Congregational	1853–91	1818	60 (1,097)
First Baptist	1835–83	1847	57 (1,051)
Wellington Street Methodist	1855; 1885	121; 481	58 (70); 69 (328)

Source: United Church/Victoria University Archives (UCA), Zion Presbyterian Church, Membership Roll, 1850–84; Wellington Street Methodist Church, Circuit Register, 1855 and 1885; First Baptist Church, Membership Roll, 1835–84, printed in T.S. Shenston, *A Jubilee Review* (1890), 141–203 (checked against Baptist Archives, McMaster Divinity School, First Baptist Church, Brantford, Membership Roll, 1836–89, (microfilm); and First Congregational Church, Church Roll, 1853–96 (typescript but checked against original, UCA, microfilm).

Brantford was not the first place that many of its female citizens had called home. Census figures in 1852 show that of the total female population, 58.5 per cent were of non-Canadian birth, with Ireland (25.5 per cent) as the major source of origin, followed by England (18.4 per cent), Scotland (7.8 per cent), and the United States (6.6 per cent); 0.2 per cent are listed as "Other."[23] Narrative sources and congregational records reveal the high transience of the town's population, especially before 1860. While membership lists and baptismal records for this period are sparse prior to the late 1850s, they support the pattern of instability that Michael Katz and David Gagan have documented elsewhere in central Canadian towns.[24] In short, for a considerable number of women, especially in the early period, life was a series of moves.

The reasons for emigration and subsequent transience were generally economic: the widespread British depression at the end of the Napoleonic Wars, the famine in Ireland, and the construction of the Grand Canal, which brought many Irish labourers to the Brantford area. The decision to move was invariably part of a wider family strategy where men decided and sometimes went ahead first, and women and children followed. While men, however, went out into the world to seek a livelihood amidst new co-workers and drew on this new identity as part of their self-understanding, women continued to identify primarily in terms of family, both those they left behind and those who accompanied them.

Religion, which played such an important role in defining relationships, was part of that continuity of identity. "You still have a fond Aunt Fanny who dearly loves you, and prays to God night and day to make you his own dear child. I hope you do not forget me, nor forget the psalms and verses I often taught you," Fanny Carroll, an evangelical Anglican, wrote from Ireland in 1837 to her young niece, Anne Good, shortly after the latter's family had immigrated to Montreal.[25] The Good family moved to Brantford a year later. Having failed to carry on his career as a banker, Anne's father, Allen Good, directed most of his energy to farming, an entirely new and more successful way of life. The challenges for his wife, Eliza, however, though no less formidable, continued to centre on family nurture; the moral help offered by religion remained, therefore, part of everyday life. Describing the development of her four children, she confided in a letter home to her sister, "My dear Fanny I have a hard task to rear them and attend to them properly, but I pray for them night and morning and talk to them and try to teach them what is right, and must only trust in the Lord to change their hearts for man cannot do that."[26] Unlike those of her spiritually minded sister, Eliza Good's letters were filled with down-to-earth household details. For her, a mother concerned to raise a young family, religion was simply a natural part of practical everyday world and easily carried over from the home country without institutional support.

Though immigration may have intensified the bonds between kinship and religion for women of all faiths, evangelicals in particular brought with them a piety already steeped in familial language. As part of a concerted onslaught against the spiritual and material dislocation of the industrial revolution, and seeking to revitalize religious life, groups such as the Congregationalists, Baptists, Methodists, and Secessionist and Free Church Presbyterians stressed the bonds of community. Within their congregations many addressed one another as "brother" or "sister" or, in the case of Methodists, entered weekly into small intimate class meetings or bands of holiness, where they recounted personal religious experiences for mutual support or correction. Human bonds were part of a wider religious family: God was their heavenly Father, from whom they had become alienated through sin. Reconciliation and forgiveness, gifts available to all who personally repented and believed, were possible only through the suffering on the cross of God's Son. Assurance of personal salvation, that supreme moment in conversion, took place when the repentant sinner experienced God, not as distant or vengeful, but as a loving Father, to be addressed in scriptural terms as "Abba." No longer wracked by guilt and doubt, the converted were now free to serve their fellows. Such an experience needed to be professed in public, and it marked the beginning of full membership in the church.[27]

Even when most of Brantford's population were Canadian-born, as was the case by 1881, structural changes, including an aging population, a high incidence of widows, and the leadership of older, well-to-do men in civic and church life, favoured the continuing influence of the first generation of immigrants.[28] Helping to preserve the memory of an earlier period of women's "prophetic role" were "mothers of Israel" such as Anna Moyle, who settled with her husband in Brantford in the early 1830s. Shortly after her conversion at age fifteen and concerned about the poverty, illness, and illiteracy in her native Dorsetshire, Moyle had begun to evangelize there and to provide material relief by setting up a Sunday school, which, in the absence of a church nearby, developed into a regular Sunday evening worship meeting.[29] Marriage and emigration did not undermine her evangelical concern, but simply transferred it to another area with similar scarcity of material and spiritual resources. Though there is no indication that she preached formally, "Sister" Moyle and her husband, Deacon William Moyle, became strong forces in the town's First Baptist Church from its early years until 1856, when they left Brantford for nearby Paris.[30]

Larger networks of immigrants transferred communal and familial expressions of evangelicalism from their native countries. Among the first wave of English immigrants to Brantford, for example, were a group of Inghamite families from Yorkshire, who had been hard hit by the economic dislocation following the cessation of the Napoleonic Wars.[31] Under the leadership of James Cockshutt and his son, Ignatius, they established the Farringdon Independent Church, located a mile outside Brantford, in 1833. Though there is no evidence of their preaching, Inghamite women played an important role in educating the young. Jane Cockshutt Laycock, for example, established a girls' school in 1861, after she was widowed. Thanks to Laycock and her brother, Ignatius, who became Brantford's leading philanthropist and was connected by marriage to a number of influential Baptist families, the Inghamites exercised a role in the town's religious life well beyond their limited numbers.[32]

Congregationalist lay leaders John Wilkes, a Birmingham gun manufacturer, and his wife, Susan Philips, who settled with their seven children in Brantford in 1825, were more representative of urban middle-class English evangelicalism. Their decision to emigrate was part of a wider kinship relocation, and as with the Inghamite group, the women were active in religious education.[33] Susan's sister, Mary

Ann Day, prematurely a widow in 1846, saw her son and grandson enter the Congregationalist ministry, and for many years she ran a day school and had a major influence on the town's youngsters.[34] An acknowledged leader within the church, she also served for years as a Congregational "lady visitor," with the task of assessing and reporting back to the male hierarchy on the spiritual maturity of women seeking church membership. In 1828 she established a union Sunday school, a favoured means of evangelical outreach, and she, with Susan Philips Wilkes, an unmarried sister, two daughters, and a son and the help of an Anglican warden, provided the teaching.[35]

The familial nature of religious life was further accentuated by the fact that, until church buildings were erected, women's hospitality contributed to the imposed informality of Sunday worship. Largely farmers, the Inghamites rotated from home to home for church services, bringing their lunches in order to attend afternoon meetings. The Congregationalists, as well, worshipped in various venues before settling in a permanent building in 1834. Other denominations followed a similar pattern: Methodists, Baptists, and United and Free Church Presbyterians all held their first services in private homes; later, eulogies would make specific mention of the hospitality given by the women of founding families.[36]

"Where there exists little differentiation between the domestic and public spheres, and thus little isolation of women,"the status of women is highest, Deborah Valenze has observed, speaking of women's central place in the household economy in early-nineteenth-century England.[37] Differentiation between places of residence and business was slow in Brantford and, it may be recalled, accounted for only 50 per cent of the living arrangements of the town's self-employed in 1852. Differentiation between the home and public places of worship, as has been observed in Brantford's early religious life, was also slow. Even when worship moved from homes to church buildings and ecclesiastical arrangements fully assumed (or resumed) their male hierarchical character, women would continue to view religion as a site at which to exercise domestic skills and family concerns in public ways. In so doing, their interest found natural expression in material forms, a dimension of religious life that historians have in large part overlooked. Measuring religious commitment primarily by the beliefs and behaviours prescribed by identifiable religious institutions and traditions, they have under-studied the complexity of communal religious expression. Against this approach, historian Robert Orsi and others have begun to recast religion as a lived experience, an examination of "how particular people, in particular places and times, live in, with, through, and against the religious idioms available to them in culture."[38] When eleven Congregational women in Brantford, for example, pooled their resources in 1836 to present to their church its first pulpit Bible, they were making an important statement about the links between spiritual priorities and their material expression.[39] Whether through offering their homes for worship or furnishing churches, women continued to weave the spiritual with the practical.

The preparation, consumption, and sharing of food offered similar possibilities for material contribution. In the early period, abundance and scarcity of food existed side by side. Irish Canadians, informed via family correspondence of the suffering that had resulted from the Irish potato crop failure, were especially aware of scarcity. "Numbers are dying in Ireland for want of food," Anne Good noted in her diary in 1847, as letters from family members in the homeland focused increasingly on their suffering.[40] Not long after, Good and her mother employed and fed some seventeen of these compatriots as labourers on the family's farm. That year, wagon after wagon laden with the cholera-stricken came into Brantford, greatly straining the resources of especially the town's Roman Catholics of St Basil's parish. In the evenings, St Basil's women, moved by the appalling suffering of the cholera victims, would dispatch their sons with pails of milk to the North Ward hospital, supervised by two church members.[41]

Although such times of acute distress were rare, providing for such basic needs as daily food and clothing remained a matter of public activity in a society where mutual dependence and responsibility were a necessary strategy for survival. Assistance to the poor was placed in the hands of a municipal poor-relief society known in Brantford, as elsewhere, as the Ladies Dorcas and Poor Society, in honour of a noted female benevolence worker in the New Testament. The society's regular collections within the various congregations, along with communal fundraising events, helped bring to public attention private family concerns.[42] That this was the one municipal organization co-administered by women underscored the fact that, while poverty might reflect the absence or underemployment of male breadwinners, female strategy was vital for the daily provision of food and other material needs.

In a voluntary society the ongoing maintenance and extension of churches was also in part dependent on women's domestic skills and organizational talents. Before the mid-1830s, in the absence of a church building and parsonage, preachers often came to new appointments unaccompanied by their families. Local women offered boarding, nursing in illness, and – in one recorded instance – a new suit of clothing as remuneration in a cash-strapped economy.[43] Early female networks, such as the Brantford Baptist Women's Sewing Society, formed in 1849 to give financial assistance to their church through the proceeds of their handiwork, offered a sociable way to combine spiritual commitment with practical fundraising. By the mid-1850s, as the town began to experience a period of economic boom accompanied by a flurry of church-building programs, Brantford's women found their domestic skills in yet more demand. Unlike the town's male civic and religious leaders, who had to rely on business leverage and moral authority to extract funds for building projects, women were able to offer an exchange of material goods and food, the product of their own hands and household skills, as their contribution to church construction. Thus in these decades of increased church-building and denominational expansion, both signs of new economic growth, they drew on a time-hallowed tradition of providing a steady round of community meals. Often combined with other forms of fundraising, such as bazaars, concerts, and evening lectures on religious topics, women's provision of food to large numbers of co-religionists and townspeople was also by its nature a valued contribution to community-building. At the same time they gave greater visibility to their various denominations, while providing "respectable" entertainment to large numbers of townfolk in a world of little organized leisure activity.

The economic expansion that fuelled church-building programs, however, also destabilized the communal religious values that stressed an intimate connection between private piety and public practice. In the booming economy of Brantford in the early 1850s, men and youth in the workplace were the first to experience the changes that undermined the godly community's moral code. At that time the front lines of church discipline were occupied by ministers and concerned women, who saw the impact of economic change upon the religious lives of their young people and menfolk, but whose own lives within the home and church had been much less affected.[44] Together they faced a twofold challenge: to bring their menfolk to conversion or reaffirmation of an earlier faith and to transform those forces in the public workplace that undermined evangelical behaviour. Given the combination of socio-economic change, a reform-minded ministry, devout, prayerful women, and an increase in population and wealth calling for church extension, the time was right for revival.

The Congregationalists in 1853 were the first to experience revival, and their recently ordained, young, single minister, the Reverend John Wood, was quite emphatic that in its origins this was a female event. Appointed to a church whose membership had dwindled through a recent schism, Wood quickly realized that the congregation's spiritual core rested in the hands – or more accurately, upon the prayers – of a number of female leaders: women such as Mrs Stephen Wickens, at whose home he boarded, and Mrs Mary Ann Day, recently widowed and actively evangelizing in her day school.[45] From its earliest beginnings, the congregation's women had outnumbered male members, but in the volatile economic climate of the early 1850s, female leaders considered the conversion of husbands and children with a new urgency. The congregation's men, young and old, soon faced a tightening discipline; minutes of the congregational business meetings after Wood's arrival show that moral infractions such as intemperance and billiard and card playing became matters of regular group censure.[46] Female prayers and clerical discipline encouraged a heightened interest in religion: extra prayer meetings were held in homes, and within this intense climate, revival began. With men numbering only six of the twenty-six recorded converts, however, the first revival remained primarily a female event.[47]

Though their relative proportion was smaller, women continued to dominate among the converts in the town-wide revivals that erupted in all the evangelical denominations, including the Congregationalists, between 1856 and 1859. Again, during this second period of revival, the behaviour and family harmony of prominent male members became a matter of special concern for church disciplinary meetings, leading at times to significant self-censure.[48] As had been the case with the Congregationalists, women were both converts and agents in conversion, in the latter case, primarily of family members. Almost one-third (32 per cent) of the converts were couples, often with wives coming first and husbands following. Even when husband and wife entered at the same time, there could be gendered differences in the trajectory of their conversion. "If Mary delays baptism until you are more in need of a saviour or until you are more worthy of a saviour, or until you can bring yourself into just a suitable frame of mind I fear it will not be in the first hundred years, resist therefore not the holy Ghost, if you do she had better go forward and take possession of the good kingdom," Benjamin Shenston exhorted his thirty-two-year-old married son, Thomas, and the latter's wife, Mary Lazenby, in 1856.[49] Soon after this warning, Thomas and Mary underwent baptism in the Grand River and entered into a lifetime of active church and civic leadership.

In asserting the need for religious continuity, wives and mothers were important, if rarely publicly acknowledged, co-agents in revival with ministers. "I pray that all belonging to me may be the subject's of God's grace and live in his fear, that the same faith and hope that

Table 2
Gender and family status of converts by denomination, 1853–59:
converts preceded by family, converts entering as married couples, and gender ratio

Denomination	Year/no. converts	Prec. by family[1] N/%	Couples[2] N/%	Gender ratio Female: male
Congregational	1853/26	10/38	2/15	20:6
	1856/78	27/35	13/33	37:41
Methodist	1856–57/243	45/19	45/37	157:86
Free Presbytarian	1857–59/124	8/6	20/32	68:56
United Presbyterian	1857–59/34	7/21	6/35	20:14
Baptist	1856–59/193	49/25	25/26	114:79
Total	698	147/21	111/32	416:282

Sources: UCA, Zion Presbyterian Church, Membership Roll 1850–84; Wellington Street United Presbyterian Church, Communicants Roll, 1843–70; Wellington Street Methodist Church, Circuit Register, 1855–57; First Baptist Church, Membership Roll, 1835–84, printed in T.S. Shenston, *Jubilee Review*, 141–203 (checked against Baptist Archives, McMaster Divinity School, First Baptist Church Brantford, Membership Roll, 1836–89, microfilm); and First Congregational Church, Church Roll, 1853–96 (typescript but checked against original, UCA, microfilm).
1 Preceded by a member of shared family name, as listed on church rolls.
2 Each couple counted as two members.

inspired the hearts of your Father and Mother and of your Grand-sires, may also be possessed by our future posterity," Mary Strachan Shenston had admonished her son three years prior to his conversion.[50] She was not alone in asserting such an expectation: 21 per cent of the converts of the 1856–59 revivals could be linked to members whose names were already on the church rolls, the majority of whom were women. Martha Woodyatt, a member of the Congregational church since 1845, finally witnessed her husband, James, a long-time adherent, seek full membership in 1856. First Baptist's Rachel Foster, commended for her prayers on behalf of her own offspring and church youth, in the course of 1856 saw three daughters and two sons baptized and received into full membership.[51]

This largely unmentioned role of women in advancing both church growth and male membership draws attention to the important ways in which religious nurture in the home found public expression in times of revival. The public nature of revival did not simply mean that men and women were examined by church officials and openly professed their faith before the gathered congregation. It also required a life of active service and acceptable moral conduct. These requirements could be more easily met if church and civic life were closely integrated. This became the case in Brantford during and after the revivals of the 1850s. Prominent male converts increasingly combined civic and church leadership in areas such as service on disciplinary committees, aggressive mission and Sunday school work, new church development, and a range of voluntary societies and institutions. Throughout this period, women were indispensable fundraisers and became increasingly active in Sunday school and mission work, opening their homes for cottage prayer groups and playing an active if informal role in maintaining church discipline. In these ways the female world of religion would extended itself and help to lay the groundwork in the mid-1870s for a reassertion of evangelical values through revival when they again became threatened by economic change in the workplace.

Thanks to steady population growth, church extension through Sunday schools and mission churches was a regular feature of the three decades following the 1850s revivals. Often originating in homes, relying on family networks and female hospitality, and concerned with religious nurture for those within and outside the church, these institutions reflected the pattern of the town's earliest informal religious gatherings. In 1870, for example, twenty-seven members of First Baptist Church met at the home of one of their members in order to establish a new church, known as Park Street Baptist; at least nine of their number were related to Baptist matriarch Rachel Foster. Her son George conducted services for several years until the arrival of a regular minister and, with his brother-in-law, William Buck, became the driving force in Park Baptist's aggressive Sunday school outreach. In 1881, when the congregation was large enough to construct a permanent church building, Foster's daughter, Mrs William Buck, in deference to her husband's work as Sunday school superintendent, was asked to turn the first sod.[52]

Cottage services, which proliferated during the 1880s, were another way in which women were able to carry on the communal vision of an earlier period when home and public place of worship were less differentiated. By 1885, for example, Anglicans had proceeded from their parish base, Grace Church, to hold cottage services in the western part of the town known as Terrace Hill. When numbers had grown sufficiently to establish a separate mission church, one of the female members offered the land on which to construct a building.[53] Making similar use of cottage prayer meetings as a means of church extension, Methodists established groups in the growing population of the Eagle's Nest area, meeting in the homes of one male and two female members.[54] Presbyterians followed the same pattern. On several occasions, church session gave permission to women whose husbands were not church members to have their children baptized at the Wednesday evening prayer meeting rather than on Sunday.[55] Baptismal records and census figures for all churches show a high preponderance of shared denominational affiliation between husbands and wives, and in marriages of mixed religious backgrounds the mother's religion primarily determined that of the children.[56] Thus, as the request for mid-week baptisms illustrates, those women and older children who fell outside the prevailing norm could feel more comfortable in the more intimate setting of a home or even the church "parlour" (itself a translation of the domestic into the public sphere) than in the formal Sunday church service.

Women also continued to play a vital role in Sunday schools, another form of church extension aimed largely at the unchurched. These often became mission churches and eventually independent, self-supporting congregations. As early as 1856, thanks to the efforts of a woman referred to in the records only as Miss Brown, Zion Free Presbyterian Church had established in one of the town's poor wards a Sunday school known as the Balfour Mission, which in 1863 became an independent congregation.[57] In the 1870s two Presbyterian women each made additional initiatives in Eagle Place, another developing suburb. The first, Mrs S. Passmore, conducted a regular Sunday school class in her home, while the second, Mrs Bennett, embarked on a more ambitious venture, a union Sunday school meeting in a house made available by Ignatius Cockshutt.[58] When, in 1877, at Mrs Bennett's request, the Zion Presbyterian Church session amalgamated the two schools, the constitution of the newly formed Eagle Place Mission Sabbath School Association expressly safeguarded its non-denominational and gender-inclusive nature.[59] As the major form of church extension, Sunday school work remained a space where women could exercise some of the prophetic and organizational skills displayed by members of an earlier generation. Though Sunday school superintendency was an all-male preserve, as teachers, women offered religious nurture and moral surveillance. Following ministerial practice, they kept public records in which they noted those who "had been brought to a saving faith," as well as striking off the names of offenders.[60]

In addition to Sunday school work, Congregationalists and Methodists also retained specific offices for women to exercise spiritual leadership among members of their own sex. Congregationalists continued the practice common in the early days in Brantford of appointing female visitors to guide and examine new converts. Methodists, following a pattern that went back to the days of John Wesley, availed themselves of a number of female class leaders. Such positions allowed for significant individual initiative, as is evident in the work of Kezia Henry, who in 1864, after the death of her mother and her father's re-marriage, moved to Brantford and joined Wellington Street Methodist Church. There she conducted a young boys' Sunday school class for a number of years; after the revival of 1875 she became class leader to a large group of young women.[61] Single and solely responsible for the support of three siblings, Henry succeeded in establishing her own dress- and mantle-making business, eventually employing a dozen women. Extending her evangelistic efforts beyond the church to the workplace, she held a prayer meeting for employees in her shop once a week after work; after her departure from Brantford for home mission work in the west, a number of her former employees continued this practice in the noon hour in their new workplaces.[62] In addition, Henry visited women in the Brantford jail on Sundays, often accompanied by one or more of her employees.

Mission work such as Kezia Henry's inevitably exposed material need. Women's concern with such need, whether of their own family or of the wider population, blurred any sharp distinction between the private and public spheres. From the time that Susan Wilkes and her family began to gather children into a union Sunday school, teachers made note of the ongoing reality that lack of suitable clothing was a major reason why some children did not attend.[63] As well, material assistance for the minister and his family was an entrenched part of congregational culture. In a denomination where the minister and his family changed at least once every three years, Methodist women or-ganized a Ladies' Aid in 1869 as an ongoing auxiliary to look after the recently built church parsonage. Baptists, who in the early period had presented their minister with a suit of clothing, thirty years later com-missioned seven female members to aid the prospective wife of a missionary to the Telugus of British India in purchasing an outfit for her marriage and departure.[64] Congregationalists annually offered their minister a "donation party," consisting of a potluck dinner and a gift to him and his family. In December 1870, for example, the Rev-erend John Wood gave grateful thanks to the congregation's young men for presenting a sewing machine to his wife and a gift of furs to his eldest daughter.[65] Though men took the public tasks of presenting and acknowledging gifts, women obviously determined their choice and thus were able to continue practices that hearkened back to a pre-cash economy.

Besides these forms of ministerial support, every congregation – formally or informally – continued to draw on female networks for fundraising and the furnishing of church buildings. When, in 1872, the town's second Methodist congregation, Brant Avenue, completed its new building, the congregation's women scrubbed the floors, tacked down the carpets, sewed the cushions, and whitewashed the walls.[66] Such female involvement remained a constant element of church life, thanks to the regular need to expand or upgrade facilities in response to the town's steady population growth and the churches' ongoing evangelistic efforts.[67] Though opportunities for leisure activity had diversified in the intervening thirty years, church socials had not receded from their place of eminence. Women's roles remained indispensable, as for example, when the women of First Presbyterian Church in 1879 prepared a bountiful dinner for a capacity crowd in the basement, who then moved upstairs for a further three hours of entertainment and lectures celebrating the completion of the congregation's new church building.[68]

In a period when churches exercised a strong civic presence, the men who planned the growing religious infrastructure in the town and the women who helped to raise the needed funds were for the most part related by marriage.[69] Among other advantages, as part of the town's financial elite, these women were able to borrow funds needed for major building projects.[70] Thus in 1882 the Ladies' Aid Society of Brant Avenue Methodist Church was able to pay the existing debt on the new parsonage through means of a $2,000 loan, supplemented by proceeds from the society's sponsorship of lectures, socials, and bazaars.[71] Harder to document but pervasive was the influence that women exercised behind the scenes, within family and informal social settings, to maintain the material fabric of the church. For example, in 1882 a sizable delegation of the Ladies' Auxiliary invaded the meeting of Zion Presbyterian Church's male Board of Management on a mission to request funds to carpet the church and repair the pew cushions.[72] Though the board tried to maintain some of its dignity by retiring briefly to deliberate separately on the matter, the wishes of the women (several of whom were the men's own wives and daughters) prevailed.[73] In a world where the shabby furnishings of a church sanctuary were a matter of female concern, the domestic sphere inevitably extended its influence into the public realm.

This domestic sphere became public as well when, Sunday after Sunday, Brantford's women attended church with their families. In the weekly Sunday services one's private family arrangements were both visible and open to comment and, where necessary, censureship. The pervasive ecclesiastical presence, undergirded by the population's daily interaction in shops and streets, offered a host of opportunities for daily moral surveillance. In an intricate interplay of popular and ecclesiastical religion, private gossip became public rumour and occasion for church censure; women's voices remained informal and unrecorded but nonetheless powerful, as perceived infractions by church members and adherents were reported to church discipline committees. Where Roman Catholics could avail themselves of the privacy of the confessional, in evangelical denominations the sins of members were a matter of communal concern. Through church discipline, such family matters as alcohol abuse, domestic quarrels, and premarital sexual activity were brought into public purview. Although accusations were investigated by a small disciplinary committee actual punishment of infractions took place before the entire congregation as sinners were reproved for the impact of their behaviour upon themselves or their family and, above all, for "having brought scandal upon true religion." Punishment was swift and clearly laid out: offenders were publicly barred from taking part in the quarterly sacrament of communion and readmitted to the next sacrament only upon confession of sin.

Denominational practices for censure varied. Methodists exercised the least overt discipline; though they were expected to receive necessary correction within the small class meeting, and church rolls show instances of names being struck off the rolls for unnamed "heinous" offences, Methodists, unlike other evangelical denominations, had no disciplinary committee. Moreover, by the 1870s the denomination had begun in the class meeting, whose female membership had expanded markedly, to stress spiritual growth through Bible study rather than shared introspection and confession. Minutes of the town's two Presbyterian sessions and of Congregational and Baptist church disciplinary meetings, however, all register strong responses to cases of sexual irregularity. In these denominations the sexual puritanism that historians have noted in the popular religion of mid-nineteenth-century Britain remained the expected norm in Brantford throughout the period under examination.[74]

Concerns about family disharmony and marital breakdown affected especially those who were already church members, with one or two cases surfacing regularly each year in Presbyterian session minutes.[75] Although these were placed before session by the minister and elders, women were often the source of the initial accusation or grievance about personal family situations, including one instance where a mother reported that her unmarried daughter had given birth.[76] Unmarried men and women who were unlucky enough to have their sexual activity exposed through pregnancy shared in the shame of "anti-nuptial fornication" or "criminal intercourse," in the trenchant ecclesiastical terminology of the period. Though a woman bore the visible shame, great care was taken to delineate the nuances of moral responsibility. In April 1856, for example, it was not Presbyterian Jessie W. who was censured but, rather, her male partner, George S., who abjectly professed before church session his "deep sorrow" at having seduced her on a Sabbath nine months earlier and his willingness to "receive admonition considered necessary for his spiritual good."[77]

Marital breakdown, where one or both partners were church members or adherents, was seen as a blight upon the congregation's spiritual well-being. Thus, though Mrs B.F. Van Brocklin had been drawn into the Congregational fold in 1856 by the fires of revival, her formal acceptance was delayed pending the receipt of acceptable evidence of her divorce from her husband.[78] In cases of family disunity, an appeal to the public tribunal of a church disciplinary committee was in itself a sign that the informal intervention of family and neighbours had been ineffective. Largely instigated by women but carried out by male church officers, such tribunals rarely produced results satisfactory to either side, and at best the outcome was ambiguous.[79] Still, only through such disciplinary investigations could grievances and the informal network of gossip be given public focus.

Female networks of moral surveillance were never to be underestimated, a point driven home to one Presbyterian clerk of session in 1884 when, thanks to a birth announcement in a Toronto paper, his son's precipitous marriage was exposed before the congregation's watchful eye. Though the facts of the case were laid out before session by a fellow male elder, female investigative skills were evident both in noting that only six months separated the dates of marriage and childbirth and in challenging the announcement of premature birth for what was clearly a "full-time" child.[80] The incident is a reminder that the much-vaunted role of woman as moral guardian was more than a literary construct, but was rooted in a real world where irregularities in "family matters" became public matters through a course that led from gossip to church disciplinary committees and public censure.

The above examples make evident that moral surveillance was part of a wider social world where women were key forces in linking behaviour in the home, the church, and public life. Within such a matrix, a second wave of revivals in the 1870s becomes easier to understand. In the revivals of the 1850s the entry of young couples in large numbers into church membership had begun to reflect the integration of domestic and public religious life; a generation later, through union revivals in 1875 and 1879, women's stamp upon the town's corporate religious life became even clearer. As in the 1850s, the later revivals occurred within a period of pervasive socio-economic change, this time resulting in young people living longer with their families of birth, decreased opportunities for male economic advancement, and a reversal of earlier gender disparity, with young women beginning to outnumber young men.[81] Whereas a major concern of the earlier revivals had been to bring in "heads of households," this time the focus was on the conversion of the town's young people. Although the later revivals drew on the services of professional revivalists – in 1875 a British Wesleyan, Henry Varley, and in 1879 an American Congregationalist, Edward P. Hammond – these men acted only as catalysts. The revivals stressed conversion as a public acknowledgment of religious nurture, with sin depicted primarily as abandonment of the values inculcated in the home and Sunday school. For example, before beginning an address aimed primarily at the town's young men, Varley, following a practice going back to the family-oriented American "businessmen's" revivals of 1857–58, read letters from mothers and sisters "craving the prayers of God's people for the rescue of their sons and brothers from the vortex of intemperance into which their fascination with the intoxicating cup was fast hurrying them."[82] Hammond, whose efforts were directed principally at children and youth and who relied heavily on song, sentimentality, and pathos, similarly emphasized that conversion was simply public assent to earlier religious socialization.[83]

By all accounts, their message found a receptive audience, with a combined total of 913 converts entering into full church membership. Of those whose gender and family name are available, 59 per cent were female, and 60 per cent shared a family name with earlier members. Selective congregational samples further indicate that the majority of converts were in their teens and early twenties, and that aggressive Sunday school work among "unchurched" young people had yielded significant results.[84] As in the 1850s, each convert, by entering into church membership, was making a public profession that religious belief was not simply a private matter. In the intervening two decades, thanks to the extension of religious institutions and female networks of moral concern and material assistance, the private and public expression of religion had become even more integrally connected.

In its focus on the religious changes within a single community over time, this study offers further evidence of the well-documented consolidation of institutional religion in Victorian Canada. It goes further, however, by drawing attention to the generally overlooked but critical role of women in this consolidation.[85] During a time of pervasive economic restructuring that resulted in increased differentiation between men's private and public lives, women drew on religion to maintain an earlier experience of communal values. Where men relied on individualism to succeed in the marketplace, for women, success continued to lie primarily in maintaining the fabric of kinship and community. Timing should not be overlooked, for the third quarter of the nineteenth century was a crucial period for the churches in central Canada. Once the formal ties between church and state were severed in the 1850s, it became more urgent to retain the moral ties of kinship and community. Under the new voluntarism, women took a central role in maintaining and extending the earlier communal nature of religion.[86] Through fundraising, Sunday school teaching, poor assistance, and moral surveillance, they transformed the traditional church-state relationship, largely a male preserve, to something dynamic and fluid which integrated domestic and civil life in new ways. As demonstrated in two waves of communal revival in Brantford, women's influence, whether through childhood nurture, marital pressure, fundraising, or moral surveillance, was pivotal in indigenizing religion and ensuring its generational transmission.

With an emphasis on relationships, women's commitment was in the first instance focused on a limited domain: family, friends, neighbourhood, and church. Theirs was, to use sociologist Stephen Warner's term, an "elective parochialism," chosen rather than ascribed.[87] In keeping with recent revisionist feminist history which has argued that "separate spheres" was more a rhetorical device than an accurate descriptor of the world of nineteenth-century women, this study has drawn attention to women's independent agency within the structural limitations of the period. These limitations, defined primarily by women's role as caregiver within the family, should not be minimized. The same Presbyterian widow, for example, whose religious commitment drove her in 1877 to establish a non-denominational Sunday school in Brantford, five years later abandoned her work to male leadership because of family illness.[88] Nevertheless, within such limitations, church involvement offered women an opportunity to craft a public life that built on, rather than challenged, their primary responsibilities to the family. Not only did they help to ensure that the church was a place where the private and the public continued to intersect, but religious involvement allowed them to escape some of the potential restrictions of a middle-class home and enter into a "larger sphere" of activity, to use their own term.

Towards the end of the period under investigation, this "larger sphere" of women's involvement in fundraising and voluntary societies was extended from home and church to the province and the nation. Again, the timing is significant. The same industrialization of the

1870s and 1880s, which in Brantford, as elsewhere, both contracted male opportunities for self-employment and concentrated wealth in fewer hands, opened up new possibilities for women. These years saw the formation of national female religious voluntary societies, such as the WCTU, the YWCA, and denominational female missionary movements. In Brantford, women organized their first WCTU in 1878, under the presidency of Methodist class leader Mrs Margaret (Judge) Jones, and a year later a female auxiliary to the YMCA (followed in 1896 by a separate YWCA) with Miss Lily Cockshutt as president.[89] In 1882 Brantford's Methodist women were among those who formed a local branch of the recently established denominational women's missionary society. Like the WCTU, whose motto was "For God, Home, and Country," they too had moved from the home and the community into a "larger sphere." Quickly establishing children's auxiliaries to these new national organizations, they continued to be guided by the same familial perspective that informed their nurturing role in the home. In response to an 1888 address on Japanese mission work by Canadian Methodist missionary Martha Cartmell, home on furlough, a female writer enthused, "Our work is to these in darkness. God has given glorious privileges in making *us*, 'whose souls are lighted,' leaders of *these*, out into the glorious inheritance of brightness and peace." Concluded with a collection where members deposited texts of Scripture and pieces of silver, the event showed that Brantford's women had indeed widened their sphere, but also that domestic interests and piety still informed their new field of activity.[90]

Such a world, in which women continued to use Scripture texts as a form of specie even as they planned to impose their peculiar "elective parochialism" upon people of a totally different culture, offers insight into the way that the religious practices and symbols of the time had become inseparably embedded in nineteenth-century middle-class domesticity and family concerns. The many instances of female religious activity outside the home examined here, therefore, offer another perspective to the historiography on "moral feminism" that explores women's work in moral reform in the final decades of the nineteenth century,.[91] and to the argument that the feminization of religion was part of a privatization of belief and practice and hence a contributor to the secularization of society. In assuming an unrelenting process of differentiation between the sacred and the secular, the private and the public, such historical analysis has overlooked the countervailing influence of women, who, by virtue of their primary location within the home and family, continued to draw on religion and on communal values. Not only did women constitute the majority of church members, but at a time when their presence in the workforce was still limited in

numbers and duration, they looked to the church and voluntary societies as a space in which to express their family concerns and strategies.
Long before the large-scale entry of the state into matters of poverty,
family relations, and substance abuse, nineteenth-century women drew
on religion to make direct connections between these broader social
matters and their own roles as primary caregivers within the home. Precisely because church involvement allowed them to place their domestic
life within a communal framework, they could assert that such apparently private concerns as intemperance, poverty, and family relations
were in fact public. Women's piety, so much vaunted by the clergy, was
more than a matter of sentiment and personal salvation; in a democratic
and voluntary society it had become a cornerstone in the public edifice
of religion.[92] If, therefore, we are to do justice to women's influence on
nineteenth-century life outside the home, the traditional distinction between the private female domestic sphere and the public male sphere of
"work" needs to be redefined to include the public locus of the church.

NOTES

Research for this essay was conducted as part of a larger project, "The Christian
Family: Evangelicalism and Community in Victorian Canada," for which time
was made available by the Pew Charitable Trusts. Grateful acknowledgment is
also made to the Advisory Research Council of Queen's University for funding
of travel costs and to R.D. Gidney and W.P.J. Millar, who generously offered me
access to their extensive data bank collected from the 1861 assessment roll and
the 1852, 1861, 1871, and 1881 manuscript censuses for the town of Brantford.

1 Walt Whitman, "A Noiseless Patient Spider," in Oscar William, ed., *A Pocket
   Book of Modern Verse* (New York: Washington Square Press, 1958), 41.
2 For the privatization-of-religion thesis, see Thomas Luckmann, *Invisible Religion* (New York: Macmillan, 1967); and Robert Bellah et al., *Habits of the Heart*
   (New York: Harper & Row, 1985). For the link between the private and the
   feminine in nineteenth-century religion, see Nancy Cott, *The Bonds of Womanhood: "Woman's Sphere" in New England, 1780–1835* (New Haven: Yale University Press, 1977); and Ann Douglas, *The Feminization of American Culture*
   (New York: Avon, 1978). For a more recent Canadian deployment of these
   constructs, see Cecilia Morgan, *Public Men and Virtuous Women: The Gendered
   Languages of Religion and Politics in Upper Canada, 1791–1850* (Toronto: University of Toronto Press, 1996); and Elizabeth Jane Errington, *Wives and
   Mothers, School Mistresses and Scullery Maids: Working Women in Upper
   Canada, 1790–1840* (Montreal and Kingston: McGill-Queen's University
   Press, 1995), p. 235.

3 José Casanova, for example, in a reconsideration of the relation between religion and modernity, has drawn attention to the "deprivatization" of religion in contemporary life and its increasingly public role as a moral voice in civil society. His compelling review of secularization, however, does not draw on gender as a significant analytical category. See Casanova, *Public Religions in the Modern World* (Chicago: University of Chicago Press, 1994), especially 3–66.

4 See, for example, Denise Riley, *"Am I That Name?"* (London: Macmillan, 1988); Joan B. Landes, *Women and the Public Sphere in the Age of the French Revolution* (Ithaca, NY: Cornell University Press, 1988); and *Feminism: the Public and the Private* (New York: Oxford University Press, 1998).

5 Mary P. Ryan, "Gender and Public Access: Women's Politics in Nineteenth-Century America," in C. Calhoun, ed., *Habermas and the Public Sphere* (Cambridge, Mass.: MIT Press, 1992), 286; Mary P. Ryan, *Women in Public: Between Banners and Ballots, 1825–1880* (Baltimore: Johns Hopkins University Press, 1990).

6 Linda Kerber, "Separate Spheres, Female Worlds, Woman's Place: The Rhetoric of Women's History," *Journal of American History* 75 (1988): 9–39.

7 For a thoughtful revisionist analysis, see Amanda Vickery, "Historiographical Review: Golden Age to Separate Spheres? A Review of the Categories and Chronology of English Women's History," *Historical Journal* 36 (1993): 384–414. I thank Nancy Christie for this citation.

8 Ann Braude, "Women's History *Is* American Religious History," in Thomas Tweed, ed., *Retelling U.S. History* (Berkeley: University of California Press, 1997), 87–107.

9 See, for example, Barbara Welter, "The Cult of True Womanhood, 1820–1860," *American Quarterly* 18 (1966): 151–74; and Susan Juster, *Disorderly Women: Sexual Politics & Evangelicalism in Revolutionary New England* (Ithaca, NY: Cornell University Press, 1994). Glenna Matthews, in *The Rise of the Public Woman: Woman's Power and Woman's Place in the United States, 1630–1970* (New York: Oxford University Press, 1992), argues that by valorizing female subjectivity, religion in the first half of the nineteenth century helped secular woman's rise to public prominence after 1850.

10 Most notably, Mary P. Ryan, *Cradle of the Middle Class: The Family in Oneida County, New York, 1790–1865* (New York: Cambridge University Press, 1981); and Catherine Hall and Leonore Davidoff, *Family Fortunes: Men and Women of the English Middle Class, 1780–1850* (London: Hutchinson, 1987).

11 For an earlier study that implicitly observes the way that religion permitted women to transcend "their proper sphere," see Hannan M. Lane, " 'Wife, Mother, Sister, Friend': Methodist Women in St. Stephen, New Brunswick, 1861–1881," in Janet Guildford and Suzanne Morton, eds., *Separate Spheres: Women's Worlds in the 19th-Century Maritimes* (Fredericton: Acadiensis Press, 1994), 93–117.

12 For economic changes, see Douglas McCalla, *Planting the Province: The Economic History of Upper Canada, 1784–1870* (Toronto: University of Toronto Press, 1993). The growth of Protestant influence is analyzed in J.W. Grant, *A Profusion of Spires: Religion in Nineteenth-Century Ontario* (Toronto: University of Toronto Press, 1988); Michael Gauvreau, *The Evangelical Century* (Montreal and Kingston: McGill-Queen's University Press, 1991); and William Westfall, *Two Worlds: The Protestant Culture of Nineteenth-Century Ontario* (Montreal and Kingston: McGill-Queen's University Press, 1989).

13 David Burley, *A Particular Condition in Life: Self-Employment and Social Mobility in Mid-Victorian Brantford, Ontario* (Montreal and Kingston: McGill-Queen's University Press, 1994), 164–8.

14 In 1852, 6.5 per cent of the male and 5.2 per cent of the female population were over age fifty; by 1871 this proportion had risen to 10 per cent and 9.7 per cent respectively. In 1852 only 39.9 per cent of single men age fifteen to thirty and 42.3 per cent of women lived with their families of birth; by 1881 this component had changed to 86.5 per cent and 83.7 per cent respectively. In 1852 the town's female population was 1,883, compared to 1,971 men; the 1861 census registered 3,085 women and 3,060 men; by 1881 the female population was 4,940, compared to 4,563 males. There were 85 widows in 1852, representing 4 per cent of the female population; in 1881, 8 per cent (379) of the female population was widowed (census returns, Brantford, 1852, 1861, 1871, and 1881).

15 Burley, *A Particular Condition of Life*, 93.

16 Ibid., 99; census returns, Brantford, 1852, 1881.

17 The 1852 census shows that adherents to these four denominations made up 47 per cent of a population of 3,854. By 1881 they made up 62 per cent of a population of 9,503 and were clearly the dominant force in the town's civic and religious life. For an analysis of the revivals and their role in extending evangelical hegemony in Brantford, see Marguerite Van Die, " 'The Marks of a Genuine Revival': Religion, Social Change, Gender, and Community in Mid-Victorian Brantford, Ontario," *Canadian Historical Review* 79 (1998): 524–63.

18 Between 1852 and 1881, Anglican adherence decreased from 30.5 per cent to 21.2 per cent of the population, and Roman Catholic adherence from 19.9 per cent to 15.4 per cent (census returns, Brantford, 1852, 1881).

19 See, for example, Anson Green, *The Life and Times of the Rev. Anson Green, D.D.* (Toronto: Methodist Book Room, 1877), 31; and *Canadian Baptist*, 22 August 1867.

20 *Home and Foreign Record of the Canada Presbyterian Church*, April 1868, 161–7.

21 Ibid., 1861–62, 60.

22 Rev. William Cochrane, D.D., *The Church and the Commonwealth* (Brantford: Bradley, Garretson & Co., 1887), 343.

23 Census returns, Brantford, 1852.

24 For example, forty of the seventy new Congregationalist members who entered the church in 1853 and 1856 could not be located in the 1852 or 1861 census. See Michael Katz, *The People of Hamilton West* (Cambridge, Mass.: Harvard University Press, 1975), chap. 3, and David P. Gagan, *Hopeful Travellers: Families, Land, and Social Change in Mid-Victorian Peel County, Canada West* (Toronto: University of Toronto Press, 1981), 95–6.

25 Beth Good Latzer, *Myrtleville: A Canadian Farm and Family, 1837–1967* (Carbondale: South Indiana University Press, 1976), 20.

26 Ibid., 30.

27 Horton Davies, *Worship and Theology in England from Watts and Wesley to Martineau, 1690–1900* (Grand Rapids: William B. Eerdman's, 1996), 184–240.

28 See David G. Burley, "The Businessmen of Brantford, Ontario: Self-Employment in a Mid-Nineteenth-Century Town" (PhD diss., McMaster University, 1983), 352–3, and Van Die, " 'The Marks of a Genuine Revival,' " 542.

29 Obituary, "Mrs. Anna Moyles," *Canadian Baptist*, 6 January 1863.

30 T.S. Shenston, *A Jubilee Review of the First Baptist Church, Brantford, 1833 to 1884* (Toronto: Bingham, 1890), 61, and membership list (10).

31 Followers of Benjamin Ingham, an associate of John Wesley, Inghamites concentrated their chapels in Lancashire and Yorkshire. See Mary P. Stedman, comp., "Farringdon Church: Its History and Background from 1833 to 1977" (typescript, Archives of Ontario). After a brief stay in York, James Cockshutt and his family settled in Brantford in 1832. See *Memoirs of Ignatius Cockshutt, Consisting Chiefly of His Own Reminiscences, Collected and Arranged by His Family* (Brantford: n.p., 1903).

32 In 1873, for example, Ignatius's liberal donation permitted the erection of the town's YMCA building, Wycliffe Hall, followed six years later by a women's auxiliary. See "Historical Sketch of Brantford Churches," *Brantford Expositor Anniversary Number*, 1 July 1927.

33 John Robertson, *History of the Brantford Congregational Church, 1820 to 1920* (Brantford: n.p., 1920), 23–6.

34 Thomas Cowherd, "To the Children in Mrs. Day's School," in *The Emigrant Mechanic and Other Tales in Verse* (Jackson, Mich., published by the author, 1884), 108–9.

35 Robertson, *History of Brantford Congregationalist Church*, 24, 31–2.

36 Ibid., 39–40; Stedman, "Farringdon Church," [6]; UCA, Zion Presbyterian Church, Minutes of Session, "Tribute to Isabella Wallace," 5 January 1882; Shenston, "Mrs. Mary Hammill," in *Jubilee Review*, 47.

37 Deborah M. Valenze, *Prophetic Sons and Daughters: Female Preaching and Popular Religion in Industrial England* (Princeton: Princeton University Press, 1985), 34.

38 Robert Orsi, "Everyday Miracles: the Study of Lived Religion," in David D. Hall, ed., *Lived Religion in America* (Princeton: Princeton University Press, 1997), 7.

39 Robertson, *History of the Brantford Congregational Church*, 42.

40 Latzer, *Myrtleville*, 39.

41 Located at the western edge of town, in the impoverished North Ward, St Basil's Church, which was constructed in 1840 to hold eight hundred people, had become the centre of Irish Roman Catholicism when many of the Irish labourers brought to Brantford to work on the Grand Canal remained behind and became members of the parish. See [W.A. Hunter], *St. Basil's Parish, Brantford, Ontario, Canada Celebrates 150 Years, 1842–1992: Parish Family Album* (n.p., n.d.), 5.

42 See, for example United Church/Victoria University Archives (UCA), Wellington Street United Presbyterian Church, Minutes of Session, 18 April 1853, noting financial support given to a woman in the congregation.

43 See, for example, UCA, Wellington Street Methodist Church, Minutes of the Quarterly Meeting, 25 August 1849, noting disbursement of money from the contingency fund to a woman boarding the three children of the congregation's widowed minister; Shenston, *Jubilee Review*, 7.

44 Evangelical women's moral concern for husbands and sons has been well laid out in Curtis D. Johnson, *Islands of Holiness: Rural Religion in Upstate New York, 1790–1860* (Ithaca, NY: Cornell University Press, 1989). Unlike Johnson's study, however, the current essay sees women as maintaining a more enduring impact on religious life in the face of socio-economic change.

45 William A. Wood, ed., *Something from Our Hands: The 19th-Century Memoirs of Rev. John Wood, 1828–1905* (Hudson Heights, Que., Wood Family Archives, 1988), 51.

46 See, for example, UCA, First Congregational Church, Minutes of Business Meeting, 31 January 1854, 3 August 1854, 3 April 1857.

47 According to Wood, another twenty-one "were brought to Christ" (and presumably joined other evangelical denominations), but these too were primarily female. Wood, *Something from Our Hands*, 55–8, and UCA, First Congregational Church, Minutes of Business Meeting, 4 November 1854.

48 See, for example, UCA, First Congregational Church, Minutes of Business Meeting, 5 June 1857; Zion Presbyterian Church, Minutes of Session, 4 September, 1862.

49 Toronto Reference Library, Thomas Shenston Papers, Correspondence, file 2, Benjamin Shenston to Thomas Shenston, 24 April 1856.

50 Ibid., Mary Shenston to Thomas Shenston, 20 November 1853.

51 Shenston, *Jubilee Review*, 97–8.

52 Shenston, *Jubilee Review*, 81–2, 97–8; Baptist Archives, McMaster Divinity School (BA), Park Baptist Church, Sunday School Minutes, 1875–1903, microfilm.

53 "Grace Church Consecration: A History of the Parish," *Daily Courier*, 7 May 1902.

54 UCA, Wellington Street Methodist Church, Minutes of the Quarterly Meeting, 4 February 1889.

56 UCA, Zion Presbyterian Church, Minutes of Session, 10 December 1889; Brantford, First Presbyterian Church (formerly Wellington Street), Minutes of Session, 12 November 1882.

56 In 1881, of the 149 families where parents did not share the same religious affiliation, children were listed under the mother's affiliation in 114 cases and the father's in 35 (census returns, Brantford, 1881).

57 *Brantford Expositor Anniversary Number*, 1 July 1927.

58 BA, Immanuel Baptist Church Records, Eagle Place Sabbath School Association. The Sunday school was eventually taken over by the Baptists.

59 According to the constitution, the association was to "consist of an unlimited number of members, male and female, and shall not be governed by any particular denomination. It shall work Independent yet with all others. It shall have the power to extend its bounds when it may deem necessary for the advancement of one cause, *Christ and his Kingdom*."

60 See, for example, UCA, Brant Avenue Sunday School Teachers' Meetings, Minutes, 12 October 1877, 2 August 1881.

61 UCA, Young People's Forward Movement, box 24, Kezia Henry, "The True Story of Kezia Henry by a Friend," 8–9 (unpub. MS). Of Wellington's eight class leaders, two were women. See UCA, Wellington Street Methodist Church, Circuit Register, vol. 2, 1882–89.

62 Henry, "The True Story," 10, which includes a lengthy letter of tribute summarizing her activities, signed by a number of prominent Methodist couples expressing regret at her departure.

63 Robertson, *History of the Brantford Congregational Church*, 32; UCA, Brant Avenue Methodist Church, Sunday School Register, 1870–90, 5 November 1875.

64 Shenston, *Jubilee Review*, 74.

65 Wood, *Something from Our Hands*, 103; *Canadian Independent*, April 1871.

66 Maria Noble, *1871–1921: Golden Jubilee Brant Avenue Methodist Church, Brantford* (n.p., n.d.), 21.

67 Though economic recession slowed down church expansion in the 1860s, subsequent decades saw a new boom in church construction, as former mission churches such as Brant Avenue Methodist, Park Street Baptist, and St Jude's (Anglican) erected their first buildings, while older denominations such as First Presbyterian Church dedicated new and larger places of worship.

68 *Brantford Weekly Expositor*, 7 March 1879.

69 Of fifty-four female office holders located for the period 1850–85, forty-six were wives or daughters of male church officers.

70 See, for a similar pattern, Lori Ginzberg, *Women and the Work of Benevolence: Morality, Politics and Class in the 19th-Century United States* (New Haven: Yale University Press, 1990), 36–66.

71 UCA, Brant Avenue Methodist Church, Brantford, 1882 Annual Report.

72 UCA, Zion Presbyterian Church, Minutes of the Board of Management, 8 September and 11 September 1882.

73 It may have been this incident that led Sara Jeannette Duncan, whose mother was part of the delegation, to note many years later in her fictitious account of life in nineteenth-century Elgin (Brantford) that "threadbare carpet in the aisles was almost as personal a reproach as a hole under the dining-room table; and self-respect was barely possible to a congregation that sat in faded pews." See Sara Jeannette Duncan, *The Imperialist* (Toronto: McClelland and Stewart, 1971), 66.

74 S.J. Connelly, *Priests and People in Pre-Famine Ireland 1780–1845* (New York: St. Martin's Press, 1982), 174–218; Hall and Davidoff, *Family Fortunes*, 26–7, 401–3. The inaccessibility of church records precludes conclusions on the extent to which the Roman Catholic parishioners of St Basil's and their priests shared in this sexual puritanism.

75 See, for example, UCA, Zion Presbyterian Church, Minutes of Session, 2 July 1861, 18 November 1887; First Presbyterian Church, Minutes of Session, 29 January 1880. Baptists, using the term "immoral conduct," reported fewer cases and, at least in the period after 1873, appear to have left these in the hands of a small disciplinary committee. See BA, First Baptist Church, Minute Book, 1873–89, 17 November 1874, 5 April, 1877.

76 First Presbyterian Church, Brantford, Minutes of Session, 1 February 1875. Session suspended the young woman from church membership simply on the basis of her mother's report.

77 UCA, Zion Presbyterian Church, Minutes of Session, 9 April 1856.

78 That she was the aggrieved party may be deduced from the fact that the church was willing to consider her for membership. See UCA, First Congregational Church, Minutes of Business Meeting, 25 March 1856.

79 For example, asked to investigate the marital difficulties of one Presbyterian head of household, two session elders concluded that though Mr J. seemed to be "the most guilty," neither party could be freed from blame. See UCA, Zion Presbyterian Church, Minutes of Session, 1 December 1856. For session's reluctance to investigate a wife's report of marital trouble, see also 31 August 1865, 20 November 1865, 20 April 1867.

80 UCA, Zion Presbyterian Church, Minutes of Session, 9 April 1884. The father submitted a letter on 27 May 1884 expressing his son's sorrow to session, which thereupon expressed its satisfaction.

81 See note 14. For the decline in economic opportunity for young men, see Burley, *A Particular Condition in Life*, 161–9.

82 *Brantford Daily Expositor,* 19 January 1875. For a superb analysis of gender issues in the 1857–58 revival, see Kathryn Teresa Long, *The Revival of 1857–58: Interpreting an American Religious Awakening* (New York: Oxford University Press, 1998), 68–92.

83 *Brantford Weekly Expositor,* 14, 21, 28 February, 7, 14, 21 March 1879.

84 For example, thirty-eight of the seventy-one new members who joined Zion Presbyterian Church on a single Sunday in 1875, shortly after the Varley revival, were female, with an average age of 17.5. Of the seventy-one converts located in the 1871 and 1881 census, fifty-one had been raised in Presbyterian homes. For greater detail on the 1875 and 1879 revivals and on the 1879 appeal to unchurched youth, see Van Die, " 'The Marks of a Genuine Revival,' " 549–55.

85 With less emphasis on women's agency, Brian P. Clarke has analyzed the place of female piety in Irish Roman Catholic consolidation in Victorian Toronto in *Piety and Nationalism: Lay Voluntary Associations and the Creation of an Irish-Catholic Community in Toronto, 1850–1895* (Montreal and Kingston: McGill-Queen's University Press, 1993), 62–96.

86 A number of Canadian studies, which have not examined the role of women, have interpreted the shift to voluntarism as part of the process of secularization. See, for example, Westfall, *Two Worlds,* 191–209, and David Marshall, *Secularizing the Faith: Canadian Protestant Clergy and the Crisis of Belief, 1850–1940* (Toronto: University of Toronto Press, 1992), 23, 127–55.

87 R. Stephen Warner, *New Wine in Old Wineskins: Evangelicals and Liberals in a Small-Town Church* (Berkeley: University of California Press, 1988), 92–3, 201, 208.

88 BA, Immanuel Baptist Church Records, Eagle Place Sabbath School Association.

89 *Brantford Expositor Anniversary Number,* 1 July 1927.

90 *Christian Guardian,* 3 October 1888.

91 For an analysis of "moral feminism" and its impetus to women's reform movements, see Wendy Mitchinson, ed., *A Not Unreasonable Claim: Women and Reform in Canada, 1880s–1920s* (Toronto: Women's Press, 1979). A revisionist perspective is Nancy F. Cott, "What's in a Name? The Limits of Social Feminism: or, Expanding the Vocabulary of Women's History," *Journal of American History* 76 (1989): 809–29.

92 This view was succinctly expressed by the Reverend William Cochrane of Zion Presbyterian Church in a sermon, "Polished Corner Stones," one of his many convocation addresses to the graduating class of the Brantford Young Ladies' College: "The true queens of society are women of christian culture … Blessed is the nation which possesses such daughters, and happy the people whose God is the Lord" (Cochrane, *The Church and the Commonwealth,* 300–1).

Redemptive Homes – Redeeming Choices: Saving the Social in Late-Victorian London, Ontario

KENNETH L. DRAPER

Late-Victorian Ontario was characterized by a wide variety of religious activity, much of which addressed what were considered major social issues.[1] A variety of concerns conspired to convince the religiously motivated that conditions then present required organized efforts outside the confines of the denominational churches. Care for the poor, reclamation of the fallen, protection of youth, and the salvation of the unconverted all represented needs that called for united action beyond the capacity of individual congregations or denominations. Thus a whole new category of lay-inspired and-led interdenominational religious activity developed. Through public meetings, union revivals, and associational life, such as the Woman's Christian Temperance Union (WCTU) and the Young Men's Christian Association (YMCA), Protestants rose to meet the challenges facing them. This study of interdenominational religious activity in London, Ontario, attempts to investigate the authority by which Protestant Christians moved to address social issues. The approach taken here is suggested by some of the conceptual tools of poststructuralist or postmodern analysis, particularly work influenced by Michel Foucault. This analysis finds the social ministrations of Protestant Christians to constitute a governing technique of the liberal society emerging in Canada. At the same time as these lay-led interdenominational religious activities opened new avenues of authority to the religiously committed, they challenged the traditional religious authority exercised by the churches. The place of the church in the lives of the faithful was now being intersected with competing opportunities for legitimate religious action and competing sites for and narratives of salvation.

A connection between Protestant religious activity and the emergence of liberal society is perhaps not obvious, since the narratives of liberal social formation are most often cast in opposition to religion. This connection is suggested by Foucault's analysis of the formation of liberal societies, which works to uncover how individuals are constructed as subjects of states.[2] Foucault uses terms such as "the arts of government" and "government rationality" to designate the particular and local techniques and disciplines by which individuals become subjects. Thus in Foucault's usage "government" is much wider that a bureaucratic entity and includes networks of power and influence that bear on all agents all the time. The role of government in liberal societies was transformed from ensuring the security of a territory under the old regime to the new and much enlarged objective of ensuring the improvement, health, and prosperity of a population.[3] This governmental objective required new and far more complex tactics and techniques for governing. A distinctive feature of the political rationality of Western societies is the constitution of its subjects as both members of the self-governing political community and members of governed populations. It is by freedom and in support of freedom that liberal governments govern.[4] The power of government is no longer understood as being centred in a sovereign, an institution, or a class, but is dispersed through the complex of social, political, and economic interactions of all members of a society.[5]

Following Foucault's analysis, Jacques Donzelot has argued that families were a primary site for governing in the name of freedom.[6] The offer of economic autonomy to the family was a strategy for managing populations. This proffered autonomy required the breakdown of traditional communities and obligations, such as those to churches. The "improvement, health, and prosperity" of the family and thus of the population as a whole was to be pursued by male initiative and independence. But masculine independence could easily be misused unless it was disciplined in the family by the economic dependence of women and children. To meet its objective of a prosperous population, liberal society required independent nuclear families in which economic incentive would stimulate male autonomy for the benefit of the men's dependents. Donzelot describes a sphere of activity in which the imperatives of liberal society meet the objectives of the family, where the public interpenetrates the private.[7] This space he designates "the social." Action in the social focused on ensuring that families and individuals fulfilled their responsibilities for the benefit of society as a whole. Where the incentives of economic and social improvement were insufficient, philanthropic associations stepped in to provide instruction on proper family organization and gender responsibilities.

The social provided a new venue for the redemptive action of religious groups. Christian charity had long motivated action among the poor. Traditional charity met immediate needs, but it did not require the uplift of those it assisted. The government of liberal society prescribed action in the social that would promote the improvement and efficiency of the population. Simple charity was understood only to encourage indigence and poverty. Saving the social gave a variety of Protestant associations the public authority to form and preserve "households of faith." The activity of women and men's associations in late-Victorian London was in support of the formation and preservation of Christian households and in order to take ameliorative action where necessary.[8] While women and men's associations shared this goal, the rhetoric that shaped their efforts was significantly different. Women's groups offered redemptive homes as their response to the social, while men's groups called their fellows to redeeming choices.

THE WOMEN'S ASSOCIATIONS

The redemptive capacity of the well-ordered Christian homes and the support of the women who managed them was the women's associations' prescription for the social ills of the day. Although they carried out their work on a number of fronts, it was the narrative of the transforming Christian home that centred their activity. The Christian women of London were called upon to enrich their lives by exerting themselves "on the broad platform of Christian love, for the moral and spiritual elevation of their less fortunate sisters." As the guardians of the home, activist women throughout the dominion claimed a large measure of social authority.[9] The women's associations worked through relational networks to support families in a number of ways. They extended short-term assistance to ensure the long-term independence of families in need, they placed women and men who had transgressed social expectations under systems of moral tutelage, and they educated the younger generation regarding its moral responsibilities.

The Women's Christian Association

The Women's Christian Association (WCA) was the mother of all the interdenominational women's associations in late-nineteenth-century

London. Although its initial attempt at founding an institution was a success, management of the Protestant Orphans' Home was lost to the association in circumstances to be considered later. Nevertheless, an impressive range of activities occupied the WCA. Temperance agitation led to the formation of a local chapter of the WCTU out of the Temperance Committee of the WCA. In due course, the WCTU gave rise to the Young Women's Christian Temperance Union, that in turn formed the Young Women's Christian Association.[10] A WCA Visiting and Relief Committee "systematically" carried out the provision of relief to the poor.[11] This activity continued at the core of the WCA's activities, and more elaborate schemes grew out of this contact. Eventually a soup kitchen, a women's refuge, visits to the hospital and jail, and homes for aged men and women would take shape as the Women's Christian Association's response to social needs.[12]

The great downfall of action in the social was the "promiscuous" provision of charity, which contemporary experts considered the cause of poverty.[13] The Visiting and Relief Committee carefully investigated the circumstances of those in need. This committee recognized that temporary distress could come upon a family from a variety of causes. For many, poverty came through "circumstances over which they have no control," such as sickness. In other cases a downturn in trade was responsible for a "scarcity of work, and caused many a heart to suffer which had never felt the pangs of want before."[14] The relief work of the WCA was to maintain the integrity of these families until circumstances allowed them to regain their independence.

There were those, however, who had "no higher ambition than to be paupers." It was the evaluation of the WCA that the main cause of poverty and want was "the love for strong drink."[15] It was this conviction that led to the association's enthusiastic embrace of the temperance cause in November 1875. Wishing to relieve the "unmitigated anguish [in] the hearts of the wives and mothers of the land," the women of the WCA devised a rather remarkable strategy. They were set to eradicate the evil of drink and relieve the anguish of women by "visiting the homes of the poor drunkard with a view to their reformation."[16] The "poor drunkard's" moral failure, together with the WCA's sense of responsibility to the dependent women and children, authorized their intervention. Women, whom decorum forbade speaking in public meetings, took it upon themselves to lecture drunkards in their own homes. In this case, gender construction sanctioned women to take direct action, in the interests of the public, upon the private sphere of the home, providing moral tutelage for those ignorant of or resistant to their social responsibilities.[17]

The 1874 constitution of the WCA set as its object the "temporal, moral, and religious welfare of women, particularly of young women who are dependent upon their own exertions for support."[18] Following Toronto's lead, the WCA proposed a boarding house for young working women. This scheme addressed the concern that young women moving to London to take up employment in the schools, shops, and factories left behind the influence of Christian homes and were subject to the dangers of city life. The attitude of the proposed home was to be "Prevention is better than cure." The features of this Christian home were clearly spelled out. It was to be centrally located, comfortably furnished, and supplied with good reading and "innocent amusements," and was to maintain "as much as possible the characteristics of a Christian home – morning and evening worship, Bible class on Sunday afternoons, and a weekly prayer meeting."[19]

At some point between October 1875 and March 1876, a change of direction occurred in the association, and the focus of the redemptive home changed from prevention to cure. At the WCA meeting of 2 March 1876 a resolution was passed which rescinded an earlier action to establish a boarding house. In its place would be "a Refuge for fallen and repentant women." The WCA was fully aware that this enterprise pushed the boundaries of appropriate activity for respectable women. The women they were newly dedicated to help were regarded as victims of male lust, but also as dangers to the purity of the community.[20] "A Member of the WCA" wrote to the editor of the London *Advertiser* inveighing against the immorality of a society in which the penalty for sexual misconduct fell heavily upon women but men suffered little. Her analysis of this problem and its solution underscored the WCA faith in the saving efficacy of the Christian home. "A Member" was motivated to write "from a sense of justice and protection to some of our sex." She unfolded a narrative of sin, its consequences, the offer of redemption, and the narrow road to salvation, expressed with the indignation of the righteous against those who would lead the innocent astray.

The problem, according to the writer, did not originate with the young women who applied to the Refuge. Rather, it was that many girls were "not blessed with happy surroundings" during their formative years. These young women came from homes headed by "unkind parents devoid of the grace of God in their hearts, and having no altar in their homes to the Lord for the proper training of their children, abuse and ill-treatment become the portion of many daughters."[21] With this inauspicious upbringing in bad homes, young women became easy prey for unscrupulous men. Against this background, "A Member" recounted the circumstances of the previous fall, when "three seduced females" applied for help within a few days. She could find no boarding house willing to admit them, nor would the city relief officer provide assistance. She told of bringing one of these young women to her own home when no other options were available. This was the redemptive moment in the narrative. The young woman's response to this act of grace was described in the language of evangelical conversion: "with tears she thanked God that she had the care of a Christian family."[22]

This incident was meant to demonstrate the necessity of the Refuge and the urgent need for a larger facility. The letter ended with a warning to the true villains, those who led susceptible women into sin and then abandoned them to the consequences: "I may state that members of our Association intend to be *vigilant*, and should the crime continue will disclose the names of those who, on the other side of the case, go unpunished, and are received into respectable homes on the same equality with the virtuous."[23] Perhaps this last phrase captures the indignity of the "double standard" most poignantly. The "seduced females" lost reputation and social position for their part in this sin. Meanwhile, the male perpetrator of the crime continued to move in respectable society, invading the sacred domestic space under false pretences.[24]

The Protestant Orphans' Home

London's Protestant Orphans' Home and Refuge for the Aged came into being on 10 November 1874, but only after a denominational turf war came close to terminating the whole enterprise. The necessity of such an institution was suggested to the public by the WCA at a meeting at city hall chaired by Mayor Benjamin Cronyn on 16 October.[25] The scheme was unanimously endorsed, and a committee was struck to work out the details. However, when the committee reported in November, management of the home was no longer to be with the WCA but had been given to a new society. Objections to this arrangement soon revealed that the women of the Church of England had refused to join with the women of other denominations in the WCA and yet felt it was their right to lead a "Protestant Home." The non-Anglicans rejected this move, but recognized that the resources, both human and material, of the Church of England were essential to the viability of the undertaking. Eventually a compromise was reached by which the president of the WCA, a Methodist, was named the president of new society and the wife of the bishop of Huron appointed lady patroness. With this issue resolved, things moved quickly; a house on Ridout Street was rented and furnished, a steward and matron engaged, and the home opened with five children on 1 December 1874.[26]

As the WCA moved on to its work of relief and refuge, the Protestant Orphans' Home and Refuge for the Aged began a period of rapid growth. Many of the principles of "home" applied by the WCA in its work were evident at the home. Its purpose was to surround the children "with moral, material and educational influences" to set them on their way in life. This moral regime included showing residents the "greatest kindness" and enforcing "strict discipline."[27] For the orphans in the home, the object of these exertions was that children should integrate into the community through either adoption or placement with a "good family." The home prided itself on the fact that those placed by "adoption and otherwise" were "giving satisfaction."[28] The language employed here presents the care of orphans as a social exchange. Support of the home by the charitable public was exchanged for assurances that those supported would "give satisfaction" rather than inhabit the jails and represent a drain on the public.[29] In keeping with the common sense of the day, it was important that conditions in the home remain austere. A London *Free Press* report noted with approval that "the ladies vie with each other in keeping the weekly expenses down."

Cost-cutting and attempts to make maximum use of the facility were aspects of a disciplinary regime that ensured that residents would be conditioned for their place in society. An enlarged home was constructed in 1877 to meet the high demand for its services. The new building opened in June, and by November 1878 the home already had eighty-three residents, and there were enthusiastic predictions that it would accommodate a hundred.[30] The population of the home, including employees, children, and the aged, ranged in the middle eighties until 1882. A serious outbreak of fever occurred that year which almost closed the institution.[31] The crisis generated considerable expenditure and some reorganization at the home. Dr Brown, the medical examiner, called for the cesspools located adjacent to the home to be drained and all the drains in the building to be cleaned and flushed. He also recommended that city water be brought to the home and a drain be constructed to take waste directly to the river.[32] The fever also brought immediate construction of an infirmary, which had been suggested by the government inspector as early as 1880.[33] With this crisis underlining the need, the infirmary was operational by November 1882.[34] Another consequence of the fever scare was an immediate lowering in the number of residents. The population was reduced from over eighty to fifty-four in 1883 by moving all the elderly men out of the facility.[35]

The women serving on the executive of the Protestant Orphans' Home were never fully reconciled with limiting the population. In the very year a bylaw restricting admission to children was passed, Dr Brown complained that three new residents of the home had been admitted by the executive as employees only to circumvent the rules. These "employees" received no wages, and one, being over eighty years of age, was physically unable to work.[36] In February 1884 members of the executive suggested that older women again be admitted since the infirmary was then being underutilized. There was not complete unanimity between the ladies of the Protestant Orphans' Home and their medical adviser even about the number of children resident. In August of 1882, with the fever just under control, Dr Brown gave strict orders that no more children were to be admitted. Mrs Hyman, the home's vice-president, argued "the children had at present more room per head than half the private families in the city." If reductions were made, she was convinced that the "citizens would cease to support the Home."[37] The doctor was able to effect some reduction in numbers on the strength of a medical emergency, but he was never successful in lowering the number of residents to his target of forty-five. During the later years of the decade, numbers were again approaching eighty. Dr Brown's concerns were heard and weighed but often disregarded. The relational networks and community connections of the trustees were a more important consideration than the opinion of the medical officer. Feminine virtue had more authority in establishing the appropriate regime for orphan children than had male expertise during the 1880s.[38]

The Woman's Christian Temperance Union

As the London WCTU began its life within the WCA, it shared many of the convictions – and indeed, many of the personnel – of the older association. The activities of the WCTU, however, were less focused on specific institutions and ranged widely wherever the temperance message or a womanly influence seemed required. Often particular issues were taken up, consumed considerable energy for a time, and then were set aside in favour of another pressing campaign. The women of the WCTU considered alcohol the major cause of ineffective families. Their activity focused on removing what they believed to be the cause of masculine failure to provide conditions for the flourishing of dependent women and children.

In November 1875 three city clergymen called on the WCA for its cooperation in the temperance movement. The new Temperance Committee of the WCA moved quickly into the political realm, collecting in short order some 1,650 signatures on a petition to the provincial legislature calling for a reduction in the number of tavern licences. Feeling that limited time had resulted in too few signatures to sufficiently represent community opinion, the committee "resolved to send a deputation to Toronto to visit the Hon. Oliver Mowat." In company with some clergymen from London's Prohibitory League, the women presented their case directly to the premier at Queen's Park. While there, they were shown around the legislature by their MPP, Robert W. Meredith, and later in the day they met with representatives of the Toronto Temperance Union. Back in London, it was discovered that the local licensed victuallers were petitioning City Council for a reduction in licence fees. This action brought a deputation of the WCA Temperance Committee to City Council, and whether as a result of the women's effort or not, the victuallers were refused the requested reduction.[39] In 1879 the very active Temperance Committee became the London branch of the WCTU after a visit from Mrs Letitia Youmans.

The authority of women in the social was considerable, but it had limits. In 1886 the WCTU took up a local issue, championing the cause of retail clerks by calling for early closing on Saturday nights. This campaign was conducted with all the techniques of public indignation, but without evident success. The matter was brought before the WCTU by its president, Mrs Ellen Gregsten, in May 1886.[40] Clerks were required to work on Saturday nights as late as midnight. Consequently, Mrs Gregsten informed the union, they "were ... too tired to attend the morning service on the Sabbath day, and too tired to enjoy the evening one."[41] Clearly, this was a situation that required the intervention of Christian women to alert merchants to their duty and ensure the attendance of clerks at service on Sunday. The women of the WCTU circulated a petition, and a public meeting was called to discuss the issue on 24 June. The well-attended meeting was strongly in favour of early closing, and with little debate, it passed motions stipulating that businesses close at seven p.m. on Saturday night and that employees be paid on Friday to allow shopping to be done early on Saturday in order to eliminate the need for late opening. It was observed at the meeting that few merchants were present and none had spoken or signed the petition.[42] The "public" who responded to the WCTU's call were those sympathetic to the cause. The merchants, who ignored the meeting, also ignored its resolutions, and business continued as usual.

At the regular July WCTU meeting, the general lack of compliance with the resolutions of 24 June was noted, along with various legitimate issues raised by merchants. It was decided to attempt a less-confrontational approach in the future as women of the WCTU pledged "themselves to do their utmost to influence their friends and acquaintances to make their purchases early on Saturday and thus endeavor to educate the public in this matter."[43] The campaign for early closing illustrated the limitations of the indignation meeting and the authority granted to benevolent women on an issue that moved beyond the redeeming qualities of the well-managed home. WCTU families included merchants, and to push the issue further would have compromised the good relations with local merchants that the women, for other reasons, would wish to preserve. WCTU reports indicate a lack of political action in later years of the decade.[44]

Education was a constant emphasis of the WCTU. Its members distributed temperance tracts, especially in the jail and the Women's Refuge, and provided the local newspapers with temperance literature for publication. A representative educational initiative was the Girls' Industrial School. It was to teach girls "industry" and was a response to an impression that many girls "lounge around their home indifferent to education of any nature." Begun in 1884, the school met on Saturdays and taught children "to make and mend their clothes, knitting, darning etc." During its first season the school enrolled sixty-five, with an average attendance of thirty. The fourth Saturday of each month featured a lunch provided by the school's president.[45] The WCTU's educational efforts were focused on reaching the coming generation with the message of temperance; it hoped to create a world that had never tasted alcohol. The disappointing level of attendance at these efforts indicated that other strategies would need to be relied upon.

Christian women's associations were the primary agents of the social in London during the 1870s and 1880s. The care they extended to the poor, the sick, those in prison, the young and old, and the victims of drink and sexual misconduct was inspired by the Christian virtue of charity. Those involved understood themselves to be obeying Christ's teaching that, in feeding the hungry, caring for the sick, and visiting the prisoners, they were ministering to Christ.[46] In so doing, they hoped that those they helped would receive their ministrations as being from Christ. The concern to express love to those in need was, at the same time, intersected by the governing imperatives of the emerging liberal society. The truth about those in need that constructed their activities counseled assistance that would lead to independent family units. Women's associations provided a range of services to support families and to provide home environments in order to repair the damage done by ineffective families. The resulting activities were not merely private charity, but were publicly constructed philanthropy to actualize the freedom and prosperity promised by liberal arts of government.[47]

While the contemporary conventions of public space required men to do the talking on behalf of women in public meetings, the gender, class, and religious discourses that constructed this deference also provided authority for women to act. They were considered to be the agents, on the public's behalf, of nurture and social discipline. While men were appointed to assist with business and legal matters, they were given no role in the actual management of the homes that women founded. The public granted full authority to women to determine what was best for those in their care. Even Dr Brown's scientific credentials could not override the authority of the Protestant Orphans' Home's benevolent women.

Gender roles were clear, but they were conflicted by social rank and behavioral expectations. The "drunkard" seemed to lose his status as a "man" on a number of counts. His victimization of his wife and children by his inability to provide for their needs resulted in a loss of independence and thus a failure to live up to the construction of manhood. Class intruded as well, as association women were committed to elevate the lower classes. Thus, the drunkard was not a man in the relevant sense, and by his own actions he became the object of social tutelage through associational ministrations of love. The manhood of the "seducer" is also brought into question. The protector of feminine virtue here became the victimizer. The WCA's weapon in these cases was to wield the conventions of respectability against seducers by disclosing their names, thereby hoping to turn them out of respectable society. Within the social constructs of the period, the women's activities both sustained and challenged conventions as they worked to protect and extend the redeeming virtues of the Christian home.

Just as men were accorded the status of their sex only as they fulfilled its obligations, so a home was redemptive only as it lived up to specific criteria. The problem of "fallen women" was the result not only of the seducer but also of homes that did not provide children with adequate religious and moral discipline. The shelters operated by the women's associations did what they could to make up this lack by integrating all the requisite features of the Christian home. The visiting committees not only provided relief but also worked to uplift those they served by elevating "the moral tone and domestic habits" of those in need.[48] The educational efforts of the WCTU focused on similar outcomes, particularly in the Industrial School. Attempts to remake deficient homes were aimed at producing conditions for instilling the disciplined autonomy required by liberal society.

THE YOUNG MEN'S CHRISTIAN
ASSOCIATION

The rhetoric of home had little place in the strategies of male-dominated organizations. Rather, the rhetorical emphasis was the independence and self-improvement that came by creating the conditions for proper choices. It was this focus that led to the organization of London's Young Men's Christian Association in 1873. The new association's first objective was to help young Christian men reach out to their fellows, especially young men new to the city and susceptible to "Satanic influences." The second objective was to provide young men from all the evangelical denominations with an opportunity to work together, enabling them to "do much more than … a single church, or several separated churches."[49] The theme of evangelical churches rising above traditional prejudices to work together for the protection and salvation of young men identified the central preoccupation of London's YMCA.

The *Free Press* was profuse in its encouragement of the work of the Y. In the view of a *Free Press* writer, many young men were being lured into places providing "companionship and amusement, which are prejudicial to their healthy future position and character, and spiritually ruinous." In defense of the young men, the writer suggested that leisure time spent in such places was not so much from choice as from necessity, for London provided no alternatives. Other speakers on this theme threw their net wider to include all the young men of the city in a rhetorical web of danger. The YMCA was in open combat against the "attractions of the devil" for the social, intellectual, and spiritual well-being of men.[50] The attractions of the devil were clearly identified as barrooms, billiard halls, and theatres. At the Y's public meeting in 1882, the general secretary of the London association identified eighty-four "places for bad influence" right in London. Against their onslaught, the forces of righteousness had only the YMCA to provide redemption. The Y reading rooms, lectures, classes, and other programs were to entice young men away from the attractions of the devil. The great service of the association to all right-thinking citizens was that it provided the "great necessity of having a place in the city where their sons can spend an evening without fear of being contaminated, but rather ennobled."[51]

The WCA and the WCTU worked to protect women who, for a variety of reasons, no longer benefited from the "natural" protection of the home and the domestic sphere. The women they deemed most at risk, and who therefore absorbed the major part of their energies, were women who had been seduced by unscrupulous men and

women whose husbands were given to drink. The WCA plan to establish a home in support of young women "dependent on their own exertions for support" was abandoned for the more immediate need of
a Women's Refuge. It is significant that young women could not be
considered "independent," a term that signified a desirable state for a
young man. Young women were always dependent, although in this
case, through some necessity, on themselves. In the gendered construction of the experience of women, "independence" was not an
option in the minds of the women of the WCA. Despite the relatively
high number of single young women working in London, the sense
of danger that Carolyn Strange finds in discourse attempting to place
single women in Toronto was not evident in London.[52] The home-
building efforts of the WCA indicated that reclaiming the fallen was
more needful than addressing the risks to single working women.
The alarmist language about the perils of the city was reserved for
young men and used consistently by promoters of the YMCA. While
young women were expected to remain dependent, with appropriate
disciplining regimes in place to ensure this status, young men were to
become independent. The passage to adulthood required them to remove themselves from the protection of home and family into public
life. The construction of masculinity demanded a period of inevitable
vulnerability from the time when a young man became independent
from his family of origin until a wife redomesticated him into the
family for which he was responsible.[53] It was into this period of transition and risk that the YMCA was dedicated to preserving young
Christian men for the Kingdom of God.

But protection was not enough; the Y focused on providing activities that ennobled and improved young men.[54] The rhetoric of self-
improvement was particularly evident as the association grew in
strength in the 1880s. The Y organized debates and encouraged
young men to develop speaking and communication skills.[55] There
were classes offering improvement in such diverse areas as arith-
metic, writing, shorthand, bookkeeping, and vocal music. A Workers'
Bible Training Class was particularly important to the Y program as it
sought to develop Christian workers by the "critical study of the
Word to fit them for its use as the Sword of the Spirit."[56] The physical
side of healthy male development was an area of some frustration for
Y organizers. They recognized the need for a gymnasium; however,
their current hall, originally a church, did not lend itself to this kind
of use.[57] In 1883 some measures were taken in this direction as hot
and cold baths were installed and Indian clubs, dumbbells, and horizontal bars were purchased. The baths proved to be very popular,

and this addition prompted the *Free Press* to conclude that Victoria Hall was now approaching "what is intended, viz: – home for young men."[58]

Interdenominational cooperation was essential to the success of the YMCA, and Y promoters were typically respectful in their statements about denominational churches.[59] But despite such statements, the project of the Y undermined the authority of the churches in a number of ways. The most common case made for the interdenominational character of the Y was that the united resources of evangelical churches were required to meet the challenge of keeping young men for the Kingdom of God. This contention was premised on the churches' presumed failure to meet the religious needs of young men. The Y's assertions of its common cause with the churches were often accompanied by claims that true religion transcended traditional denominational lines. It claimed to save and protect young men where the churches had failed and to represent a truer, more inclusive Christianity than that of the churches. At the same time, Y promoters chided the clergy for their lack of sufficient sympathy with and support for Y causes, contending that denominational prejudice was inhibiting the work of the Lord.[60] Those involved in the Y were continually being offered new avenues for "usefulness," which meant that they were less available for the growing number of programs being developed in the churches. Annual meetings in London's churches often heard pastors complain and plead for the young men to take a more active role. The same could be heard from the general secretary of the YMCA. Even while Y organizers were careful to claim that allegiance to the church should be primary, loyalty was clearly the issue.[61] As the network of interdenominational associations grew in the 1880s, the direction that an active Christian's energy should take was under negotiation. The churches made a variety of claims based on particular traditions and grounded in practices of worship and congregational life. The Y evoked a universal faith, transcending traditions and contributing to the spiritual, intellectual, and physical improvement of the nation's young men. YMCA promoters framed their claims in the progressive discourse of the universal over the particular, pulling their version of religious improvement out of the tradition-bound churches. In calling Christian men to labour for a faith that transcended the particulars of denominational traditions, they held a rhetorical advantage. However, in constructing a faith divorced from the particular doctrines and practices of congregational life, the Y risked calling young men to no faith in particular.

UNION REVIVALS

Like the Protestant associations, union revivals increased religious activity and did so in a very public way. Union revival meetings also brought churches together to carry out religious work that transcended the reach of local congregations. Thus religious activity was consciously moving outside the churches and laying claim to a supra-denominational faith. This faith was grounded on an individual choice in conversion, expressed in rhetoric that paralleled the freedoms central to liberal techniques of government.

The scale of union revivals made them major community events. Edward P. Hammond drew four thousand to the under-heated drill shed in December 1879. D.L. Moody preached to six packed crowds on the Sunday of his London appearance, and by the final day the police had been called upon to limit entrance to the meeting. The revivals were in part spectacle, in part a connection with a wider evangelical world, in part a call to individual introspection, and in part a rehearsal of and challenge to community standards of propriety. The revival meeting constructed its own reality in which the out-of-the-ordinary became the expected.

Union revivals were self-consciously interdenominational. The clergy of all denominations viewed union meetings as an effective, even essential, aspect of the religious nurture of their congregations. The Reverend W.H. Porter, pastor of Talbot Street Baptist, introduced the meetings, arranged by the YMCA with H.W. Brown, by suggesting that revival needed to break out of the narrow circle of religious interest. This could only occur as all the churches participated in the great work of "saving souls for Christ." On the same occasion, Presbyterian minister Murray expressed his hope that every "unconverted man or woman in his church would come here tonight." Murray had heard good reports of meetings of this kind in other parts of the country, particularly as regards the conversion of young men. Beyond conversion, he believed that long-time church members could also benefit spiritually from the meetings.[62]

The Narrative Thought World of Revival

The narrative that animated revival understood the world to be entrapped in sin, a condition that separated people from God and from one another. Salvation from sin and reconciliation with God were available because of the atoning work of Jesus Christ. The way to conversion was to believe that this narrative of sin and salvation described the real world. God offered salvation to all, but people must believe and enter into this reality for him or herself.[63] After conversion, the benefits of the Christian life became available. These included peace and comfort and an ability to love as Christ loved; indeed, all the virtues of Christ were to characterize the Christian. The presence of the Holy Spirit brought these benefits into the life of the individual and provided power over sin and human frailties. The message of the revivalist was that the sinner must respond now, before it was too late.[64]

Those attending revivals could expect to be called to a change. The change was grounded on belief and intellectual acceptance of the evangelical narrative. However, it was not the offer of new knowledge that made the difference. Henry Varley urged his hearers "to seek the truth, not as a theory, but as a living truth."[65] What revival offered was a "new birth," a new quality of experience and meaning. The revival meeting was the place of decision, a symbolic space constructed between the old life and the new where actions had ultimate, eternal import. Revivalists and pastors, as well as critics of revival, recognized that many who responded would not follow through. Hammond referred to these as "professors and not possessors of religion."[66] Moody emphasized that conversion was not primarily changing one's mind but changing one's ways. The first without the second would never endure.[67] The work of the revival was to construct the symbolic space within which fundamental spiritual and moral change was possible. Conversion narratives such as those of William Stevens, the Brantford "infidel," and a violent husband now sharing the faith of his believing wife, provided an empirical verification of the narrative of restoration.[68] The testimonies of women, silenced by the conventions of public space, were welcomed and honoured as evidence and vehicles of divine grace.[69] Tears and weeping, which accompanied revival meetings, spoke of an extraordinary power at work, particularly when they broke through gender constructs, allowing strong men to weep like little children.[70] The private and hidden world of confession and reconciliation was, for a time, made the focus of the city's public life.

The actual message of salvation proclaimed at the revival was not markedly different from that preached regularly in the local churches. Revival meetings, however, could create a different reality that lifted people out of their regular religious duties and social conventions and urged upon them a new or a deeper commitment. One of the express purposes of revivals was that they reached a "different class" than was regularly to be found in the churches.[71] Revivals attempted to identify and break down the hindrances to the new life and to create a shared sense of urgency in all who attended to take their religious responsibilities more seriously.

Ironically, one of the hindrances most often cited by revival preachers was regular church involvement. Hammond warned against those who "talk of their respectability, but will not admit their sinfulness" as being in particular danger.[72] Moody argued that many considered themselves good Christians because they went to church, read the Bible, were baptized, or were "turning over new leaves." While these activities were good in themselves, he declaimed them as false religion and hindrances to the new birth if they were trusted for salvation.[73] Evangelists proclaimed that external ceremonies and rituals did not bring the experience of the presence of God, which alone was evidence of inner change. Upsetting respectable Christianity and abandoning denominational traditions and forms, revivals attempted to divest the faith of its incidental trappings and impress upon seekers the pure and simple reality of an individual, unmediated encounter with God. In breaking down denominational barriers at the altar, the individual was brought before God without Christian history or identity.

At the inquiry meetings, which those under conviction were invited to attend following the main meeting, groups numbering in the thousands were reduced to isolated individuals confronted by zealous Christian workers as the time of ultimate religious choice was upon them.[74] The urgency and weight of the decision bore upon the individual human will, and in the narrative of evangelical encounter, there was no one to help. Those clustered around the seeker could pray and encourage and cajole, but not even God could make this decision. The choice was to let go of an old identity, one that was marred by sin, and receive a new birth, a new life. Revivalists used few images of hell fire and brimstone. The common images of the consequences of sin were gender-specific; unrepentant men were destined to intemperance and dissipation and women to frivolousness and novel-reading. Both sexes were warned against a wasted life and offered instead a life of usefulness. To reject the new birth was to leave with the old identity and its attendant problems unimproved by the offer of salvation. This narrative gave the individual ultimate and autonomous responsibility for his or her place in this world and the next.

In his final sermon to the men of London, Moody focused on what he believed to be the greatest hindrance to the conversion of young men – fear of ridicule. He revealed sensitivity to the contemporary construction of maleness and religion. Courage was not only one of the cardinal virtues; it was to be a characteristic of the male of the race that would empower him in his role as protector and leader. A lack of courage was a lack of manliness; thus, Moody called on young men to have the courage of their convictions and to act as men in not being "ashamed to come to Christ."[75] But the same gender construction that assigned men courage assigned women religion. Thus, Moody's prediction that young men were "afraid of the jeers" of their companions was directly related to the fact that confession of wrongdoing, asking forgiveness, and submission to Christ in a life of obedience could hardly be construed as manly. Independence of thought and action were the hallmarks of masculinity. To the degree that revival was about stripping away the dominance of tradition and dogma and choosing a new life by a heroic act of the individual will it was congruent with manhood. However, the language that emphasized humility, submission, and self-giving love held little appeal. Moody's suggestion that standing up to ridicule for the sake of Christ revealed manliness attempted to extend the accepted gender constructs towards a distinctively Christian manhood. Moreover, he presented this kind of ridicule as a discipline creating an authentically independent manhood equal to the task of providing for dependents in a healthy and prosperous family.

Churches and Revivalists

London's local clergy were organizers and promoters of union revivals. They repeatedly endorsed revival meetings as an essential part of the religious culture of the city, and each course of meetings added new adherents to their churches.[76] Yet, differences between the practices of church life and those of the revival meeting reflected underlying tensions. One of the surest techniques for moving religion from the routine to the extraordinary was to condemn the "religiosity" of respectable church members and to mock preachers. Most revivalists had these somewhere in their arsenal, but Sam Jones developed ridicule of religion to an art form. Fashionably attired, charitable women were criticized for distributing second-hand clothing, wives' lack of ability in the kitchen was regarded as the cause of the irreligion of husbands, and ministers were prescribed opiates to bring some life to their "one-legged sermons."[77] The revivalist's tendency to diminish regular religious activity in contrast to their own offerings undermined the local clergy and congregational life as sources of spiritual nurture and development. This was not the intention of the majority of revivalists, who showed more reserve and respect than Jones did. Moody suggested that the success of his work was up to the pastors who would follow through on the good that was done. However, it was not the intentions of revivalists but the power of their narrative that undermined local religious practices. The effect of their rhetoric of extraordinary religion was to construct religious experience as a product served up to individuals by professionals at large gatherings for a limited time. The weekly diet of worship and community attempts to live by particular beliefs and practices was thereby devalued as sectarian and uninspiring.

The revivalists made consistent use of the Christian belief in the essential unity of the faith and the need for harmony among the denominations. Brown hoped that during his meetings "sectarian differences would be forgotten."[78] He invited others to join him in the inclusive space constructed by the revival meeting, where salvation was offered "only through faith in Christ" without reference to sectarian considerations.[79] The maintenance of this inclusive space required constant vigilance. Points of dispute, especially age-old theological differences, could not be allowed to disrupt the work of revival. Moody would not allow questions to be put to him that "involved disputed points in theology, such as baptism by immersion or sprinkling." The children of God were "bound to keep the peace," he argued, rather than concern themselves with matters as peripheral as the rite of initiation into congregational life.[80]

Before the union revivals became the vogue in London, the Reverend Dr Cooper of Talbot Street Baptist Church presented a paper to the Baptist conference in which he referred, in a distinctly negative light, to the work of revivalists. He characterized revivalist preachers as "men belonging to no church, and glorying in their freedom from all sectarian trammels." The irony of their claim was that they refused to extend to others the freedom they claimed for themselves. Cooper argued that, "while professing in high sounding words their utter dislike of all sectarianism, we found them the most sectarian and the most uncharitable people with whom we have had anything to do."[81] This comment captures the tension between the revivalist and the churches rather well. In breaking down the particular in favour of a universal experience of religion, the revivalists constructed a new particularity in competition with, even as it sought to support, the churches. People saved at the revival meetings rather than in their churches continued to seek religious nurture in an abstract, spectacular, unmediated faith. As at the point of decision at the altar, this revival faith allowed no connection with a particular community and amplified the privatization of religion. Revivalism increased church membership while at the same time aiding the removal of religion from corporate to privatized experience. Rather than building a community of faith, it encouraged a consumerist conception of religion as meeting personal needs and offering improvement and success in an often hostile world through inner resolve and force of will.

CONCLUSION

Gender-specific themes emerge from the discourses and practices of the associations and union revivals in late-Victorian London, Ontario, particularly with regard to redemptive interventions in the social. The focus of the YMCA, the principal male association, was the improvement and protection of other males. Its activities were to provide constructive alternatives to the many temptations of the world resulting in independent moral men ready to take on the responsibilities of family. The support of the public was urged to preserve and strengthen the virtue of its male leadership through the auspices of the Y. The rhetoric of independence and improvement assumed that men required associational life to provide positive influences and activities to those of similar social status. The women's organizations sought to uplift rather than improve. The rhetoric of uplift so prevalent among women's associations indicated that much of their work was among those who would not be considered their social equals. The work of middle-class women provided for the social and moral tutelage of the young, the old, the sick, and the poor. The conventions of male authority were preserved in that women's power extended only over those whose masculinity had been brought into question by some moral lack, most often signaled in a loss of independence. The WCA threat to expose seducers and the WCTU attempt to direct when merchants should pay their employees and close their establishments pushed the limits of these conventions, without evident success.

Both male and female associations were dedicated to saving the social, yet the saving strategies their practices embodied are grounded in gendered difference. The public authority of women was premised on the redemptive nature of the home. The institutions built by women's associations were invariably "homes," and the solution to social issues being addressed was to provide the discipline and care of an effective and healthy household. This approach to salvation emphasized relationships and provision of good influences over time to train the young or raise up the fallen. Conditions of poverty and want were understood by these women to be complex. Their solutions to social problems included providing soup to the hungry, lecturing drunkards as to their responsibilities as men, carrying petitions to legislators in Toronto, giving shelter to the marginalized, providing educational opportunities for the young, and in everything working for the salvation of souls. The salvation of individuals and the social was understood to take place within networks of nurture and regulation.

In support of, as well as in contrast to, this activity was the saving strategy of the male-dominated YMCA and revival meetings. In these locations the way to salvation was by heroic individual choice and moral renewal, if necessary in the face of ridicule and persecution. Networks of relationships were considered to be hindrances to salvation, since such considerations might cause the seeker to resist or delay the moment of decision. Everything had to be peeled away as the individual came alone and unaided into a discursive space that constructed the encounter with the divine in conversion. Testimonies at revivals emphasized the moment of choice as the change that brought the new birth. However, accounts of inquiry meetings emphasized the presence and encouragement of family and friends in the drama leading to conversion.[82] While the rhetorics of the redemptive home and the redeeming choice were widely divergent, in practice they supported each other. Women used the authority of their relational networks to bring their households to the revival meeting in order to force or inspire a choice, particularly among their young men.

Both these saving strategies found salvation outside the church. This perhaps had the most far-reaching significance for nineteenth-century Protestantism. Salvation through the home required the church only as a support to the family. The introduction of varied-age-level programs for children and adolescents during this period indicated the churches' initial attempts at this new role.[83] On the other hand, salvation through individual choice required the church to meet the spiritual needs of an assembly of religious individuals rather than to form them into a community. The call of both was to leave behind doctrinal and liturgical traditions in order to more adequately serve individuals and the family. Conforming to the orthodoxy of liberal society, the Protestant world devised a way of speaking religion in public that claimed to transcend particularities, and in so doing, it bleached the particular out of its faith. The redemptive home and the redeeming choice were themes that came to define religious activity to a degree that it was confused with Protestantism itself. Protestantism continued to flourish in congregational life; however, this life became increasingly difficult to sustain as the discourse of interdenominational activity contested the legitimacy of denominational particularity. The rhetorical power of this lay-led interdenominational religious activity silenced its critics, who could only look sectarian, narrow, and anti-family and anti-choice in raising their objections. The church could make no exclusive claim to be the place in which the divine was encountered, and thus, congregations and their clergy were forced to question exactly what it was for. Public claims for the authority of Christianity were now to be cast in support of the family and individual choice.

NOTES

1 John Webster Grant, *A Profusion of Spires: Religion in Nineteenth-Century Ontario* (Toronto: University of Toronto Press, 1988).
2 Colin Gordon, "Governmental Rationality: An Introduction," in Graham Burchell, Colin Gordon, and Peter Miller, eds., *The Foucault Effect: Studies in Governmentality* (Chicago: University of Chicago Press, 1991), 7–8. The themes that surround Foucault's thinking on governmentality were discussed primarily in his lectures and seminars towards the end of his life, many of which are unpublished; see ibid., 1–8.
3 Michel Foucault, "Governmentality," ibid., 98–100.
4 Nikolas Rose, "Towards a Critical Sociology of Freedom," in Patrick Joyce, ed., *Class* (Oxford: Oxford University Press, 1995), 215.
5 Nikolas Rose, *Governing the Soul: The Shaping of the Private Self* (London: Routledge, 1990), 4–5. On Foucault's use of the concept of power, see C.G. Prado, *Starting with Foucault: An Introduction to Genealogy* (Boulder: Westview Press, 1995), esp. chap. 4.
6 Jacques Donzelot, *The Policing of Families*, trans. Robert Hurley (New York: Pantheon Books, 1979), 53–4.
7 Ibid., 88. Gilles Deleuze's foreword, "The Rise of the Social," to Donzelot's work is also helpful in defining "the social."
8 Donzelot, *The Policing of Families*, 92–4.
9 A large varied of literature on "maternal feminism" has emerged over the last two decades has established this point. See Wayne Roberts, " 'Rocking the Cradle for the World': The New Woman and Maternal Feminism, Toronto, 1877–1914," in Linda Kealey, ed., *A Not Unreasonable Claim: Women and Reform in Canada, 1880s-1920s* (Toronto: The Women's Press, 1979). Denise Riley, in *"Am I That Name?" Feminism and the Category of "Women" in History* (London: Macmillan, 1988), 50, argues that the space created by the social was peculiarly feminized, given its primary concern with familial standards.
10 Mark Greenberg and Edward Phelps, *The Young Women's Christian Association of London, Ontario, Canada: A Century of Faith, Hope and Good Works, 1889–1951 (YMCA-YWCA) (London, 1989), 1–2, 6.
11 Donzelot, *The Policing of Families*, 69. System was essential if assistance was to "teach" its recipients the path to uplift.
12 "The City Charities," London *Free Press*, 19 March 1890, 3.
13 Donna Andrew is very helpful in charting the changing attitudes to charity in the eighteenth century, contrasting a concern for the character of the giver and the welfare of the recipient with the later concern for the character of the recipient and the welfare of society. See Donna T. Andrew, *Philanthropy and Police: London Charity in the Eighteenth Century* (Princeton: Princeton University Press, 1989), 3–4. Similar themes are explored for the late nineteenth century in Garth Stedman Jones's early work, *Outcast*

London: A Study in the Relationship between Classes in Victorian Society (Oxford: Claredon Press, 1971), especially chap. 13, 14, and 15. Contemporary analysis argued, according to Stedman Jones, that it was the "indiscriminate almsgiver" motivated by Christian charity who was the cause of the "demoralisation" of the poor and thus the perpetuation of poverty. The solution was to organize philanthropy to produce desired behaviors in the recipient. This shift in focus gave rise to the founding in 1869 of the Society for Organising Charitable Relief and Repressing Mendicity. See Stedman Jones, *Outcast London*, 245–56.

14   "Women's Christian Association," *Free Press*, 3 May 1889, 6.

15   "The Sixth Anniversary," *Free Press*, 19 May 1880, 3, and "The W.C.A.: Proceedings of the Anniversary," London *Advertiser*, 10 May 1876, 1.

16   "The W.C.A.: Proceedings of the Anniversary," 1.

17   Donzelot, *The Policing of Families*, chap. 4, "The Tutelary Complex."

18   "Women's Christian Association," *Advertiser*, 15 June 1874, 3.

19   "Women's Christian Association," *Free Press*, 9 October 1875, 4.

20   Carolyn Strange, *Toronto's Girl Problem: The Perils and Pleasures of the City, 1880–1930* (Toronto: University of Toronto Press, 1995), 53–4.

21   This device allows "A Member" to distance her own world and, if not her own daughter, at least the daughters of her peers from the world they entered in their charitable endeavours. It is the daughter of the "other" who is subject to seduction, while the Christian home of women in her condition provides an effective prophylactic to the advances of "the lewd."

22   "Need of a Woman's Refuge," letter, *Advertiser*, 15 March 1878, 4.

23   The emphasis is that of the original. It is clearly men of her own class whom "A Member" is charging with misconduct. There is no evidence that this threat was carried out, at least through the two daily newspapers. Since the continued existence of the Refuge would indicate that the "crime" did persist, either the women found it impossible to carry out their threat or they used informal methods of protecting "respectable homes."

24   This theme emerges consistently as members of the WCA reflected on their work. In defending the work of the Refuge, a WCA speaker from Toronto gave the following directive: "Some said that showing kindness and extending the comforts of a home to those erring sisters was only making the life which they lead easy. This was a manifest error. No Christian woman would spurn from her door a fallen woman, and welcome to her parlor an immoral man" ("Christian Work," *Free Press*, 15 April 1880, 4).

25   This account follows the fuller account of the London *Advertiser*: "Aged and Orphans," 17 October 1874, 2; also see "The Orphans' Home," 17 October 1874, 4.

26   "The Protestant Home," *Free Press*, 10 November 1875.

27   "The Protestant Home," *Free Press*, 9 November 1877, 1.

28 "Protestant Orphans' Home," *Free Press*, 3 November 1882, 3. Also see "The Protestant Orphans' Home," *Advertiser*, 5 November 1880, 2.

29 Jails were supported by the government at a much higher subsidy than orphanages, giving Hannon's argument the force of social efficiency as well as moral sense. See Mariana Valverde, "The Mixed Social Economy as a Canadian Tradition," *Studies in Political Economy* 47 (1995): 46.

30 "Protestant Home," *Advertiser*, 8 November 1878, 4. For suggestions as to the home's capacity, see "The Orphans," *Advertiser*, 17 November 1880, 4.

31 "The City Charities: The Origins and Work of the Protestant Orphans' Home," *Free Press*, 1 March 1890, 3.

32 The work to bring water to the home was completed by August 1882; see "The Protestant Orphans' Home," *Free Press*, 19 August 1882, 4. The drain was considerably more expensive, estimated at $500, and took considerably longer to complete. The annual report of 1885 indicates that this work had been completed during the year (see *Free Press*, 6 November 1885, 3).

33 Mr Langmuir's recommendation is noted in the annual report for 1880; see "The Protestant Orphans' Home," *Advertiser*, 5 November 1880, 2. Cost estimates and building designs for the infirmary were matters for discussion at a number of meetings; see, for example, "Protestant Orphan's Home," *Free Press*, 14 May 1881, 4.

34 "Protestant Orphans' Home," *Free Press*, 3 November 1882, 3.

35 "Protestant Orphans' Home," *Free Press*, 3 November 1883, 2.

36 Ibid.

37 "The Protestant Orphans' Home," *Free Press*, 19 August 1882, 4.

38 These women were resisting the movement away from a religiously inspired benevolent institution towards a social-work model. For this process at work in Toronto, see John R. Graham, "The Haven, 1878–1930 – A Toronto Charity's Transition from a Religious to a Professional Ethos," *Histoire sociale/Social History* 25 (1992): 283–306.

39 "The W.C.A.: Proceedings of the Anniversary," *Advertiser*, 10 May 1876, 1.

40 Ellen Gregsten served as the founding president of the Women's Christian Association and the Protestant Orphan's Home. Upon retirement from the presidency of the Orphan's Home in 1883, she took on the presidency of the WCTU in 1884, a position she retained until 1890.

41 "Early Closing on Saturday," *Free Press*, 12 May 1886, 7.

42 "Earlier Closing Hours," *Free Press*, 25 June 1886, 3.

43 "The W.C.T.U.," *Free Press*, 14 July 1886, 3.

44 Sharon Cook finds this decline of interest in political activity at the local level to be widespread. See Sharon Anne Cook, *"Through Sunshine and Shadow": The Woman's Christian Temperance Union, Evangelicalism, and Reform in Ontario, 1874–1930* (Montreal and Kingston: McGill-Queen's University Press, 1995), 114.

45 On the founding and functioning of the Girls' Industrial School, see
    "W.C.T.U.," *Free Press*, 5 March 1884, 6; "The W.C.T.U.," *Free Press*,
    10 September 1884, 8; and "Women's Temperance Work," *Free Press*,
    8 September 1886, 6. Although the number of students seems to have
    dropped off, the school was still functioning in 1890; see "The
    W.C.T.U.," *Free Press*, 28 November 1890, 3.
46 Matthew 25: 34–6.
47 On the distinction between charity and philanthropy, see Donzelot, *The
    Policing of Families*, 66–7.
48 "Women's Christian Association," *Free Press*, 9 October 1875, 4.
49 "Young Men's Christian Association," *Advertiser*, 8 September 1873, 3.
50 "Y.M.C.A.," *Advertiser*, 22 April 1874, 1.
51 "Y.M.C.A.," *Free Press*, 22 October 1885, 5.
52 The 1891 census records 794 single women under thirty working in enter-
    prises other than domestic service in London. This figure is a significant
    increase from the 296 in 1871. See Strange, *Toronto's Girl Problem*, chap. 2.
53 E. Anthony Rotundo, *American Manhood: Transformations in Masculinity
    from the Revolution to the Modern Era* (New York: Basic Books, 1993), 172–4.
    Donzelot, in *The Policing of Families*, 36, suggests that dependent women
    provided an effective means of curbing masculine independence, particu-
    larly among the working classes in France.
54 Patrick Joyce, *Democratic Subjects: The Self and the Social in Nineteenth-
    Century England* (Cambridge: Cambridge University Press, 1994), 171–6.
55 "Y.M.C.A. Work," *Free Press*, 27 February 1884, 1; "Y.M.C.A.," *Advertiser*,
    26 July 1884, 1; and "Our Young Men," *Advertiser*, 15 October 1884, 3.
56 "The Association's Work," *Free Press*, 16 October 1886, 5; also see "Young
    Men's Work," *Free Press*, 10 October 1883, 2.
57 "Y.M.C.A. Work," *Free Press*, 11 October 1882, 4.
58 "Y.M.C.A. Work," *Free Press*, 27 February 1884, 1.
59 "Y.M.C.A.," *Advertiser*, 21 October 1876.
60 "Y.M.C.A.," *Free Press*, 22 April 1874, 4.
61 "Y.M.C.A.," *Free Press*, 21 October 1876.
62 "Union Revival," *Free Press*, 27 September 1886, 5.
63 See, for example; "Varley," *Advertiser*, 1 February 1875, 1; "The Tabernacle,"
    Advertiser, 25 December 1879; and "Mr. Moody's Message," *Free Press*,
    8 January 1890, 5.
64 "Varley," *Advertiser*, 1 February 1875, 1; "The Tabernacle," *Advertiser*,
    22 December 1879, 4; "Unabated Interest," *Advertiser*, 8 January 1890; and
    "Evangelist Moody," *Advertiser*, 7 January 1890.
65 "Varley," *Advertiser*, 1 February 1875, 1.
66 "The Revival Wave," *Free Press*, 9 December 1879.
67 "Mr Moody's Message," *Free Press*, 8 January 1890, 5.

68 On the story of William Stevens's conversion, see "The Revival Wave," *Advertiser*, 4 December 1879; and "The Revival Wave," *Free Press*, 5 December 1879. On the story of the threat of violence and reconciliation, see: "The Revival Wave," *Free Press*, 5 December 1879; "The Hum of the Revival," *Free Press*, 6 December 1879; and "The Tabernacle," *Free Press*, 12 December 1879.

69 "The Tabernacle," *Free Press*, 12 December 1879.

70 "The Revival," *Advertiser*, 12 December 1879.

71 Moving the Hammond meetings to the drill shed was to attract those who would not be likely to attend a church; see "The Revival Services," *Free Press*, 4 December 1879. Lynne Marks, in *Revivals and Roller Rinks: Religion, Leisure, and Identity in Late-Nineteenth-Century Small-Town Ontario* (Toronto: University of Toronto Press, 1996), 205–6, discovered a high percentage of working-class people among the converts at the Crossley and Hunter revival in Thorold in 1893. Although recognizing the complexity of identity construction, she flattens her explanation of the phenomenon to economic distress.

72 "The Revival Meetings," *Free Press*, 29 November 1879.

73 "Evangelist Moody," *Advertiser*, 7 January 1890.

74 The methods used in the inquiry meeting at the Hammond revival are described in "The Revival Wave," *Free Press*, 9 December 1879, and "The Story of the Cross," *Free Press*, 14 December 1879.

75 "Mr. Moody Has Gone," *Free Press*, 10 January 1890.

76 Marguerite Van Die, " 'The Marks of a Genuine Revival': Religion, Social Change, Gender and Community in Mid-Victorian Brantford, Ontario," *Canadian Historical Review* 79 (1998): 550, and Marks, *Revivals and Roller Rinks*, 258–9.

77 "How to Win," *Free Press*, 22 September 1887, 7, and "Sam Jones – 'Getting Thar,' " *Free Press*, 24 September 1887.

78 "Union Revival," *Free Press*, 27 September 1886, 5.

79 "Mr. Brown's Revival," *Free Press*, 29 September 1886, 4.

80 "Words of Warning," *Advertiser*, 9 January 1890.

81 "Evangelists and Their Work," *Free Press*, 17 October 1877, 4.

82 "The Story of the Cross," *Free Press*, 14 December 1879.

83 Marguerite Van Die, " 'A March of Victory and Triumph in Praise of The Beauty of Holiness' ": Laity and the Evangelical Impulse in Canadian Methodism, 1800–1884," in G.A. Rawlyk, ed., *Aspects of the Canadian Evangelical Experience* (Montreal and Kingston: McGill-Queen's University Press, 1997), 84–6.

Reinventing Christian Masculinity and Fatherhood: The Canadian Protestant Experience, 1900–1920

PATRICIA DIRKS

Leaders of Canada's major Protestant denominations entered the twentieth century already deeply worried that their churches were losing ground individually and collectively. A significant proportion of every denomination's children were never brought into Sunday school, the agency generally recognized as the chief membership source. In addition, many who entered Sunday school left before becoming church members. These conditions generated great anxiety about Sunday schools' weaknesses, particularly their inability to hold those who were enrolled once they reached puberty.[1] Concerns about the membership implications of "teen age leakage" intensified after the 1901 census, which revealed that the combined growth of Canada's major Protestant denominations over the preceding decade had not matched that of the Roman Catholic Church.[2] This trend threatened the position of Protestant churches in Canadian society and the dream, shared by the growing ranks of social gospellers in the major denominations, of making Canada into a great twentieth-century power led in all walks of life by active Protestants.[3] Overcoming this threat would require finding ways of keeping adolescents, especially boys, in Sunday school and bringing them into their respective churches.

In the socially disruptive and materialistic environment of the opening decades of the century, unsatisfactory Protestant church membership gains were increasingly linked to a deterioration in family life and parental neglect of children's religious training. More and more church leaders argued that the actions and attitudes of Canada's

Protestant parents determined what Sunday schools could accomplish as religious-education and membership-recruitment agencies. This conviction fostered increased efforts to reawaken parents to their primary responsibility for religious education and to ensure that fathers as well as mothers fulfilled their respective duties in this regard. As the new century dawned, Presbyterian parents were already being castigated for shifting their "God-given parental responsibility" onto the Sabbath school, "where the father and mother in the vast majority of cases never go."[4] Writing just a few years later, the editor of the *Canadian Churchman*, the Anglican church's national publication, declared that the "evil effects" of "[t]he neglect of the modern professing Christian parent of his responsibility" were "everywhere evident."[5] Protestant parents of all major denominations, including those of the growing urban middle class, were criticized for allowing outside activities to keep them away from their homes and children. Mothers, even those who were heavily involved in church work, were warned against taking too much time away from their primary duties as homemakers. Fears about the feminization of the church, however, focused more and more attention on fathers, who were admonished to put family responsibilities ahead of all other interests, business included. The inability of Sunday schools to hold adolescents, particularly boys, was attributed to fathers' shortcomings as adult Protestant role models.

Church criticisms of early-twentieth-century parents were clearly tied in with attempts to redefine Christian masculinity for the modern age.[6] As the Reverend W.H. Hincks explained in 1900, "the mother alone cannot bring her boy to a virility, a masculinity, a manhood of Christian life and thought unless she has her husband by her side."[7] And how, Protestants asked, could Sunday schools bring adolescent boys into the church if their fathers were not already there? Was it any surprise that even the sons of church members identified the church as an institution for girls, women, and "little" boys? What their fathers did was crucial if boys were to be convinced that religion was a man's concern.[8] While mothers continued to be recognized as the formative influence in the religious lives of young children, worries about Christianity's lack of appeal among men and boys stimulated efforts to place fathers at the centre of family religious life at home and in the church. The almost exclusive focus on the "big" boy problem and its relationship to the inadequacies of modern parents, fathers especially, reflects increasing Protestant preoccupation with these issues. Even those Protestants who argued that equal attention should be paid to the Christian training of women and girls did not want any less effort to be expended on boys and men.[9]

The widespread social dislocation of the early 1900s thus fuelled Protestant attempts to link masculinity and religious faith. Like American proponents of the social gospel, Canada's emerging class of professional religious educators sought to define a new masculine ideal based on "personality and social involvement."[10] Their efforts included the definition of an ideal of Christian fatherhood suitable for the modern, urban industrial world. With the help of preachers and editorial writers, they spread the message that good fathers were well-rounded individuals who devoted time and energy to fulfilling their essential and unique duties, upon which the religious health of their families, and ultimately their churches and the nation, depended.

Increased church pressure on Protestant fathers, as well as mothers, to fulfill their religious-education duties coincided with the development in Canada of non-denominational Christian training programs for adolescents. The lead in this area was taken by Canadian branches of the Young Men's Christian Association (YMCA), the Young Women's Christian Association (YWCA), and the International Sunday School Association (ISSA). Protestants active in these non denominational organizations presented Canadians with answers to church membership recruitment problems which put the blame for past failures on out-of-date theories and methods. Without absolving parents of all responsibility, they claimed that after puberty successful religious education had to be incorporated into training programs designed to perfect every facet of human nature, including the physical. Families had an important part to play in the moral and religious education of children, but once the crucial teenage years arrived, programming designed by outside experts had an essential contribution to make to their development. In the view of the young men who ran and worked for the nation's popular, well-funded YMCAs, their association had the virile image and the resources needed to save Canada's "big" boys for Protestantism.[11] The YWCA's female leaders were similarly convinced that their association was best able to provide Canada's future wives and mothers with the different, but no less essential, training required to win the nation's girls for their churches and Christian service in their homes and the broader community.[12]

Church leaders were not immediately convinced that non-denominational involvement in religious education offered the way out of their membership-recruitment problems. Suspicion of such involvement had in fact prompted Protestant denominations to put church-run Sunday school agencies into place during the late nineteenth century. The popularity of the YMCA boys' programming and its promise to overcome the male indifference to religion and the upbringing of children associated with the arrival of modernity in Canadian society, however, forced Protestant churches to re-evaluate their position in the religious-education field. Without abandoning their respective efforts to reinvigorate family religious life, Canada's major Protestant denominations had, by World War I, joined forces with non-denominational religious-education agencies in a national campaign designed to help parents and Sunday schools turn Protestant adolescents, boys especially, into efficient, effective church members.

THE FAMILY AND RELIGIOUS EDUCATION

Accounts of the shortcomings of Protestant homes in the areas of religious and moral training abounded in early-twentieth-century Canada. Even church families were accused of disregarding the religious education of their children because of the increased worldliness of Canadian life. In their 1902 report to General Conference, Methodist Sunday school officials called upon ministers to warn parents about these dangers and pressure them to maintain homes where children would learn what it meant to be a Christian.[13] At the same time Canada's largest Baptist convention was being told that family life was "far from ideal" and that reformation was essential because "homes [were] better training agencies than even the best of Sabbath Schools," and could become "more assuredly successful as soul-winners than any teacher or evangelist."[14] Anglicans also expressed worries about "influences at work disintegrating the home." Like other Protestants, they impressed upon parents that "no subsequent training [could] make up for the lack of proper culture in the most impressionable period of human life."[15]

An October 1900 editorial in the national Methodist publication, the *Christian Guardian*, made very clear why the family received all the attention it did from early-twentieth-century Protestant leaders. "When the great purpose of the parent becomes the development of the child up into a true and worthy and Christ-like character and personality, rather than the gaining by it of mere learning or money or social position, then there will be some chance of our modern civilization overtaking and overcoming that spirit of materialism that at times seems to threaten the very existence of all that is true and noble among us. The ideals of home become the ideals for life."[16] Only weeks later an entire issue of the *Christian Guardian* was devoted "to awaken[ing] mothers, fathers and pastors to a sense of their solemn responsibility and great opportunity in relation to the children of our Methodist homes." A front-page editorial entitled "This Issue for the

Parents" emphasized that "healthy children and ones in hovels" both required careful nurturing because of the dangers of the urban environment, and it offered three lines of advice under the headings "Begin Early," "The Power of Example," and "Maintain Fellowship." The message of the final section was that "[p]arents and children should be each others best and closest companions."[17] Fathers and mothers were constantly reminded that their children had first call on their time.

Instead of alleviating Protestant fears about parental neglect of their children's spiritual training, the expansion of Sunday schools exacerbated them. Methodist worries that parents had turned "the responsibility of caring for their children in spiritual matters" over to Sunday schools were shared by the Reverend Principal Macvicar, who warned Presbyterians in October 1901, "It is a notorious and deplorable fact ... that many parents culpably relegate" the religious education of their offspring to Sunday schools.[18] As the *Canadian Baptist* explained, the problem was that this outside institution could only benefit "the children of Christian parents, if it [was] made supplementary to home instruction, not a substitute for it."[19] This point was reiterated by the *Christian Guardian* of February 1902: "The family cannot shirk or shake off or ship over upon the church the share of responsibility which rests upon it in the ordering of God's providence."[20] Without denying that the church had an essential role to play in the religious-education field, Methodists, from editorialists to Sunday school officials and pastors in the field, argued that the efficacy of the church's work in this realm depended ultimately on the family. Anglicans voiced similar attitudes towards the role that Sunday schools should play in the religious education of the church's children. "If the child is a 'lamb in the fold,'" a 1903 *Canadian Churchman* editorial argued, "the fact that it is entrusted to an earthly father and placed in an earthly home makes the home, and not the Sunday school, the real battleground in the arduous work of training children." Sunday schools were "a useful adjunct to the Church, but the home [was] the nursery of the Church."[21] Anglicans were exhorted therefore to "[l]et the home be what it should be, a place for the teaching and illustration of the Christian graces and virtues."[22]

Protestant parents in early-twentieth-century Canada were left in no doubt about either their deficiencies as religious educators or the dire consequences of their failures. D. Torrance Fraser concluded his 1901 analysis of the problems facing Presbyterian Sabbath schools by asking, "[h]ow can we elevate the children with the parents acting as dead weights?"[23] An August 1902 *Canadian Baptist* editorial entitled "Who Are to Blame?" found the nation's parents responsible for the perceived deterioration of family life. The presence on the streets of villages, towns, and cities of "boys, and, in too many cases, girls, of young years, engaged in the wildest kind of romping and play after hours when it would be best for them and best for the citizens if they were at home," inspired the editorialist to ask rhetorically: "Are there no comforts at home? Are there no parents there who are thinking about the associations of their children and who are seeking to guide their companionships? ... Are the children to blame, or their parents?"[24] Just a month earlier a *Canadian Churchman* editorial, "Duty of Fathers to Their Children," had expressed astonishment at the apathy that parents showed about providing religious teaching in their homes and warned fathers and mothers that they would "have to answer before God for the religious instruction given to their children." As the editorial's title indicates, fathers were already being singled out as the weakest link in the religious education of Canada's Protestant children. Men, therefore, had to be convinced to fulfill the important role they alone could play in the religious life of their families.[25]

According to a 1905 edition of the *Christian Guardian*, the home had "lost its grip" on Methodists, prompting the editor to contend, "The healthiest revival that could come to us, the most fundamental and far-reaching would be a revival of the sense of responsibility among parents." When it came to identifying the causes of home "decay," the increased strenuousness of life in early-twentieth-century Canada ranked highest. "Fathers are off to business, mothers are off to social engagements."[26]

The importance attached to fathers accepting their parental responsibilities, which had come in for special attention before the turn of the century, increased as the idea spread that mothers alone could not bring their sons to virile Christian manhood. Pressure on fathers to become more involved in the upbringing of their children, sons especially, mounted. An April 1908 editorial in the *Christian Guardian* addressed the issue of "The Boy and His Father," and after noting a previous tendency to say that "a boy is what his mother makes him," it declared, "[I]t is probably quite as near the mark, and possibly just a little nearer to it, to say that a boy is what his father makes him." Fathers must therefore devote more time and attention to their sons. "To know the boy, ... to be his friend and comrade and chum – to do this the father may have to make some sacrifice of time and effort, and even of money occasionally, but it is the one first thing to be done."[27] Throughout the opening decades of the twentieth century, Protestant leaders urged fathers to take on a greater role in the upbringing of their children, particularly in the religious realm. "It is the father's business and the mother's business to look after the moral well-being of their child."[28] While the central role of mothers in child rearing continued to be acknowledged, a larger role for fathers was increasingly recognized as key to the successful parenting of teenage boys.[29] Fathers alone could convince boys that religion was a man's concern. Men were needed in Sunday schools, for instance, because boys generally had a low opinion of the schools and of Christianity, which they considered "a very appropriate thing for children, women and people who are about to die; but hardly the thing for youthful men who ... have things to do in an active busy world."[30]

The family's weaknesses generated repeated calls for reform. The *Christian Guardian* of October 1907 drew on "recent ethnological research ... as to the place which the family has occupied in the history of the race" to argue:

The Christian teaching and practice gave a unique place to the home and the family, ... Jesus established the family ... as the unit of religious worship and service ... Christianity has ... attempted to make the home and the family the sacred things of life ... But in this connection some dangerous tendencies are manifesting themselves in our modern life. An extreme of individualism is threatening the family ... There is need, even great and pressing need, that the church lay increasing emphasis upon the home, home life, home religion, home obligations and opportunities, and that she point out with ever-increasing clearness the religious significance and importance of the family.[31]

At the same time church leaders increasingly felt that the institutions they directed must intervene to compensate for the failures of Canada's Protestant families in the realm of religious and moral education. The Reverend C.H. Huestis's 1907 explanation of the Methodist Church's dilemma with respect to the provision of religious education reveals the ambiguous position into which this issue put Canadian churches during the opening decades of the twentieth century: "The true place for the religious culture of children is the home ... But the home has proved incapable of caring for the religious nurture of the children, hence the church has come in to supplement the home. The church ... must continue to set before parents the responsibility of the home for the moral nurture of its inmates."[32] The appearance of new boys' and girls' organizations and of sports teams in the early twentieth century added weight to the argument that Protestant churches must reconsider the roles their religious-education agencies played in the lives of Canada's adolescents. Churches were encouraged to take control of movements such as the Boy Scouts and Girl Guides and to set up church sports' teams in order that such activities might help, rather than hinder, their membership-recruitment efforts. Denominational religious educators argued that their churches must expand Sunday school work to include mid-week programming, even though these agencies had still not been given the resources to enrol all the nation's Protestant boys and girls. The call for immediate church action resulted from the serious challenge being mounted by non-denominational organizations in the field of Protestant religious education.

NON-DENOMINATIONAL INVOLVEMENT IN RELIGIOUS EDUCATION

The Protestants who ran Canada's leading non-denominational voluntary associations – the YMCA, the YWCA, and the Canadian branches of the ISSA – agreed that the family had a pivotal role to play in the religious-education field. They too traced the hemorrhage of adolescents from Sunday schools back to the poor examples set by their parents and to the failure of Protestant homes to instill religious knowledge and patterns of worship in children during their earliest, formative years. What the Ys also did was to offer the fathers and mothers of Canada's early-twentieth-century teenagers a final chance to turn their sons and daughters into competent, committed Christian men and women. While the initial focus was on saving the boys, who deserted Sunday school at puberty in even greater numbers than their sisters, religious educators were always cognizant of the need to ensure that the standards of twentieth-century Protestant girls also improved. As the future wives and mothers of Canadian Protestants, girls would play a crucial role in determining the quality of Canadian home life and the health of the nation.

From the late nineteenth century on, professional boys' workers and non-denominational Sunday school officials, armed with the latest child-development theories, argued that the weaknesses of the "modern" family could be overcome by outside intervention during the crucial teenage years. They made extensive use of the well-known child psychologist G. Stanley Hall's version of the recapitulation theory, which argued that children went through the successive phases of human evolution on the way to becoming adults.[33] According to Hall, boys between eight and twelve were like the early pygmies; after that stage they experienced a rebirth, emerging as adolescents capable of unselfishness and thus amenable to religious education. Adolescence was a period of emotional turmoil during which individuals made their lifelong decisions about religion and morals. But as Hall and his popularizers made clear, it was by no means certain that the religious potential of adolescents would be realized, because adolescence was also the period when boys, and even girls, were most susceptible to evil influences. Moreover, such theories warned, if adolescents were not won by their late teens, they were likely lost forever.

Hall's theories supported the position that the best way to win teenage boys for Christ was to organize them into "gangs" and allow them to follow their instincts under the watchful eyes of virile Christian role models. His location of the crucial period of religious decision-making in adolescence, the very time when teenagers – boys especially – fled Sunday schools, prompted non-denominational attempts to use organized leisure programming to win adolescents for Christ. Support for these efforts persisted even after Canadian Protestants came under the influence of George Coe, a prominent American religious educator who rejected Hall's recapitulation theories. Although Coe stressed continuity in religious education and warned against moves which allowed parents to transfer their educational responsibilites to outside "experts," he did admit that the recapitulation theory had led to improved methods of moral training in Sunday school classes and organizations such as the YMCA.[34] In the opening decades of "Canada's century," the YMCA and the YWCA, in conjunction with denominational religious educators, applied their understandings of such theories in an effort to improve the nation's Protestant adolescents physically, intellectually, and socially as well as spiritually. Without challenging the concept of separate spheres, Canada's evangelical Protestants developed training programs that promised to help parents and Sunday schools turn adolescents into committed Christians who were both well prepared and willing to fill their respective roles in family, church, and state. The roots of the unique Canadian cooperative Protestant religious-education movement that emerged as a result stretch back to the country's incorporation into the North American operations of the ISSA and the YMCA.

Non-denominational Sunday school work expanded rapidly in eastern and central Canada in the decades following Confederation under the auspices of the Illinois-based voluntary association, which worked outside the framework of churches to promote and improve Sunday schools. Canada's Sunday school teachers and administrators eagerly joined Canadian branches of the movement, which became part of the appropriate American regional organizations. By 1875 Canadian involvement merited adoption of the label "International" by the American association.[35] Participation in the ISSA increased Canadian awareness of the seriousness of such problems as teenage leakage and of the urgent need for solutions. At the same time the very growth of the movement and its monopoly in vital areas, including Sunday school lesson preparation and teacher training, persuaded Canada's major Protestant churches that Sunday school weaknesses were related to a lack of denominational control. By the opening decade of the twentieth century, consequently, church religious-education agencies had entered into competition with Canadian branches of the non-denominational Sunday school association. The response of the Ontario Sunday School Association (OSSA) turned out to be a crucial step in how Canadian Protestants tried to overcome the perceived inability of families to meet the religious-education needs of their teenagers.

In the first instance, the entry of Protestant churches into areas of Sunday school work monopolized for decades by the ISSA led to suggestions that there was no longer any need for the association.[36] In Ontario, the site of over half the ISSA's Canadian operations, officials responded by taking steps to overcome existing association weaknesses.[37] Their first move was to bring the Reverend E.W. Halpenny, a Canadian Methodist, back from Indiana to head up the OSSA. Within two years of his arrival, the OSSA had expanded its membership and embraced the idea that Sunday school work must incorporate a midweek training program designed to turn Canadian boys into virile Christians. To this end, the reinvigorated OSSA joined forces with YMCA boys' workers, who, under the leadership of Taylor Statten, were preparing to embark on a nationwide campaign to win Canada's teenage boys for Christian service by means of a fourfold develpment program.[38] The country's Protestant churches by 1910 faced competition from very popular, broadly based non-denominational organizations in the crucial area of boys' work.

The growth after 1890 of boys' work in Canada's burgeoning YMCAs worried both Protestants who were convinced that outside activities contributed to the decline of family life and those who advocated church sponsorship of such activities. Neither group accepted YMCA claims that teenagers who fled denominational Sunday schools would be transformed into virile Christians by YMCA boys' departments. Such claims did not mean that YMCA boys' workers disagreed entirely with what Protestant churches had to say about the importance of proper parenting. Will Dakin of Truro, Nova Scotia, for example, called the attention of delegates at the first Maritime conference of YMCA boys' departments, held in January 1897, to the powerful "influence for good or evil" that parents, fathers as well as mothers, had on their sons prior to adolescence. He emphasized that it was therefore every father's responsibility to "be in a position to train and ... to use his power aright."[39] While Canada's YMCAs continued to make it very clear after 1900 that the family remained the primary and most powerful influence on younger children, they maintained that this pattern changed after puberty. YMCA programs, based on the latest findings of child psychologists and religious-education experts, did not supplant but, rather, supplemented home training in the critical adolescent period. Indeed, boys' work pamphlets with titles such as "Father: What about the Future of That Boy of Yours?' and"Is Your Boy Handicapped?"asserted that"every father should be anxious that his boy be given a good start"and argued that fathers owed their sons, and their sons' mothers, the cost of"surround[ing] them with healthful recreation, manly sports and moral influences."[40] The YMCA promised parents that its programs could turn the adolescent boys who fled Sunday school into "Christian" gentlemen.[41]

However, the YMCA also wanted fathers to make the lifestyle changes demanded by church leaders. Indeed, they reinforced Protestant arguments that fathers had to become more involved parents. The "Parents Column" of a 1909 Ottawa YMCA boys' publication, for example, maintained, "Most boys would prefer to stay around home with a group of neighbor companions if they were given a little encouragment." Parents generally were admonished, therefore, not to "think more of their carpets and furniture than their boys." Once these boys had entered their teens, the argument continued, only fathers could keep them around home. After urging parents to organize home-based alternatives to the attractions of city streets, the article warned, "The success of such a plan for boys over twelve years of age will largely depend on whether 'father' gets into the game or not." The road to successful fatherhood was obvious: "Be the leader of your boy and you will know where he is being led."[42] From the YMCA's perspective, boys' programming was intended to help Canadian parents meet the religious, social, physical, and intellectual needs of their sons and not to do their work for them. Churches nevertheless continued to have doubts about the efficacy of non-denominational religious-education efforts.

The expansion of boys' work in Canada's YMCAs coincided with the boom years of the Laurier era. The steadily rising numbers of male white-collar employees flocked to YMCAs for recreational and social activities.[43] These young adults saw themselves as manly Christian achievers and viewed boys' work as an opportunity to mould future national leaders in their image. And like the YMCA's first dominion boys' work secretary, they regarded the association's non-denominational character as peculiarly suiting it to play a pivotal role in meeting the challenge that the half-million adolescent boys presented to Canada as a Christian country.[44] These "big" boys, who associated religion and church membership with femininity, would be attracted to the Christianity espoused by the manly YMCAs that they were so eager to join.[45]

Toronto was at the forefront of YMCA boys' work in Canada partly because of the large consistituency of Protestant schoolboys, who, it was generally agreed, faced rapidly growing forces of evil in the city. Association directors impressed upon Toronto parents that failure to provide their boys with the benefits of YMCA membership threatened both their salvation and the moral fibre of the nation. This was a view shared by Taylor Statten, that epitome of a manly Christian, whose volunteer work with boys at Toronto's Central YMCA earned him appointment as that associations's first full-time boys' work secretary in 1905.[46] Statten's preparation of a "made-for-Canadians" boys' program moved a step closer in 1907 when he heard the secretary of the Chicago Central YMCA expound on "The Four-Fold Development of Boys" and the secretary of a boys' work department in Cleveland explain a system of tests and badges based on the Y triangle. In the following season Statten set out to combine the merits he saw in these American schemes.[47] Five years later, when he assumed the position of national boys' work secretary following creation of a Canadian YMCA, he came to the job armed with a draft training program for Christian boys called "Canadian Standard Efficiency Tests" (CSET), the first version of which was published in October 1912.[48] By the middle of the next year Canada's National YMCA Council had a special subcommittee at work on the development and promotion of CSET. Under the chairmanship of H.H. Love, president of the W.J. Gage Company, the YMCA's Standard Efficiency Tests Sub-committee, into which Love had drawn a group of prominent young businessmen, endeavoured to ensure widespread Protestant acceptance of its boys' program.[49]

Like other early-twentieth-century Protestant religious educators, CSET's designers wanted to convince adolescent males that the church and religion were legitimate masculine concerns. To do so, they presented an ideal of virility attainable only through symmetrical development of all four aspects of life: the physical, mental, social, and spiritual. Religion was an essential element in a fourfold regime that would transform Canada's teenage boys into self-motivated and self-regulated all-round men who would rise to leadership positions throughout Canadian society. In the words of CSET's promoters, "Any Canadian boy who is ambitious to be the most successful man possible should strive for four-fold growth." They went on to explain, "In this twentieth century, masterful men of powerful influence possess strong bodies with sound minds and they must maintain an unselfish brotherly interest in their fellowmen and strive to be in harmony with the great will of God." But while religion was essential to achievement of a boy's potential, overdevelopment of the spiritual side of one's nature and underdevelopment of the body, mind, and social nature was dangerous.[50] The message was clear: unless Christian men maximized their physical, mental, and social strengths, their religious development would go to waste. Religion, in other words, was not for sissies; only the strong could hope to attain Christian manhood. Thus CSET integrated Sunday school with mid-week evening sessions at which boys, under the guidance of virile young men, strove for overall improvement and had fun.

By July 1913 the National Boys' Work Committee of the Canadian YMCA had conferences planned for western Canada and the Maritimes at which CSET would be featured. The committee's recommendation to National Council that preparations be undertaken for increased community work had also received approval. The Canadian YMCA's endorsement of boys' work expansion into areas without association buildings meant that churches in many more communities across the nation would face competition from the much better funded and popular YMCA boys' work programming.[51] In the fall, when Statten toured western Canada to explain and promote implementation of CSET, he was accompanied by John L. Anderson, the former boys' work secretary of the Philadelphia Central YMCA, who had recently been appointed secretary of the Secondary Division of the ISSA. Plans were reportedly being laid during this tour to have the non-denominational ISSA join the National YMCA in its efforts to persuade Canadian Protestants to adopt CSET as their religious-education program for boys.[52]

Such an arrangement, which would have precluded direct denominational participation and input, never materialized. Instead, on Statten's return the YMCA's National Boys' Work Committee instructed him to try to involve the major Protestant churches in the development, operation, and promotion of the program that he and other Canadian boys' workers believed would provide the nation with well-rounded, manly Christian leaders. The committee's view "that there should be more unity of effort and programme on the part of the various bodies endeavouring to promote the Kingdom of our Master through work with boys in Canada" was shared by the Reverend E.W. Halpenny, who by 1914 headed not only the Ontario section of the ISSA but also the newly created Canadian Council of Provincial Sunday School Associations.[53] It remained to convince Canada's small band of professional denominational Sunday school secretaries that their churches could safely enter into cooperative arrangements with non-denominational religious-education organizations. The success of subsequent negotiations reflected denominational Sunday school officials' common dissatifaction with church backing of religious education, which many church leaders and clergy continued to regard as "women's work". The churches' undervaluing of their agencies convinced denominational religious educators to join forces with the self-financing non-denominational voluntary associations, which enjoyed widespread Protestant support and respect in the opening decades of the twentieth century.

CHURCH ENTRY INTO COOPERATIVE RELIGIOUS EDUCATION

The difficulties that denominational religious-education officials experienced getting their respective churches to devote financial and human resources to their field severely limited what they could accomplish in the early 1900s. Persistent – and indeed, intensifying – claims about the centrality of the family's role in religious education, moreover, put Protestants charged with responsibility for denominational Sunday schools in a difficult position. While agreeing that the family's role was crucial in religious education, Sunday school officials from the late nineteenth century on were engaged in a continuous campaign to convince church decision-makers that the organizations they headed were the key to the successful religious education of Protestant youth. Much of the effort of denominational religious educators at the beginning of the new century went into trying to persuade church leaders and pastors to devote more of their time and money to work with children, especially teenagers. They tried unsuccessfully to get the men who ran their respective churches to give priority to this work which child psychologists and religious-education experts agreed was necessary in order to bring young people into church membership.

Weak church support for Sunday school work was highlighted in reports that the governing bodies of Canada's Presbyterians and Methodists received at their respective annual meetings in 1914. The Presbyterian Commission on Religious Education, struck in 1912, delivered a blunt message to the 1914 General Assembly: Presbyterian Sunday schools remained educationally deficient because too little of the church's resources went to them. Not surprisingly, minimal progress was reported in the areas of Sunday school expansion and improvement. The work of those responsible for bringing youth into the church was neither adequately supported nor fully appreciated. According to the Presbyterian commissioners, "Perhaps the greatest danger is that so many people in the Church do not see the vital importance of religious education ... [I]n their conception Sunday School work is more or less childish and unimportant ... Twin brother to this is indifference and easy-going satisfaction with the school as it is and was."[54] Successful membership recruitment, however, depended upon the adoption of new methods and an expanded role for the church in the lives of more of Canada's youth. Given these circumstances, the Presbyterian commission advised entry into cooperative schemes with other denominations and better use of non-denominational institutions such as the YMCA.[55]

Canada's Methodists received an equally depressing report at the July 1914 annual meeting of the General Board of Sunday Schools and Young People's Societies. They too were advised to incorporate mid-week programming into Sunday school work and to do so in cooperation with the non-denominational YMCA and ISSA.[56] Conditions were no better for the country's Anglicans, whose Sunday school secretary was arguing for that church's entry into cooperative boys' work by the spring of 1914. The Sunday School Commission of the Church of England in Canada remained short of funds and served Sunday schools that, at most, enrolled only 135,000 of the approximately 200,000 Anglicans between the ages of five and twenty.[57] The Reverend R.A. Hiltz, the commission's general secretary, concurred with experts who maintained that "the activities of boy life must be made to centre around the Sunday school class ... if they are to be productive of the best results." To achieve this end, he advised Anglicans to cooperate with the YMCA in the hope that denominational Sunday schools offering the association's comprehensive training program might hold adolescent males. According to Hiltz, suspicions that the YMCA led Anglicans into acceptance of "nonconforming principles, ... dissenting doctrines and methods" were no longer valid and must be put aside in favour of a united campaign against teenage loss.[58]

Given these conditions, it is not surprising that the YMCA persuaded Canada's denominational religious-education agencies to enter into cooperative boys' work. The resulting formation of the National Advisory Committee for Co-operation in Boys' Work (NACCBW) transformed CSET from a YMCA boys' program into a religious-education program promoted by all of Canada's major Protestant churches and the ISSA. The leaders of all these organizations agreed with YWCA claims that turning Protestant boys into virile Christian men would accomplish little unless the girls who would one day become their wives and the mothers of future generations of Canadian Protestants were equal to the challenges of Christian womanhood in twentieth-century Canada.[59] By 1915 the YWCA, Canada's major Protestant churches, and the ISSA were hard at work developing a parallel program for the nation's girls, Canadian Girls in Training (CGIT). The persistence of belief in the family's primacy in the field of religious education is reflected in the care that CGIT's formulators took to reassure Protestants that their training program would not compete with the home for the time and loyalties of girls.[60]

The conviction that Sunday school must incorporate a mid-week training element and disillusionment with what churches were doing in this regard had brought Canada's denominational religious educators into cooperation with the nation's leading non-denominational organizations involved in the religious-education field. The denominational boards responsible for Sunday schools felt that they lacked the prestige and financial backing required to meet the challenges posed by twentieth-century urban adolescents. The leaders of these agencies consequently endorsed cooperative religious-education efforts. In their view, professionally designed, cooperatively developed, all-round training schemes offered the best chance of turning Protestant boys and girls into efficient, energetic, and committed church members. Such endorsements, however, in no way lessened church efforts to improve the parenting and home lives of Protestant children.

THE PERSISTENCE OF PARENTAL RESPONSIBILITY

The expansion in organized leisure activities for youth fuelled Protestant fears that increased outside activities were undermining family life. In November 1912 such worries prompted the *Christian Guardian* to ask: "Is it not time that we began a serious 'back to the home' movement? ... [O]ught not our children to be in their own homes more than they are? ... Boys' and girls' clubs are good, and there are a multitude of outside attractions for our children to-day that in their way are wholesome enough, but are we not in danger of having too many of them?" The answers provided for these questions gave clear directions to Protestant parents. It was they who must create the attractive atmosphere required to keep their sons and daughters at home.[61] Not surprisingly, therefore, anxieties about the deterioration of Canadian home life intensified during and after World War I, in spite of the cooperative development of religious-education programming for Protestant boys and girls. While the themes were not new, the sense of urgency was greater. Even church work came in for more criticism because, like "[t]he theatre, the card party, the social function, ... the religious gathering ... claim[ed] more and more the evenings of our people." Husbands as well as wives were taken to task for putting any outside activities before home life. "And there are men and women who are exceedingly active in church work and all kinds of philanthropic and missionary enterprise, who do not seem to show half as much enthusiasm in caring for the needs of their own home circle."[62] The Presbyterian Church's Commission on Religious Education began its 1914 report by "re-emphasizing the primacy of the home in character formation"; it then declared, "To-day, too often business, pleasure or indifference is allowed to crowd group worship and religious and moral training out of the home." Parents, the report continued, were responsible for this "very unsatisfactory" situation and needed the church's help.[63] The head of Canada's Anglicans made the same points in his 1915 address to the General Synod. Admitting that it was up to the church to lead a campaign to reintroduce "religious practices that [had] been allowed to slip out of ... modern life," he argued that its success would depend upon the involvement of the laity, whom he urged to accept their parental duties for religious education. The occasional nature of church influence could not counteract the daily influence exerted by a child's family.[64]

Church pressure on fathers to become more involved in the upbringing of their sons steadily mounted. In 1917 the *Christian Guardian* stated bluntly that the best mothering possible could not overcome the failure of fathers to fulfill their parental responsibilities. On 22 August 1917 an editorial entitled "Wanted! A Father" declared: "We believe in mother love, and we believe that a mother exercises a wonderful influence over her boys, but we know that the time comes in every boy's life when he needs the stimulus, the strength, the inspiration of his father's unfailing friendship, and just at that time the father may be too busy with his business, his lodge, ... or even with church duties, to be a true comrade to his boy. Is it any wonder that the boy drifts?" The problem was that "God-fearing men ... failed to realize that fatherhood means responsibility for growing up with our boys." The solution was recognition that "There is no more important duty than of being father to our own boys."[65]

The importance attached to the family, and to fathers in particular, in the fulfilment of Protestant religious-education objectives strengthened church interest in shaping family relationships and lifestyles. Some churches, including Central Methodist of Toronto, adopted the "Father and Son" movement to this end; in 1915 it held a banquet for boys and their fathers which was described as "epoch-making in the church's history." "Never before had the sons of some of the fathers and the fathers of some of the sons enjoyed companionship together under the church's hospitable roof. Many testified that the evening had meant a social and religious awakening to them, fathers recognizing a new responsibility to their sons and to the church, and the boys finding unexpected good fellowship with their elders."[66]

The suspicion that Protestant mothers and fathers were guilty of putting social, business, and church obligations before home duties were not assuaged by such developments. Parents who spent too much time away from home were reminded that successful parenting depended upon mothers and fathers being with their children. The expansion of mid-week programming for Sunday school classes renewed attacks on parents for shifting responsibility for their children's religious training onto pastors and churches.[67] Fathers' failings came in for special attention in a 1918 *Christian Guardian* editorial on the proposal that 7–14 April be observed as a National Father and Son Week. After pointing out the futility of any father trying to do a year's work in one week, the editorial continued:

It is a good time ... to stir up this question of the boy and his dad, and to really realize that we have been altogether too prone to lay responsibility over on the boy's mother. We men often think that we are getting off a beautiful sentiment when we quote "the hand that rocks the cradle rules the world," but what we really are doing is laying off responsibility that we ought to bear. Far be it from us to belittle the power and influence of the mother, but the task of bringing up the boys and girls in the home isn't all hers, and oughtn't to be more than half hers, and the father that leaves it with her is a coward and a shirk.

In other words, devoting time and effort to parenting and home life established one's masculinity. It was courageous men who "ma[d]e friends of [their] boys and honestly and self-sacrificingly tr[ied] to play a friend's true part toward them."[68]

Protestant churches struggled through the opening decades of the twentieth century to convince parents that the fortunes of the church and the state depended ultimately upon the nature and quality of the home life they created for their children. The view that the church needed the assistance of the home in religious education gave way over time to the belief that the home was "the larger instrument" in this field. This change meant that churches had to move beyond the Home Department and the Adult Bible Class, which had sought to bring the entire family into the Sunday school. As the Anglican church's official Sunday school publication put it in 1916, "even the Church cannot supplant the influence of the Home or its position ... the supreme training ground for the young Christian must be the

Home."[69] Satisfactory Sunday school results could only be achieved by recognizing "the Home's fundamental position." This conviction forced Sunday school officials who believed that "[t]he Home has become, too often, simply a boarding-house" to intensify their efforts to revive "the Religious Life of the Home." For Sunday schools to succeed, officials had to work with parents to ensure that they laid the foundations upon which church religious education had to rest.[70] Speaking from the parish perspective, the Reverend A.L. Beverly of St Mark's Church, London, Ontario, blamed the church's loss of adolescents on the "irreligious, critical and indifferent religious influence of many homes. Father and mother do not go to Church, why should the grown-up boy or girl go?" Fathers came in for the greatest criticism, however, because the inability to hold "big" boys remained the church's most serious problem. "Sunday School and Church are all right for kids and women, but boys – they want something different. The business man does not trouble about Sunday School or Church, except to pay his dues. Why should he? 'Stepping in the steps of Father' is not so much a fancy as a fact ... When father says, 'Come,' instead of 'Go,' more boys will step in the path of Sunday School and Church blazed by fathers, instead of running in the opposite direction."[71]

Increased emphasis on the key importance of parents' "function as religious educators" translated into calls that churches should prepare adult members for this work. Recognition that "the home stands supreme for good or ill in life culture" drove Presbyterian religious-education advocates to urge their church to provide parents with the assistance they so obviously needed to fulfill their duties in this regard.[72] In the same vein, Methodist congregations were urged to set up a parents' class where church members could be trained "to better perform their work as teachers of religion in the home."[73] Anglicans similarly were being told by 1917 that fulfillment of their church's mission in Canada depended upon "a great revival of spiritual power, and a renewed hold upon the life of the people," which could only be brought about by the revival of family worship.[74] In his charge to the committee struck to achieve these ends in British Columbia's Diocese of Columbia, the bishop declared that wherever the devotional life of home had waned "it must be revived ... whatever changes in family habits may be necessitated by new conditions and modes of living."[75]

The professional religious educators who headed denominational Sunday school agencies endorsed efforts to revivify family religion, as did the non-denominational agencies with an interest in religious education. Children whose parents brought them up in a religious environment were much more likely to enrol in the training programs they designed. Denominational Sunday school officials could not, however, fail to see that their churches' increased emphasis on parental responsibility was matched by a persistent refusal to provide their agencies with adequate funds. According to the 1914 report of the Presbyterian Church's Commission on Religious Education, a study of church budgets revealed that total Sunday school expenses amounted "to only 43 per cent of what is spent on church music."[76] After a decade in operation, the Anglican Sunday School Commission's officials claimed that progess had been made in spite of the fact that "we have been handicapped in our work by lack of funds."[77] The clearest expression of this sentiment came in the Reverend S.T. Bartlett's explanation in 1918 that he had resigned at the end of ten years as the Methodist Sunday School Board's general secretary because he could no longer bear to have his leadership "seriously hampered by unreasonable financial stringency."[78] The men who ran Canada's Protestant churches, like fathers, had to be convinced that children's work was worthy of their attention and support.

A *Christian Guardian* editorial the week following Bartlett's resignation outlined the frustations experienced by Protestants who had been trying for over two decades to convince the male leaders and members of Canada's churches that maintaining the strength of these institutions into the new century depended upon the attention they paid to children, especially adolescent boys.

In the home, in the school, in the church, we find that only too often the boy is looked upon almost as the devil in disguise, and not so very much disguised at that ... The truth is we haven't time to waste on boys. We have time galore for prayer-meetings and committee meetings, time for regenerating the slums and evangelizing the heathen ten thousand miles away; time for gossip and time for fashion; time for mental improvement and time for recreation; we can go to the seaside, the mountains, the forest, we can fish and hunt, play bowls and golf, make money and spend it; these all take time, and they take so much time that we haven't time for our own boys, and so they are not brought up, but just grow up.

The responsibility and the power to right this wrong belonged to fathers and the church's male pastors.

What a great revival it would be for Canada if the promise were fulfilled and hearts of the fathers turned towards their children and the hearts of the children turned towards their fathers! ... We venture to say that the pulpit has no more important note to strike than this very one, the note ... that insists on the value of the boys and girls. Our boys are worth more than our banks, our factories, our fisheries, our mines and our farms all rolled into one. Our boys are too good to be lost, too valuable to be neglected, too useful to be wasted, and altogether too lovable to be forgotten. What are we doing with them?[79]

CONCLUSION

Canada's major Protestant denominations emerged from World War I more convinced than ever of the need to reverse the decline of religion in twentieth-century family life. In September 1918 R.A. Hiltz, general secretary of the Church of England's Sunday School Commission, reported the reception of a letter from the Reverend W.J. Knox, who headed the Presbyterian board responsible for Sunday schools, asking the Anglicans to copy his church's effort to "devis[e] plans by which the home may realize more fully its fundamental place as an agency in religious education." The Anglican Sunday school officials endorsed Knox's suggestion: "If a number of churches would emphasize the importance of home religion and give guidance and inspiration to the homes of the nation at the same time much more good would be done than if any one church would alone."[80] The church's General Synod concurred, and it struck a special committee to inaugurate a campaign in the interests of "Home Religion," which it was hoped would yield "some very practical results."[81]

The "readiness of the Home to hand over the religious training of its children to outside institutions," a recognized problem by 1900, had grown with the expansion of church religious-education programming to the point where it could only be reversed by "concerted action on the part of the Church." Past efforts at reform of twentieth-century family life had produced only limited results because they were "largely spasmodic."[82] Canada's major Protestant churches entered the 1920s with renewed determination to reverse the secularization of family lifestyles and to reshape parent-child relationships. Those Protestants who focused on training future generations of Canadian parents faced the post-war world equally convinced that the time had come for the "big push" that would bring them success.

From the turn of the century on, concerns about Christianity's lack of appeal, especially among men and boys, and parents' neglect of their religious-education responsibilities inspired Protestant attempts to influence social norms in the realms of parenting, masculinity, and femininity. Great importance was attached to making Christianity and family life a primary focus of Canada's twentieth-century Protestant males and to ensuring that Protestant women were better prepared and more willing to carry out their essential roles as Christian homemakers and mothers. What Protestant leaders said and did to achieve these ends in the opening decades of this century profoundly influenced definitions of masculinity and fatherhood and femininity and motherhood in interwar Canada.

NOTES

1 See, for example, United Church Archives, Toronto (UCA), Presbyterian Church of Canada, General Assembly, *The Acts and Proceedings* (*APPC*), 1900, appendix 2, Synodical Sabbath School Missionaries, 262–6; *APPC*, 1901, Committee on Sabbath Schools (PCSS), Report ... , 1900–01, 252; *APPC*, 1903, PCSS, Report ... , 1902–03, 234–41. See also F. Yeigh, "The Problem of the Young Man," *Presbyterian Record* (*PR*), May 1904. For Methodist expressions of these concerns, see editorial, *Christian Guardian* (*CG*), 4 July 1900, and W.B. Kerby, "The Young Man Problem," *CG*, 23 July 1902. The *Canadian Baptist* (*CB*), June 1900, carried a report of similar concerns expressed by the chairman of the Toronto Sunday School Association's annual meeting. Anglican concerns were expressed by the editor of the *Canadian Churchman* (*CC*), 8 January 1903.

2 *CC*, editorial, 13 March 1902.

3 These developments within the Presbyterian Church and their relationship to the rise of the social gospel are discussed in Brian Fraser, *The Social Uplifters: Presbyterian Progressives and the Social Gospel in Canada, 1875–1915* (Waterloo: Wilfrid Laurier University Press, 1988), 35, 43, 83–5, 94–5, 100, 118–19. With respect to the Methodist experience, Marguerite Van Die, *An Evangelical Mind: Nathanael Burwash and the Methodist Tradition in Canada, 1839–1918* (Montreal and Kingston: McGill-Queen's University Press, 1989), 10–13, traces that denomination's commitment to Christianizing the nation back to John Wesley's desire to "win the world for Christ." Phyllis Airhart, *Serving the Present Age: Revivalism, Progressivism, and the Methodist Tradition in Canada* (Montreal and Kingston: McGill-Queen's University Press, 1992), 117–22, analyzes early-twentieth-century Methodist attempts to link the emerging social gospel to that church's evangelical tradition and relates transformations within Methodism to the emergence of different approaches to work with children championed by the new religious-education specialists and increasingly by W.B. Creighton, editor of the *Christian Guardian*. For a discussion of the historiographical debate on the relationship between Protestantism and social reform in Canada, see Nancy Christie and Michael Gauvreau, *A Full-Orbed Christianity: The Protestant Churches and Social Welfare in Canada, 1900–1940* (Montreal and Kingston: McGill-Queen's University Press, 1996), xi–xiv.

4 "The Home and the Sabbath School," *PR*, January 1900.

5 *CC*, 26 July 1906.
6 For an analysis of Christian attempts to link masculinity and religious faith in a Canadian context, see Lynne Marks, *Revivals and Roller Rinks: Religion, Leisure, and Identity in Late-Nineteenth-Century Small-Town Ontario* (Toronto: University of Toronto Press, 1996), 3–37, 112–13, 211–13. Similar trends in the United States are discussed in Margaret Marsh, "Suburban Man and Masculine Domesticity, 1870–1915," and Susan Curtis, "The Son of Man and God the Father: The Social Gospel and Victorian Morality," in Mark Carnes and Clyde Griffen, eds., *Meanings for Manhood: Construction of Masculinity in Victorian America* (Chicago: University of Chicago Press, 1990).
7 UCA, Ontario Council of Christian Education, 1865–1967 (OCCE), Sunday School Association of Ontario (SSAO), "Convention Proceedings," 1900, 83, W. H. Hincks, "Decision Sabbath, or Decision Day."
8 Margaret Marsh, "Suburban Men and Masculine Domesticity, 1870–1915," in Carnes and Griffen, *Meanings for Manhood*, 116–17, 122–3, discusses the appearance by the early twentieth century of advice emphasizing the father's role within the family and the importance of the father-son relationship.
9 See, for example, "The Family: Our Young Women," *CG*, 9 January 1901.
10 Curtis, "The Son of Man and God the Father," 67–8, 71–5, discusses the early-twentieth-century rise in the United States of a new masculine ideal based on "personality [and] social involvement" and notes the relationship between its definers and the primarily urban, middle-class social gospel movement. These views were widely shared by the new class of professional religious educators which was emerging in Canada by the early twentieth century. See, for example, Fraser, *The Social Uplifters*, 118–19, and Airhart, *Serving the Present Age*, 121–2.
11 For elaboration, see David Macleod, "'A Live Vaccine': The YMCA and Male Adolescence in the United States and Canada, 1870–1920," *Histoire sociale/Social History* 11 (May 1978): 5–25; and David Macleod, *Building Character in the American Boy: The Boy Scouts, YMCA and Their Forerunners, 1870–1920* (Madison: University of Wisconsin Press, 1983). For the Canadian context, see C.A.M. Edwards, *Taylor Statten, a Biography* (Toronto: Ryerson Press, 1960). See also E. Anthony Rotundo, *American Manhood: Transformations in Masculinity from the Revolution to the Modern Era* (New York: Basic Books, 1993), especially chap. 10 and 11, for analysis of the changing definitions of masculinity in North America and the emergence of the idea of muscular Christianity.
12 See Diana Pedersen, "'On the Trail of the Great Quest': The YWCA and the Launching of Canadian Girls in Training, 1909–1921" (paper read to the Canadian Historical Association, Ottawa, 1982); Margaret Prang, "'The Girl God Would Have Me Be': The Canadian Girls in Training, 1915–1939,"

Canadian Historical Review 66 (June 1985). The YWCA's move into programming for middle-class adolescent girls was informed by the association's
earlier attempts to save working girls from urban dangers. These dangers
and the YWCA's work are discussed in Carolyn Strange, *Toronto's Girl Problem: The Perils and Pleasures of the City, 1880–1930* (Toronto: University of
Toronto Press, 1995), 14–8 and 118–27. For an analysis of mounting Protestant concerns about leisure activities in smaller centres, see Marks, *Revivals
and Roller Rinks*, 3–21.

13 Methodist Church Records (MCR), *Journal of Proceedings of the General Conference of the Methodist Church* (JPMGC), 1902, Sunday School and Epworth
League Report (SSELR), 129.

14 *CB*, 13 February 1902.

15 *CC*, 17 October 1902.

16 *CG*, 3 October 1900.

17 *CG*, 7 November 1900.

18 MCR, *JPMGC*, 1898, SSELR, 201. See also *PR*, October 1901, 389.

19 *CB*, 15 February 1900.

20 *CG*, 5 February 1902.

21 *CC*, 29 October 1903.

22 *CC*, 22 January 1903.

23 *PR*, January 1901, 10.

24 *CB*, 21 August 1902.

25 *CC*, 24 July 1902.

26 *CG*, 19 July 1905.

27 *CG*, 29 April 1908.

28 *CG*, 16 February 1910.

29 See, for example, "What a Boy Needs," *CG*, 18 October 1911, and "Tobacco,
Pool-Rooms, Profanity and Boys," *CG*, 8 May 1912.

30 Rev. S.T. Bartlett, "The Man, the Woman and the Sunday School," *CG*,
11 March 1908.

31 *CG*, 9 October 1907.

32 *CG*, 11 September 1907.

33 For elaboration on the theories and influence of G. Stanley Hall and his
followers, see J.H. Kett, *Rites of Passage: Adolescence in America, 1790 to
the Present* (New York: Basic Books, 1977), 204–11. See also, for example,
F. Tracy, "The Child's Growth with Its New Problems for the Teacher,"
Ontario Sunday School Association (OSSA), Convention Proceedings
(CP), 1904, 100–5; M.S. Lamoreaux, "The Sunday School and the Boy,"
OSSA, CP, 1905, 124–7, and "A Study of the Juniors," ibid., 129–33.

34 George A. Coe, *A Social Theory of Religious Education* (New York: Charles
Scribner's Sons, 1920), 163.

35 For elaboration, see R.W. Lynn and E. Wright, *The Big Little School: Sunday
Child of American Protestantism*, 1st ed. (New York: Harper and Row, 1971),

chap. 4; and G.E. Knoff, *The World Sunday School Movement* (New York: Seabury Press, 1979), 29–36.

36 See, for example, UCA, *OCCE*, SSAO, box 3, file 10a; "Minutes of Meeting of Special Com. to consider the relations of the work of the Ontario Sunday School Association with the denominations," 1 June 1909.

37 Ibid., "Text of Memorandum from Mr. Gibson re Interview with Mr. Glassford," Gibson to Hamilton, 27 November 1909.

38 YMCA, National Historical Library, New York (YMCA, NHL), Canada-Boys' Work Publications, I 240, "Report/Proceedings, Fifth Annual Boys' Work Conference of the Provinces of Ontario and Quebec ... under the auspices of the Ontario Sunday School Association and the Ontario and Quebec Provincial Committee of the YMCA," 55.

39 YMCA, NHL, Canada-Maritime Provinces Boys' Conferences, 1895, Proceedings of the First Separate Maritime Boys' Conference, YMCA, Amherst, NS, 1897, 19–21.

40 YMCA, NHL, Canada-Ontario-Toronto, I 321, Taylor Statten, secretary, Boy's Club, Central YMCA, "Father: What about the Future of That Boy of Yours?" and I 322, West End Branch, YMCA, A Good Season Start, 1905–06, "Is Your Boy Handicapped?"

41 YMCA, NHL, Canada-Ontario-Ottawa, I 308, "Something Attempted, Something Done, 1906–07," Ottawa YMCA, Boys' Section folder.

42 YMCA, NHL, Canada-Ontario; *Boys Herald*, vol. 1, no. 1 (Ottawa, October 1909).

43 YMCA, NHL, Canada-Ontario and Quebec pamphlet, "Meeting a National Need" (June 1910), noted that between 28 April and 9 May 1910, $650,000 had been raised by the YMCA Building Campaign in Toronto. For Ontario and Quebec together, over $1.5 million had been invested in YMCA buildings and equipment and over $1 million pledged for new buildings and equipment. See also National Archives of Canada (NA), YMCA of Canada Records, MG 28 I 95, vol. 300, "Minutes of the Provincial Executive Committee," 20 January 1910, 26 January 1911, and 28 September 1911.

44 F.H.T. Ritchie, "A Challenge to a Christian Nation," *Association Boys* (*AB*), 9 (October 1910).

45 For an analysis of changing conceptions of fatherhood, the role of the North American YMCA in redefining masculinity, and the emergence of "manly Christianity" in the late nineteenth century, see Michael Kimmel, *Manhood in America: A Cultural History* (New York: The Free Press, 1996), especially 159–62, 167–71, and 175–81.

46 Edwards, *Taylor Statten*, 24–6.

47 Comité Universel Chrétiennes de Jeunes Gens, Bibliothèque, Geneva, pamphlet 21246, "Young Men's Christian Association: Boy's [sic] Work in Canada–May 1923" (n.p., n.d.).

48 Edwards, *Taylor Statten*, 47.

49 NA, YMCA of Canada Records, vol. 234, "Minutes of the Executive Committee of the National Council of the YMCA," 3 July 1913.

50 YMCA, NHL, Canada-Boys' Work Publications, *The Canadian Standard Efficiency Tests for Boys* (proof ed.), cover page.

51 NA, YMCA of Canada Records, vol. 234, "Minutes of the Executive Committee of the National Council of the Y.M.C.A.," 3 July 1913.

52 Ibid., 3 July 1913 and 10 December 1913. See also Edwards, *Taylor Statten*, 47.

53 *Canadian Manhood* I (October 1914). See also NA, YMCA of Canada Records, vol. 234, "Minutes of the Executive Committee of the National Council of the Y.M.C.A.," 10 December 1913; and Edwards, *Tayor Statten*, 46–8.

54 UCA, APPC, 1914, "Report of the Commission on Religious Education."

55 Ibid., Board of Sunday Schools and Young People's Societies (BSSYP), "Report: 1913–14," 231–2, 235–6, 240.

56 UCA, MCR, BSSYP, Annual Meeting, 7–8 July 1914, "Report of the Committee on Boys' and Girls' Work."

57 Anglican Church of Canada, General Synod Archives (GSA), Sunday School Commission of the Church of England in Canada (SSC), *Commission Bulletin*, May 1914.

58 Ibid., January 1914.

59 Diana Pedersen, "'The Power of True Christian Women': The YWCA and Evangelical Womanhood in the Late Nineteenth Century," in Elizabeth Muir and Marilyn Whiteley, eds., *Changing Roles of Women within the Christian Church in Canada* (Toronto: University of Toronto Press, 1995), especially 323–5. Arguments that Pedersen makes about YMCA work with men being undermined without the uplift of women holds true for work with middle-class boys and girls.

60 NA, Canadian Girls in Training (CGIT) Records, MG 28 I 313, vol. 1, "Minutes of the Adjourned Session of Called Meeting in the interests of Co-operation in Girls' Work," 9 September 1915; Dr Winnifred Thomas, "Summary of Minutes of the CGIT Movement, 1915–55," 1–3.

61 *CG*, 6 November 1912.

62 *CG*, 16 April 1913.

63 UCA, APPC, June 1914, "Report of Commission on Religious Education," 231.

64 Anglican Church of Canada (ACC), Diocese of Columbia Archives, Victoria, BC (DCA), *Diocesan Gazette*, 5 (November 1915).

65 *CG*, 22 August 1917.

66 *CG*, 21 April 1915.

67 *CG*, 14 November 1917.

68 *CG*, 20 February 1918.

69 GSA, SSC, *Commission Bulletin*, 5 (July 1916).

70 Ibid. See also *Commission Bulletin*, 8 (February 1917), 28–30.

71 Ibid., 9 (March 1918), 39.

72 UCA, "The Conservation of Young Life," prepared by the Board of Sabbath Schools and Young People's Societies, and issued by the Committee of the Forward Movement of the Presbyterian Church in Canada, September, 1919, and *APPC*, June 1914, "Report of Commission on Religious Education."

73 *CG*, editorial, 20 February 1918.

74 ACC, DCA, *Diocesan Gazette* 6 (February–March 1917), 20.

75 Ibid., 6 (May 1917), 7.

76 UCA, *APPC*, June 1914, "Report of Commission of Religious Education," 235–6.

77 GSA, SSC, "Report of the Work of the Sunday School Commission for the Nine Months ending December 31st, 1918, Being a Supplementary Report to the Tenth Annual Report," 29.

78 *CG*, 23 October 1918.

79 *CG*, 6 November 1918.

80 GSA, SSC, "Minutes, Executive Committee, 9 September 1909."

81 GSA, SSC, "Report of the Work of the Sunday School Commission for the Nine Months ending December 31st, 1918, being a Supplementary Report to the Tenth Annual Report," 28.

82 GSA, SSC, "Minutes, 7 May 1919, 18th Report of the General Secretary of the SSC," 17.

Modernity, Sexuality,
and the Individualist Temper

The Emergence of Personalist Feminism: Catholicism and the Marriage-Preparation Movement in Quebec, 1940–1966

MICHAEL GAUVREAU

On a hot summer's day in July 1939, thousands of Montrealers participated in a carefully choreographed public spectacle designed to reinforce the identity of Catholicism, family, and national values. One hundred and four automobiles, each containing a chosen engaged couple who had completed a rigorous study session on the Catholic doctrines of marriage and family, led a procession from Parc Lafontaine to Delorimier Stadium, the home of the Montreal Royals baseball team. There, in front of an audience of fifteen thousand people, the couples exchanged their marriage vows in a mass marriage ceremony presided over by Monseigneur Gauthier, the archbishop of Montreal. The wedding ceremony, followed by a parade and scenic tableaux, powerfully underscored the place of marriage and family within a wider Catholic vision of social reconstruction. Led by five hundred flags bearers, participants in the Jeunesse Ouvrière Catholique (JOC) movement, organized into various trades and occupations, marched into the stadium through the triumphal promenade of flags and proceeded to erect on a stage at the centre a symbolic "New Society."[1] The chaplain of the JOC, Father Henri Roy, then preached a sermon highlighting the spiritual values of Catholic marriage and the central role that Catholic families must play in preserving society from the false promise of materialist ideologies. Social reconstruction, Roy stated, moved "neither right nor left, but forward," and was not to be accomplished by violence or class conflict, but through "the conversion of *souls.*"[2] Later that evening, as the stadium lights were darkened, the 104 newlywed couples, each holding a lighted torch, marched towards a massive cross at centre stage. The silence was broken only by the voice of a young woman singing the hymn "Salve Regina."[3]

At one level, this great Catholic spectacle can be read as the swan song of a traditional order that was soon to disappear under the assaults of modernity. Indeed, the three decades following 1939 witnessed the rapid transformation of Quebec in what historians tell us was a response to the new urban industrial realities. The Roman Catholic Church, increasingly perceived as the sclerotic guardian of the traditional culture, was being challenged and its authority eroded by new secular ideologies articulated by new elites and borne by the rising mass media. By the end of the 1960s the de-confessionalization of public institutions appeared simply to reflect the wider de-Christianization of Quebec culture, with plummeting birth rates indicating a mass popular rejection of Catholic teachings on marriage and family.[4] However, the dichotomy pitting Catholic traditionalism against secular modernity, which has become the common coin of historical discussion, was not so apparent to those who lived through the era between World War II and the 1960s. Speaking in 1966, the Montreal psychiatrist Camille Laurin, later to be famous as minister of culture in the first Parti Québécois government and architect of its controversial language legislation, stated, "Our Quebec is certainly still Catholic and even if Catholicism offers to the world a new face it remains Catholic."[5] Laurin's emphasis on the ability of Catholicism to adapt and innovate had found expression a few years earlier in an influential work on the French-Canadian family by Philippe Garigue, professor of sociology at the Université de Montréal. Rejecting the existence of a "traditional" type of French-Canadian family, Garigue likewise absolved Catholicism from a blinkered adherence to the past in its teachings on family relationships. Indeed, he concluded, the reverse was true: in its teachings on love, marriage, and birth control, Catholicism was actually in advance of public values in Quebec.[6]

These statements on the place of Catholicism in Quebec society by two prominent representatives of the rising "secular" intelligentsia prompt a reassessment of the decades between 1940 and 1966 as characterized by a simple opposition between religious immobility and a flood tide of "modern" values. Popular attitudes to matters such as marriage and birth control underwent substantial transformation in Quebec during these decades. At the focal point of change was the redefinition of marriage away from its earlier function as a relationship directed towards procreation – a rational, prudential alliance of families and generations – towards an ethic of personal fulfillment, in which marriage was an emotional, affective partnership characterized

by sexual intimacy between man and wife, with the birthing and raising of children an important, but increasingly secondary, consideration. This essay argues that the impetus, definition, and institutional
promotion of these "modern" attitudes came from within Catholicism
itself, but not from the institutional hierarchy, whose outlook on most
social questions remained exceedingly conservative. A new, progressive Catholic attitude to questions of family and sexuality was articulated by women, who dominated the various Catholic Action
movements which flourished during this period as expressions of lay
initiative. One of the most popular of these was an organization, the
Service de Préparation au Mariage (spm), entirely devoted to marriage preparation and counselling. In this respect, it is important to
distinguish between the church as an institution dominated by a professional clergy and "Roman Catholicism," which in Quebec after
World War ii also meant a welter of movements and ideologies that
incarnated the values, aspirations, and ambitions of large numbers of
Catholic lay people but did not often fit smoothly with the prescriptions of the clerical hierarchy. Indeed, it would be fair to say that between 1940 and 1966, on issues involving the dynamic relationship of
women, family, and Quebec society, Roman Catholicism, rather than
party politics, articulated the language and defined the issues in
which the ideological struggle between left and right in Quebec was
waged.

The Catholic Church's involvement in the sphere of marriage preparation was the logical outgrowth of its encouragement of Catholic Action, a wider movement aimed at enlisting the energies of lay people
in the re-Christianization and social reconstruction of Quebec society
during the economic crisis of the 1930s. These various movements, the
most prominent of which were the Jeunesse Ouvrière Catholique, the
Jeunesse Étudiante Catholique (jec), and the Jeunesse Agricole
Catholique (jac), were specifically designed to meet the spiritual
needs of modern youth. In 1938 an inquiry conducted under the auspices of the joc revealed that many young workers were entering
married life without adequate emotional or financial preparation, and
chaplains of these youth groups urged the necessity of a permanent
service to make married couples aware of the psychological, economic, sexual, and religious demands imposed by modern marriage.[7]
The mass marriage ceremony of July 1939 was the culmination of
these early efforts at marriage counselling, but the initiative was allowed to lapse during the early stages of World War ii. By 1944,
however, the Service de Preparation au Mariage was formally established as a branch of the joc and accorded official recognition by

Archbishop Joseph Charbonneau of Montreal.[8] In creating this organization, Roman Catholicism was at the forefront of a wider movement to redefine the nature and role of the family in Canadian society. By the end of World War II, in both English Canada and Quebec, a chorus of clergy, social scientists, and social workers had launched a critique of what had become the new orthodoxy in federal government circles, that the family was essentially an economic unit concerned only with the material welfare of its members.[9] The opposition to this "materialist" definition of the family crystallized around a vision of the modern family as the locus of "personal relationships" in an impersonal urban and industrial civilization. The primary function of the family was no longer as unit of production or reproduction but as "a socialising influence and a source of affectional ties."[10] While, at one level, it appeared to be the reassertion of an older domestic ideal in which women were the primary guardians of the spiritual character of the home, this new definition of the family was largely shorn of its maternalist overtones. Central to the proper functioning of the modern family was the nature of the relationship between husband and wife, now defined in terms of sexual and psychological intimacy. If the modern family was to succeed in providing "emotional security" to its members, the partnership between husband and wife must be founded upon "affection, confidence, and mutual respect."[11]

This new sensibility regarding the emotional and affective nature of the family placed a high premium upon the avoidance of marital breakdown, and this, in turn, necessitated strategies of psychological preparation for marriage that ensured there would be harmony from the beginning between husbands and wives, based upon a new awareness of each sex's emotional and sexual needs and desires. However, this new vision assumed a heightened and more institutionalized form in Roman Catholicism because the doctrines of the church placed a firm prohibition against divorce. After 1944 the SPM elaborated a comprehensive fourteen-week marriage-preparation course designed to address the issues of psychological, sexual, and emotional adjustment between men and women, to inform them of the teachings of the church on the nature of marriage, and to prepare the newly-weds to assume the financial responsibility of establishing a household and the complex task of parenting and raising a family.[12] From the outset, the SPM defined its role as both apostolic and educational, and as a branch of Catholic Action, which sought to promote the social teachings of the church, it taught that the family was the primary cell of society, which must radiate a Christian spirituality that would infuse modern life. Thus the SPM attempted to combine within the framework of the course both "sacramental and conjugal" love and to show newlyweds how to found Christian households.[13] Those princes of the church such as Cardinal-Archbishop Paul-Émile Léger of Montreal saw in the promotion of Christian marriage a front-line defence against "libertarian anarchy" and "totalitarian tyranny."[14]

Despite this rather lofty clerical agenda, the leaders of the SPM made it clear from the outset that, given the medical, psychological, and legal implications of marriage, the bulk of the instruction would fall to lay experts,[15] and after 1949 the key role was played by experienced married couples themselves, whose personal testimony provided the centrepiece of the course. Until that year the entire course was divided along male-female lines, but the use of married couples as team leaders compelled the creation of coeducational sessions, to the point where by 1958 four of the fourteen courses were given to mixed groups of men and women.[16] Indeed, the expectation of lay participants was that the clergy would be, by and large, an "invisible presence" and would confine themselves to the treatment of Christian morals, the rights and duties of spouses, and the laws of the church regarding marriage and male and female psychology, and that they respect the expertise of those who had either the knowledge or the experience to pronounce on marriage.[17] As Jean-François Durand, one future husband who participated in the 1950 SPM session, observed, a successful course required a "radiant, energetic couple," and he had high praise for Mr and Mrs Philippe Laroche, the group leaders. "Nothing," Durand concluded, "affects young people more than the lived experience of others."[18] One husband-and-wife team, who taught a session at a parish in Montréal-Nord, recalled that the bulk of their effort was directed to instilling in the engaged couples a sense of how male and female roles complemented each other in the home. This part of the course, which treated the psychology of men and women, was appreciated far more than doctrinal teaching, because it dealt with the actual problem of how to create and maintain sexual intimacy on a daily basis and in real-life financial situations.[19] By 1955, five courses, those dealing with the experience of married life, were given by married couples themselves, and specialized courses on the civil laws of marriage, psychology, and the medical aspects of male and female anatomy and sexuality were taught by a growing cohort of lay professionals.[20]

By the early 1960s the SPM was clearly the most successful of the Catholic Action movements in terms of popular participation. While those movements directed towards working-class and rural youth failed to become the mass organizations envisioned by their founders,[21] Catholicism's activities in the sphere of marriage preparation had a wide base of popular support. From small beginnings in

Montreal in the mid-1940s, the SPM by 1955 was active in fifty-three parishes in the Montreal diocese. Of 11,000 marriages celebrated that year, 5,925 followed the marriage-preparation course. Between that date and the mid-1960s, from 45 to 50 per cent of all Catholic couples followed the program in premarital counselling,[22] a very high rate considering that participation in the program was not obligatory, and the courses were given on weekday evenings, which involved a sacrifice of leisure time for young working people. In a very real sense, the SPM and its courses were by the early 1960s termed "a national institution," although its activities were at times disrupted by that other national passion, hockey, in the glory days of the Montreal Canadiens.[23] In the Montreal diocese alone, the program enlisted the energies of nearly 800 volunteers, 150–200 married couples, 75 doctors, and 75 nurses, as well as priests, psychologists, notaries, and teachers. The appeal of the SPM was cross-class; indeed, because it had originated under the auspices of a movement directed to working-class youth, it remained popular during its first decade among young couples drawn from this social stratum. However, there was a clear sense that by the early 1960s the social transformation of post-war Quebec was itself affecting the participants in the SPM. Surveys conducted in 1962 and 1968 revealed the increasing presence of what organizers termed the "middle class," which they defined, not in terms of occupation, but according to level of education, a criterion that would have included a large working-class component. Indeed, 75 per cent of the participants had more than ten years of schooling, and it was observed that the idea of premarital education under Catholic auspices appealed to nearly everyone in Quebec, failing to resonate only among either unskilled workers or the upper-middle-class professionals of Quebec society.[24]

It has become a commonplace of recent historical scholarship that the years between the end of World War II in 1945 and the great youth rebellion of the mid-1960s were dominated by a "cult of marriage." This characteristic was emblematic, in terms of family life in North America, of a period of passivity, conformity, and attempts by political and cultural elites to enforce traditional norms of gender relationships and sexual behaviour in a quest for security from the subversive dangers of communism or the spectre of economic recession.[25] Historians have been particularly savage towards that much-vaunted post-war achievement, the "normal democratic family," which under their scrutiny has been revealed to be little more than empty rhetoric, the authoritarian construct of Anglo-Saxon social scientists concerned to ensure conformity to middle-class values. Indeed, these scholars have contended that those who defined the "democratic family," far from promoting a genuine quest for equality between men and women, sought to enforce marital stability, the hallmark of a stable society, through the harmonization of traditional, complementary male and female roles.[26] At first sight, the marriage ideal promoted through the SPM by Catholics in Quebec appears to be a simple variant of the conservative North American pattern. It might well be expected that, given the reputation of Roman Catholicism for authoritarianism and hierarchy, the reinforcement of traditional values would be amplified in Quebec society during the two post-war decades. Indeed, one would not have to look far to find diatribes from Catholic commentators on the selfishness and superficiality of the values of modern youth, the "unhealthy" influence of the mass media and its portrayal of love as sexual adventure,[27] and the threat to family stability posed by the work of married women outside the home. Activists for the SPM were constantly urged to exert themselves to criticize the craze for consumerism and material comfort, which they believed lay at the root of the desire of wives to work after marriage. This quest for luxury could only result in the "mediocrity of a home that cannot meet its primary task: to be an educational framework for its children."[28]

However, what the teachings and activities of the SPM reveal is less a concern for the preservation of tradition than the articulation of a concept of sexual relations and family life that its leaders believed was in firm opposition to the practices and values of the pre-war generation. Two themes occurred again and again in post-war Catholic discussions of youth and marriage. First was the conviction that the present represented a clean break with the past: the social and cultural experience of an earlier generation was an abject failure and could not be relied upon to guide human beings in the modern age. Closely linked to this view was the belief that in a rapidly evolving society, lacking the guidance of the past, young people were suffering from an inability to locate a precise sense of identity, an identity that was defined in terms of sexual self-awareness and emotional fulfillment. For this new generation of Catholics, sexuality was essential for the flowering of the human personality under modern conditions; only through its proper cultivation and expression, within the sacramental relationship of marriage, could the family realize its modern task as the guardian of the emotions and affections, and thus effectively nurture the personality of the next generation.

Speaking to the SPM in 1954, Marcel Clement, a French-born Social Catholic commentator identified with the political right, stressed the novelty of the marriage-preparation movement. "If we had told our grandmothers about such an institution," he declared, "they would have laughed until they died." Clement forcefully drew the contrast between an older rural society, characterized by family solidarity, where preparation of the young for marriage occurred "spontaneously" and "empirically," and the modern urban, industrial world, where the education of youth now occurred outside the home and beyond the purview of parents, and was sadly deficient in terms of psychology and religion. Given the specialization of modern life, Catholicism's premarital counselling program, he concluded, was a permanent necessity.[29] Clement's was no isolated voice; indeed, his comments simply articulated the dominant sensibility of the post-war decades: that the present was culturally and spiritually severed from the past and needed entirely new values and institutions to give it form and expression. On the issues of sexuality, family, and gender relations, Quebec Catholicism after 1945 did not articulate, as it had done in the aftermath of World War I, a nostalgia and a veneration for past traditions.[30] What gave particular intensity, even the edge of anger, to this post-war Catholic imperative was the belief, expressed over and over again in surveys and inquiries conducted by the SPM, that parents whose upbringing lay in the pre-war decades had lamentably failed young people, particularly young women, in the sphere of sex education.

The sexual relationship between husband and wife, for these Catholic activists in the post-war decades, was regarded as the fundamental basis of marriage. "Human sexuality," stated the Reverend Bernard Mailhiot, "is a psycho-sexuality that is bound up with the mystery of the human soul,"[31] an observation that precisely expressed the activits' new definition of marriage as a sexual, psychological, and spiritual partnership which had less to do with reproduction than with an ongoing cultivation of intimacy. Married love, the premarital course never tired of repeating, was "a gift of the self."[32] Only by establishing a satisfactory sexual partnership founded upon the union of two well-developed personalities could young couples overcome selfishness and the lust for dubious gratification and material possessions and direct their energies to saving and sound financial administration which would ensure the establishment of independent and successful households. The great barrier to this cultivation of marital intimacy, in the estimation of SPM leaders, was what they regarded as the appallingly low level of sexual knowledge and self-awareness exhibited by young men and women who frequented the marriage-preparation courses. The recurring phrase was that "sexual education and thus emotional maturity is clearly unsatisfactory,"[33] an impression borne out in surveys conducted at the end of the fourteen-week courses. It was thus hardly surprising that, for their sheer novelty, the most popular courses were those (numbers 10 and 11) on anatomy and health, where the technical and medical aspects of human sexuality and reproduction were explained, and number 13, on Catholic teaching concerning sexual practices. Even as late as 1962, 55 per cent of women and 57 per cent of men attending the courses stated that they had not been well informed by either parents or teachers about sexuality.[34] Of those who felt that their knowledge of these matters was adequate, what was more telling was that only 61 per cent of women and 34 per cent of men credited their parents with providing them with such information. A shocking 18.5 per cent of young men and women had *never* been informed about marriage, sex, and reproduction before attending the SPM seminars.[35]

The leaders of Catholic Action placed the blame for such deplorable conditions squarely upon the parents of youth and upon the puritanical cultural values of the pre-war era, which, in a modern era of social change, were constraining the development of independent personalities among young men and women. For the SPM activists, the ideal of marriage that they advocated, based upon personal choice, love, and sexual fulfillment, was a response to what they believed was the "acceleration of history"[36] which was in the process of transforming the fundamental nature of Quebec Catholic society. The marriage-preparation movement was initially established by clerical authorities who wished to contain the forces of change, and in a post-war environment where they believed that many lay Catholics were seduced by the easy lure of consumerism and an amoral self-gratification of desire, divorce, separation, and illicit sexual expression on the part of young people, which would weaken the foundations of Quebec society. Thus, in part, the SPM reflected this more traditional agenda, insisting throughout its courses upon Christian marriage as the only context in which sexual desire could be gratified. However, lay activists and participants in the premarital courses did not unquestioningly accept the clerical, puritanical definition of marriage. They aimed to promote a refurbished ideal of Christian marriage, one that balanced sexuality with spirituality and defined marital intercourse as an occasion for "mutual enrichment" that should be prepared for as one would for "an act of contemplation."[37] In the eyes of these Catholic activists, it was the sexual satisfaction of spouses that would affirm family harmony, which in turn would maintain the Catholic doctrine of the sacramental vocation of spouses as a remedy to the "Social Cancer" of family breakdown.[38]

While ostensibly defending the traditional Roman Catholic ideal of marriage as an unbreakable, sacramental bond, those involved in the new marriage-preparation movement did not blindly subscribe to the clerical values of the past. Those who frequented the courses in the post-war decades would have heard the message that in the modern era a successful marriage did not necessarily mean simply that it was permanent. Rather, as Madeleine Trottier, the secretary of the Montreal SPM, wrote in 1965, factors such as the happiness of the couple, sexual satisfaction, unity, and self-adjustment had to be considered as crucial standards in evaluating marriage.[39] Here was not an evocation of tradition, but a rather open critique of what the older generation had considered important about marriage and family life. To unquestioningly follow these pre-war prescriptions, SPM activists believed, would betray modern youth. The marriage-preparation courses provided an occasion for young people themselves to vent their frustrations at the traditional and unhappy marriages of their parents, which they believed were due to psychological and sexual incompatibility. In 1962 an astounding 39 per cent of women and 66 per cent of men claimed to know at least one married couple that did not get along, and 11 percent of young men stated that their own parents did not set them a good example of married life.[40] Catholic commentators frequently cited the failure of parents, raised under an older cultural dispensation, to provide the understanding and emotional guidance that young people needed in the critical years to achieve sexual and psychological maturity.

The result was a failure to project a firm identity, which resulted in evasion, the masking of sentiments, and a lack of intimacy that would fatally compromise a marriage.[41] Gérard Pelletier, who later founded the periodical *Cité libre*, which was to articulate the critical mindset of the Quiet Revolution, declaimed sarcastically on the rigid social customs of the older generation, "where marriages are still undertaken to serve the needs of family considerations or strategies. These are completely contrary to the will of the spouses. It is a scandal among us that there are parents who allow their children no freedom of choice, even that most basic one of choosing their life's companion."[42] In defending the new personalist vision of marriage based upon love and individual freedom of choice, Pelletier openly mocked the experience of those who assumed that the values of 1910 or 1925 were proper guides for modern youth, and he lambasted as hypocrisy the silence that surrounded the sexual facts of marriage, which then contrived to blame young people for moral lapses and early pregnancies while failing to educate them on facts of sexuality and family management. "In the past," he declared, "we supposed that only haste was responsible for so many bad marriages. But we did not think of helping young people to prepare for married life. The entire discussion of marriage was taboo. We only sought to ensure that the trousseau of the bride was in order and that the groom was chaste. We never stopped to ask how young people, in a working world that is largely indifferent to their needs, and often morally suspect, could find the means to prepare themselves emotionally and spiritually for the greatest decision of their life. Abandoned and ignorant, a large number of young people were literally forced to the altar."[43]

Indeed, a critique of the values of the older generation was integrated into the marriage-preparation courses themselves. The particular target of the SPM was the old interdependent family, in which young men and women contributed much of their wages and labour to support an intergenerational household. This was a social reality that had enjoyed a particularly long lease on life in urban Montreal.[44] But the new generation of Catholic laity emphatically rejected the church's time-honoured injunction regarding the intergenerational solidarity of families, which lay at the base of Quebec's traditional structure of local parishes.[45] The new Catholic ideal of the modern family was emphatically nuclear, not multi-generational. A home, in the view of Catholic Action, "must shelter all the members of the *same* family, otherwise its solidarity is in danger." Normal family development required a separate dwelling; only thus would the "emotional and moral life" of all its members find satisfaction.[46] The course on budgeting the family finances aimed at enabling the newlyweds to secure their own separate dwelling. Indeed, many of these young people came to the courses expressing considerable frustration at the fact that they were unable to own their own homes and thus establish an independent identity as a married couple. One survey done in the mid-1950s revealed that only 5 per cent of newlyweds would be homeowners; another 10 per cent would live in a single room, 16 per cent with parents or in-laws, and 69 per cent in apartments.[47] They were emphatically advised by the SPM that living with parents or in-laws was a prime cause of marital dispute and would merely extend the problem of insufficient sexual education to their own children. The sessions on intimacy and harmonization of personality had as their aim the resolution of conflict by the couple themselves, and young women, in particular, were advised not to divulge anything about their intimate lives to their mothers. Doing so, it was categorically stated, was a principal cause of disharmony and loss of mutual trust. The ideal was the independence of the couple's household as the bedrock of a solid marriage, and this was interpreted as the breaking of intergenerational solidarity. Family self-sufficiency meant independence from the interference of parents.[48] However, from the standpoint of young women, the new Catholic ideal of the nuclear

family, by rupturing both the economic and the emotional connections between generations, created greater isolation, rendering them
more dependent psychologically upon their husbands for satisfying
personal relationships.

The new Catholic ideal of the family founded upon love, personal
choice, and sexual fulfillment within the context of marriage marked a
radical departure from tradition. Histories that treat of life among
Quebec Catholic families during the period before 1939 have outlined
that, in the early part of the twentieth century, marriage was not regarded as an intimate partnership of personalities based upon love or
personal choice; rather, as Philippe Garigue observed in his 1962
study, French-Canadian family traditions did not treat marriage as an
end in itself, but as a "universe of rules" characterized by formalism
and lack of intimacy between spouses.[49] Courtship and marriage frequently involved the intervention of extended family networks, which
at times exerted not so subtle pressure to determine the choice of a
"proper" spouse. Sex was rarely spoken of, and female sexuality was
defined solely in terms of duty and obligation to produce children,
while male desires were regarded as the gratification of animalistic
lust. For those women who married just before or during the Depression, there was a widespread lack of knowledge about their own sexuality, which extended to such matters as the menstrual cycle and
pregnancy.[50] In the early stages of married life, both the middle and
working classes exhibited a lack of desire to forge an independent
identity, a problem reinforced by the shortage of housing in the me-
tropolis of Montreal. The common pattern was for young couples to
live for several years with the husband's parents, a situation that
seems not to have resulted in the transmission of much wisdom, sexual or otherwise, from one generation to the next, and merely retarded
the development of the sexual personality and served as a barrier to
intimacy.[51] It was for this reason that, in addition to marriage preparation, one of the main thrusts of the Catholic Action movement was the
advocacy of affordable housing for young working-class families,[52]
which would allow them the proper environmental setting to put into
practice the new ideal of marital intimacy.

That the SPM's promotion of a modern concept of Christian marriage and the nuclear family was regarded as the focal point of a challenge of post-war youth culture in the process of self-definition to the
values of the pre-war generations of parents was made abundantly
clear in one outraged article to the Catholic periodical *Front ouvrier*.
An anonymous parent accused the SPM activists of "making young
girls wild to sleep with men and to have children quickly ... You have
no business in these matters ... and instead of bothering young

women with this nonsense about marriage preparation, you should be teaching them how to earn an honest living ... You are no better than Italian Fascists ... in allowing young men and women to associate in your Catholic youth groups; you are corrupting the young generation; you are simply making them horny." More tellingly, this writer declared that the new Catholic youth culture "want to leave parents completely out of the picture, as though parents had nothing more to do with their children ... Tachez de vous trouver un autre job. Au revoir."[53]

What particularly outraged this critic of the new Catholic youth movements was that, under the sanction of religion, young *women* were in the process of acquiring for the first time an equal access to sexual knowledge and self-expression and the means to acquire psychological independence from the authority of their mothers. This development, it should be stressed, was something entirely new in the context of Quebec society and culture. Indeed, the central dynamic of the entire Catholic marriage-preparation movement involved the redefinition of Christian marriage in personalist terms of love, free choice, sexual intimacy, and personal fulfillment, rather than motherhood and reproduction. The placing of these ideals at the centre of Roman Catholicism was driven by the large numbers of young women who not only comprised the receptive audience of the premarital counselling courses but also held positions as rank-and-file activists, group leaders, and directors of the various Catholic Action movements. Contemporary observers of Catholic Action were well aware of the fact that, as a general rule, women far outnumbered men, usually in the ratio of 2 to 1.[54] As one anguished priest privately confided, "the 'feminized' nature of our J.O.C. has always troubled me. Are we to be spiritual directors for a worker's movement of young women rather than of young men?"[55]

Clerical concern was amplified by the fact that women participants did not see their role as subordinate or as merely echoing clerical dictation. In a 1957 survey of twenty-two women activists, they cited their own superior organizational skills and a well-developed experiential grasp of the Catholic Action philosophy of spiritual community as reasons for their ability to take on leadership roles within this traditionally male-dominated institution. They viewed their participation in this lay movement as a self-enriching process, one that offered them a transformed spiritual life, a capacity for adaptation and for understanding people, and the opportunity to place to the fore their personal discoveries, devotion, and spirit of service.[56] The impact that this new Catholicism could have on women's self-perception was effectively illustrated by Madeleine Meloche, one of the seminar leaders in the SPM program. Called upon to accompany her husband as a lecturer, she stated that she at first did so, thinking that she would be a moral support for him. However, during the course of the evening she held a number of informal conversations with the new couples and discovered that she had a gift for putting them at their ease and engaging them in discussions about their hopes and fears for married life. Meloche soon concluded that her presence at the course was as necessary as that of her husband. As she informed the SPM directors, "I know that there are women here that can play a role at least as equal as that of their husbands."[57]

Particularly after 1949, when the SPM began to recruit married couples as group leaders, women such as Madeleine Meloche seized the opportunity to transform the initially rather conservative clerical agenda that sought to reconstruct marriage as a spiritual bastion against communism and modern influences. Under the leadership of Catholic lay women, the program of premarital counselling was increasingly oriented towards the needs of women within marriage. These Catholic women emphatically rejected an "economic feminism" that advocated the equality of women outside the home and in the workplace, and they exalted the role of the woman as resisting the "materialist" imperatives in modern society. Women, they believed, would find their personal fulfillment as the spiritual, emotional, and educative centre of the modern family: the integrity of a woman's personality was best achieved through "dialogue with those that she loves ... her husband and children."[58] Woman's work outside the home, declared one SPM activist in 1957, "hampers woman's adaptation from the perspective of sexuality, culture, and society," and she urged an ever-greater insistence upon "the spiritual beauty of woman's role within the home."[59] While certainly conservative in prioritizing the spiritual role of women and the family, the post-war advocates of Catholic marriage engaged in a subtle, yet palpable, reworking of an older "maternal feminist" concern that defined women totally within the framework of her reproductive role.[60] Though it certainly agreed with the idea that women had a special "vocation for motherhood,"[61] the new Catholicism argued for a wider social and cultural role for women in modern society beyond simply reproduction and child care. As the leaders of the marriage-preparation movement stated, they sought "a richer conception of the role of woman, one in which she was both mother and queen of the family circle, but also as a human person."[62] This "personalist feminism," which desired for woman "a status worthy of her dignity as a human person,"[63] attempted to steer a middle course between "that feminism which wants to impose upon woman tasks for which she is not suited" and "male tyranny which seeks to prevent the flowering of the female personality."[64] The outlook promulgated by the Catholic social movements was directed at developing a new, self-reliant individuality among Quebec Catholic women,[65] and to achieve this, they advanced the notion of modern marriage, particularly the relationship between husband and wife, as a fulfilling emotional and sexual partnership in which women would, through knowledge of and control over sexuality and reproduction, both realize their distinctive personalities and acquire equality and power within Quebec culture and society.

The key to the realization of this vision lay in popularizing, through the framework of the marriage-preparation courses, an awareness of the different psychological needs of each sex. spm activists stated that the foundation of the home was intimacy, which grew out of mutual awareness between husband and wife of each other's needs; this awareness would then lead to the sharing and cooperation that alone could build a happy marriage.[66] A successful marriage, it was now believed, "depends upon a constant, objective dialogue between the couple themselves at the heart of the home."[67] The courses were carefully structured around the idea of the "complementarity" of male and female roles, which explicitly rejected the achievement of equality through the competition of men and women in the workplace; such competition would "deprive woman of her soul, of her spirituality."[68] However, priority was placed on the fostering of discussion and intimacy between husbands and wives, and it was this reason that group leaders were emphatically instructed to "get at least one word out of each of them, make them advance their opinions" on matters ranging from budgeting to their emotional needs to their ideas about sex and their aspirations for married life.[69]

It is apparent that the prospective brides who attended these courses regarded the frankness that the lectures and discussions encouraged, together with the emphasis on intimacy and partnership, far from being an intrusive clerical imposition, as something both novel and refreshing. Writing in 1947, one young woman, "Marie-Ange," stated that "the study of the psychology of the male simply stunned me. What a revelation for me – and how useful – to learn that men think and act differently than we do." For her, this new psychological self-awareness encouraged a new intimacy with her fiancé: "we have often discussed together the subjects treated in the course. We are very happy to have settled before our marriage a host of problems: balancing a family budget, mutual trust, a proper sense of our sexual life and of its responsibilities, and child rearing."[70] Another participant in the courses praised the premarital counselling "for having opened my eyes and making me realize that I was about to make the biggest mistake of my life. I thus broke off with my fiancé and I am completely happy in my 'old-maidhood.' "[71] And throughout the history of the SPM, it was invariably the women who appreciated that the focus on the psychology of the sexes and the cultivation of intimacy was particularly tailored to their needs and desires.[72]

While, from the perspective of the 1990s, the psychological and physiological advice offered to these young women would appear both patronizing and designed to keep them in a state of economic and sexual subordination to their husbands, participation in the SPM went far to reassure these young Catholic women that, in a conservative society in which marriage was still regarded as the *sine qua non* of adulthood, the choice of a husband was not simply a "roll of the dice" that might confine them to a lifetime of emotional and sexual unhappiness. The premarital courses enabled many women to reject the values of the pre-war generation of women, whose marriage ideals seemed to extend only to finding a husband who did not drink, held a steady job, and did not cheat, but who was not terribly intimate or communicative.[73] However, it was in the area of sexuality and control of reproduction that the SPM courses, with their core of personalist feminism, had their greatest influence over the mindset of many postwar Quebec women. From a very early date, it was clear that what the prospective brides attending the sessions most appreciated and desired was the message that both women and men had entirely natural sexual urges which did not have to be repressed, but could be openly discussed and satisfied within the context of marriage.[74] Most novel about the SPM's approach, when compared with pre-war attitudes, was the fact that, while the courses assumed that women's sexual knowledge was not as well developed as that of their prospective husbands and that they should let men take the initiative in sexual matters, they also emphatically taught that woman's sexuality existed independently of reproduction. Therefore the new Catholicism declared that it was the responsibility of the husband to respond to the wife's needs. Indeed, it was bluntly stated to husbands that those sexual acts which led to male ejaculation without intercourse were not permitted by the laws of the church, but that foreplay which did "not lead to ejaculation and is not prolonged to the point of ejaculation" was allowed, and indeed, encouraged by the laws of the church.[75] The SPM organizers were well aware of the Kinsey Report and its implications regarding the promiscuous sexual behaviour of North American youth. For this reason, lecturers stressed the duty of both spouses to ensure frequent and fulfilling sexual relations. To this end, they argued from traditional Catholic moral teaching that it was sinful for a spouse to refuse the natural and legitimate sexual desires of the other.[76] Thus the marriage-preparation movement not only tacitly recognized the nature of women's sexual needs, but also bluntly informed husbands that "it was a duty of conscience to see to and further the complete orgasm, the physical and psychological satisfaction of your wives."[77] It was small wonder, then, that SPM organizers at times complained that young people were "flocking to the courses for sexual information and not to explore the spirituality of marriage."[78]

Between the end of World War II and the mid-1960s, the personalist feminism of Catholic Action decisively reoriented Quebec Catholic teaching on marriage towards a recognition of the psychological, sexual, and emotional needs of women within a sacramental institution that was still viewed as a lifetime partnership. However, personalism's emphasis upon the dignity of the human person and respect for individual decision-making over blind adherence to past traditions, as well as the powerful presence of women in the marriage-preparation movement, played a crucial role in articulating and popularizing what was perhaps one of the most central attributes of modernity in the Quebec culture that emerged after 1945: women's control over reproductive choice, one of the most fundamental elements shaping modern feminism. Again, the role of a Roman Catholic movement in such a cultural process may seem paradoxical, given the church's prohibition on many forms of birth control and the often-perceived link between Catholicism and the tradition of having large families. It forcefully demonstrates, however, the power of laywomen to effectively tailor and direct an institution towards the promotion of an emphatically feminist agenda.

A surface reading of the SPM's marriage-preparation course would indicate that it was firmly anchored in the traditional Catholic notion that the purpose of marriage which legitimated the sexual relationship was child-bearing and parenthood; these must remain the great ends of marriage for the modern husband and wife.[79] Group leaders regularly told their audiences that the child was the confirmation of the marriage bond, and that from the perspective of marital harmony, it was unwise to delay the birth of the first child unduly; doing so, the SPM maintained, would merely prolong a species of "egotism" and prevent the psychological growth of husband and wife as a couple.[80] Indeed, most of the young men and women who attended the premarital counselling sessions appear to have been quite traditional in their attitudes regarding size of family. As late as 1962, even after the beginning of the political "Quiet Revolution," those questioned in a survey indicated that they desired a family of approximately four or five children.[81] However, from a very early stage in the history of the SPM, the presence of a large number of doctors and nurses as course lecturers was intended not merely for the purpose of informing prospective brides and grooms about human anatomy and the technical aspects of sexual intercourse or reassuring prospective mothers about the naturalness and safety of childbirth, but in order to popularize the Ogino-Knauss (rhythm) method of birth control,[82] based upon determining the fertile and sterile days in the female cycle. This was the only means for regulating birth, other than total or periodic abstinence, sanctioned by the doctrines of the church, because it avoided the use of artificial or chemical means while fostering the self-control so essential to a Christian way of life.

During the "sexual revolution" that followed upon wide access to the birth control pill after the late 1960s, the rhythm method was much ridiculed as both ineffective and a symbol of women's subjection to patriarchal clerical dogma, but its promotion by the SPM must be placed in the context of the period before 1960. Given the high level of popular unawareness about sexual reproduction itself and the lack of access in Quebec to reliable means of birth control, knowledge of the rhythm method gave Catholic women, for the first time, a sense that they possessed the technical means, sanctioned by religion, to determine the timing of conception and thus, ultimately, the power to control the size of their families. In this respect, there was a gap between the official teaching of the spiritual directors and chaplains of the SPM and the attitudes of the Catholic laity who dominated the movement. Clergy such as Father Jules Paquin, who lectured to the SPM in 1960, explained that Catholic doctrine permitted the use of contraception to allow for the spacing of children so as to ensure their proper care and education: "the church has never advocated giving birth to the most children in the quickest possible time."[83] However, the lay activists and group leaders, most of whom were women, celebrated the access to contraceptive information that their movement offered as a step out of the dark ages and a recognition of the human personality. Despite the SPM's claim that "our traditions regarding large families have been respected,"[84] the tenor of the movement after the late 1950s emphasized a "prudent" attitude to family size and reproduction. "It is nearly impossible," declared the SPM directorate, "to determine today what is the ideal family size. All that we can say is that for a couple to voluntarily limit themselves to a single child might suggest a lack of generosity and that, on the other hand, consecutive maternities every ten months might not be a prudent use of human reproductive capacity."[85] The ability to plan and space births that the rhythm method seemed to promise was, for this post-war generation of Catholic women, simply a confirmation of human freedom, and in light of the priority that women within the movement placed upon sexuality and personal satisfaction within marriage, no longer would men and women have to rely upon the denial of sexual appetite in order to limit family size: "the human heart, human reason, and human sense of responsibility can now intervene to assure a sensible birth control. This human progress in the mastery of fertility is possible thanks to recent scientific advances ... With the progress of science, the time is not far off when humanity will become more completely the master of fertility."[86]

That clerical teaching on birth control clearly took second place to the desire of Catholic women for control over reproduction was evident in the SPM's attitude to the advent of the birth control pill in the early 1960s. Although clearly unhappy about the fact that the pill might free female sexuality from any restraint, the clergy seemed most intent on preserving good relations with the laity, and they tried to accommodate the use of this new birth control method with Catholic doctrine. In the years before the absolute papal prohibition was imposed in 1968, it was possible for both clergy and laywomen to reach a workable compromise on the use of the pill. Even Father Jules Paquin, while clearly preferring abstinence as the best alternative to the rhythm method, stated that, according to Catholic doctrine, use of the pill was sanctioned as a means of regularizing the female cycle in those cases where medical problems existed.[87] For the Catholic women who directed the organization, the pill was an *aide à la nature* because it assisted breast-feeding and regularized the female cycle. For them, however, the decision to use the pill was increasingly not a matter of Catholic doctrine or morality but a private decision to be determined by the woman herself in consultation with medical professionals.[88]

Here was the clearest articulation of a personalist feminism, as distinct from the older maternalist imperatives of pre-war Catholic Quebec. Driven by the presence of women within Catholic organizations such as the SPM, not only had a fundamental transformation in the self-perception of many Quebec women occurred between 1940 and the mid-1960s, but a shift from reproduction to equality and personal fulfillment had taken place, increasingly sanctioned by the wider society. It is clear from the larger demography of Quebec after 1945 that a "contraceptive revolution" ensued among the cohorts of women born between 1921 and 1935, and that this "revolution" was largely accomplished without the use of the pill – that is, through the supposedly "traditional" methods sanctioned by Roman Catholicism.[89] And significantly, it was achieved by the very group of women who were affected by the attitudes to marriage and family promoted by the Catholic marriage-preparation movement. For Quebec women in this period, Catholicism may at one level have served as a repository of traditional values, but it also functioned as the vehicle for an increasingly modern view of marriage and woman's personality. As the psychiatrist Camille Laurin aptly stated in 1966, the SPM, with its popularization of the different male and female psychologies, had actually paved the way for the modern feminist movement and for the enshrinement of formal legal equality within the civil code in 1964. The organization, he stated, was to be praised for promoting a more dynamic knowledge of women which had opened a creative dialogue between the sexes. However, a woman's future would, in Laurin's estimation, be bound up less with motherhood than with her self-awareness as an independent personality and as an equal partner in the marriage.[90]

By the late 1960s the creative synthesis between Roman Catholicism and the initiative and aspirations of laywomen that had launched the marriage-preparation movement in Quebec had broken down in the wake of the papal encyclical *Humanae vitae*, which categorically condemned all forms of "artificial" birth control. As the lay directorate of the SPM sought to jettison official affiliation with the church in response to what it believed was the more "pluralist" nature of Quebec society in the wake of de-confessionalization, the clergy themselves attempted to reassert tighter control over definitions of marriage and sexuality by launching their own courses in premarital counselling.[91] What this attempt to reimpose clerical authority indicated was that by the late 1960s Catholicism, particularly in the area of marriage and sexuality, no longer mediated between tradition and modernity. In light of an increasingly strident youth culture that exalted pluralism and freedom of choice, the church's teachings had become a hotly contested terrain. Writing in 1971, Father J. Alphonse Beaulieu of Mont-Joli savagely lampooned the efforts of groups such as the SPM to synthesize Catholic doctrine and modern sexual science. "To experience God through sex," he stated, "is pure moonshine." The SPM's program, which stressed sexual education, family planning, anatomy, and sexual role-playing, was dismissed as a humanistic gospel of liberation at odds with the traditional teachings of the church.[92]

However, it would be a superficial reading of the personalist feminism incarnated in the SPM to dismiss it as merely a naive maternalism, a code word for the conservative family ideologies and the supposed female passivity of the post-war decades that was simply consigned to oblivion in the face of a more radical, and hence more legitimate, "economic feminism" which arose in the 1960s. Nor was personalist feminism a symptom of creeping secularization, as Claude Ryan, the national secretary of Catholic Action, contended in 1954. In articulating what has become the current historical orthodoxy regarding the relationship between Catholicism and the Quiet Revolution, Ryan sounded the warning that religion, because it enlisted the energies of so many women, was naive, dependent upon tradition, and infantile, and that it was rapidly becoming divorced from the rational, forward-looking "male" world of politics, business, labour unions, and universities.[93] His comments should remind historians that the way in which they have interpreted the relationship between religion and society in this period is itself a gendered construct. To adopt such a view uncritically would simply be to fall into the historiographic trap of positing a dichotomy between Roman Catholicism and modernity. If the personalism that inspired the various Catholic Action movements constituted an intellectually respectable attempt to defend individuality in the modern world, to navigate a "third way" between capitalism and communism,[94] then a similar argument can be made about personalist feminism, which sought to preserve links to Quebec's religious past by exalting women as a "spiritual" presence within home and society, while defining an ideology that placed a high priority on personal choice and liberty, particularly over women's sexuality and reproduction. If, as Leonore Davidoff has argued, a crucial attribute of modern individuality in the twentieth century has been the turning away from mere material survival towards the affirmation of a private and ultimately sexual self,[95] then Roman Catholic efforts to redefine marriage in Quebec after 1940 must be regarded, not as part of an apparatus constructed by repressive elites, but as central to the social and cultural modernization that we call the Quiet Revolution.

NOTES

I would like to thank Denyse Baillargeon, Nancy Christie, and Roberto Perin for their comments on an earlier draft of this essay and the Arts Research Board of McMaster University for financial assistance that facilitated the research.

1 For contemporary accounts of this famous mass marriage spectacle, see Archives Nationales du Québec à Montréal (ANQM), Fonds Mouvement des Travailleurs Chrétiens, P257, art. 12, "Scrap-Book, Les cents-mariés, 1939," "La digne apothéose du travail chrétien," *La Presse*, 24 juillet 1939; ibid., art. 13, "20ᵉ anniversaire, 1959"; ibid., art. 13, Bill Bantey, "Mass Marriage Couples Renew Vows," *Montreal Gazette*, 31 August 1959.

2 Ibid., art. 12, "Scrap-Book: Les cents-mariés, 1939," "La reconstruction sociale par la Jeunesse Ouvrière Catholique," *Le Devoir*, 24 juillet 1939.

3 Ibid., "La digne apothéose du travail chrétien."

4 On the origins and progress of this "quiet revolution," see P.-A. Linteau et al., *Histoire du Québec contemporain: Le Québec depuis 1930* (Montréal: Boréal, 1989); and Michael Behiels, *Prelude to Quiet Revolution: Liberalism vs. Neo-Nationalism, 1945–1960* (Montreal: McGill-Queen's University Press, 1985). The effects of this period on the Roman Catholic Church as an institution are explored in Jean Hamelin, *Histoire du catholicisme québécois*, tome 2, *De 1940 à nos jours* (Montréal: Boréal, 1984).

5 ANQM, Fonds Service de Préparation au Mariage, P116, art. 24, Camille Laurin, "Conférence, banquet annuel," 4 juin 1966.

6 Philippe Garigue, *La vie familiale des Canadiens-français* (Montréal: Les Presses de l'Université de Montréal, 1962), 26–7.

7 ANQM, P116, art. 18, Michel Haguette, "FAVIC ou la nouvelle orientation de Service de Préparation au Mariage de Montréal," 30 mai 1973. For a historical sketch of the various Catholic Action movements created during the 1930s, see Gabriel Clement, *Histoire de l'Action Catholique au Canada français* (Montréal: Fides, 1972).

8 ANQM, P116, art. 1, "Historique du S.P.M."

9 For the promotion of this view by a social science elite in the 1930s and its subsequent entrenchment in government policy, see Nancy Christie, *Engendering the State: Family, Work, and Welfare in Canada, 1900–1945* (Toronto: University of Toronto Press, 2000), chapter on the 1930s.

10 National Archives of Canada (NA), Canadian Council on Social Development (CCSD), MG 28 I 10, box 62, Marriage Counselling file 44/45, "The Social Worker Tackles the Problem of Marital Conflict"; Canadian Youth Commission (CYC), *Youth, Marriage and the Family* (Toronto: Ryerson Press, 1948), vii–viii. It was no coincidence that the Catholic Church's efforts in the field of education for family life won high praise from the CYC and that Protestant churches were urged to follow this example; see *Youth, Marriage and the Family*, 166–7. The fundamental opposition between "spiritual" and "material" interpretations of the family was eloquently expressed in 1942 by Father Émile Bouvier, who incorporated it into a social philosophy of conflicting national ideals between French Canadians and Anglo-Saxons. See Archives de l'Université de Montréal (AUM), Fonds Action Catholique Canadienne, P16/K, 1.11, Émile Bouvier, "Votre tâche, jeunesse," *Le Devoir*, 18 novembre 1942.

11 NA, CCSD, "The Social Worker Tackles the Problems of Marital Conflict"; CYC, *Youth, Marriage and the Family*, ix.

12 The marriage-preparation course itself was designed as follows: (1) Sens des fiançailles; (2) La psychologie complémentaire des deux; (3) L'amour et le bonheur; (4) Accord des personnalités; (5) L'administration financière du

foyer; (6) Lois civiles du mariage; (7) Lois écclesiastiques du mariage; (8) La cérémonie du mariage; (9) La mystique, Le sacrement; (10 and 11) Anatomie, hygiène et santé – relation des époux; (12) Les premiers temps du mariage; (13) La morale conjugale; (14) L'attente de l'enfant. The course underwent several revisions between 1944 and 1966. See ANQM, Fonds Jeunesse Ouvrière Catholique, P104, art. 4, "17ᵉ session intensive, 1952," Jacques Champagne, "Le Service de Préparation au Mariage," 1952.

13 ANQM, P116, art. 2, Germain Lemieux, "Allocution," 1950; ibid., art. 1, "Journée d'étude, 28 sept. 1952"; ibid., P104, Fonds Jeunesse Ouvrière Catholique, art. 4, "Rapport de la 17ᵉ session intensive, 1952," Jacques Champagne, "S.P.M. Service de la J.O.C."

14 ANQM, P116, art. 24, "Conférences données au service, 1954 à 1958," "Fiancés d'aujourd'hui ... époux de demain," Conférence de Mgr Léger, 11 janvier 1954, au Plateau (in which he saw civilization threatened by "anarchie libertaire" and "tyrannie totalitaire"). See also ibid., P116, art. 1, "Allocution de Mgr. Leger," 28 septembre 1952.

15 ANQM, P116, art. 1, "Session d'étude, 1954," "Résumé de l'allocution de M. l'abbé Gérard Lalonde"; ibid., art. 2., "Allocution du président du S.P.M. à la clôture de la semaine des fiancés," le 15 janvier 1950.

16 ANQM, P116, art. 36, "Spicilèges," "Mémoire sur le Service de Préparation au Mariage de la J.O.C. canadienne," janvier 1958.

17 ANQM, P116, art. 6, "Appréciation des cours," Marcel Lefebvre, rue Marquette, Montréal, à rédacteur, Le Petit Journal, 19 juin 1952; AUM, P16/D5,1, "Fonction des foyers responsables – exposé présenté par M. Paul Meloche, lors de la réunion du 13 décembre, 1963."

18 ANQM, P116, art. 6, "Appréciation des cours," Jean-François Durand, Ville St Michel, à Gilberte Rivest, secrétaire, SPM, 3 mai 1950.

19 Ibid., art. 2, "Semaine des fiancés, 1949," "Un professeur et un élève," Le Devoir, 8 janvier 1949.

20 Ibid., art. 24, "Résumé de l'allocution de M. l'abbé Gérard Lalonde, aumonier diocesain du S.P.M., à la recollection des couples-conférenciers," 6 mai 1955.

21 As Jean Hamelin notes, at the peak of their effectiveness, these movements never enlisted more than 32,000 people, the bulk of them concentrated in the Jeunesse Étudiante Catholique. See Histoire du catholicisme québécois, 126.

22 ANQM, P116, art. 1, "Semaine des fiancés, 1955," Marie Bourbonnais, "Les fiancés d'aujourd'hui sont les parents de demain," La Presse, 8 janvier 1955; ibid., art. 19, "Aumoniers," ca. 1968–69; ibid., art. 36, "Spicilèges," n.d.; AUM, Fonds Action Catholique Canadienne, P16/D5, 3.1, "Réunions 15 déc. 1955–16 mars 1964."

23 ANQM, P116, art. 19, Raymonde Charron, "Le Service de Préparation au Mariage: Une institution nationale," ca. 1962; ibid., art. 1, "Remarques extraites des rapports des conférenciers, série Janvier 1956."

24 Ibid., art. 1, "Situation des fiancés, 1955–56," noted that of the young men, 7.6 per cent were students, 15.7 per cent office workers, 30.6 per cent skilled workers, 27.6 per cent unskilled workers, and 15.5 per cent in miscellaneous occupations. Of the young women, 6.2 per cent were domestics, 8 per cent students, 34.5 per cent office workers, 25.8 per cent manual workers, 18.8 per cent "ouvrières mixtes," and 6.7 per cent in miscellaneous occupations. See also ibid., art. 19, "Communiqués aux journaux," Renaude Lapointe, "Les cours de préparation au mariage déglamorisent–ils l'amour," *La Presse*, 19 janvier 1963, "Aumôniers," ca. 1968–69; Charron, "Le Service de Préparation au Mariage: Une institution nationale."

25 This argument has been advanced in the American context in Elaine Tyler May, *Homeward Bound: American Families in the Cold War Era* (New York: Basic Books, 1988); and James Gilbert, *Cycle of Outrage: America's Reaction to the Juvenile Delinquent in the 1950s* (New York: Oxford University Press, 1986); and for Canada in Doug Owram, *Born at the Right Time: A History of the Baby Boom Generation* (Toronto: University of Toronto Press, 1996), 10–30; and Owram, "Canadian Domesticity in the Postwar Era," in Peter Neary and J.L. Granatstein, eds., *The Veterans Charter and Post-World War II Canada* (Montreal: McGill-Queen's University Press, 205–23.

26 Mona Gleason, "Psychology and the Construction of the 'Normal' Family in Postwar Canada, 1945–1960," *Canadian Historical Review* 78 (September 1997): 442–77; Mariana Valverde, "Building Anti-Delinquent Communities: Morality, Gender, and Generation in the City," in Joy Parr, ed., *A Diversity of Women: Ontario, 1945–1980* (Toronto: University of Toronto Press, 1995), 19–45; Mona Gleason, *Normalizing the Family: Psychology, Schooling, and the Family in Postwar Canada* (Toronto: University of Toronto Press, 1999); Mary Louise Adams, *The Trouble with Normal: Postwar Youth and the Making of Heterosexuality* (Toronto: University of Toronto Press, 1997), 53–106.

27 See, for example, ANQM, P104, art. 4, "Suggestions de programme d'action, 1961," "Programme social de 1961–62, projet de la JOC et JOCF, la Préparation au Mariage"; ibid., "L'amour entre garçons et filles"; P104, art. 176, "Rapport de la J.O.C. canadienne d'expression française préparé pour la réunion du Bureau International de la J.O.C., tenue à Rome, les 6–10 nov. 1954"; P116, art. 2, "Semaine des fiancés, 1948," "Sermon prononcé par le R.P. Lorenzo Gauthier, c.s.v., à la clôture de la semaine des fiancés du S.P.M., le 18 janvier 1948."

28 AUM, P16/H18.84, "Le S.P.M. de Montréal et le travail de la femme mariée," ca. 1963–64. See also P16/D6, 5.2, Marcel Clément, "Chômage et travail féminin," *L'Action catholique*, 31 mars 1953; ANQM, P116, art. 24, "Conférences, 1954–1958," "La crise de l'amour dans le monde moderne," Résumé de la conférence de M. Gustave Thibon, 1 novembre 1956; P104, art. 4, "17e session intensive, 1952," Champagne, "S.P.M.," 1952.

29 ANQM, P116, art. 24, "Conférences données au Service, 1947–1954," "Substance de la conférence de M. Marcel Clément," novembre 1954. Clément was born in France in 1921 and graduated in political economy from the Faculty of Law at the Sorbonne. During World War I he served in the French Resistance, and in 1943 he was in charge of research into the problem of French forced labour in Germany. In 1946 he was named to the faculty at the Université de Montréal. For his identification with the Catholic right, see Leon Dion, *Quebec 1945–2000*, tome 2, *Les intellectuels et le temps de Duplessis* (Québec: Les Presses de l'Université Laval, 1993), 233.

30 For this nostalgia, which persisted throughout the 1920s and 1930s, see Andrée Lévesque, *Making and Breaking the Rules: Quebec Women, 1919–1939* (Toronto: McClelland & Stewart, 1994), 19–21.

31 ANQM, P116, art. 24, "Conférences 1960–1966," Bernard Mailhiot, "De l'esprit de géométrie en psychologie," n.d.

32 ANQM, P104, art. 4, "17ᵉ session intensive," Champagne, "S.P.M.," 1952.

33 Ibid., art. 171, "Rencontre nationale des responsables et aumoniers du S.P.M.," 3–4 décembre 1955. See also ibid., art. 4, "Suggestions de programme d'action, 1961," "Amour entre garçons et filles"; art. 176, "Enquête auprès de 329 fiancés qui ont suivi le S.P.M. sur la préparation économique des jeunes au mariage," 1954.

34 AUM, P16/D5, 1.14, "Compilation du sondage auprès des fiancés sur l'amour," 1962. This was a study based upon the responses of 133 couples in five Quebec dioceses and eight cities. See also ANQM, P116, art. 1, "Situation des fiancés, 1955–56," which pointed to the very late sexual awareness of Quebec youth. Fully 60 per cent of young people questioned stated that they had acquired their sexual knowledge after age fourteen.

35 AUM, P16/D5, 1.14, "Compilation du sondage," 1962; P16/H18.84, "Conclusion du Comité Exécutif du S.P.M., Jan–Mai 1956."

36 The phrase was used by Camille Laurin in his speech to the SPM in 1966; see ANQM, P116, art. 24, "Conférences 1960–1966," Camille Laurin, "Les services que le S.P.M. rend à la société," 4 juin 1966.

37 Ibid., art. 2, "Semaine des fiancés, 1951." Roman Catholicism's marriage-preparation courses were, in this respect, a variant of a wider North American movement that began on a small scale in American colleges in the 1930s and blossomed after World War II. See Beth L. Bailey, *Front Porch to Back Seat: Courtship in Twentieth-Century America* (Baltimore and London: Johns Hopkins University Press, 1989), 125–39. These courses, according to Bailey, stressed the "personal" rather than academic knowledge.

38 ANQM, P257, art. 3, "Semaine de la famille ouvrière 1955," "Panne de foyer – pourquoi?"; ibid., "Semaine de la famille ouvrière 1954 – déclaration du président national," *Le Devoir*, 11 octobre 1954.

39 AUM, P16/H3, 18.86, Madeleine Trottier, André Normandeau, "Le mariage d'adolescents à Montréal: Étude sociologique sur leurs chances d'ajustement marital," mars 1965.

40 AUM, P16/D5, 1.14, "Compilation du sondage auprès des fiancés sur l'amour, 1962."

41 AUM, P16/H18.83, "Les cours du S.P.M. sont-ils adaptés aux fiancés," juin 1960.

42 ANQM, P116, art. 2, "Semaine des fiancés 1949," Gérard Pelletier, "Reflexions sur un mot malheureux," Le Devoir, 8 janvier 1949. For Pelletier's status as one of the chief intellectual progenitors of the Quiet Revolution, see Behiels, Prelude to Quiet Revolution; and Dion, Les intellectuels et le temps de Duplessis.

43 ANQM, P116, art. 2, Pelletier, "Reflexions." For similar views, see art. 1, "Semaine des fiancés, 1955," Marie Bourbonnais, "Les fiancés d'aujourd'hui sont les parents de demain," La Presse, 8 janvier 1955; and ibid., "Semaine des fiancés 1950," Chanoine Clavel, "La semaine de la famille et la préparation au mariage," Le Canada, avril 1950.

44 For the breakdown of the concept of the interdependent family during the 1930s and 1940s, see Christie, Engendering the State, chapters on the Depression and World War II. See also Bettina Bradbury, Working Families (Toronto: McClelland and Stewart, 1994); and Denyse Baillargeon, Ménagères au temps de la crise (Montréal: Éditions du Remue-ménage, 1991), 28, 71. Baillargeon notes that this pattern persisted well into the 1930s in Montreal.

45 Hamelin, Histoire du catholicisme québécois, 2, notes the breakdown of the traditional parish structure in urban Montreal during the 1940s and 1950s, but explains it through demography and urbanization, rather than culture.

46 ANQM, P257, art. 13, "Crédit à l'habitation," "Conférence au poste CKCV," ca. 1947–48; italics mine.

47 ANQM, P104, art. 171, "Rapport national," 1954.

48 ANQM, P116, art. 2, "Semaine des fiancés, 1949," "Quelques conseils pratiques."

49 Garigue, La vie familiale des Canadiens-français, 79–81.

50 Denise Lemieux and Lucie Mercier, Les femmes au tournant du siècle, 1880–1940 (Montréal: Institut Québécois de Recherche sur la Culture, 1989), 110–12, 125, 155, 179, 235; Lévesque, Making and Breaking the Rules, 26–7; Baillargeon, Ménagères au temps de la crise, 102. Lemieux and Mercier have noted the emergence of a new sensibility regarding love. They fail, however, to link it to the formation of a youth culture under the auspices of Catholicism.

51 On the cohabitation of generations, see Lemieux and Mercier, Les femmes au tournant du siècle, 168–71; Baillargeon, Ménagères au temps de la crise, 94–6.

52 It should be noted in this context that as late as 1961, over 67 per cent of the population of Montreal rented, rather than owned, their dwellings, and much of even the new construction consisted of multi-family dwellings. See Linteau et al., *Histoire du Québec contemporain*, 279–80. On the Catholic Action crusade for working-class housing, see Jean-Pierre Collin, "La Ligue Ouvrière Catholique et l'organisation communautaire dans le Québec urbain des années 1940," *Revue d'histoire de l'Amérique française*, 47 (automne 1993): 163–91.

53 ANQM, P116, art. 6, "Appréciation des cours," anonymous letter to rédacteur, *Front ouvrier*, n.d.

54 ANQM, P104, art. 4, "Rapport de la 17ᵉ session JOC canadienne," 27 juin – 1 juillet, 1952; P115, art. 2, "Historique du S.P.M." Subsequent historical research revealed that these estimates were far too conservative. In examining the Catholic Action membership figures for the 1950s, Jean Hamelin has determined, in averaging all movements, that the figure was at times closer to 75 per cent. See *Histoire du catholicisme québécois*, 2: 127.

55 ANQM, P104, art. 181, "Correspondance 1950–1959," Rev. Gérard-Marie Coderre, évêque-coadjuteur, St Jean, à Rev. Père Pierre-Paul Asselin, chief chaplain, JOC, 21 août 1954.

56 AUM, P16/A1, 19, "Secteur féminin en AC," mars 1957.

57 AUM, P16/D5,1, Madeleine Meloche, "Les fonctions particulières de l'épouse responsable," 13 décembre 1963.

58 AUM, P16/D5, 1.10, "Travaillera-t-elle?" n.d.

59 ANQM, P116, art. 1, "Session d'étude 1957," Solange Pitre à Madeleine Trottier, secrétaire, SPM.

60 For a discussion of the relationship between the rise of maternal feminism in the early twentieth century and the definition of the "spiritual" family, see Christie, *Engendering the State*, chapter 1, "The Evangelical Morphology of the State." For an account of the impact of "maternal feminism" on the position of women in Quebec before World War II, see Lévesque, *Making and Breaking the Rules*, 23–52; and more recently, Karine Hébert, "Une organisation maternaliste au Québec: La Fédération Nationale Saint-Jean-Baptiste et la bataille pour le vote des femmes," *Revue d'histoire de l'Amérique française* 52 (hiver 1999): 315–44. Post-war Quebec Catholicism did not entirely abandon "maternalist" discourse, but it mingled it with newer variants of Catholic personalism, which over the next decade subtly recentred the priority on the rights and spiritual satisfactions of women as individuals.

61 AUM, P16/D5, 1.10, "Travaillera-t-elle?" n.d.

62 Ibid.

63 AUM, P16/J22,2, "Cours donné par Mme. Thais Lacoste-Fremont au Cercle de l'Amicale J.M. de Sillery, Quebec," 23 octobre 1947; also P16/D6, 10.1, "Commission sur le statut juridique de la femme mariée dans le

Québec," avril 1947, which proposed the legal recognition of women as full partners in marriage.

64 AUM, P16/D5, 1.10, "Psychologie de l'homme et de la femme," n.d.

65 AUM, P16/A1, 19, "Secteur féminin, mars 1957."

66 Ibid.; ANQM, P257, art. 3, "Semaine de la famille ouvrière, 1955"; ibid., "Semaine de la famille ouvrière, 1957," "Causerie prononcée par Mme. Albina Arcand, CKCV, 11 oct. à 4.50 hres."

67 AUM, P16/D5, 1.10, "Psychologie de l'homme et de la femme," n.d.

68 ANQM, P104, art. 4, Champagne, "S.P.M., 1952."

69 Ibid.

70 ANQM, P116, art. 6, "Appréciation des cours," Marie-Ange à "Ma chère Reine," 28 novembre 1947. See also ibid., Madeleine à "Chère Marie-Paule," 26 novembre 1947.

71 Ibid., C. Frappier, Montréal, à directeur, SPM, 31 août 1961.

72 ANQM, P116, art. 22, "Sondage auprès les fiancés," 1963–64.

73 ANQM, P116, art. 6, "Appréciation des cours," Jeannette Gingras, Montréal-Nord, à Père J. de B. Laramee, 24 juin 1946. In her study of working-class women in Montreal during the Depression, Denyse Baillargeon has observed that, for the pre-war generation, the qualities of a good husband were defined in negative terms, and many of the women of this generation referred to lack of communication or discussion with their husbands. Most cited the lack of marriage-preparation courses. See Baillargeon, *Ménagères au temps de la crise*, 82–4.

74 ANQM, P116, art. 6, "Appréciation des cours," Pauline Fontaine à Mlle G. Bates, 29 mai 1947; Therese Brault à SPM, 10 mai 1947; Lucille Ducharme à Julienne Croteau, 20 mars 1947.

75 ANQM, P116, art. 24, "Conférences données au Service, 1960–1966," "Compte-rendu de la rencontre des conférenciers du S.P.M. avec le Révérend Père Jules Paquin, s.j.," 16 mars 1960.

76 ANQM, P116, art. 24, Mailhiot, "De l'esprit de géométrie"; "Compte-rendu … Jules Paquin, s.j."

77 ANQM, P116, art. 2, "Semaine des fiancés 1951."

78 ANQM, P115, art. 1, "Session d'étude 1955," commission des couples.

79 ANQM, P104, art. 4, "17e session intensive," Champagne, "S.P.M., 1952."

80 AUM, P16/D5, 1.10; ANQM, P116, art. 24, "Différents articles sur la préparation au mariage … 1942 à 1960," lettre de Jean Lemieux, "On accepte les enfants que le bon Dieu envoie," *Le Devoir*, 9 septembre 1959.

81 AUM, P16/D5, 1.14, "Compilation du sondage," 1962; ANQM, P116, art. 6, "Appréciation des cours," Madeleine à "Chère Marie-Paule," 26 novembre 1947.

82 AUM, P16/H18.83, "Commission médecins-infirmières," 2 octobre 1955.

83 ANQM, P116, art. 24, "Compte-rendu de la rencontre des conférenciers du S.P.M. avec le Révérend Père Jules Paquin, s.j.," 16 mars 1960.

84 AUM, P16/D5, 1, "Nouveaux résumés," ca. 1963–64, "Famille nouvelle."

85 AUM, P16/D5,1.10, "S.P.M. de Montréal," s.d., "Pour un amour enrichissant (morale conjugale)."

86 Ibid.

87 ANQM, P116, art. 24, Paquin, "Compte-rendu," 1960.

88 AUM, P16/D5, 1.12, "S.P.M. de Montréal," n.d.; P16/D5, 1.10, "S.P.M. de Montréal," "Pour un amour enrichissant."

89 For this demographic discussion, see Danielle Gauvreau and Peter Gossage, " 'Empêcher la famille: Fécondité et contraception au Québec, 1920–60," *Canadian Historical Review* 78 (September 1997): 478–510. Of those born 1921–25, 47 per cent used some form of contraception; those born 1926–30, 59 per cent; those born 1931–36, 64 per cent. These figures have been confirmed by Jacques Henripin et al., *Les enfants qu'on n'a plus au Québec* (Montreal: Les Presses de l'Université de Montréal, 1981), 162, which states that only 28.7 per cent of women married before 1946 used contraception, but 58.7 per cent of those married between 1946 and 1960 did. This was the focal point of the revolution. On the almost exclusive use of the Ogino-Knauss method or abstinence by those practising contraception before 1962, see Garigue, *La vie familiale des Canadiens-français*, 89.

90 ANQM, P116, art. 24, Laurin, "Les services que le S.P.M. rend à la société," 4 juin 1966.

91 ANQM, P116, Haguette, "FAVIC." For an earlier example of clerical appropriation of lay initiative, see Bryan Clarke, *Piety and Nationalism* (Montreal: McGill-Queen's University Press, 1994).

92 Archives Nationales du Québec à Québec, P428, S2, Action Sociale Catholique, *Action Catholique* (journal), file "La parole est aux lecteurs," 1968–73, J. Alphonse Beaulieu, ptre, Mont-Joli, ca. 1971.

93 AUM, P16/D6, 5.2, Claude Ryan, "Dangereuse prédominance de l'élément féminin dans l'A.C.," ca. 1953–54.

94 See John Hellman, *Emmanuel Mounier and the New Catholic Left, 1930–1950* (Toronto: University of Toronto Press, 1981), 5.

95 Leonore Davidoff, *Worlds Between: Historical Essays on Gender and Class* (New York: Routledge, 1995), 263.

Sacred Sex: The United Church and the Privatization of the Family in Post-War Canada

NANCY CHRISTIE

Christianity looks upon sex as one of the basic factors in human experience. The Word became flesh in Christ, thereby manifesting the truth that the physical can be the vehicle of the spiritual ... Sex is God-given and as such we must seek to understand its meanings and manifestations in physical development, physiological reactions and spiritual potentiality.[1]

This remarkable statement by the Board of Evangelism and Social Service of the United Church of Canada suggests that what has come to be known as the "sexual revolution" was not simply the product of the liberal youth culture of the 1960s, as some historians have maintained.[2] As this essay will argue, mainstream institutions such as the Protestant churches, which otherwise have been mythologized as the vessels of the conservative social mores so characteristic of the 1950s, were in fact agents of cultural change and were at the forefront in redefining the nature of the family and the purpose of sexual relations, as well as more relativistic conceptions of morality. Between 1945 and 1966 the United Church's perception of sex changed radically from epitomizing original sin to symbolizing the highroad to the Kingdom of God, a transformation that calls into question the easy generalizations about the 1950s as a somnolent and conservative era that have been offered by the snapshot analysis of generational historians.[3] Their emphasis upon mega-trends and their propensity to juxtapose the domestic ideology of the post-war era against the liberal aspirations of 1960s youth have masked the complex undercurrents of cultural change that percolated beneath the surface. Moreover, their descriptive narrative, which rightly points out that the family was re-conceived as a haven of emotional and psychological retreat, rather than primarily as an economic unit, during this period, fails to explain why there was a heightened emphasis upon the centrality of the domestic sphere during these post-war decades.

Indeed, one of the striking lacunae in the historiography of the baby-boom generation is the virtual absence of any lengthy discussion of Canada's Protestant churches, institutions that traditionally have seen marriage, children, and family as crucial to sustaining evangelical faith. By focusing upon an institution that had for generations spoken about the theme of family, separate spheres, and sexual conduct, we can more precisely discern what was indeed novel about the discourse on family after World War II, and more importantly, we can discover some of the reasons why the Canadian family was reinterpreted as occupying a distinctly private realm, and why sex became elevated from an act circumscribed by prohibitions to the centrepiece of religious experience, the development of a healthy personality, and the hallmark of individual liberty, especially for women. The idea of domesticity, I argue, was not consensual; rather, it was a contested terrain and thus a receptacle for a multiplicity of ideological perspectives. While it may be said that the Protestant churches participated in the general discourse on the family, their preoccupation with it was not simply a consequence of concerns over wartime instability and fears regarding the rise of delinquency; nor were they concerned with the containment of the sexual energies of modern teenagers in the face of the Cold War threat. Rather, their elevated concern for the family was a response to uniquely Canadian events, such as the emergence of the welfare state – most notably, the Family Allowances Act of 1944 – the consequent spectre of the political power of Roman Catholicism in Quebec, and the realization that, by entering the workforce in ever larger numbers, married women were transgressing traditional gender categories. Though the impulse of Protestantism to resist these disruptive social forces was an essentially conservative one, the very attempt to control and contain what were viewed as direct challenges to the authority of the Protestant churches had peculiarly liberal results and were instrumental in establishing the cultural preconditions for modern sexual mores.

In the years immediately after World War II the problem of how to stabilize the family was under discussion, a debate well documented by several historians, including Annalee Golz, Doug Owram, and Elaine Tyler May. Post-war commentators fretted over normalizing gender relations within the family and thus directed their attention to the problem of whether married women would choose the workplace over the home, or whether returned soldiers would rejoin their families and once again take up their responsibilities to work and support their dependents. As well, a host of social commentators saw in the escalating divorce rate and the increase in juvenile deliquency and illegitimate births distinct signs of moral and social decay.[4]

Although the notions that the family was merely a microcosm of society and that home and nation were interdependent were not new ideas,[5] the public insistence that domestic values determined social stability and economic progress reached a fever pitch in the first few years after the war. Indeed, the idea that domestic economic prosperity, the upholding of gender boundaries between the workplace and the home, and a stable family life were all interdependent variables was frequently evoked during the public debate on family allowances between 1942 and 1944.[6] However, the heightened focus upon the importance of marriage and family to the social order was not simply a response to the supposed instability of family life during the war; many of the concerns voiced at the conclusion of war found their provenance in social trends which had emerged during the thirties. Thus, while the Canadian Youth Commission, one of the most concerted efforts to study the interconnection between employment, women's work, Christian belief, and family relations, was established in 1943, the actual impetus behind its existence hearkened back to concerns arising out of the Depression, when social scientists first uncovered the troubling connection between youth unemployment, the postponement of marriage, and the development of deviant sexual behaviour.[7]

Like many other commentators at the time, the authors of the various reports of the Youth Commission adumbrated a decidedly public conception of family, viewing it as the most fundamental cell of all social relationships. In *Young Canada and Religion*, published at the end of the war in 1945, the commission concluded that the home promoted "unselfishness and a sense of responsibility," and because of its singular ability to establish "Christian principles," the family was "the oustanding institution and the most powerful influence in society."[8] In drawing a direct connection between the character of the family and national well-being, the Youth Commission echoed a set of beliefs that had been frequently articulated in Canada since the turn of the twentieth century, when industrialization and the apparent increase in poverty and social inequality, together with the assertion of women's rights, were seen to be potent forces creating family disarray. In this way the statement offered by the United Church that the "life of the nation cannot rise above the level of life in its homes"[9] was not a novel one. Indeed, the Protestant churches were but one among a host of voices that stressed the home as a nursery for the development of notions of thrift, work, and responsibility which were so crucial to sustaining national economic progress and that placed an overwhelming emphasis upon the moral economy of the family with its important "emotional or personality functions."[10]

If the church's insistence that the primary function of the stable, Christian family was to forestall social collapse replicated a conservative ideological position indistinguishable from the broader culture, its preoccupation with the interconnectedness of marriage and nationalism was a direct response to the anti-Catholicism that was unleashed by the implementation of the Family Allowances Act of 1944. While anti-Catholicism has always simmered just beneath the surface of the Protestant creed, it was catapulted to the centre of public debate with the implementation of government family allowances. Old-style conservative nationalists erroneously believed that this social legislation would reward large Catholic families, and it had, in their estimation, the potential to trigger a birth explosion in Quebec of such enormous proportions that not only would the balance of political power within the dominion be irreversibly altered, but Protestantism would be overcome by the sheer numerical preponderance of Catholics.[11] Whereas Mackenzie King and the Liberals argued that welfare measures would bring about national unity by creating equal opportunities for all, Conservative thinkers such as the Reverend Edwin Silcox, Charlotte Whitton, and Premier George Drew adhered to an older vision of nationalism which conceived of the nation in terms of linguistic and religio-cultural traditions and thus saw in family allowances the spectre of destabilizing the balance between French and English Canada. Birth control, observed Silcox, would allay Protestant fears and create national unity, for it would "obviate the suspicion that one ethnic group was trying to outbreed the other." Family allowances, on the other hand, simply inflamed a pre-existing "cultural incompatibility" between Protestant and Catholic.[12] While he recognized that tension existed between the pervasive natalist propaganda, which equated family reproduction with economic prosperity and the necessity to combat Roman Catholic "totalitarian sacerdotalism"[13] perceived by mainline Protestantism, he nevertheless proclaimed the Malthusian argument that overpopulation was the main source of poverty and that an alternative to government relief and family allowances would be a rigorous system of birth control for all families, Protestant and Catholic.[14]

For Protestant leaders, family limitation and the containment of sex even within marriage had distinct social and political consequences.

Not only would a national – preferably, government – commitment to birth control solve the problem of the supposed fecundity of the Roman Catholic family, but by permitting families to relate the number of children they produced to the family budget, it would obviate the need for government intervention in family welfare. Social conservatives such as Whitton and Silcox abjured any state intervention in the family because, in their estimation, it allowed governments to tamper with the "natural" responsibility of the male breadwinner to support his dependents. Removing the state from the sphere of family self-sufficiency, Silcox also believed, would eliminate the modern emphasis upon economic over moral imperatives not only from the family circle but also from public discourse and national policy. Moreover, by conveniently demolishing what he castigated as the false god of economic security, he promoted birth control as the true prophylactic against the "acids of modernism," for it would inhibit the need and desire for married women to enter the workforce; not only would it serve to remove the spectre of want and the "lust" for material possessions, but at the same time it would tend to elevate the spiritual and emotional relationship between husband and wife by alleviating the burden of reproduction.[15]

What is compelling about the Protestant churches' response to the threat of Catholic ascendancy is that they did not simply recapitulate the nexus of family and nation which has come, in the common coin of historical discussion, to denote the conservative, complacent culture of the 1950s. Rather than reaffirming the long-held notion that the family was a public institution, anti-Catholicism was in fact the catalyst that decidedly shifted the whole bias of evangelicalism and the very question of the survival of the church towards the issue of reproduction and sexuality. By so doing, the United Church began to carve out a new sensibility in which the family looked inward to the private relationships of its members, rather than outward to the world of public duties and ideologies. By 1945 this movement from public to private was in its incipient stage, for leading commentators in the United Church began explicitly to proclaim that the family was a "divine institution" based on love and fidelity. However, some continued to maintain that personal values and individual rights must be preserved and exalted in the interests of sustaining democracy. The high-water mark of this congruence between family and society, private and public values, and the sacred and the secular, which formed the foundation of social evangelism, was represented by the wartime United Church Committee on Mixed Marriages, one of whose architects, the Reverend Hugh Dobson, reported that the "Family to a far greater degree than the State determines the shape of things to come and the nature of the civilization which is on the way ... If we can produce a democratic and Christian family life – Democracy and a Christian civilization to that degree is on the way!"[16] In this statement, Dobson unwittingly identified what would become the catalyst for the privatization of the family – namely, the modern state.

His insistence that an individual's experience within the family was a more direct route to achieving the Kingdom of God than her or his participation in the wider society represented a crucial break with the tradition of social Christianity which had formed the core of the United Church's outlook since the turn of the twentieth century. What was especially remarkable about this abrupt about-face undertaken by Dobson at the end of World War II was that he was one of the principal exemplars of the ideal of a full-orbed Christianity, in which evangelicalism and social reform constituted a seamless whole. In this formulation the state was perceived as part and parcel of a broader Christian culture and was thus regarded as an institution both complementary and subordinate to Protestant church authority.[17] This equipoise between church and state, in which both institutions functioned amicably within an interdependent culture and society characterized as "an organic whole," was breached with the launch of the Liberal government's social security legislation in 1943–44. In the view of conservative clergymen such as Edwin Silcox, by defining familial security and stability wholly in terms with economic well-being, the Beveridge and Marsh reports threatened to reconceive society as "an economic machine."[18] With the emergence of a social security state, not only did church leaders suddenly recognize that the goals of government were singularly economic and thus amoral in their attitudes in that they gave little recognition to the spiritual and emotional contexts of family life, but the weakening authority of Protestantism within the realms of government and social reform were forcefully brought home by the fact that the Liberal reconstruction and social security proposals had been devised by university-trained economic experts such as Leonard Marsh, F. Cyril James, A.E. Grauer, and George Davidson, who were indifferent, to the United Church's traditions in the field of family social policy.

Not only had Protestant church leaders been excluded from the inner circles of government policy-making during the war, but – more disturbingly for the influence of Protestantism in Canadian society as a whole – clergymen believed that, although in practice the creation of a cadre of elite experts, the modern security state had garnered such a large degree of mass support that, from their point of view, the emergence of the welfare state had been transformed into a broad cultural movement. It was this aspect of the welfare state that most threatened the cultural edifice of Christianity and prompted the United Church Committee to Arrange for a Forward Movement after the War to declare that "this is what makes the real crisis of our time a cultural as well as a moral one."[19] In many ways, the Liberal government's own propaganda that the very essence of the nation grew out of its offer of social security to the masses was immensely successful. What induced clergymen such as Silcox to equate family allowances with the demise of Protestantism and to rail against the "doctrinaire apotheosis of the common man,"[20] an attitude that ran directly counter to Protestant traditions of incorporating the aspirations of the Canadian working class, was that public debate over the Liberal welfare intitiative reinterpreted human personality and identity wholly in terms of government provision of material security. Indeed, much of the public commentary on social security involved finding the intellectual means by which to directly link the ideal of individual self-determination with the drastic expension of government authority. Thus Paul Martin, himself a former labour activist in Windsor, observed that the true realization of "man's personality"[21] lay with government welfare schemes. Not only did he maintain that the idea of "liberty for all"[22] was derived from economic variables, but he, like other defenders of the new social security state, postulated that, because the government was the only institution in modern society which could provide equal access to economic abundance, it alone defended the "democratic way of life."[23]

The way in which the crucible of welfare discussion redefined democracy as a economic creed was anathema to the principles of Protestant belief.[24] The emphasis that social security now placed on the rights of the masses to economic prosperity threatened the very essence of Christian endeavour. By rejecting the idea that individuals had a responsibility to society, it not only nullified the Christian ideal of social service, but it eviscerated the notion that all social relations flowed from an inherently moral core. Under this new dispensation, the individual had a prior right to government assistance irrespective of any obligation to society, a modern idea of citizenship that totally expunged any necessity for a moral community. It was for this reason that Silcox denounced "the arms of the paternal state" and its privileging of economic security, for not only had this virus of materialism begun to infect "even religious people," but it threatened "to take the place of salvation as the highest good."[25]

The creation of social security profoundly unsettled the Protestant mindset, not simply because legislation such as the Family Allowances Act appeared to diminish the conservative ideal of family self-sufficiency, but because post-war welfare, in identifying the state and economic security with the totality of social and cultural experience, seemed to the beleaguered leaders of the United Church completely to eradicate Christian ethics from Canadian culture. Unprecedented wartime state growth redefined the boundaries between church and state and compelled the United Church to retreat from culture into the precincts of a narrowly defined institutional church, guarded by the ramparts of a neo-orthodox theology which insisted upon a radical disjuncture between the secular and the sacred. The modern welfare state thus destroyed the concept of a full-orbed Christianity which had so well sustained the authority of Protestantism for four decades. In January 1943, the very month in which Leonard Marsh began to write his famous *Report on Social Security*, the United Church attempted to stave off the forces of economic materialism by establishing a Commission on Church, Nation and World Order. The stated objectives of this Protestant commission were to establish "the RIGHT of the Church to speak on political, economic and social problems."[26] However, that the church felt compelled to enunciate reasons why it had a claim upon the public sphere was telling evidence of the rapidity with which its broader cultural authority had been eroded during wartime.

The commission ultimately failed miserably in its attempt to temper the implications of Marsh's conclusions, for in their desire to counter what they termed "modern economic thinking" – "modern Beveridgian philosophy"[27] – church leaders were forced into an increasingly conservative bunker. In final analysis, the commission's report was feeble and merely restated the verities of nineteenth-century moral philosophy, which exalted the doctrine of self-help, and its remedy for the deficiencies of modern, mass culture was to retreat into a parody of Matthew Arnold's Oxbridgean elitism, in which the quest for high art and culture would evoke "the deep moral undertones"[28] of society. While church leaders hoped to deploy the commission as a means of propping up its message of social evangelism in order to deflate the popular movement for government social security, the commission's backlash against modernism propelled it into an ultimately defeatist attitude, in which its members declaimed against environmentalist explanations of poverty, concluding that the ills of society were the result of disobedience to God, a position unheard of in mainstream Protestantism since the palmy days of the age of atonement in the mid-nineteenth century.[29] In attempting to assuage the impact of "secular and materialistic" forces, one of its prominent lay advisers, Arthur Lower, who taught at United College, Winnipeg, actually protested against any intervention, whether by private or by public means, which might raise the general standard of living, claiming that "a facile materialism is no answer to life's problems," because history had taught that only through tragedy and struggle did individuals find spiritual awakening.[30]

The increasingly conservative direction of the United Church was not merely a temporary aberration, but gained force throughout the decade following the war. Indeed, by 1950 the Commission on Culture, a precursor to the Massey Commission, replete with a similarly elitist bias, released a report entitled *The Church and the Secular World*, in which it defined "our modern cultural crisis" as the result of forces that had divorced religious faith from "all other matters pertaining to human life." Although at specific junctures throughout the report the commission's members, who included Mary Q. Innis, John Irving, Northrop Frye, Professor John Line (a former member of the left-leaning Fellowship for a Christian Social Order), Lorne Pierce, and Principal Graham of United College, spoke of their desire to reintegrate science and religion, the secular and the sacred; but so completely had modern, conservative theologies such as neoorthodoxy come to define the United Church's identity that the commission could only declare that, because "in modern thinking God has been dethroned," the church's survival depended upon its standing "over-against the world."[31]

The fact that United Church leaders now maintained that there existed an unbridgeable gap between the secular and the sacred and had effectively relinquished the wider culture of politics, social reform, and education as a sphere of Christian influence constituted the intellectual watershed which was instrumental in compelling the Protestant churches to seek out a new relationship between the institutional church and the family. If the wellspring of the church's sustenance and the means of finding the Kingdom of God could no longer be ensured through an individual's participation in the larger society, a new vessel for Christian renewal must be sought. Since the symbol of modernism, according to Protestant thinkers, was the erosion of "personality" – this word occurs again and again throughout their perorations against the palliative of economic security, state control of marriage laws, the overweening demand for emotional stimulants, the increasing dependence upon the machine, economic and psychological definitions of history, and the growing depersonalization and alienation of modern urban living[32] – then it followed that the family must be exalted as the supreme focus for Christian endeavour. Indeed, if the solution to all modern ills rested upon the recoving of what was "uniquely personal,"[33] Protestant leaders concluded that the home was the haven for protection against secularization, for it was the only institution that emulated personality, freedom, and spiritual values, and only there were individuals free from the tyranny of utilitarian concerns.[34]

In 1946 the United Church's Commission on Christian Marriage and the Christian Home reported that "the life of the family is being threatened at its source by secularism and materialism, and that the Church has a great responsibility in combatting the disintegration of the home."[35] The preoccupation with marriage, family, and the domestic sphere and the tendency throughout the 1950s to reinterpret these as a private realm in which spiritual and emotional values flourished were not, as recent historians have suggested, a merely secular response to war and international instability; rather, the reconceptualization of the home as the "plumbline of those ultimate [spiritual] values"[36] was a creation of mainstream Protestantism, and its provenance lay in concerns peculiar to problems of religious faith in a secular world. If the supposed "acids of modernity" and the "secularization of modern social services"[37] were acting primarily upon the family, it was imperative that the United Church capture the domestic sphere and transform the cultural attributes of family life into the central redemptive force in society.

In the United Church discourse the family – and with it, the rights of personality – was commonly juxtaposed against the "absolute value of the state."[38] Increasingly, the family was seen as the singular pathway to faith, superior to even church worship itself. Having relinquished the public sphere to modern "barbarism,"[39] Protestant church leaders felt compelled to elevate the home to a position equivalent with the divine. Thus they concluded that the answers to all ultimate spiritual questions could be found only "through our own hearths,"[40] and homes were celebrated in terms of "domestic ties" that bound its individuals together with God.[41] As never before, the Kingdom of God was understood solely in terms of the home: Christ was the exemplary family-builder; the earthly family mirrored divine domesticity, in which heaven was the ideal home; God was the Father; the church was called the "Mother Church."[42] In short, spiritual efflorescence no longer occurred in the nexus between individual and community; rather, one's whole personal development and the accretion of piety occurred within through one's personal fulfillment and emotional satisfaction within the domestic sphere. Domestic security, however, was not the fruit of either maternal morality or the work ethic of the male breadwinner, the traditional gender divisions within the family. Rather, the idea of the world becoming a "household of faith"[43] was guaranteed by sexual intimacy. Increasingly, the ideal Christian and the wellspring of spirituality came to be wholly identified with the sexual act itself, for as Edwin Silcox concluded in his lecture "Toward a Philosophy of Christian Marriage," sex was the "most dynamic and constructive force in the building of personality and in the integration of society."[44]

Immediately after World War II the identification of sex as the central dynamic of society had not as yet taken hold in the United Church. As Arthur Lower, one of the prominent lay leaders of the Commission on Church, Nation and World Order, declared, marriage was still primarily a social act, and for this reason he adamantly opposed divorce on any grounds. Preoccupied with the growth of materialism and hedonism, Lower maintained that the ultimate test for divorce "must be social utility and the spiritual health of society rather than the fate of individuals."[45] Indeed, the report of this commission offered reluctant support to the principle of family allowances because at the very least they reinforced the notion that the family – and more particularly, parenthood – was important to the commonweal.[46] In the years immediately after the war the Protestant conception of the family studiously emphasized the production of children. Lower himself recommended that, at the very least, Protestant families should have three children and preferably five in order to keep abreast of the natural fecundity of Catholics.[47] Moreover, the moral education of children was seen as the centrepiece of evangelical renewal and the primary means of fighting "secular attitudes of life" during wartime.[48] The crucial role played by children in the conversion of adults was evoked in a Mother's Day poster for the Christian Education Advance movement which showed a young girl standing with her parents on their front doorstep and beseechingly asking, "Why don't you come with me to Sunday School?"[49]

This emphasis upon Christian nurture had, since the late nineteenth century, formed a large dimension of evangelical theology, wherein the primary relationship of faith was seen to be between God and his children.[50] In this traditional conceptualization of the Christian home, the family cleaved to the central figure of the moral mother, whose primary role was to use her maternal instincts to promote Christian values throughout society. In turn, the sexual needs of both men and women were considered to be antithetical to the development of spirituality and thus destructive of the Kingdom. This attitude generally held sway within the mainline Protestant denominations until World War II. Thus in 1940 Edwin Silcox protested against the growing tendency throughout society "to minimize procreation or the rearing of a family as the end of marriage, and to consider the question of sex-adjustment as a matter to be solved wholly by the individual according to his own tastes and with little or no sense of social responsibility."[51] Indeed, during wartime, Protestant commentators were somewhat preoccupied with the problem of sex containment for youth,[52] but this never formed a dominant theme even during the 1950s, when popular attitudes regarding sexual discipline were believed to be at their height. Certainly, Silcox, whose wife had recently died, did exclaim, after seeing a "bevy of buxom young girls" passing by with "their skirts swishing rhythmically with the vital abandon of their walking," that if "it weren't for the women, we could extend the Kingdom of God almost indefinitely."[53] And the 1939–40 United Church Committee on Mixed Marriages did warn against the modern emphasis upon "sex gratification" outside of marriage.[54]

What is remarkable about even these conservative commentators is that the concept of original sin occupied an increasingly minor place in their thought. While Silcox may have castigated Freudian psychology for insisting that sex was indispensable to an individual's psychological health,[55] he at the same time called upon the United Church to advance a new sex morality, one that would extoll sex as the primary "spiritual agency," and to reconceive marriage, not as a social unit of reproduction, but as the personification of personality, in which the physical sharing of husband and wife would in and of itself be symbolic of "Creative love itself." Thus, while marriage was deemed to be the means by which to regulate and channel these dangerous sexual appetites, the libido, thus constrained, was regarded as a determinedly spiritual force, while sexual union itself was reconceived as even "sacramental in its nature."[56]

What then prompted the leaders of opinion within the United Church to so drastically reinterpret the functions of marriage and family and the relationship between sex and spirituality? Male leaders in the church were driven to reconceptualize the purpose of marriage in terms of sexual satisfaction largely because they recognized that the future of the institution of marriage now centred upon the attitudes of women. While it is true that in the past the church had been receptive to feminist demands for the ideal of a companionate marriage where, through the use of birth control methods, women could exert control over male sexual passion,[57] the impetus to convert the home and family into a haven of emotional and sexual satisfaction for women reached its apex during the 1950s and was directly related to new patterns of women's work. Indeed, the creation of the United Church Commission on Marriage and Divorce in 1957 coincided with a drastic upsurge in married women's work. Although its stated aim was to find a means to reform the divorce laws and at the same time preserve the institution of marriage, its real intent was to reinstate the gender boundaries, which the commission's members believed had been transgressed by the modern, materialistic woman. Women's economic independence could be circumscribed, they believed, if their sexual freedom could be enhanced within the family. Post-war sexual containment was thus not an end in itself, as many have argued; rather, it was a means to the economic containment of married women.

As married women began to enter the workforce in increasingly large numbers by the late 1950s, churchmen recognized that the economic independence which work conferred on women created a vast potential for the option of divorce. Declarations such as that issued in 1954 by the Reverend Harriet Christie to the effect that her colleagues would just have to accept the fact that 20 per cent of the working population of Canada now consisted of women did little to allay the rising anxiety within the ranks of the United Church clergy.[58] Apart from a few references to the fact that families with working mothers could potentially produce more homosexuals,[59] the United Church objected to mothers working, not because this would detract from their moral and educative role, but because the fact of married women's work directly challenged the authority of their husbands. The reaction of the United Church during the 1950s contrasted volubly with the immediate post-war mentality as articulated by the Canadian Youth Commission, which inveighed against married women's work primarily because it caused delinquency and diminished the religious function of family life.[60] By the fifties the primary focus of concern was no longer the family as a unit, but the nature of the marital relationship itself.

That the authority of men was thought to reside in *both* the public sphere of the workplace and the private sphere of the home may be explained by a massive cultural shift which occurred in Canadian society following the Depression. Even though Protestant clergymen may have protested against the concentration that the modern welfare state appeared to place upon economic security, they neverthess accepted the reinterpretation of the ideal of separate spheres that came about during the thirties. As I have argued in *Engendering the State*, the traditional notion of separate spheres, in which the home was dominated by the moral mother and the workplace by the breadwinning father, was irrevocably transformed. By the end of the Depression, both the workplace and the home had been reconceived as legitimate domains of the breadwinner; but more signficantly, where the borderlines between gender spheres had previously allowed some space for women's work, following the crisis of the thirties the ideal male head of the household was intended to be the sole breadwinner in the family.[61] But what made the economic and social trends of the 1950s even more problematic for defenders of this patriarchal home was that for the first time married women were directly challenging the exclusivity of this male domain, which transcended both the public and the private. It is not without significance then that the United Church's Commission on Marriage and Divorce began to solicit reports from clergymen across the nation in 1958, the very year that witnessed the beginning of one of the severest economic recessions since the war.[62] But because male dominance in the family had become so thoroughly identified with a man's dominance in the workplace, any assaults on his status in the workplace were thought to automatically undermine his status in the home. Thus one submission to the Commission on Marriage and Divorce concluded that, because of the recent explosion in married women's paid labour, a man could not "carry his 'role' as earner in the home."[63]

What the convenors of the Commission on Marriage and Divorce feared, therefore, was the end of the patriarchal family, which had hitherto been guaranteed by the pre-eminent status of the husband. Between 1958 and 1966 the commissioners launched a massive research program in order to find ways to deflect the impact of women's work upon male authority in both the workplace and the home. As early as 1950 the report of the United Church Commission on Culture, *The Church and the Secular World*, had identified the problem of "a modern matriarchy,"[64] and by 1957 the spectre of "the difficult masculine wife"[65] had become a reality, as statistics indicated the awful truth that fully one-half of all women in the workforce were married.[66] Even female commissioners, such as Dr Patricia White, concluded that the fundamental problem posed by "modern society" revolved around the question of gender relations: "In today's society man has lost his former place of authority because, one by one his sources of authority have been taken over by other people and organizations. With the development of Government, Religion, Education and other things man has not the authority that he once had."[67]

While White praised the modern recognition of women in industry and extolled the work of sociologists and anthropologists because they concluded that women were indeed the stronger sex, her male colleagues reached very different conclusions. R.S. Hosking, for example, penned an article in the Toronto *Star Weekly* in 1959 called "What's the Matter with Father." In it he presented an analysis of modern social trends similar to White's. However, he blamed the changing status of men on the changing role of women. In fact, he, like other United Church clergymen, conceived of the post-war juggernaut of secularization as a decidedly gender-specific process. Indeed, Edwin Silcox equated modernity with matriarchy. In his peroration "The Menace of Modernity to Christian Life," he concluded that the battleground between the secular and the sacred, between material and spiritual values, was merely a reflection of a deeper warfare between biology and economics. That pagan ethics were in the ascendancy Silcox attributed to the disturbing new reality of the working "Magna Mater."[68] For the United Church clergy, then, there was no greater symbol of the modern excesses of materialism and the consequent loss of spiritual values than the trend towards married women's work.[69] The increasing depersonalization of life, the obsession with material things, birth control, and the emphasis on personal satisfaction were attributed to women – in particular, their temptation to enter the workplace. The congruence many believed existed between women's desires and modern materialism was clearly enunciated by Hosking. He contended that the primary culprit in the post-war disequilibrium of traditional gender spheres was the modern domestic appliance. Not only did the purchasing of these appliances fuel the desire for more consumer items, but the consequent pressure upon the family budget caused friction between husband and wife. Moreover, in saving women's labour in the home, appliances produced an abundance of leisure time for then, which caused wives to become bored and dissatified with their homes, thus propelling them to seek personal satisfaction in the workplace.[70]

It followed from these assumptions that women's sexual gratification was the key to overcoming the temptations of material gratification and the desire for economic independence. What better way to ensure that the sexes are once again "clearly defined" than through the experience of sex itself.[71] Male clergymen believed that establishing an ideal of equality through difference within the sexual relationship would solve the problem of the economic disequilibrium between the sexes outside the home. Thus, while the United Church Commission on Marriage and Divorce addressed the issue of sexual containment among single young people, both heterosexual and homosexual,[72] its real focus was upon the "fundamental satisfactions"[73] experienced by adults within marriage. The enunciation of the modern democratic family, in which husbands and wives were equal but separate in their sexual and emotional temperaments, thus became the means by which the patriarchal family could be defended and the status of the sole, male breadwinner preserved. Ideally, if women were treated as equals within the sexual relationship, thus completing their sense of personal achievement and individuality, male clergymen were convinced, the need to seek economic independence would be negated. This was what was meant when contributors to the Commission on Marriage and Divorce such as R.S. Hosking and Leonard Marsh stated that a new balance had to be found between freedom and discipline within the Canadian family: women were to be given unlimited personal freedom in terms of sexual and emotional satisfaction so that men could regain their role as sole provider and thus rediscover their own sense of authority.[74]

Because the family no longer nourished traditional gender divisions between work and home, sex became the only means for men and women to "discover the meaning of the manhood and womanhood through the various relations in which they fulfil one another."[75] The modern Canadian family was no longer united by the economic contribution of all its members; rather, its interdependent nature flowed from the "personal fellowship" of the husband and wife alone, in which sex was the dynamic for "creating a new union between man and woman."[76] What the members of the Commission on Marriage and Divorce wished to make abundantly clear, however, was that the personality of each partner was not diminished, for in the modern theology in which "sex is sacred," sex became a substitute for evangelical faith in so far as it accentuated "personality and self-realization."[77] Nevertheless, sexual intercourse was believed to be the highest sacramental act, where through "self-abandonment"[78] one found a higher "spiritual integrity"[79] with God. Churchmen, anxious to proffer a new prescription for marriage that would salve women's desire for equality and independence and did not involve economic competition with men, declared that sexual relations must reflect the notion that a woman was a "person with rights."[80] They adamantly rejected the traditional master-servant concept of the marital relationship and maintained that henceforth the basis of marriage must be sexual intercourse, not for procreative purposes, but as an activity in which the consent of the wife was imperative and which would ideally lead to "personal satisfaction"[81] and amplify her sense of individuality, freedom, and creativity. Sexual containment within marriage was an avenue of woman's assertiveness and equality because she, and not the husband, determined the sexual relationship. However, the personal gratification she derived from an equal sexual relationship within marriage was also touted as a relief from the cultural poverty of the modern, technologically driven home and as the spiritual counterpoint to the alienation of modern industrial automation. Sex was thus the surest pathway that would lead the modern woman back to the welcoming family circle.

The novelty of such a positive revalorization of sex, especially a new concern with the importance of female sexuality, within the official thinking of the United Church should not be underestimated. It did not simply constitute an extension of pre-war ideals of "companionate marriage" or the interest of certain clerics such as Edwin Silcox in the question of birth control, evident in the 1930s. While a number

of American historians began in the 1980s to insist that, within the
wider culture, positive views of female sexuality became the mainstream in the 1920s and 1930s, reversing the nineteenth-century association of sexuality with maleness,[82] a more nuanced revisionism has
suggested serious qualifications to this chronology. Indeed, it would
seem that in both Britain and the United States any severing of female
sexuality from reproduction did not permeate the social strata beyond rather limited segments of upper-middle-class, urban bohemi-
ans or Ivy League college youth before the 1940s. Working-class
attitudes firmly condemned casual sex, and there was little evidence
for a widespread culturally accepted notion that marriage was based
solely on sex.[83] Likewise, the historical definition of "companionate
marriage," promoted by the Protestant churches in the era before
World War II, is itself the subject of considerable misunderstanding.[84]
Companionate marriage had its origins in an insistence on egalitarian
and emotional compatibility, and it was only in the 1930s that sexual
compatibility was added to this equation,[85] a view that did not reach
Canada until after World War II. More significantly, a commitment to
birth control, usually regarded as the harbinger of more positive notions of female sexuality, seems not to have fulfilled this function in
the Canadian Protestant churches. Until 1932 the United Church remained officially committed to large families, and although by the
later 1930s the church could speak in terms of "voluntary parenthood," there seems to have been little connection between birth control and acceptance of sexual pleasure. In the immediate post-war
period there was something of a backlash against the idea of birth
control in some sections of the United Church, and although clearly
liberal views prevailed by the early 1960s, with the United Church
well in advance of the Anglican Church on such matters, the impetus
from Anglicans and other Protestants seems not to have stemmed
from the need to accommodate the notion of female sexual desire but,
rather, from concerns over global overpopulation.[86]

While the impetus behind the United Church's Commission on
Marriage and Divorce to regularize the concept of the "two-sex society"[87] was decidedly conservative, the underlying implications were
much more liberal in orientation and led rapidly to the jettisoning of
traditional standards of morality and a new sexual ethic for Canadian
society. Where old-style evangelicals continued to associate the sins
of the flesh with the devil,[88] the younger cadre of United Church clergymen asserted the view that sexual intercourse itself was a sacred
act. If sexual behaviour was reinterpreted as an actual positive force,
"especially but not exclusively within marriage,"[89] it was difficult to
maintain the older view that sex was immoral. Moreover, because

this new theology of sex was so identified with female desire for emotional satisfaction, personal development, and the woman's very sense of individuality, it was likewise impossible to sustain the conception of woman as the temptress. In 1958 United Church clergymen began to warn against sermons that superficially drew an equation between "sin and sins of the flesh."[90] By 1960 the whole Protestant tradition of moral theology had been recast. "Christianity at its best," commented one clergyman, "has never considered the human body evil ... Sex, being part of the order of God's creation, is good and not evil."[91] By conceiving of sex as a divine gift and the body as a thing to be enjoyed, clergymen were compelled to abandon the very concept of original sin and to maintain that the real message of Genesis was that Adam and Eve had simply disobeyed God.[92] Thus promiscuity and homosexuality were now deemed to be merely symptoms of "a disturbed personality," which could be easily forgiven and remedied through Christian counselling.[93] Even the very notion of monogamy came under scrutiny by clergymen such the young John Webster Grant, who castigated the first drafts of the report of the Commission on Marriage and Divorce for their "pious spirituality" and called for the Scriptures to be reinterpreted in terms of "the newest discoveries in the social sciences," which postulated that the concepts of monogamy and sexual chastity were not eternal moral verities but merely cultural constructs relative to time and place.[94]

By 1960 moral relativism had become the watchword of the new theology of the United Church. Driven by the increasing emphasis that Protestantism placed upon "the freedom of the individual,"[95] church leaders in turn dropped the traditional moral sanctions against divorce. By 1966, in their landmark submission to the Special Join Committee of the Senate and House of Commons on Divorce, United Church leaders were no long arguing that divorce was a "social disease"[96] but, rather, that the inability to dissolve a marriage was the main source of "festering sores in our society and a threat to the sanctity of marriage."[97] The very basis of the church's argument for widening the grounds for divorce rested upon two fundamental beliefs: that sexual incompatibility was the primary cause for marital breakdown and that marriage was a private and not a social contract. As Dr Thomas G. Donnelly noted in 1958, "Certainly, marriage is increasingly being regarded as an area of private choice where the *collective* concern that marriage as an institution be stable is yielding to the *individual* that marriage be rich, rewarding and fulfilling to each of the two participants separately."[98] Some clergymen may have been more comfortable with the accepted view that marriage was a public matter for the state, but as the Reverend R.C. Chalmers hastened to add, neither Calvin nor Luther had envisioned "our secular state."[99] Marriage was now the arena of "personal and domestic morals,"[100] a position lent a scriptural gloss by the work of the neo-orthodox theologians Karl Barth and Emil Brunner, who insisted that marriage was a covenant between two individuals before God and thus a matter wholly outside the purview of public legal sanctions.[101] From this position, clergymen were easily led to the conclusion that all marriages could be dissolved by mutual consent. But more problematical still, the overwhelming preoccupation of the United Church with shoring up the institution of marriage and the increasing need to assert the relevance of the church to those who had been separated and divorced[102] led them to eviscerate the concept of sin from sex and marriage. This development in turn ineluctably propelled the United Church to evacuate the core of Protestant evangelicalism, which rested upon the notion of universal moral principles and the ever-present reality of sin from which the individual must be redeemed, and to embrace Protestant modernism, in which "the conscience of the sincere individual"[103] remained the fundamental anchor of Christian commitment. By 1966, after two hundred years of forming the core of Methodist and Presbyterian theology, evangelicalism in mainline Protestantism foundered upon the rock of modern gender identities and human sexuality.

The discourse on family that occurred immediately after World War II, in which domestic ties were believed to mirror the broader social order, was not emblematic of cultural attitudes throughout the 1950s. But as the debates about family within the United Church reveal, there was a perceptible disjuncture between the concerns of wartime culture, which had focused upon the problem of juvenile delinquency and the sexual containment of teenagers and had celebrated the family as a primarily reproductive unit, and those of the mid-1950s, in which the family had been reinterpreted as a distinctly private entity, bereft of any public significance, in which the personal emotional and sexual relationship between husband and wife was the central pillar. Not only has this essay called into question the prevailing historical characterization of the 1950s in positing that it was a period of considerable cultural variegation and considerable social flux, but it has also challenged the notion that Canadian discussions on family life were but an echo of American trends. The retreat towards the sexually charged, private family was not hastened by the threat posed by international Cold War politics in a nuclear age, nor was the sexual revolution the consequence of youth culture, feminism, or a lifestyle defined by the Kinsey Report.[104] Rather, the reformulation of the Canadian family as a haven of spiritual and moral nourishment occurred within the context of the precipitous growth of the "secular" welfare state, while the exaltation of sex as a primarily sacramental act was intended to offset the transgression of gender boundaries caused by the new social reality of married women's work in the rapidly expanding consumer economy of the late 1950s.

Although the motivation underlying the position of the United Church regarding marriage and sex was a conservative one, its preoccupation with reasserting the status of the sole, male breadwinner led to a paradoxical view that equated personal freedom with sexual fulfillment, thus unleashing a dynamic which created a mindset in mainstream culture that actually facilitated something of a groundswell of sympathy for the radical youth culture of the 1960s, with its open celebration of sexuality.[105] Cultural change was thus not simply the reflection of the baby-boom generation, as Doug Owram has contended, for cultural innovation also occurred in the more traditional corridors of mainstream Protestantism. Our contemporary cultural attitudes did not suddenly appear on the scene in the 1960s, but were the by-products of a peculiar alchemy of conservative reaction to modern bureaucratic collectivism, secularization, and consumerism, questions that revolved around the issue of rapidly changing gender identities between adults within marriage. This response, in turn, precipitated a new theological construct whose emphasis upon sex as the preserve of individual identity was distilled into a clearly modernist sensibility.

NOTES

1 United Church of Canada, *Report of the Commission on Christian Marriage and the Christian Home* (Board of Evangelism and Social Service, 1946), 132.
2 See, for example, Doug Owram, *Born at the Right Time: A History of the Baby Boom Generation* (Toronto: University of Toronto Press, 1996), 262.
3 Ibid., 90; Elaine Tyler May, *Homeward Bound: American Families in the Cold War Era* (New York: Basic Books Inc., 1988); Wini Breines, *Young, White and Miserable: Growing Up Female in the Fifties* (Boston: Beacon Press, 1992); Veronica Strong-Boag, "Home Dreams: Women and the Suburban Experiment in Canada, 1945–60," *Canadian Historical Review* 62 (December 1991) 5–25; Strong-Boag, "Canada's Wage-Earning Wives and the Construction of the Middle Class, 1945–60," *Journal of Canadian Studies* 29 (1994); Valerie J. Korinek, "Mrs. Chatelaine vs. 'Mrs. Slob': Contestants, Correspondants and the *Chatelaine* Community in Action,

1961–1969," *Journal of the Canadian Historical Association* 7 (1996): 251–76. For a more nuanced perspective on this period, see Neil Sutherland, *Growing Up: Childhood in Canada from the Great War to the Age of Television* (Toronto: University of Toronto Press, 1997); and Joan Sangster, *Earning Respect: The Lives of Working Women in Small-Town Ontario, 1920–1960* (Toronto: University of Toronto Press, 1995). See also the essays in Joy Parr, ed., *A Diversity of Women: Ontario, 1945–1980* (Toronto: University of Toronto Press, 1995); John Murphy, "Shaping the Cold War Family," *Australian Historical Studies* 26 (October 1995): 566; and Gaile McGregor, "Domestic Blitz: A Revisionist History of the Fifties," *American Studies* 34 (spring 1993): 5–33. For a critique of the views of those historians who have adopted Betty Friedan's evaluation of post-war domesticity as a conservative phenomenon, see Joanne Meyerowitz, "Beyond the Feminine Mystique: A Reassessment of Postwar Mass Culture 1946–1958," *Journal of American History* 79 (March 1993): 1455–82.

4 For a discussion of these themes, see Annalee Golz, "Family Matters: The Canadian Family and the State in the Postwar Period," *Left History* 1 (1993): 9–49; Owram, *Born at the Right Time*, 31–53; May, *Homeward Bound*; Mariana Valverde, "Building Anti-Delinquent Communities: Morality, Gender, and Generation in the City," in Parr, ed., *A Diversity of Women*, 19–45; Nancy Christie, *Engendering the State: Family, Work, and Welfare in Canada, 1900–1945* (Toronto: University of Toronto Press, 2000), chapter "Reconstructing Families"; Owram, "Canadian Domesticity in the Post-war Era," in Peter Neary and J.L. Granatstein, eds., *The Veterans Charter and Post-World War II Canada* (Montreal and Kingston: McGill-Queen's University Press, 1998), 205–23.

5 See, Christie, *Engendering the State*, chapter 3.

6 For a discussion of this theme, see Christie, *Engendering the State*, .

7 H.A. Weir, "Unemployed Youth," in L. Richter, ed., *Canada's Unemployment Problem* (Toronto: MacMillan, 1939), 159–60. See also United Church Archives UCA), Silcox Papers, 8: 36, "Youth's Eye View of Some Problems of Getting Married," YMCA, 1936, in which Silcox connects the "sublimation of the sexual impulse" caused by delayed marriage in the thirties to the kind of mass psychosis that gave rise to fascism. By the end of the war he was arguing that democracy and national unity depended upon the containment of sex.

8 Canadian Youth Commission, *Young Canada and Religion* (Toronto: Ryerson Press, 1945), 72.

9 E. Gilmour Smith, "The Christian Home," *United Church Observer*, 1 July 1945, 9.

10 Canadian Youth Commission, *Youth, Marriage and the Family* (Toronto: Ryerson Press, 1948), 28. See also Owram, *Born at the Right Time*, 134.

11 Silcox had been an advocate of Catholic-Protestant cooperation prior to the Family Allowances Act of 1944. See Silcox, "Religious Peace in Canada," *Food for Thought* 11 (October 1941). For the Protestant backlash against the Catholic church, see UCA, Inter-Church Committee in Protestant-Roman Catholic Relations (which equated Catholicism with communism), Watson Kirkconnell to Rev. Dr H.H. Bingham, 10 November 1945. See also UCA, United Church Committee on Mixed Marriages, 1939–40. Mixed marriages were castigated as hastening secularization, loss of faith, and an anti-religious climate within the home. See also UCA, Commission on Marriage and Divorce, 2: 21, Rev. John Shearman, "Mixed Marriages in Quebec," April 1959.

12 UCA, Silcox Papers, 11:5, Silcox to Arthur Maheux, Archives de Séminaires de Québec, 8 July 1942; 9:20, Silcox, "Will Canada Split," 10 September 1944.

13 Ibid., 11:5, Philip Quebec to Silcox, 17 November 1941; Silcox to Rev. Carrington, 8 December 1941. On the economic necessity for post-war population growth, see Silcox, "Population Problems," Anglican Church of Canada, Council of Social Service, *Bulletin*, 15 October 1941. Silcox was a great advocate of British immigration.

14 Silcox, "Family Allowances and the Population Question", *Saturday Night*, 23 October 1943. Silcox was a frequent contributor to this popular journal largely because the father of its editor, B.K. Sandwell, a Congregational minister, had worked alongside Silcox's father in Toronto.

15 Silcox, "Birth Control: Bane or Blessing," *New Outlook*, 15 January 1937, 29; Silcox, "What is Wealth and Poverty?" *Mentor*, 1938; UCA, Silcox Papers, 8:45, "Transcript of Mr. Silcox's Testimony during the Eastview Trial, 1937," 17.

16 UCA, United Church Committee on Mixed Marriages, 1939–40, 1: 1, Hugh Dobson to J.R. Mutchmor, 20 June 1939.

17 Nancy Christie and Michael Gauvreau, *A Full-Orbed Christianity: The Protestant Churches and Social Welfare in Canada, 1900–1940* (Montreal: McGill-Queen's University Press, 1996), 197–223.

18 UCA, Silcox Papers, 13: 16, "Private Enterprise and Social Ownership of Control," in *Private and Public Enterprise* (Church of England publication), no. 113 (10 April 1944): 5.

19 UCA, Committee to Arrange for a Forward Movement after the War, 1:2, *Report of Committee* (n.p).

20 Silcox, "Family Allowances and the Population Question," *Saturday Night*, 23 October 1943, 1.

21 Paul Martin, *Labour's Post-War World* (Toronto: Canadian Institute of International Affairs and Canadian Association for Adult Education, 1945), 3, 7–8, 12–13.

22 Ibid.

23 Advertisement for lipstick, *Canadian Home Journal*, October 1943, 25. For a larger discussion of the modern democratic state, see Christie, *Engendering the State*, chapter "Reconstructing Families."

24 UCA, Silcox Papers, 13: 1, Silcox, "Why Anti-Semites Hate Christ: A Study in Hitleresque Pathology," *Churchman*, 1 January 1941, 13; 13:8, Silcox, *The Atlantic Charter and Christian Concern* (Church of England pamphlet, 14 February 1942), 4.

25 Ibid., 5:15, "Living Dangerously," CBC Radio Pulpit, 27 March 1937.

26 UCA, United Church Commission on Church, Nation and World Order, 1: 3, C.E. Silcox, "Memorandum," 11 October 1943, 1.

27 Ibid., 1:8, Hugh Wolfenden to Gordon A. Sisco, 2 September 1943.

28 Ibid., 1:3, Silcox, "Memorandum," 11 October 1943, 3.

29 For a discussion of social and economic attitudes typical of this older evangelicalism, see Boyd Hilton, *The Age of Atonement* (Oxford: Oxford University Press, 1988).

30 UCA, Commission on Church, Nation and World Order, 1: 10, Arthur Lower, "Memorandum re: the Basic Memorandum," 9 August 1943; 1:7, Lower to Sisco, 25 March 1943.

31 United Church, Commission on Culture, *The Church and the Secular World* (Board of Evangelism and Social Service, 1950), vii, 34, 70.

32 UCA, Silcox Papers, 9: 28, Silcox, "The Interest of the Christian Churches in Marriage and the Home," *Home and School Review* (n.d.), 2.

33 Commission on Culture, *The Church and the Secular World*, 70.

34 United Church, *Report of the Commission on Christian Marriage and the Christian Home* (1946), 116; Anglican Church, *Social Service Annual Report* (1958), 18; UCA, Silcox Papers, 9:19, Silcox, "Canadian Churches and Postwar Reconstruction," *Religion and Life*, 1943, 3.

35 United Church, *Report of the Commission on Christian Marriage and the Christian Home*, 106.

36 Ibid., 111.

37 UCA, Commission on Christian Marriage and the Christian Home, 1.1, "Untitled Memorandum," 1946.

38 UCA, Silcox Papers, 9: 19, "Canadian Churches and Postwar Reconstruction," *Religion and Life*, 1943, n.p.

39 Commission on Culture, *The Church and the Secular World*, 70.

40 UCA, Silcox Papers, 9: 29, "Toward a Philosophy of Christian Marriage," 22 January 1946, 4.

41 Ibid., "The Menace of Modernity to Christian Life" (n.d.), 11.

42 Anglican Church of Canada, *Social Service Annual Report*, 1958, 17; UCA, Silcox Papers, 9:28, "The Interest of the Christian Churches in Marriage and the Home," 2; United Church, *Report of the Commission on Christian Marriage and the Christian Home*, 118.

43 UCA, Silcox Papers, 9:28, "The Interest of the Christian Churches in Marriage and the Home," 2.

44 Ibid., , 9:29, "Toward a Philosophy of Christian Marriage," 22 January 1946, 3.

45 UCA, Commission on Church, Nation and World Order, 2: 15, Lower, "Comments and Suggestions on the Ninth Draft," 2.

46 United Church, *Church, Nation and World Order: A Report of the Commission on Church, Nation and World Order* (Board of Evangelism and Social Service, 1944), 25, 28. Although it was a minority perspective by the 1950s, a few Protestant clergymen still linked the family with the creation of national values. See UCA, Commission on Marriage and Divorce, 4: 38, F.W.L. Bailey, "Why Divorce," 1953.

47 UCA, Commission on Church, Nation and World Order, 2:15, Lower, "Comments and Suggestions on the Ninth Draft," 2.

48 "Backing Up the Sunday School," *United Church Observer*, 1 Novenber 1940; "Prayer for the Children," *United Church Observer*, 15 January 1941.

49 "Mother's Day Poster," *United Church Observer*, 1 May 1942, 5.

50 See Marguerite Van Die, *An Evangelical Mind: Nathanael Burwash and the Methodist Tradition in Canada, 1839–1918* (Montreal and Kingston: McGill-Queen's University Press, 1989); Neil Semple, *The Lord's Dominion: The History of Canadian Methodism* (Montreal and Kingston: McGill-Queen's University Press, 1996); UCA, Commission on Marriage and Divorce, 4: 39, "The Meaning and Responsibility of Christian Marriage," 1932, 6.

51 UCA, Silcox Papers, 9: 13, "Some Moral Aspects of Birth Control," 1940, 5.

52 Muriel Jacobson, "The Church and the Teenage Girl," *United Church Observer*, 1 August 1942, 15, 18. There were very few examples of a discourse regarding sexual containment, and most of these were written during wartime and not into the 1950s. Indeed, one later article, "Should Teen-Agers Go Steady?" (*United Church Observer*, 1 July 1958, 7), argued that early teenage dating made for healthier and happier marriages. For a contrasting view on the fifties discourse on teenage sex, see May, *Homeward Bound*, 94, 101.

53 UCA, Silcox Papers, 5:12, "Possibilities and Limitations of Social Planning in a Dynamic World," speech to Winnipeg Central Council of Social Agencies, 21 October 1935.

54 UCA, Committee on Mixed Marriages, "The Meaning and Responsibilities of Christian Marriage," 1940; Social Service Council of Canada, "The Trend of Family Life and Marriage in Our Times," n.d., 27. By war's end the United Church, though generally supportive of the concept of birth control, also feared that it would unleash a popular emphasis upon sex.

55 UCA, Silcox Papers, 9: 4, Silcox, "The Oxford Group Movement," 31 July 1934. Silcox opposed this movement because he believed that it led to public declarations of sexual improprieties.

56 Ibid., 9:13, Silcox, "Some Moral Aspects of Birth Control," 1940, 5–6; 5:22, Silcox, "Constructive Birth Control and Tomorrow's Children," January 1940, 14–15.

57 Ibid., 9:13, "Some Moral Aspects of Birth Control,", 18; UCA, Committee on Mixed Marriages, 1:4, "Birth Control and Sterilization."

58 UCA, Rev. Harriet K. Christie Papers, 1: 23, "Men and Women in the Church," 1954. See also "Canada's Working Women," *Globe and Mail Magazine*, 20 May 1961; United Church, *Married Women Working: Report of the Commission on the Gainful Employment of Married Women* (1962); and Canadian Association for Adult Education, *The Real World of Women* (1967).

59 UCA, Commission on Marriage and Divorce, 3:35, J. Alex Edmison, National Parole Board, to Rev. Frank Morgan, 15 February 1961, 3; 2:20, W.E. Boothroyd, "Homosexuality in Marriage," 3.

60 National Archives of Canada (NA), MG28 I 11, Canadian Youth Commission, series C-7, vol. 42, file "Family Report," Margaret S. Davis to Dr S.R. Laycock, University of Saskatchewan, 12 April 1946, R.E.G. Davis to Eugene Forsey, director of research, Canadian Congress of Labour, 1 February 1946; ibid., file "Effects of War on Family Life," L.W. Skey to R.E.G. Davis, 21 March 1947, "Findings of the Youth and Family discussion held in Budge Hall, Central Y.M.C.A., Westmount," 21 October 1944, "Brief Submitted by Winnipeg Group on Family Life," 26 September, 1944.

61 Christie, *Engendering the State*, chap. 6, "'Not Only a Living Wage, but a Family Wage."

62 On the connection between women's work and unemployment among men, see Jean Shilton, "Prudence in the Parsonage," *United Church Observer*, 1 May 1957; R.B. Craig, "A Married Woman's Place Is in the Home," *United Church Observer*, 1 November 1957; "On Unemployment," *United Church Observer*, 15 March 1959.

63 UCA, Commission on Marriage and Divorce, 3: 28, Canadian Welfare Council, "Family Desertion," May 1961, 3. On post-war North American concerns to define a domestic, rather than a purely economic, role for fathers, see Jessica Weiss, "Making Room for Fathers: Men, Women and Parenting in the United States, 1945–1980," in Laura McCall and Donald Yacovone, eds., *A Shared Experience: Men, Women, and the History of Gender* (New York: New York University Press, 1998), 359; Robert L. Griswold, *Fatherhood in America* (New York: Basic Books, 1993), 189; and Robert Rutherdale, "Fatherhood, Masculinity, and the Good Life during Canada's Baby Boom, 1945–1965," *Journal of Family History* 24.3 (July 1999): 351–73.

64 Commission on Culture, *The Church and the Secular World*, 33.

65 United Church, *Report of the Secretaries of the Board of Evangelism and Social Service* (1957), 8. This phrase was coined by the Reverend J.R. Mutchmor.

66 United Church, *Married Women Working* 9. See also Canadian Association for Adult Education, *The Real World of Women*, 119, 128, which reported that in 1961 fully 47 per cent of married women were in the workforce and that wives had become at the very least "partial breadwinners." Significantly, this publication noted that there was no significant increase in juvenile delinquency as a result, showing the length of the route travelled since World War II.

67 UCA, Commission on Marriage and Divorce, 2:22, Dr Patricia White and R.S. Hosking, "The Changing Role of Women in Modern Society," 2 November 1959.

68 UCA, Silcox Papers, 9: 39, "The Menace of Modernity to Christian Life," 1946, 17.

69 Since the war there had been a constant campaign in various United Church commissions against the increasing trend of married women in the workplace. See UCA, Commission on the Ministries of Women, which aimed to undo the ten-year experiment in women's ordination. There was considerable response from women in the church on these questions. See ibid., 1.2, Sisco to Marion Hilliard, 18 January, 1947; Gerturde L. Brooks to Gordon Sisco, 15 February 1947; UCA, Commission on Church, Nation and World Order, 1.9, Mary A. Endicott to Sisco, 11 March, 1944.

70 R.S. Hosking, "What's the Matter with Father," *Star Weekly*, 21 November, 1959; UCA, Commission on Marriage and Divorce, 1.6, Dr R.S. Hosking, "The Family in Modern Society," 12 January 1960, n.p.; 2:22, Dr W.G. Scott, "The Changing Role of Women"; 3:28, "Family Desertion," 4.

71 UCA, Commission on Marriage and Divorce, 2:25, James Anderson, "Charts on the Psycho-Sexual Differences between Men and Women"; College of Worcester, Department of Sociology, "Preparation for Marriage," Course 366.

72 The issue of homosexuality formed a central point of departure, but the emphasis placed by some of the members of the commission upon this theme was not without controversy, since many clergymen did not believe this was a crucial dimension of the modern issue of marriage and divorce. See UCA, Commission on Marriage and Divorce, 1:2 "Minutes," 16–17 June 1959. The reorientation from marriage for reproduction towards an ideal of personal fulfillment did at the very least move the church towards the conclusion that homosexuality was not immoral. See ibid., 1:7, "A Christian Understanding of Marriage and Sex," 2.; 2:20, W.E. Boothroyd, "Homosexuality and Marriage." This position caused great controversay; see ibid., 3:35, J. Alex Edmison, National Parole Board, to Rev. Frank Morgan, 15 February 1961.

73 UCA, Commission on Marriage and Divorce, 2:18, Morrison Kelly, "Marriage and Divorce," 9 October 1958, 4.

74 Ibid., 1.6, R.S. Hosking, "The Family in Modern Society," 12 January 1960; 1:4, Minutes, 11–12 April 1961, 150. For the view that the patriarchal family was in decline, see C.W. Topping, "The Egalitarian Family as a Fundamental Invention, " *Canadian Journal of Economics and Political Science* 8 (1942): 598.

75 UCA, Commission on Marriage and Divorce, 1:7, "A Christian Understanding of Marriage and Sex," 8 January 1958, 7; 2:17, E.S. Lautenslager, "A Re-Study of Christian Marriage and Divorce," n.d., 3.

76 Ibid., 3:28, "North American Conference on Church and Family," 30 April–5 May 1961; 1:7, "A Christian Understanding of Marriage and Sex," 8 January 1958, 7.

77 United Church, *Report of the Commission on Christian Marriage and the Christian Home*, 108; UCA, Commission on Marriage and Divorce, 2:17, Rev. R.H.N. Davidson, "Christian Marriage and Divorce," July 1958, 11.

78 UCA, Commission on Marriage and Divorce, 1:7, "A Christian Understanding of Marriage and Sex," 7.

79 Ibid., 1:6, "First Draft of Report," 29 March 1960, n.p.

80 Ibid., 2:20, R.S. Hosking, "The Changing Role of Women," 28 January 1959, 2; 2:17, Hosking, "Standards of Morality," July 1958.

81 Ibid., 2:19, Patricia White, "Men and Women in Society," January 1960, 1; 1:7, "A Christian Understanding of Marriage and Sex," 8 January 1958, 7–8; 1:7, Dr W.E. Boothroyd, "Marriage and Interpersonal Relationships," 125–6; 4:39, David W. Gaulke, "A Christian Approach to Sex in Marriage," 1959, 1.

82 Christina Simmons, "Modern Sexuality and the Myth of Victorian Repression," in Barbara Melosh, ed., *Gender and American History since 1890* (London and New York: Routledge, 1993), 17; Carroll Smith-Rosenberg, "The Body Politic," in Elizabeth Weed, ed., *Coming to Terms: Feminism, Theory, Politics* (New York: Routledge, 1989), 109; Anita Grossman, "The New Woman and the Rationalization of Sexuality in Weimar Germany," in Ann Sitow, Christine Stansell, and Sharon Thompson, eds., *The Politics of Sexuality* (New York: Monthly Review Press, 1983), 158; Barbara Epstein, "Family, Sexual Morality, and Popular Movements in Turn-of-the-Century America," in Sitow, Stansell, and Thompson, *The Politics of Sexuality*. On nineteenth-century notions of female asexuality, see Nancy Cott, "Passionless: An Interpretation of Victorian Sexual Ideology, 1790–1850," *Signs* 4 (1973) Carl Degler, *At Odds: Women and the Family in America from the Revolution to the Present* (New York: Oxford University Press, 1980); and Judith Walkowitz, *City of Dreadful Delight: Narratives of Sexual Danger in Late-Victorian London* (Chicago: University of Chicago Press, 1992).

83 John D'Emilio and Estelle B. Freedman, *Intimate Matters: A History of Sexuality in America* (New York: Harper and Row, 1988), 271; Mary Jo Maynes,

Taking the Hard Road: Life Course in French and German Women's Autobiographies in the Era of Industrialization (Chapel Hill and London: University of North Carolina Press, 1995), 136–41; Ellen Holtzman, "The Pursuit of Married Love: Women's Attitudes toward Sexuality and Marriage in Great Britain, 1918–1939," *Journal of Social History* 16 (winter 1982): 42; Cate Haste, *Rules of Desire: Sex in Britain, World War 1 to the Present* (London: Chatto & Windus, 1992).

84 A misunderstanding perpetuated most recently in Canada by Mary Louise Adams in *The Trouble with Normal: Postwar Youth and the Making of Heterosexuality* (Toronto: University of Toronto Press, 1997), 9.

85 D'Emilio and Freedman, *Intimate Matters*, 266. In the Canadian context, it is significant that even the lectures of Beatrice Brigden to groups of young women and married women were less celebrations of female sexuality than expositions on reproduction. Indeed, Brigden never overtly referred to human sexuality, preferring to draw her examples from the animal kingdom. On this point, see Christie and Gauvreau, *A Full-Orbed Christianity*, 49.

86 For a survey of the principal shifts in Canadian opinion and legislation on birth control, see Brenda Margaret Appleby, *Responsible Parenthood: Decriminalizing Contraception in Canada* (Toronto: University of Toronto Press, 1999), 31, 62, 70.

87 UCA, Commission on Marriage and Divorce, 2:19, Patricia White, "Men and Women in Society," January 1960, 1.

88 UCA, Crusade for Christ, 1:2, J.R. Mutchmor to Rev. Moorehouse, 16 November 1944.

89 UCA, Commission on Marriage and Divorce, 1.7, "A Christian Understanding of Marriage and Sex," 7.

90 "Evangelism in Our Time," *United Church Observer*, 15 March 1958, 7.

91 UCA, Commission on Marriage and Divorce, 2:19, Frank H. Morgan, "Responsible Parenthood," 20 January 1960, 1.

92 Ibid., 1:7, "A Christian Understanding of Marriage and Sex," 8; 2:19, National Council of the Churches of Christ in the U.S.A., Carson McGuire, "The Cultural Sources of Our Sex Attitudes and Behavior," 7.

93 Ibid., 2:21, "A Christian Understanding of Sex and Marriage," April 1959, 8.

94 Ibid., 3:32, John Webster Grant, Ryerson Press, to Frank Fidler, 16 November 1959; 1:3, Minutes, 25–27 April 1960, 117.

95 Ibid., 1:7, "A Christian Understanding of Marriage and Sex," 41.

96 Ibid., 3:35, Milton Weber to Rev. Berry, 20 April 1961.

97 Ibid., 2:16, "Brief of United Church of Canada to the Special Joint Committee of the Senate and House of Commons on Divorce," 22 January 1966, 2. Whether the submissions presented by organizations such as the United Church or the "'plot' element" of life stories presented in personal letters to Prime Minister Lester Pearson were more effective in altering the divorce law remains an open question. See Christina Burr, "Letters to

Mike: Personal Narrative and Divorce Reform in Canada in the 1960s,"
in Lori Chambers and Edgar Montigny, eds., *Family Matters: Papers in
Post-Confederation Canadian Family History* (Toronto: Canadian Scholars'
Press, 1998), 396.

98 UCA, Commission on Marriage and Divorce, 2:18, Dr Thomas G. Donnelly, Untitled submission, 28 August 1958, 7.

99 Ibid., R.C. Chalmers, "A Brief on Divorce," August 1958, 3–4.

100 Ibid., 2:16, Mervin Bury, "The Meaning and Responsibilities of Christian
Marriage," 13 May 1958, n.p.

101 Ibid., 1:7, Rev. Professor David Cairns, Christ's College, Aberdeen, "The
Teaching of Brunner and Barth on Marriage and Divorce," 171–3. A host
of Scottish professors were consulted by the United Church commission
because its secretary, Frank Fidler, a Scotsman, had himself written a
similar report for the Church of Scotland in May 1957.

102 Ibid., 2:16, Rev. E. Gilmour Smith, Timmins, "Common-Law Partnerships
and Morals," 2; *Toward a Christian Understanding of Sex, Love and Marriage*
(1960), 121–2.

103 UCA, Commission on Church, Nation and World Order, 2:15, Lower,
"Comments and Suggestions on the Ninth Draft," 2. Lower intended
this focus to serve conservative purposes, but by 1960 the implications of
this priority of the United Church were very different.

104 United Church clergymen read and reacted to the Kinsey Report, but its
findings regarding female sexuality were not the primary engine behind
the church's exaltation of sexual relations. See UCA, Commission on
Marriage and Divorce, 4: 38, Richard E. Lentz, "The Challenge of the
Kinsey Report," n.d.

105 On this development within the broader framework of Western society,
see Arthur Marwick, *The Sixties: Cultural Revolution in Britain, France, Italy, and the United States, ca. 1958–ca. 1974* (Oxford and New York: Oxford
University Press, 1998), 19, 111. Marwick notes that "many of the excit-
ing developments in the sixties, and much of its unique character are due
to the existence of a genuine liberal tolerance and willingness to accommodate to the new subcultures, permitting them to permeate and transform society" (19). He observes that simultaneously with the youth
revolution there was considerable activism also among young married –
and indeed, middle-aged – individuals throughout Western society, especially on issues regarding sex and personal behaviour. "The liberation
of the sixties," concludes Marwick, "affected, and was participated in by,
majorities: it was not the prerogative of ultimately frustrated revolutionary minorities" (694).

Conclusion: "Patriarchal Piety" and Canada's Liberal Tradition

In many respects, the central problem posed by this volume relates to that raised by Gad Horowitz[1] in the late 1960s when he sought to account for the conservative nature of both liberalism and socialism in Canada. Where Horowitz approached the issue of communitarian values from the perspective of political philosophy, *Households of Faith* has employed the lens of culture – namely, the religious culture of Canada – to explore the changing relationship between family, church, and state. Thus the arguments contained in this study have direct implications for our understanding of the changing nature of the Canadian polity insofar as the family is seen as a distinctly "political" institution whose relations, as they were both idealized and experienced, reflected and shaped broader social and public values. Like Horowitz, the conclusions reached by this collective work point to the persistence of a "tory," or what we term a "patriarchal," set of hierarchical social and political relations which, even as they intersected with liberal or Lockean notions of familial equality and individualism, continued to be ideologically dominant.

Because the vast majority of the essays focus both on the prominence of fathers and husbands within the family and on the mutuality and interdependence of gender roles, both in terms of ideological discourse and in practice, it becomes imperative to cast off the accepted conceptual framework of the binary opposite of "separate spheres," with its notion of a gendered division between the private world of the home and the public sphere of work and politics, which cannot be reconciled with the way in which people in the past understood how relationships within the family functioned or how the family intersected with the larger society. Rather, I have used the notion of patriarchy to explain how visions of the social order were founded upon authority, which was believed to flow naturally from the heavenly Father, God, to earthly fathers, whose governance of their household dependents became the metaphor, by analogy, for the organization of church and state. Within this ideological formulation, the family was ineluctably connected to the public sphere, while the importance it placed upon male headship within families fostered the complementarity of men and women, because both derived their self-identity from their participation in the primary sociability of the family. Thus while traditionally, historians have equated the rise of the affectional family with a growing emphasis on the moral mother, this investigation of religious discourse has demonstrated that the language of domesticity is not the necessary corollary of notions of gendered divisions between public and private spheres. Because church discourse on domesticity focused on idealizing male roles within the family as much, if not more, than on defining women's roles, which remained largely static, it is more appropriate to employ the concept of patriarchal domesticity[2] as an interpretive framework that better captures the masculine nature of households in the past. In other words, because this communal model of the close interconnectedness of family, church, and society, and the model of domesticity it elaborated, allowed little space for a "modern" concept of the private or the individual, it arrested the development of a strict gendering of the private and the public, as has been conceived for the past twenty years by feminist historians.

While most historians would concur that a patriarchal society obtained in Britain, France, and the United States until the end of the eighteenth century, when a series of political revolutions overthrew the set of assumptions upon which it was founded, their periodization is largely defined by political events. Even the latest and arguably the most sweeping of these historical revisionists, J.C.D. Clark, has only pushed forward the chronology to 1832, an end point also bracketed by a distinctly political event, parliamentary reform.[3] When society is viewed from the perspective of cultural history and, more particularly, through the ideological discourse and practice of the Protestant and Roman Catholic religious traditions in Canada, a new historical trajectory is revealed. Between 1660 and the 1850s patriarchal definitions of society remained in the ascendancy; from the 1850s until the 1880s, with the injection of liberal individualism, familial communalism became a somewhat more contested terrain which, however, was quickly compromised in the early twentieth century by a renewed emphasis of both church leaders and social reformers on the role of fathers in the family. If historians of Britain and the United States have begun to problematize the "long eighteenth century," this study of social ideologies demonstrates that such a concept is even more relevant to interpreting Canada's historical experience, where the peculiar configuration of religious diversity, a non-revolutionary tradition, and the persistence of Old World communal ethnic identities, combined with an enduring commitment to preserving a small state, placed inordinate cultural weight on maintaining the family and the reality of paternal power as the mainstays of the social order.

While it is not surprising to find a patriarchal family entrenched in New France or in the Eastern Townships of Lower Canada in the opening years of the nineteenth century, when the promise of a state church still defined the political terrain, what is path-breaking about the findings of this volume is that, even at the level of lay experience and popular religious culture, "tribalism," rather than individualism, continued to define the terrain of religion and society well into the mid-nineteenth century, when historians have traditionally "discovered" the flowering of a coherent separate-spheres ideology. As several essays in this collection underscore, the persistence of a communal, rather than an individualistic, conception of social relationships was not imposed on a passive, churchgoing community by clerical elites; rather, the prolongation of patriarchy within the family was sustained from below by the interests and needs of ordinary men and women. Indeed, intercultural contact from the mid-nineteenth until the mid-twentieth century, between Protestant missionaries and Aboriginal communities, French Catholics and Protestant converts, and southern Italian immigrants and Irish Roman Catholic clerical elites was not the impetus for change or "modernization"; for the interests of cultural assimilation, the preservation of family stability through migration, and ethnic cultural priorities were instrumental in enhancing patriarchal leadership and gender interdependence. And even in an era of unprecedented religious choice, the dictates of family preservation overrode the centrifugal pull of individual desire.

Similarly, the self-identity of women who utilized evangelicalism as a vehicle to extend their domestic roles into the public sphere of social reform did so within the parameters of a continuing patriarchal discourse. Thus, just as a new maternal voice began to assert itself in the political domain, it was truncated in the late nineteenth century when the increased geographical mobility of young men, together with fears regarding the peaceful integration of the classes, aroused new anxieties concerning the socialization of youth, which in turn prompted a rehabilitated discourse of patriarchy and family governance. If, as Carole Pateman has argued, the implications of Lockean thought tended to eviscerate women from the public sphere,[4] it might just as fruitfully be argued that the protracted Filmerian paradigm in Canada ensured that any vestigial concept of the "moral mother," derived from evangelical female activism, could not be translated into a political argument in favour of individual, rights-based feminism.

Thus in 1878 the Reverend J. Lanceley, influenced by state imperatives for responsible citizenship and national prosperity, revalorized the Filmerian social order defined by hierarchical social relations and the interdependence of family, church, and government. True to the tory Filmerian legacy, and echoing the Catholic clergy of New France, twentieth-century clerics drew direct analogies between family, church, and state authority when they admonished fathers to discipline children and gather them in the family pew on Sunday. Lanceley's evocation of Adam Smith's description of family authority as that of husbands over wives, fathers over sons, and masters over servants and his statement that in the "constitution of the home," as in the church polity, the mother has no place, together with his observation that "all governments originated in patriarchal or parental authority," should alert us to the realization that, even when young men were being admonished to develop individual aspirations in the workplace, their public rights as citizens derived principally from the cultivation of family responsibilities.[5] And as the mainline churches promoted social reform and their interests became more closely aligned with the goals of the state, their spiritual purposes became more closely wedded to the breadwinner ideal.[6] As a consequence, both the mainline churches and the state remained committed to limited government, an outlook that further enhanced reliance on patriarchy for maintaining social order. Only when the churches jettisoned their close relationships with government over the issue of post-war welfare planning did the family, in religious discourse, become severed from public priorities and the notion of the family as a private entity emerge.

Significantly, because the priorities of public values in Canada remained centred upon the problem of political order and on authority based upon the hierarchical duties and obligations rooted in the family, a Lockean vision of democratic individualism founded upon gender equality within the household was attenuated here. Although the ideal of the "democratic family" as promulgated by church leaders after World War II, with its emphasis upon the rights of wives and children to self-expression and fulfillment, may not have corresponded to the lived experience of the majority of Canadians, the fact that it was only enunciated at this particular juncture is a signal reminder of the degree to which the sphere of liberalism had until then been subsumed within a broadly tory, patriarchal cultural system. Only in the 1950s did liberalism shed these restraints and its conservative carapace become the subject of noisy jeremiad and historical curiosity.[7]

NOTES

1 Gad Horowitz, *Canadian Labour in Politics* (Toronto: University of Toronto Press, 1968), especially chap. 3, "Conservatism, Liberalism and Socialism in Canada."

2 Carole Shammas, "The Domestic Environment in Early Modern England and America," in Michael Gordon, ed., *The American Family in Social Historical Perspective*, 3rd ed. (New York: St. Martin's Press, 1983), 129.

3 J.C.D. Clark, *English Society, 1688–1832: Ideology, Social Structure, and Political Practice during the Ancien Regime* (Cambridge and New York: Cambridge University Press, 1985).

4 Carole Pateman, *The Sexual Contract: Aspects of Patriarchal Liberalism* (Stanford: Stanford University Press, 1988).

5 Rev. J. Lanceley, *The Domestic Sanctuary; or, the Importance of Family Religion* (Hamilton: Spectator Publishing, 1878); D.C. Hossack, *The Gospel of the Home* (Toronto: William Briggs, 1903).

6 Nancy Christie and Michael Gauvreau, *A Full-Orbed Christianity: The Protestant Churches and Social Welfare in Canada, 1900–1940* (Montreal: McGill-Queen's University Press, 1996), chap. 3 and 6; Nancy Christie, *Engendering the State: Family, Work, and Welfare in Canada, 1900–1945* (Toronto: University of Toronto Press, 2000).

7 George P. Grant, *Lament for a Nation: The Defeat of Canadian Nationalism* (Toronto: McClelland and Stewart, 1965); Carl Berger, *The Sense of Power: Studies in the Ideas of Canadian Imperialism, 1867–1914* (Toronto: University of Toronto Press, 1970); Horowitz, *Canadian Labour in Politics*.